Focus in Hausa

Publications of the Philological Society, 40

Focus in Hausa

Melanie Green

Publications of the Philological Society, 40

Oxford UK & Boston USA

Blackwell Publishing Ltd
9600 Garsington Road, Oxford, OX4 2DQ, UK

and
350 Main Street,
Malden, MA 02148, USA

Library of Congress Cataloging-in-Publication Data

Green, Melanie.
   Focus in Hausa / Melanie Green.
     p. cm. – (Publications of the Philological Society ; 40)
   Includes bibliographical references and indexes.
   ISBN-13: 978-1-4051-5626-4
   ISBN-10: 1-4051-5626-0
   1. Hausa language–Syntax. I. Title.
   PL8232.G74 2006
   493'.725–dc22

                                 2006032065

A catalogue record for this publication is available from the British Library.

Set in Times by SPS (P) Ltd., Chennai, India
Printed and bound in Singapore by
Seng Lee Press Pte Ltd

The publisher's policy is to use permanent paper from mills that operate a
sustainable forestry policy, and which has been manufactured from pulp processed
using acid-free and elementary chlorine-free practices. Furthermore, the publisher
ensures that the text paper and cover board used have met acceptable environmental
accreditation standards.

For further information on Blackwell Publishing, visit our website:
http://www.blackwellpublishing.com

For my mum and dad

For my mum and dad

CONTENTS

CONTENTS

PREFACE

This book grew out of my (1997) SOAS Ph.D. thesis *Focus and copular constructions in Hausa*, but differs from the thesis in a number of ways. Firstly, it has been reorganised and rewritten with a different reader in mind. Although the study is approached from a broadly Principles and Parameters/Mimimalist perspective, there is less emphasis upon the intricacies of the theoretical analysis, and more emphasis upon the description of the data. In part, this has been made possible by the recent publication of two substantial reference grammars of Hausa by Paul Newman (2000) and Philip Jaggar (2001). These invaluable resources have made a far richer set of data available for scrutiny, which has been fully exploited in this book.

Secondly, this book departs from my 1997 thesis in incorporating new research, which emerges from two recent collaborative projects that explore focus in situ (Green and Jaggar 2003) and the syntactic conditioning of 'special inflection', or focus/relative aspect marking (Green & Reintges 2004; 2005a; 2005b; Reintges & Green 2004). This new research develops the original project by attempting to answer some of the questions that were raised there.

Thirdly, the book reflects my growing interest in comparative Afroasiatic syntax by placing greater emphasis on the identification of cross-linguistic and typological patterns. In attempting to set the Hausa facts within their broader (within-family) comparative and typological context, I have included surveys of some of the available data on focus constructions and copular/non-verbal clauses in Chadic, as well as data from some other Afroasiatic languages. While I have attempted to provide a sense of the range of variation in focus and copular/non-verbal clauses within Chadic and, more broadly, within Afroasiatic, I have not attempted to extend the theoretical analysis proposed here beyond the Hausa data. In particular, because descriptive work on many Chadic languages remains at a relatively early stage, some of the available grammatical descriptions are sketchy. Although the inclusion of these data sometimes raises more questions than it answers, it nevertheless provides a glimpse of the patterns of similarity and variation that exist in this language family.

Finally, it is also worth emphasising that empirical and theoretical questions are sometimes raised but left unanswered here regarding the nature of the relationship between prosody and syntax in Hausa focus constructions. This is the subject of ongoing research (Green, in preparation).

ACKNOWLEDGEMENTS

I was fortunate enough to be educated at the School of Oriental and African Studies, University of London, in an environment where descriptive and theoretical linguistics are both valued. Phil Jaggar, who taught me Hausa during my undergraduate years at SOAS, and who gave me the linguistics bug in the first place, has been generous with his advice and encouragement in the years since. Phil was also kind enough to read through the draft and correct errors of transcription in the Hausa data (although I remain responsible for any errors that crept back in). Wynn Chao introduced me to syntactic theory and supervised my 1997 thesis, helping me to develop many of the ideas that are explored in this book. Jamal Ouhalla and Laurie Tuller, who examined my 1997 thesis, also provided me with much useful advice and, together with Phil Jaggar, were kind enough to provide detailed readers reports on the book proposal and draft chapter I submitted to the Philological Society. Fellow linguists Malami Buba, Andrew Haruna and Mohammed Munkaila have taught me a great deal about Hausa, and have all been most generous with their time in patiently answering my data questions. Paul Newman and Russell Schuh kindly responded to my queries about Chadic languages, and Russell Schuh read through parts of the draft and provided me with much useful information and advice.

I have also learnt a great deal from working with Chris Reintges, who also read through most of the draft, providing invaluable criticism and encouragement, and who helped me keep my research interests alive during periods when I was overwhelmed by other work-related pressures. I have enjoyed many helpful discussions with members of the Sussex Meaning and Grammar Reading Group, including my colleagues Vyv Evans, Lynne Murphy and Max Wheeler. Lynne Murphy also read and commented on parts of the draft. My colleagues in the Department of Linguistics and English Language at the University of Sussex took on my teaching and administrative commitments during a period of sabbatical leave that finally enabled me to complete this book. My late colleague and mentor Larry Trask, who passed away during the preparation of this book, was an instructive reader and guided me through the early years of my career at Sussex with patience and with humour.

At the Philological Society, Keith Brown provided me with generous guidance in the early stages of preparing the manuscript, Paul Rowlett and Delia Bentley guided me through the latter stages, and Lutz Marten provided me with valuable comments on the pre-final draft of the manuscript. The people whose help I have acknowledged here do not necessarily agree with the theoretical position advanced in this book, nor are they responsible for any of its shortcomings. Finally, I want to thank my children for their affection and humour along the bumpy road to my career in academia, and my mum and dad, to whom this book is dedicated, for their kind and quiet support throughout my studies and the early years of my career.

LIST OF TABLES

ABBREVIATIONS, SYMBOLS AND TRANSCRIPTION

ACC	accusative	OBJ	object
ADV	adverb	OBL	oblique
AGR	agreement	OPT	optative
ALLAT	allative	PART	particle
AP	adjective phrase	PASS	passive
ASP	aspect marker	PF	perfective
AUX	auxiliary	PL	plural
CM	contrastive marker	POSS	possessive
COMP	complementiser	POT	potential
CONJ	conjunction	PP	preposition phrase
COP	copula	PREP	preposition
CP	complementiser phrase	PRES	presentational predicate
CP	clefting particle	pro	null pronominal
DD	definite determiner	PRO	pronoun
DECL	declarative	PROG	progressive
DEM	demonstrative	PRO.REL	pro-relative (TAM)
DO	direct object	PRS	present tense
DP	determiner phrase	Q	interrogative particle
EXIST	existential predicate	REFL	reflexive pronoun
f	feminine	REL	relativiser
FM	focus marker	REL.PRO	relative pronoun
FOC.IMPF	focus imperfective	RHET	rhetorical
FOC.PF	focus perfective	RM	relative tense marker
FP	focus phrase	RP	resumptive pronoun
FUT	future	SID	specific indefinite determiner
GEN	genitive	s	singular
H	high tone	spec	specifier
HAB	habitual	STAT	stative
ICP	intransitive copy pronoun	SUB	subjunctive
IMPF	imperfective	SUBJ	subject
INDEF	indefinite determiner	t	trace
INF	infinitive	TAM	tense/aspect/mood category
INFL	inflection	TOP	topic/topic particle
INTER	interjection	TOT	totality marker
IOM	indirect object marker	TP	tense phrase
IP	inflection phrase	VENT	ventive
L	low tone	VN	verbal noun
LOC	locative	VNP	verbal noun phrase
m	masculine	vP	light verb phrase
NEG	negation marker	VP	verb phrase
NOM	nominative		
NOMIN	nominaliser		
NP	noun phrase		

1	first person
2	second person
3	third person
4	impersonal
*	ungrammatical/proto-form
?	marginal
#	unacceptable

Hausa transcription

v̄	long vowel
v̀	low tone vowel
v̂	falling tone vowel
ɓ	implosive bilabial stop
ɗ	implosive alveolar stop
ƙ	ejective glottalised velar
ts	ejective alveolar sibilant
'y	laryngealised palatal glide
'	glottal stop
j	voiced alveopalatal glide
r̃	alveolar tap/roll

1

INTRODUCTION

This book sets out to achieve two main objectives: first, to provide a thorough and in-depth description of the morphosyntax, semantics and pragmatics of focus and copular constructions in Hausa and secondly, to provide a theoretically oriented syntactic analysis of these constructions from a current generative perspective. The book is intended to be broadly accessible within the linguistics community, serving to introduce readers to aspects of the syntax of Hausa, a major world language, and containing material of relevance not only to those interested in generative syntax but also to those interested in the typology of focus constructions and non-verbal clauses. For this reason, the descriptive sections are presented in theory-neutral terms and can in principle be consulted independently of the theoretical sections.

The remainder of the book is organised as follows. Chapter 2 provides a descriptive overview of the Hausa language, focusing mainly on the morphosyntax, and introduces readers to the data that form the focus of the present study. Chapter 3 explores definitions of focus, a linguistic phenomenon that involves the complex interaction of phonology, morphosyntax, semantics and pragmatics. This chapter also charts the development of generative theories of the syntax of focus, and sets the scene for the theoretical exposition that forms parts of the following chapters.

Chapter 4 explores the syntax, semantics and discourse properties of focus fronting constructions in Hausa, and the empirical and theoretical implications of a Principles and Parameters approach are discussed. In particular, an analysis is proposed wherein the focused constituent is displaced to the left periphery, where it targets the specifier of a functional projection Focus Phrase (FP). This projection is headed by the copular focus marker *nē/cē*, which is analysed as a grammaticalised focus marker that occurs optionally in monoclausal focus/*wh*-fronting constructions. The properties of focus fronting and *wh*-fronting are also compared and contrasted in this chapter. The analysis developed here owes much to the analysis proposed by Tuller (1986a), which is developed and extended in a number of ways to enable a fuller explanation of the empirical facts. This chapter also discusses the properties of in situ focus/*wh* in Hausa, and compares and contrasts these with the properties of ex situ focus/*wh*. In particular, the chapter addresses the question of whether, in addition to the obvious syntactic differences, the two types of focus construction are distinct in terms of semantics or discourse function. Finally, the syntactic conditioning of 'special inflection' (relative aspects) is explored.

Chapter 5 investigates the syntax, semantics and information packaging properties of non-verbal copular sentences in Hausa, the other major context in which the non-verbal focus marking copula $n\bar{e}/c\bar{e}$ occurs. The main empirical question addressed in this chapter is whether the reanalysis of $n\bar{e}/c\bar{e}$ as a grammaticalised focus marker is upheld by its function in the non-verbal clause. While the non-verbal copula shows a 'less grammaticalised' status in the non-verbal clause in the sense that its function is partly to license predication or equation, there is also evidence in the non-verbal clause of its evolving function as a focus marker, hence the fact that there is a designated focus position in both canonical and non-canonical non-verbal copular clauses. The theoretical discussion in this chapter demonstrates that the FP analysis developed in Chapter 4 can be usefully extended to the non-verbal copular clause, enabling a simple account of these constructions that accurately captures both their morphosyntactic properties and their information packaging properties.

Chapter 6 takes a within-family cross-linguistic perspective on the construction types discussed here, and presents a comparison between focus constructions in Hausa and some of its closer Afroasiatic relatives (Chadic), as well as three of its more distant Afroasiatic relatives, Arabic, Hebrew and Coptic Egyptian. In addition, this chapter compares and contrasts Hausa non-verbal clauses with those in Chadic and in Arabic, Hebrew and Coptic Egyptian, where the discussion reveals that although Hausa is one of a minority of Chadic languages with copulas, there are some striking patterns of similarity between Hausa and some of its closer and more distant relatives both in terms of the properties of non-verbal clauses and in the participation of copulas in focus marking.

Finally, Chapter 7 presents a short summary of the descriptive and theoretical conclusions reached in this book, and indicates directions for future research.

1.2 THE DATA

The Hausa data in this book are taken from a number of sources. The bulk of the descriptive data is either taken from or adapted from Newman (2000) or Jaggar (2001), two impressive recent reference grammars that provide a considerable body of data transcribed with tone and vowel length diacritics. Some Hausa examples, including the ungrammatical examples (unless otherwise indicated), have been constructed and discussed with native Hausa speakers. The sources of any other examples are acknowledged in the text.

The Hausa examples are all provided in standard Hausa orthography rather than IPA. However, neither tone/vowel length nor the distinction between retroflex flap (r) and alveolar tap/roll (ř) are marked in standard Hausa orthography. Diacritics are therefore used to indicate these features, which, in the case of tone and vowel length, are frequently relevant to morphosyntactic analysis. Finally, while there is considerable dialect variation across the Hausa-speaking area, which can be broadly divided into 'eastern' and 'western' dialects (see Jaggar 2001: 2), the Hausa data in this book, unless stated otherwise, can be considered Standard (Kano) Hausa.

Sources are cited in the text for data from all other languages discussed, and the author's transcription is reproduced as in the original (some authors, for example, mark tone and vowel length differently from the system adopted here for Hausa, and some authors mark tone and vowel length in some publications but not in others).

2

THE HAUSA LANGUAGE

2.1 Introduction

This chapter provides a brief introduction to the Hausa language, with the objective of making this book accessible to those unfamiliar with the language. In this section some general background information about Hausa is presented (§ 2.1), followed by a brief overview of the Hausa linguistics tradition (§ 2.2). The remainder of the chapter summarises the main linguistic features of the language (§ 2.3), and introduces the types of construction that are the focus of this book (§ 2.4).

Hausa is spoken mainly in northern Nigeria as a first language, but also widely in surrounding parts of west Africa, including Niger, where it is also the majority language. Hausa is estimated by Jaggar (2001) to have in excess of 30 million first-language speakers. Hausa is a Chadic language belonging to the larger family of Afroasiatic languages, which, in addition to the Chadic branch, also includes Ancient Egyptian/Coptic, Berber (e.g. Tamazight, Turareg), Cushitic (e.g. Somali, Oromo), Omotic (e.g. Maale, Benchnon, Wolaytta), and Semitic (e.g. Akkadian, Arabic, Hebrew). The Afroasiatic group is the major language family of north Africa, although it is not confined to the African continent, counting Hebrew and Arabic among its members.

The status of the Chadic group within the Afroasiatic family has been the subject of some debate dating back over 100 years, but is now widely accepted on the basis of lexical, phonological and morphosyntactic similarities that point towards a common inheritance.[1] For example, there exist well-attested cognates between the core vocabulary of Chadic and a number of well-established Afroasiatic languages (Newman 1980). With respect to phonology, Schuh (2003: 57) describes a 'rather sparse vowel system with a length distinction in the low vowel, which is typologically similar to the vowel systems of Semitic and Berber, ... widespread in Chadic despite millennia of contact with Niger-Congo languages, which typically have five, seven and even nine vowel systems and no distinction in vocalic length'. With respect to morphology, Schuh (2003) also describes distinctive Afroasiatic features such as the *n/t/n* marking of masculine, feminine and plural respectively in the demonstrative system, and common morphology in the pronominal systems (§ 5.3; see also Chapter 6). In terms of syntactic

---

[1] For further details see Newman (1980); Schuh (1982b; 2003); Pawlak (1994).

features, the Chadic languages lack morphological case on lexical noun phrases, relying instead on word order, which is predominantly SVO, with some VSO languages within the Biu-Mandara sub-group (among these are Gude, Lamang, Margi and Podoko). Schuh (2003: 58) argues that the VSO Chadic languages may be remnants of the proto-Chadic word order, given that 'VSO is the prevalent order in Berber and older Semitic languages', and that the historically common shift from VSO to SVO could be accounted for by contact with non-Chadic SVO languages.

The Chadic group covers an area beginning in northern Nigeria and southern Niger and stretching eastwards across northern Cameroon into Chad. Schuh (2003) estimates that there are in excess of 150 Chadic languages. Hausa is the best described of the Chadic languages, although substantial reference grammars exist for a small number of others, including Frajzyngier (1989) on Pero, Frajzyngier (1993) on Mupun and, most recently, Schuh (1998) on Miya and Schuh & Gimba (forthcoming) on Bole. While Hausa has millions of native speakers, most of the other Chadic languages, according to Schuh (2003), have fewer than 100,000.

The Chadic group has been subject to various classifications since Lukas (1936) and Greenberg (1950), and remains the topic of some debate in the literature.[2] In his widely accepted classification, Newman (1977) divides the Chadic group into three main branches: West Chadic (languages spoken in northern Nigeria, including Hausa); Biu-Mandara (north-eastern Nigeria and northern Cameroon); East Chadic (Chad); and a fourth branch, Masa, containing six closely related and poorly documented languages spoken mainly in western Chad. Newman further divides each of the three main branches of Chadic into two sub-groups of closely related languages; Hausa belongs to the West A group, together with the Bole-Tangale, Angas and Ron sub-groups. The closest 'relative' to Hausa is Gwandara, which Newman (2000) describes as a 'creolized offshoot'.

A competing Chadic classification is that of Jungraithmayr & Shimizu (1981), which recognises Newman's West Chadic and East Chadic branches, but instead of Newman's Biu-Mandara and Masa branches has a third main branch, Central Chadic.

Hausa is without question the most widely spoken Chadic language. Indeed, Schuh (1982b) describes it as second only to Arabic in terms of the number of native speakers on the African continent. Hausa is an official language of Nigeria (together with Igbo and Yoruba, inter alia) and is, aside from English, the lingua franca of northern Nigeria, widely used as a language of administration and education. There are a number of Hausa newspapers, and Hausa is also broadcast widely on the television in Nigeria and Niger, as well as on the radio, both nationally and internationally (by the BBC World Service and Voice of America, among others). Hausa is also

---

[2] See Schuh (2003) for a more detailed overview of Chadic classification.

taught in a number of universities, both within Nigeria and around the world, including Europe and the USA.

The Hausa language has a well-documented written tradition, including an abundance of written literature. Due to the spread of Islam in west Africa dating back to the 14th century, Hausa was originally written in Arabic script (*Ajami*), and there are historical, religious and folklore texts dating back to the early 19th century. Since the time of British colonial influence in the early 20th century, Hausa has been written in Roman script, and there now exists a considerable body of modern Hausa literature.[3]

There is considerable dialectal variation to be found in a language as widely spoken as Hausa. The dialect spoken in the Kano area is considered 'Standard Hausa' and, together with other eastern dialects, is broadly distinguishable from the western dialects (such as the Sokoto dialect), as well as from the dialects spoken in Niger.

2.2 HAUSA LINGUISTICS

Descriptive grammars and dictionaries of Hausa date back as far as the work of Schön (1843). Major Hausa dictionaries appeared in the earlier part of the 20th century, notably Bargery (1934) and Abraham (1946; 1962). There are also a number of pedagogical dictionaries, grammars and readers, including Skinner (1965; 1979), Cowan & Schuh (1976), Newman & Ma Newman (1977), Furniss (1991) and Jaggar (1992). Major grammars include Abraham (1941; 1959) and, most recently, Wolff (1993), Newman (2000) and Jaggar (2001).

In addition to grammars, readers and dictionaries, a good deal of linguistic research has been carried out into Hausa phonology, morphology and syntax. Pre-eminent Hausa linguists of the twentieth century include F.W. Parsons and Paul Newman. A large body of descriptive material was collected and analysed by Parsons from the 1950s onwards, a comprehensive collection of which can be found in Parsons (1981). Parsons's work includes his widely adopted 'grade system' classification of Hausa verbs into categories based on the correlation between morphological and semantic features (§ 2.3.2). Since the 1960s, an impressive and wide-ranging body of research has also been produced by Paul Newman, culminating in his recent (2000) encyclopedic reference grammar.[4]

Other well-known and prolific researchers in the field of Hausa (and Chadic) linguistics include Russell Schuh and Philip Jaggar.

---

[3] For further details on Ajami and the development of Roman script for Hausa, see Jaggar (2001: 698–714) and references cited there. For a survey of modern Hausa literature, see Furniss (1996).

[4] For further details see Jaggar (2001: 3–4) and references cited there, and Newman (1996) for a detailed bibliography of Hausa.

A number of theses on various aspects of Hausa linguistics have appeared over recent years and include, among those relevant to syntax, McConvell (1973), Jaggar (1985), Tuller (1986a), Junaidu (1987), Yusuf (1991), Abdoulaye (1992) and Yalwa (1995). However, in comparison to the European languages, which tend to represent the focus of current theoretical linguistics, particularly where syntax is concerned, many aspects of the Hausa language remain to be fully researched.

2.3 MAIN LINGUISTIC FEATURES

In this section a brief descriptive overview of the linguistic features of Hausa is presented, in order to familiarise the reader with the salient features of the language and to facilitate the understanding of the data presented throughout this book. The descriptions and the examples here owe much to Newman (2000) and Jaggar (2001), and further detail on all the facts presented in the remainder of this chapter can be found in these two volumes.

2.3.1 *Phonology*

Hausa is a tone language with a relatively elaborate phonemic inventory. At the segmental level, Hausa has 32 consonants including glottalised (ƙ), palatalised (c, j) and laryngealised (ɓ, ɗ) consonants. The vowel inventory is moderate, but at the suprasegmental level, tone and vowel length are both phonologically contrastive. Hausa has a ten-vowel phoneme system, five short vowels (a, e, i, o, u) and five long vowels (ā, ē, ī, ō, ū), in addition to two diphthongs (ai, au).[5] Hausa has a three-tone system: vowels can be either high (v), low (v̀) or falling (v̂). Tone and vowel length therefore combine to indicate both lexical and grammatical (derivational and inflectional) information, as the following examples illustrate:

(1) a. sāƙò   'corner'
     b. sàƙō   'message'
     c. fādà   'palace'
     d. fâdā   'priest'
     e. maƙērā   'forge'
     f. maƙèrā   'blacksmiths'

Typologists have traditionally classified languages as either TONE or INTONATION languages. In an intonation language like English, pitch (relative highness or lowness of a sound) is used mainly at the utterance level,

---

[5] Newman (2000: 398–403) provides a detailed discussion of the allophonic realisation of the Hausa vowels and diphthongs.

resulting in a pitch pattern that may, for example, distinguish a statement from a question. In a tone language like Hausa, pitch functions mainly at the word level to mark lexical or grammatical contrast, although, as Newman (1995) points out, the combination of sound properties that characterise tone may be more complex than pitch alone. The word-internal phonology of Hausa tone is well understood.[6]

The tone/intonation dichotomy has received little empirical support, however: tone and intonation are not mutually exclusive. Intonation in Hausa was the subject of much research during the 1980s.[7] This research focused particularly on the intonational patterns that distinguish clause types such as declaratives, yes-no questions and *wh*-questions, and revealed that Hausa 'clause type' intonation is consistent with cross-linguistic patterns. For example, statements are characterised by 'downdrift' (a progressive lowering of pitch over the utterance as a whole) and yes-no questions by the suspension of downdrift and the raised pitch of the final high tone.

2.3.2 *Word order and the verbal-inflectional complex*

Hausa is an SVO language in which inflection occurs as an independent lexical item preceding the verb but not cliticised to it. Example (2) illustrates a canonical active declarative (mono)transitive clause with an overt lexical NP subject, an independent pronominal object and a third person plural perfective INFL morpheme, which agrees in person and number with the subject (gender is not marked in the plural).

(2) yârā   sun   dòkē shì
     children 3pl.PF   beat   PRO.3ms
     'the children beat him'

Hausa verbs are not inflected for person, number, gender, tense, aspect or mood. (An exception to this generalisation is the imperative, which affects the tone pattern of the verb as well as licensing the absence of the INFL word.) The conjugation base or person-aspect complex (henceforth INFL) is a free functional morpheme that occurs independently from the verb, and consists of a subject agreement morpheme (marking person, number and gender) and a tense/aspect/mood (TAM) morpheme, although not all forms of INFL involve discrete morpheme boundaries. With the exception of the future and allative forms, the subject agreement morpheme precedes the TAM morpheme. There are 16 distinct inflectional paradigms, with 11 for affirmative and five for negative conjugation patterns, and INFL imposes

---

[6] See e.g. Hyman and Schuh (1974); Leben (1978); Schuh (1978); Newman (1995).
[7] See e.g. Newman & Newman (1981); Miller & Tench (1980; 1982); Lindau (1986); Inkelas et al. (1987).

Table 2.1 Hausa 3pl INFL paradigms (Jaggar 2001: 153).

	GENERAL	FOCUS	NEGATIVE
PF	sun	sukà	bà sù ... ba
IMPF (+ V PRED.)	sunà	sukè̀	bā sà̀
IMPF (−V PRED.)	sunà	sukè	bā sà̀/bâ su (dà...)
SUB	sù	–	kadà sù
HAB	sukàn	sukàn	bà(a) sukàn ... ba
POT	sâ	–	bà(a) sâ ... ba
RHET	–	sukà̀	–
FUT	zā sù	zā sù	bà(a) zā sù ... ba
ALLAT	zâ sù	zâ sù	bà(a) zâ sù ... ba

selectional restrictions on its complement: the allative selects only non-verbal locative predicates in Standard Hausa; the imperfective selects either complements headed by verbal nouns or non-verbal complements; the remainder select VP. A range of temporal, aspectual and modal distinctions are expressed by INFL, and the perfect and imperfect paradigms show a morphological alternation between 'general' and 'focus' forms (traditionally referred to as 'relative aspects'), where the latter occur in typical exemplars of *wh*-constructions: relative clauses, *wh*-questions and focus fronting constructions (§ 2.4).[8] The focus perfective also occurs in narrative sequences (see Chapter 4). Table 2.1 represents the 16 distinct paradigms, exemplified by third person plural forms. As the table shows, the subjunctive and potential forms are not licensed in 'focus' contexts, whereas the rhetorical is restricted to such contexts.

Hausa reflects a mixed system of both tense and aspect, with the major aspectual distinction between perfective and imperfective, where the former indicates a completed event and the latter a non-completed event. Each of these may be used with reference to past, present or future time, which is established by linguistic context. In addition, Hausa has a future paradigm, but even this is not restricted to future time reference. The following examples (adapted from Jaggar 2001: 155) illustrate:

(3) a. Mūsā yanà̀ cîn àbinci
    Musa 3ms.IMPF eat.VN.of food
    'Musa is/was eating'

---

[8] 'Focus form' is a term coined by Jaggar (2001) for what is traditionally described as 'relative aspect'. In Jaggar's view, this term provides a more accurate descriptive label for the syntactic contexts in which this 'special' inflection occurs, but this term is not yet widely adopted (see e.g Newman 2000: 567 and Jaggar 2001: 162). Jaggar's terminology will be adopted throughout this book.

    b. ìdan kin   kāwō aikìn   gòbe,   zân   dūbà shi
        if   2fs.PF bring work.DD tomorrow FUT.1s look   PRO.3ms
        'if you bring (lit. 'have brought') the work tomorrow, I'll look at it'
    c. jiyà   wàr̃hakà   zâi   dāwō
        yesterday at.this.time 3ms.FUT   return
        'yesterday at this time he was going to come back'
        (lit: 'will come back')

The subjunctive is very commonly used, given the absence of any infinitival form, and is essentially a modal (irrealis) category, used in speech acts such as commands, prohibitions, intentions and wishes (4).

(4) a. kì   kāwō àbinci!
        2fs.SUB bring food
        'bring the food!'
    b. kar̃ kì   mântā!
        NEG 2fs.SUB forget
        'don't forget!'
    c. munà   sô   mù   tàfi yànzu
        1pl.IMPF want.VN 1pl.SUB go   now
        'we want to go now'

The potential is also a modal category, expressing uncertainty or doubt (5a). The allative expresses imminent future events (5b). Finally, the rhetorical, which Jaggar (2001: 205) describes as 'somewhat archaic and stylistic', is nevertheless a feature of both written and spoken Hausa, although syntactically restricted to 'focus' environments (5c). Observe that the person/number/gender morpheme is dropped from the INFL word in example (5c), a particularly common feature of the rhetorical (Jaggar 2001: 205).

(5) a. wata rānā nâ   kōyà mikì   *potential*
        SID.fs day 1s.POT teach PRO.2fs
        'one day I may teach you'
    b. zâ   mu   gidā   *allative*
        ALLAT 1pl house
        'we're off home'
    c. rashìn sanì   nē   kà   jāwō irìn   *rhetorical*
        lack.of knowledge FM.m RHET cause kind.of
        wannàn rìkicī
        this   crisis
        'it's ignorance that causes this kind of crisis'

Negation in Hausa verbal sentences involves the discontinuous negative morphemes *bà(a) … ba*, with the exception of the negative imperfective, which uses only an initial negative morpheme, and the subjunctive, which has a distinct negation morpheme. The initial *bà(a)* occurs between subject and INFL, although in some paradigms (e.g. negative perfective and imperfective) the initial negative morpheme and INFL show distinct morphology from the corresponding affirmative forms. The final *ba* morpheme usually occurs clause-finally, but adverbial phrases can occur to the right of the final *ba* morpheme:[9]

(6) a. bã zā sù amìncē dà wannàn ba
NEG FUT 3pl agree to this NEG
'they won't agree to this'

b. bā nà̃ sôn hakà
NEG 1s.IMPF like.VN.of thus
'I don't like this'

c. bài taɓà zuwã̀ makaɽantā ba
3ms.NEG-PF ever go school NEG
'he has never been to school'

d. bà mù fàhìnci muhummancìnsà sôsai ba /
NEG 1pl.PF understand importance.of.3ms completely NEG
ba sôsai
NEG completely
'we didn't understand its importance completely'

Although Hausa verbs are not marked for person, number or TAM features, they nevertheless show systematic morphological features reflecting argument structure syntax. Parsons (1960) classified Hausa verbs into seven 'verb grades'. Each grade shows a templatic form in terms of syllabic structure, tone and vowel length. This system therefore shows some similarity to the templatic morphology of the Semitic verb system. According to Newman's revised version of this system (see Newman 2000), verbs are classified in terms of a primary stem (grades 1–3), whose final vowel and tone is replaced by an extension in the secondary (derived) grades (grades 4–7). In addition, Newman incorporates monosyllabic verbs into the primary system (grade 0).

Primary grades 0–3 are defined on the basis of morphological features and argument structure syntax. Grade 0 contains eight monosyllabic tone verbs (e.g. *ci* 'eat', *shā* 'drink', *yi* 'do, make', *ji* 'hear, feel') and four disyllabic HH tone verbs (*kirā* 'call', *biyā* 'pay', *jirā* 'await' and *rigā* 'precede). Verbs in this set are predominantly transitive. Grade 1 contains HL(H) verbs ending in final -*a* (e.g. *gyārà* 'repair', *kaɽàntā* 'read'). Verbs in this set are either transitive or intransitive. Grade 2, which contains transitive verbs, is the most morphologically complex, since both tone pattern and final vowel is determined by syntactic context. For example,

---

[9] See Jaggar (2001: 453–6) for further discussion of the position and scope of negation morphemes in complex clauses.

grade 2 verbs show a distinct tone pattern and final vowel alternation depending on whether the complement is direct object pronoun ((L)LH-*ē*), nominal or clausal complement ((L)LH-*i*), indirect object (HL(H)-*ā* and/or (H)HH-*ař*), or extracted object or discourse-linked null object (LH(L)-*ā*). The following examples illustrate the various forms of the grade 2 verb *sàyā* 'buy'.

(7) a. zân   sàyē sù   *pronominal direct object*
         FUT.1s buy   PRO.3pl
         'I'll buy them'

     b. zân   sàyi r̀gā   *nominal direct object*
         FUT.1s buy   dress
         'I'll buy a dress'

     c. zân   sayà̀ wà màtātā r̀gā   *indirect object*
         FUT.1s buy IOM wife.1s dress
         'I'll buy a dress for my wife'

     d. mề   zā   kì   sàyā?   *extracted object*
         what FUT 2fs buy
         'what will you buy?'

     e. kin   sàyā?   *null object*
         2fs.PF buy
         'did you buy (it)?'

Grade 3 contains intransitive verbs mainly with final -*a*. These have either LH(L) tone patterns (e.g. *shìga* 'enter', *zàmanà* 'become') or HH tone patterns (e.g. *girma* 'grow up', *tsūfa* 'grow old'), although there is a small set with a HL pattern (e.g. *ɓatà* 'get lost', *gudù* 'run', *mutù* 'die').

While the primary grades are not always easy to classify according to semantics or valency features, the secondary grades (4–7) are derived grades where the suffix affects either the semantics or the valency of the primary grade base form in systematic ways. Grade 4 verbs have the tone patterns HL(H) and suffix -*ē*, and derive 'totality-conclusive' semantics (e.g. grade 1 *kōnà̀* 'burn' → grade 4 *kōnề* 'burn up'), 'separative-deprivative' semantics (e.g. grade 2 *bùgā* 'hit' → grade 4 *bugề* 'knock down/over'), or unaccusatives (e.g. grade 1 transitive *fasà̀* 'break' → grade 4 *fashề* 'explode'). Grade 5 verbs have all H tones and suffix –*ař*, and derive 'efferential' or 'action away' semantics (e.g. grade 2 *sàyā* 'buy' → grade 5 *sayař* 'sell'). Grade 6 verbs have all H tones and suffix -*ō*, and derive 'ventive-centripetal' or 'motion towards deictic centre' semantics (e.g. grade 1 *kōmà̀* 'go back' → grade 6 *kōmō* 'come back'). Grade 7 verbs are characterised by (L)LH tones and suffix -*u*, and derive what Jaggar (1988; 2001) describes as 'affected subject' semantics, which affects the argument structure by detransitivising the verb (e.g. grade 1 transitive *fasà̀* 'smash' → grade 7 *fàsu* 'be smashed (up)'). Finally, Hausa also has a set of 'pluractional' verbs, which involve partial or full reduplication of the base form of the verb, and express plurality of events/participants (e.g. grade 3 [irregular] *mutù* 'die'→ *mummutù* 'all die').

A further important issue relevant to the verbal-inflectional complex in Hausa is the derivation and function of VERBAL NOUNS. In addition to their other functions, verbal nouns occur after imperfective INFL, where they perform a function like that of the progressive *-ing* participle in English. Like common nouns (§ 2.3.3), the verbal noun shows grammatical gender (final *-ā* usually denotes a feminine noun form). The verbal noun also takes the nominal genitive linker (§ 2.3.4) before objects. Compare the following examples:

(8) a. nā   nèmi   aikì
         1s.PF   seek   job
         'I looked for a job'
     b. inà   nēma-n   aikì
         1s.IMPF seek.VN-of job
         'I'm looking for a job'

Verbal nouns are further subdivided into 'weak' and 'strong' classes. The weak verbal noun is restricted to occurring after imperfective INFL in constructions without an object (either intransitive constructions or those in which the object has been displaced). In constructions with an object, the (non-nominalised) verb is used, regardless of the TAM properties of the clause:

(9) a. mè   takè   dafà-wā?
         what   3fs.FOC.IMPF cook-VN
         'what is she cooking?'
     b. tanà   dafà   àbinci
         3fs.IMPF cook   food
         'she is cooking food'

The weak verbal noun is derived from the verb by suffixation of *-wā*. The 'floating' L tone is redundant when affixed to a final L tone verb, but changes a heavy syllable verb-final H to a falling tone (e.g. *tattàunā* 'discuss'→ *tattàunâwā*). Most grade 1 verbs and all secondary grades (4–7) derive this kind of verbal noun, as well as three irregular monosyllabic verbs *cê* 'say' (→ *cêwa*), *kai* 'reach, take' (→ *kâiwā*) and *sâ* 'put' (→ *sâwā*).

The strong verbal noun is a feature of grade 0 and grade 3 verbs, which take regular strong verbal nouns. These occur after imperfective INFL in all syntactic contexts apart from preceding indirect objects, where the verb form is used. Grade 0 verbs derive (masculine) verbal nouns by lengthening the final vowel (sometimes redundantly) and adding a low tone. Monosyllabic H tone verbs become HL:

(10) a. ci 'eat'   → cî   c. biyā 'pay'   → biyà
      b. yi 'do'   → yî   d. kirā 'call' → kirà

Grade 3 verbs form (feminine) strong verbal nouns by lengthening the final vowel:

(11)   a.   fìta   'go out'   →   fìtā
          b.   tsūfa   'grow old'   →   tsūfā

When regular strong verbal nouns precede objects, they take the nominal genitive suffix:

(12)   inà   bî-n   wannàn   hanyà
        1s.IMPF   follow.VN-of(m)   this   road
        'I'm following this road'

Grade 2 verbs (together with a number of grade 1 verbs) derive irregular strong verbal nouns, which are not predictable in terms of phonological or morphological form. However, like regular strong verbal nouns, these also suffix the genitive linker before an object:

(13)   a. sunà   sàye-n   àbinci   (< sàyā)
            3pl.IMPF   buy.VN-of(m)   food
            'they're buying food'
          b. sunà   sātà-ř   kāyā   dà   yawà   (< sàtā)
            3pl.IMPF   steal.VN-of(f)   goods   with abundance
            'they're stealing a lot of things'

2.3.2 *Non-verbal clauses*

Non-verbal clauses in Hausa can be divided into those that are formed with imperfective INFL followed by a non-verbal predicate, and those that lack INFL altogether. Non-verbal clauses that are formed with imperfective INFL fall into four types according to whether the predicate is possessive prepositional phrase (*dà* + NP), locative adverbial, stative adverbial or 'equational-like' NP or AP. The latter construction (14d) is described by Jaggar (2001:472) as 'marginal' in comparison to the non-verbal copular construction (described below):

(14)   a. Bintà tanà   dà   mōtà   *possessive*
            Binta 3fs.IMPF with   car
            'Binta has a car'
          b. Bintà tanà   gidā   *locative*
            Binta 3fs.IMPF   house
            'Binta is at home'
          c. Bintà tanà   zàune   kân   kujèrā   *stative*
            Binta 3fs.IMPF sit.STAT   on   chair
            'Binta is sat on a chair'
          d. Bintà tanà   mālàmā   à   lōkàcîn   *'equational-like'*
            Binta 3fs.IMPF teacher(f)   at   time.DD
            'Binta was a teacher at the time'

In addition, there is an emphatic non-verbal construction formed with the focus-imperfective TAM morpheme *kè* followed by the deictic adverbial *nan* 'there':

(15) halinsà kè̀ nan
    character.of.3ms FOC.IMPF there
    'that's just his character'

Non-verbal clauses that lack INFL altogether fall into three types: existential clauses, presentational clauses and non-verbal copular clauses.[10] Existential clauses are formed with the existential expressions *àkwai* or *dà*, with negative forms *bābù* or *bâ*:

(16) a. àkwai wuƙā kân tēbùr̃
       EXIST knife on table
       'there's a knife on the table'
    b. bābù kuɗī
       NEG.EXIST money
       'there's no money'

The forms *dà* and *bâ* must have an overt complement, whereas the alternative forms *àkwai* and *bābù* may have null complements if the referent can be recovered from the discourse context.

Presentational clauses are formed with the presentational expression *gà̀*, which Jaggar (2001: 468) suggests is derived from an imperative form of the verb *ganī* 'see':

(17) gà̀ kuɗîn
    PRES money.DD
    'there's the money'

Non-verbal copular clauses are formed with NP subject, NP or AP predicate, and non-verbal copula *nē/cē/nē* (m/f/pl). The copula usually agrees in gender/number with the subject, as does the nominal or adjectival predicate, and the tone on the copula is polar (opposite to that of the preceding syllable):

(18) a. Audù **ɗālìbī** nè̀
       Audu student(m) FM(m)
       'Audu is **a student**'

---

[10] Jaggar (2001: 428) describes Hausa as having a number of copular verbs, such as *kōmà̀* 'become', defined as those verbs that take a subject complement:
  (i) ruwā zâi kōmà̀ ƙanƙarā
      water FUT.3ms become ice
      'the water will turn into ice'
Jaggar lists further examples including *zama* 'become', *kàsāncē* 'become, turn out', *rikìɗē* 'change into' and *zaunà̀* 'remain'. These copular verbs are distinct from the non-verbal copula in Hausa in two important ways. Firstly, these verbs have semantic content, and as such may be described as quasi-copulas. Furthermore, like all verbs in Hausa, these quasi-copular verbs co-occur with INFL.

b. Audù   **dōgō**   nè̀
   Audu   tall(m)   FM(m)
   'Audu is **tall**'

c. Kànde **ɗālìbā**   cè̀
   Kande student(f)   FM(f)
   'Kande is **a student**'

d. Kànde **dōguwā**   cè̀
   Kande tall(f)   FM(f)
   'Kande is **tall**'

The non-verbal copula is glossed throughout this book as 'focus marker' (FM), since it marks the left-adjacent constituent as the focus of the clause (henceforth indicated by boldface), both in non-verbal copular clauses and in focus fronting constructions (§ 2.4.3). It follows that non-verbal copular constructions allow a range of word order permutations dependent on discourse context. This is the subject of Chapter 5, where the similarities between the focus properties of these constructions and focus fronting constructions (Chapter 4) are shown to justify a unified syntactic analysis.

Negation of non-verbal copular clauses involves the constituent negation morphemes *bà̀...ba*. These may occur in a range of positions; the initial negative morpheme directly precedes the focus of the clause and the second morpheme either directly follows the focus of the clause or occurs clause finally:

(19) a. bàbānā   bà̀   **mālàmī**   ba   nè̀
        father.1s NEG   teacher(m)   NEG   FM(m)
        'my father isn't **a teacher**'

    b. bàbānā   bà̀   **mālàmī**   nè̀   ba
        father.1s NEG   teacher(m)   FM(m)   NEG
        'my father isn't **a teacher**'

    c. bà̀   **Audù**   nē   dà̃raktà̀   ba
        NEG   Audu   FM(m)   director   NEG
        '**Audu**'s not the director'

2.3.4 *The noun phrase*

Hausa preserves the Afroasiatic binary distinction between masculine and feminine nouns in the singular. Masculine gender is the unmarked default, whereas feminine gender is usually marked by final -*ā*. Grammatical gender triggers agreement on adjectives, determiners, subject–INFL agreement and genitive markers in complex NPs. Specific indefinite determiners, interrogative determiners and distributive universal quantifiers precede the head, whereas definite determiners, genitive phrases, numerals and relative clauses follow the head. Demonstratives, adjective phrases and collective universal quantifiers may optionally precede or follow the head. The definite determiner -`n/-`r̃/-`n (m/f/pl) is a bound morpheme (observe that final vowel shortening results from this affixation):[11]

(20) a. mōtà̄   'car'(f)   →   mōtà-r̃   'the car'
     b. yārò̄   'boy'(m)   →   yārò-n   'the boy'
     c. rīgunà̄ 'gowns' (pl)   →   rīgunà-n 'the gowns'

The presence of the definite determiner indicates 'unique identifiability' (Jaggar 2001: 317), but the absence of the definite determiner does not necessarily correlate with indefiniteness; an unmarked NP may still be interpreted as definite in appropriate discourse contexts. The definite determiner shares some of its morphology (and its historical deictic source) with the gender and number morphology also seen in the free genitive morphemes na/ta/na (m/f/pl), the bound genitive morphemes -n/-r̃/-n (m/f/pl) and in the non-verbal copula nē/cē/nē (m/f/pl) (for more detail see § 5.3).

The specific indefinite determiner (SID), which precedes the head noun, is a morphologically complex word containing a wa- deictic morpheme followed by a person/number morpheme -ni/-ta/-su (m/f/pl). This element can also function as a pronoun (but is glossed as 'SID' throughout):

(21) a. nā   ga   wasu   awākī   à   gōna-r̃-kà
        1s.PF   see   SID.pl goats   at   farm-of-2ms
        'I saw some goats on your farm'
     b. wasu   sunà̄   nēma-n-kà
        SID.pl 3pl.IMPF   seek.VN-of-2ms
        'some (people) are looking for you'

In possessive NPs the possessed (head) noun is phrase-initial and either contains the genitive linker -n (m/pl) or -r̃ (f) or precedes the free genitive morpheme na (m/pl) or ta (f) which precedes the possessor NP:

(22) a. kuɗi-n   Audù
        money(m)-of(m)   Audu
        'Audu's money'
     b. r̃ìgâ-r̃   ta   Audù
        gown-DD(f) of(f)   Audu
        'the gown of Audu's'

---

[11] A recent development in generative syntax involves the reanalysis of noun phrases (NPs) as determiner phrases (DPs), where the functional head D takes an NP as its complement (Abney 1987). Yusuf (1991) argues that since Hausa is a consistently head-initial language we would expect a structure in which D precedes its complement. On this basis, he proposes a structure in which the head of NP left-adjoins to D, deriving the order of constituents we find in the definite NP-DP complex in Hausa. The term NP will be used throughout this book, with the exception of some discussion in Chapter 5 (§ § 5.2; 5.4)

Adjectives can be either prenominal or postnominal, where the prenominal position is unmarked and the postnominal position usually expresses emphasis or contrast. Prenominal adjectives incorporate the same genitive morpheme found in possessive NP constructions:

(23) a. nā   sàyi   fara-r̃   mōtā̀
         1s.PF   buy   white(f)-of(f)   car(f)
         'I bought a white car'

     b. nā   sàyi   mōtà̄   farā   (bà   baƙā   ba)
         1s.PF   buy   car(f) white(f)   NEG   black(f)   NEG
         'I bought a white car (not a black one)'

Hausa has a rich deictic system, most elements of which can function both as determiners and as pronouns. The demonstrative system is based on person-oriented deixis (closeness to speaker/hearer), and encodes a proximal vs. distal distinction. This system also reflects the relative newness of the referent in the discourse context. Demonstrative determiners can precede head nouns, in which case they occur as full forms consisting of deictic morpheme *wa-*, genitive linker/plural infix *-ɗan-*, and spatial deictic morphemes *nân* (near speaker), *nan* (near hearer), *cân* (distant from speaker and hearer) or *can* (remote from speaker and hearer). These forms can also function as pronouns (24c):[12]

(24) a. wannàn   aik̀ī   /   wannàn   aikì-n
         this(m) work(m)   this(m) work(m)-DD(m)
         'this work'

     b. waccàn   r̃gā   /   waccàn   r̃ga-r̃
         that(f) gown(f)   that(f) gown(f)-DD(f)
         'that gown'

     c. sai   wannàn   ya   dùbi   wannàn...
         then   this(m) 3ms.FOC.PF look   this(m)
         'then this one looked at that (this) one...

Demonstratives can also follow the head noun, in which case they occur as reduced forms consisting of the genitive morpheme (suffixed to the head noun), followed by the spatial demonstrative morpheme:

(25) a. r̃gar̃-nàn
         gown(f).of(f)-this
         'this gown' (near speaker/just mentioned)

     b. r̃gar̃-càn
         gown(f).of(f)-that
         'that gown' (distant from speaker and hearer)

---

[12] See Jaggar (2001: 325) for a description of the phonological processes that derive the surface forms of these demonstratives, concerning both tone patterns and the surface form of the feminine genitive morpheme.

The major division within the pronoun system is between personal and non-personal pronouns. Non-personal pronouns lack distinct person forms, but are marked for gender and number. This set includes demonstratives (e.g. *wàncan* 'that (ms)', *wàccan* 'that (fs)', *wàɗàncan* 'those'), interrogatives (e.g. *wằ* 'who?', *mề* 'what?'), specific indefinites (e.g. *wani* 'someone (ms)', *wata* 'someone (fs)', *wasu* 'some (people)'), relatives (e.g. *wandà* (ms), *waddà* (fs), *waɗàndà* (pl)) and universals (e.g. *kōwā* 'everyone', *kōmē* 'everything').

The personal pronoun set includes eight sub-classes: independent pronouns (e.g. *nī* (1s), *kai* (2ms), *ita* (3fs)); strong (free) direct object pronouns (e.g. *ni* (1s), *ka* (2ms), *ta* (3fs)); weak (bound suffix) direct object pronnouns (e.g. *-nì* (1s), *-kà* (2ms), *-tà* (3fs)); indirect object pronouns (e.g. *minì* (1s), *makà* (2ms), *matà* (3fs)); free possessive pronouns (e.g. *nằwa* (1s), *nākà* (2ms), *nātà* (3fs)); bound (suffix) genitive pronouns (e.g. *-nā* (1s), *-nkà* (2ms), *-ntà* (3fs)); reflexives (e.g. *kâinā* (1s), *kânkà* (2ms), *kântà* (3fs); lit. 'my/your/her head') and reciprocals (e.g. *jūnanmù* (1pl), *jūnankù* (2pl), *jūnansù* (3pl)). Each subclass contains eight forms, five singular (1s; 2ms; 2fs; 3ms; 3fs) and three plural (1pl; 2pl; 3pl). While common and proper nouns are not marked for case in Hausa, there are some grounds for describing the Hausa personal pronominal system as a case system, although the 'independent' pronouns, which perform the subject function, also occur in a range of non-subject positions, e.g. indirect object position; following core prepositions.[13]

2.3.5 *Null subjects and objects*

Like many languages with a rich inflectional system, Hausa is a pro-drop language: sentences can occur without overt NP subjects, as long as the referent can be retrieved from context. Hausa also allows null object NPs, with some restrictions: there is a strong tendency for null objects to have non-human referents, but null objects may have human referents in consecutive clauses:[14]

(26) a. Q: kā   sàyi   r̃gā?
           2ms.PF   buy   gown
           'did you buy the gown?'

     A: ī,   nā   sàyā
           yes   1s.PF   buy
           'yes, I bought (it)'

---

[13] See Tuller (1986a: 19–50) for an analysis of the free genitive morpheme *na/ta/na* (m/f/pl) as a 'dummy case marker'. Tuller argues that the bound genitive morpheme, in all its functions, is a compound marker rather than a case morpheme.

[14] For further discussion see Jaggar (1985) and Tuller (1986a).

b. sukà   taraɽ dà shī   kwànce... sukà   kìnkimà,
   3pl.FOC.PF find PART 3ms.PRO prostrate 3pl.FOC.PF lift
   sukà   kai gidā,   sukà   binnè
   3pl.FOC.PF take house   3pl.FOC.PF bury
   'they found him lying dead... they lifted (him) up, took (him)
   home, (and) buried (him)'

2.3.6 *Modal/adverbial particles*

Hausa has a small set of particles that have been variously described as 'adverbial',
'modal' or 'topic' particles: *dai* 'just, really, actually'; *fa* 'indeed, certainly'; *kuma*
'also, and'; *kàm* 'as for'; *kùwa/kɔ̀* 'and, moreover'; *mā* 'also, too, even'. These
particles may appear in various positions within the clause, including between
topic and clause (27a), between subject and INFL (27b), between INFL and verb
(27c), and between verb and nominal direct object (27d).

(27) a. nī   kàm, bàn   san   shī   ba
        1s.PRO PART 1s.NEG.PF know 3ms.PRO NEG
        'as for me, I don't know him'
     b. wasu kuma sunà   ganin   shī   tsōhon ministà...
        SID.pl PART 3pl.IMPF feel.VN.of 3ms.PRO old.of minister
        'and some feel that the former minister ...'
     c. bài   dai   sanì   ba
        3ms.NEG.PF PART know NEG
        'he just didn't know'
     d. nā   sàyi mā   ɽìgā
        1s.PF buy PART gown
        'I also bought a gown'

2.4 *WH*-TYPE CONSTRUCTIONS

Relative clauses, *wh*-questions and focus fronting constructions are
described here as '*wh*-type' constructions since they share common syntactic
properties. First, these constructions all involve 'displacement': a dependency between a constituent in the left periphery of the clause and a
corresponding gap in the position in which that constituent is interpreted. In
the case of relative clauses, the gap corresponds to the modified head noun,
sometimes mediated by a relative pronoun. Secondly, these constructions
are united by the presence of 'special inflection': the 'focus' form of INFL.

2.4.1 *Relative clauses*

Restrictive relative clauses are formed either with the relativising
complementiser *dà* (the most 'natural' or prototypical relative clause
construction, illustrated by (28a) and (29a)), or (marginally) with the full

relative pronoun *wandà/waddà/wadàndà* (m/f/pl) (illustrated by (28b) and (29b)). The full relative pronoun consists of the deictic morpheme *wa(a)*, the definite determiner, the plural morpheme *đàn* (in the case of the plural relative pronoun) and the relativiser *đà*.[15] Relative clauses condition the focus form of INFL, and the relative pronoun agrees in gender and number with the head noun, which may be definite or indefinite:

(28) a. [yāròn dà sukà   dòkā] yanà   asibitì
        boy.DD REL 3pl.FOC.PF beat 3ms.IMPF hospital
        'the boy that they beat up is in hospital'
     b. [yārò wandà   sukà   dòkā] yanà   asibitì
        boy RELPRO(m) 3pl.FOC.PF beat 3ms.IMPF hospital
        'the boy that they beat up is in hospital'
(29) a. [wani yārò dà kè   nan   a lōkàcîn] yā   ga
        SID(m) boy REL FOC.IMPF there at time.DD 3ms.PF see
        kōmē
        everything
        'a boy who was there at the time saw everything'
     b. [wani yārò wandà   kè   nan à lōkàcîn] yā   ga
        SID(m) boy RELPRO(m) FOC.IMPF there at time.DD 3ms.PF see
        kōmē
        everything
        'a boy who was there at the time saw everything'

The relative pronoun may also substitute for the head noun:

(30) wadàndà   sukà   mutù
     RELPRO(pl) 3pl.FOC.PF die
     'those who died'

Jaggar (1998; 2001) observes that non-restrictive relative clauses, which are typical of more formal spoken and written styles, differ from their restrictive counterparts in three main respects. First, non-restrictive relative clauses are distinguished by pause intonation, which is represented by orthographic commas. Secondly, some speakers prefer an all-low-tone relative pronoun *wàndà/wàddà/wàdàndà* (m/f/pl). Thirdly, and most interestingly, some speakers also allow the non-focus form of INFL in non-restrictive relatives:

(31) đàlìbân,   wàdàndà sukà/sun   gamà aikìnsù,   duk
     students.DD RELPRO(pl) 3pl.FOC.PF/3pl.PF finish work.of.3pl all
     sun   tàfi
     3pl.PF go
     'the students, who have finished their work, have all gone'

---

[15] See Jaggar (2001: 528) for a description of the phonological processes that derive the surface forms of these relative pronouns, concerning both tone patterns and the surface form of the feminine definite determiner morpheme.

2.4.2 Wh-*questions*

While declarative word order and the general form of INFL are maintained in
yes-no questions, which are marked either by question intonation or by a
dedicated interrogative particle such as *kō* (32a), canonical *wh*-questions
involve fronting of the *wh*-phrase to clause initial position, accompanied by
the obligatory presence of the focus form of INFL (32b),(32c):

(32) a. yârā   sun   tàfi   kàsuwā kō?   yes-no *question*
         children 3pl.PF go   market Q
         'did the children go to market?'
     b. wà   yârā   sukà   ganī?   *object* wh-*question*
         who   children 3PL.FOC.PF   see
         'whom did the children see?'
     c. su-wànē sukà   tàfi   Amìrkà?   *subject* wh-*question*
         3pl-who 3pl.FOC.PF   go   America
         'who went to America?'

Observe that while subject questions do not show any surface departure
from the unmarked declarative word order, the focus form of INFL is
nevertheless obligatory, which suggests 'string vacuous' displacement.

   Although Hausa is traditionally described as a language that does not
allow *wh*-in situ questions in non-echo contexts, Jaggar (2001; 2006a)
argues that these are attested in spontaneous discourse. These constructions
are characterised by the presence of the *wh*-phrase in its canonical
(declarative clause) position, and by the non-focus form of INFL:

(33) a. kin   ga   dà wà dà wà   à   wh-*in situ (object)*
         2fs.PF   see   who.pl   at
         makàrantā?
         school
         'whom did you see at school?'
     b. sunà   inā   yànzu?   wh-*in situ (locative)*
         3pl.IMPF where   now
         'where are they now?'

Wh-in situ subject questions are not attested, however: subject *wh*-questions
require the focus form of INFL for grammaticality. Although Jaggar (2001:
496–8) suggests that dialect variation may explain the fact that some
speakers accept *wh*-in situ constructions while others reject them, Jaggar
(2006a: 5) states that 'it now seems that this strategy is not as dialect-
specific as I had earlier thought'. The pattern that emerges from Jaggar's
recent study is that there is evidence of an argument–adjunct asymmetry in
wh-in situ, with more speakers accepting *wh*-adjuncts in situ (e.g.
expressions of place, time and manner) than *wh*-arguments. In addition,
wh-in situ is also widely accepted in the case of non-verbal clauses with

locative predicates (§ 2.3.3). For example, even speakers who reject *wh*-in situ in most other contexts find constructions like (33b) well-formed. Despite the fact that *wh*-in situ is attested in spontaneous discourse, it is important to emphasise that *wh*-fronting is a strongly preferred option for all speakers, and the only option for *wh*-arguments for most/ many speakers. *Wh*-questions are discussed in detail in Chapter 4 (§ 4.4; § 4.6).

2.4.3 *Focus constructions*

Focus fronting constructions in Hausa, like *wh*-fronting constructions, involve movement of the focused constituent to clause-initial position, and obligatory use of the focus form of INFL. In addition, the non-verbal focus marking copula *nē/cē* may optionally follow the focused constituent, in which case it agrees in gender and number with the head of the focused constituent. The following examples illustrate contextually determined new information focus and contrastive focus (focus is indicated by boldface):

(34) Q: wà   kukà   ganī   à   kàsuwā?
        who   2pl.FOC.PF see   at   market
        'who did you see at the market?'

    A: **yārònkà**   (nē)   mukà   ganī   *new information focus*
        boy.of.2m   (FM.m)   1pl.FOC.PF   see
        'we saw **your boy**'

(35) Q: kun   sàyi   bakāř   mōtà?
        2pl.PF buy   black.of   car
        'did you buy a black car?'

    A: ā'à,   **faràř   mōtà**   (cē)   mukà   *contrastive focus*
        no   white.of   car   (FM(f))   1pl.FOC.PF
        sàyā (bà   bakā ba)
        buy   NEG   black NEG
        'no, it was a **white car** we bought (not a black one)'

The hypothesis that *wh*-fronting and focus fronting share a common syntactic derivation is supported by the possibility that fronted *wh*-phrases may also be followed by the non-verbal copula:

(36) su-wànē   nè   sukà   tàfi   Amìřkà?
     3pl-who   FM(pl)   3pl.FOC.PF   go   America
     'who went to America?'

Focus fronting constructions in Hausa share superficial similarities with topic constructions. Both are characterised by a 'prominent' constituent in clause-initial position. There are a number of important differences between

the two construction types, however. First, the topic is optionally followed
not by the non-verbal copula *nē/cē*, but by a modal/adverbial particle
(§2.3.6). Secondly, the topic construction is characterised by the non-focus
form of INFL:

(37) a. Mànsûr̃ kùwa, yā   sằmu   bàbban dìgìr̃î   *topic*
         Mansur TOP   3ms.PF   get   big.of degree
         'as for Mansur, he got a PhD'

    b.   **Mànsûr̃** nē   ya   sằmu   bàbban dìgìr̃î   *focus*
         Mansur   FM(m)   3ms.FOC.PF   get   big.of degree
         '**Mansur** got a PhD'

Finally, there is a preference for (object) resumption over gapping in topic
constructions, particularly for animate referents. These differences between
focus fronting and topic constructions are discussed in more detail in
Chapter 4 (§ 4.2.2). The syntactic parallels between focus and *wh*-
constructions are not restricted to fronting constructions. Although Hausa
has until recently been described as a language with obligatory focus
fronting, Jaggar (2001; 2006a) also shows that focus in situ is attested. The
following examples illustrate new information and contrastive focus in situ:

(38) Q: wànè   kāyā   kikà   mântā?
         which things   2f.FOC.PF   forget
         'which things did you forget?'

    A: nā   mâncē   **jàkātā**   **dà**   **hùlātā**   *new information focus*
         1s.PF   forget   bag.of.1s   and   hat.of.1s
         'I forgot **my bag and my hat**

(39) Q: kā   aikằ   dà   takàr̃dâr̃?
         2m.PF   send   with   paper.DD
         'did you send the paper?'

    A: ā'ằ, nā   aikằ   dà   **littāfìn**   (bằ   *contrastive focus*
         no   1s.PF   send   with   book.DD   NEG
         takàr̃dâr̃   ba)
         paper.DD   NEG
         'no, I sent **the book** (not the paper)'

As with *wh*-in situ constructions, focus in situ constructions show a
canonical (declarative clause) word order and lack the focus form of INFL. A
further similarity is that in situ subject focus is ungrammatical: subject
focus always co-occurs with the focus form of INFL, suggesting vacuous
displacement. Finally, as with *wh*-in situ constructions, focus in situ is
subject to certain restrictions, although it appears to be less restricted than
wh-in situ. Focus constructions are discussed in detail in Chapter 4.

3

FOCUS IN GENERATIVE GRAMMAR

3.1 INTRODUCTION

The objectives of this chapter are threefold. First, the chapter provides a short overview of the Chomskyan framework (§ 3.2), in anticipation of the syntactic analysis of focus and copular constructions that will unfold in Chapters 4 and 5. To this end, the emphasis is on providing a sketch of the framework rather than elaborating its finer technical details. Where necessary, certain theoretical assumptions are elaborated later in the book. The second objective of this chapter is to provide some background information about focus, a linguistic phenomenon that involves the complex interaction of phonology, morphosyntax, semantics and pragmatics (§ 3.3). This section sketches out a cross-linguistic typology of the morphosyntax of focus, together with some discussion of its phonological correlates and the semantic/pragmatic subtypes of focus. The final section of the chapter explores generative approaches to focus, and maps out a generalised theory of focus within a broadly Principles and Parameters/ Minimalist framework, outlining the theoretical model of focus constructions that will be assumed in the remainder of this book (§ 3.4).

3.2 THE GENERATIVE FRAMEWORK

This section presents a brief historical overview of the generative enterprise and maps out recent models within this framework, particularly those aspects relevant to the syntax of focus and related constructions. Throughout the remainder of this book it is argued that this approach provides a simple and explanatory model of the syntax of focus, which also enables predictions to be articulated and tested with respect to cross-linguistic variation and the typology of focus.

3.2.1 *Philosophical assumptions*

As is well known, the generative framework has its origins in Chomsky's earliest work (Chomsky 1957; 1959), where he stated the logical problem of language acquisition, or the poverty of the stimulus argument: the idea that, given finite linguistic input, the speaker acquires the potential for infinite linguistic output. In addition, imperfect input does not result in imperfect knowledge of language in the mind of the speaker: although much everyday language consists of utterances that contain incomplete sentences, slips of the tongue, and so on, speakers still know how to construct complete and well-formed sentences. According to Chomsky, it follows that the principles of grammar are underdetermined by the input, or primary linguistic data (PLD), and therefore that the speaker must bring some innate linguistic knowledge or competence to the process of language acquisition. The idea that linguistic knowledge arises from 'drawing out what is innate in the mind' (Chomsky 1965: 51) represents what philosophers call the rationalist view, and contrasts with the empiricist view, which holds that linguistic knowledge is constructed on the basis of experience, and is independent of any specialised cognitive system. In modern linguistic theory, the empiricist view is represented by the usage-based model of language acquisition favoured in cognitive linguistics (see Langacker 2000). Chomsky's model was the first truly 'cognitive' theory of human language in the sense that it attempted to integrate explanations of human language with what is known about other aspects of human mind and cognition. For this reason, Chomsky's early work is often described as one of the catalysts of the 'cognitive revolution': the birth of cognitive science as a discipline in its own right, uniting through common goals and research questions disciplines such as philosophy, psychology, linguistics and artificial intelligence.

The model of the initial state of the innate language faculty posited by Chomsky is known as Universal Grammar, and assumes a modular model of mind (see Chomsky 1986: 13, 150; Fodor 1983; 2000), according to which the language faculty represents an encapsulated system of specialised knowledge that equips the child for the acquisition of language. The language system itself is viewed within generative theories as a modular system, due to the assumption that the principles and processes, and the primitives over which they operate, are different in kind from one area of language (e.g. phonology) to another (e.g. syntax). A simple model of the language module is shown in (1). The levels of Phonological Form (PF) and Logical Form (LF) operate over the output of the syntax (sentence-level structures) with respect to phonological and semantic principles, respectively:

In developing this mentalist theory of language, Chomsky asserts that the only revealing object of linguistic study, given the objective of characterising competence, is the system of linguistic knowledge in the mind of the idealised individual speaker. This system of internalized linguistic knowledge is known as I-language (Chomsky 1986: 19–56), and generates the expressions uttered by the speaker. The theory of this system is referred to as the grammar, hence the term generative grammar. The system is not open to conscious introspection, nor does it correlate with any single local function in the physical brain. Rather, it is one aspect of a complex model of mind, and can only be reconstructed on the basis of its output: human language itself. For this reason, native speaker intuition and judgement play

(1)

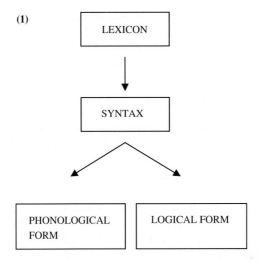

a central role in this model: speakers can rarely explain the rules that govern their native language, but can rapidly judge what is possible in the language and what is not, thereby providing a body of data on the basis of which the linguist can attempt to model the system itself. From this perspective, the externalised language of the speech community (E-language) is merely epiphenomenal, in the sense that it arises as the output of individual I-languages. It is I-language that underlies the native speaker's intuitions concerning grammaticality.

The generative model is built upon principles of language: statements that aim to characterise the linguistic knowledge or competence that underlies the individual speaker's I-language. Since Chomsky's early work (see e.g. Chomksy 1965: 24–37), levels of adequacy have played a central role in the design of the generative model of language. According to Chomsky, an adequate theory of language must meet three criteria. The weakest of these criteria is observational adequacy, which is likely to be (at least partially) met by any grammar of any language. However, descriptive adequacy and explanatory adequacy are more stringent criteria, which must be met by 'a genuine theory of human language' (Chomsky 2000: 7). A grammar of a particular language attains observational adequacy if it specifies which strings of words are and are not well-formed in that language. For example, an observationally adequate grammar of English would distinguish between the grammatical sentences in (2a) and (2b), on the one hand, and the ungrammatical string in (2c), on the other.

(2)   a. Bill loves her
      b. Bill loves himself
      c. *Bill loves herself

The grammar of a particular language attains descriptive adequacy if it specifies which sentences are and are not well-formed in that language *and* accounts for the speaker's intuitions concerning grammaticality by accurately modelling the tacit knowledge that underlies the (un)grammaticality of those strings, and by describing their properties in terms of principles of language. For example, a descriptively adequate grammar of English would account for the (un)grammaticality of the examples in (2) in terms of principles governing the distribution of pronouns like *him, himself* and *herself* across the language as a whole. In Binding Theory (Chomsky 1986: 164–84), these principles are stated in terms of co-reference and locality. *Bill* can be co-referential with *himself*, since both expressions are third person, singular and masculine. *Bill* is therefore a potential binder for *himself*, but not for *herself*, which explains why (2b) is grammatical while (2c) is not. In addition, reflexive pronouns like *himself* need to be bound locally: compare (2b) with (3a), where brackets indicate an embedded clause. In (3a), the main clause subject *Bill* cannot bind the reflexive pronoun *himself* in the embedded clause. In contrast, pronouns like *him* do not tolerate local binding. This explains why (2a) is grammatical (*Bill* cannot bind *her*), and why (3b) is only grammatical if *him* is not co-referential with *Bill* (this sentence cannot be interpreted to mean that Bill loves himself).

(3) a. *Bill said [himself was tired]
     b. Bill loves him

Finally, a grammar attains explanatory adequacy if it provides a descriptively adequate account of each individual language *and* explains how knowledge of language is acquired via the interaction of the input (PLD) and the innate endowment (Universal Grammar). For example, an explanatorily adequate model of grammar must represent the binding principles described above in terms that are sufficiently general to account for the distribution of pronouns in all human languages, and sufficiently simple and economical to account plausibly for the acquisition of this knowledge on the part of the child, given exposure to everyday spoken language. In Binding Theory, the statement of principles capturing the distribution of both types of pronoun in (2) and (3) in terms of a single local binding domain represents an attempt to meet these objectives: while reflexive pronouns like *himself* must be bound within this domain, pronouns like *her* must not be bound within this domain.

As this discussion indicates, it is necessary to distinguish between a grammar of a particular language and a theory of human language in general (see Radford 1988: 28–30). While the latter represents the ultimate objective of modern linguistic theory, it cannot be achieved independently of the former: any theory of human language that attains explanatory adequacy must also contain the basis for a descriptively adequate account of each particular language. As has often been observed, there is a tension between the two objectives of descriptive and explanatory adequacy (see Chomsky 1986: 51–2; 2000: 7; 2002: 31): while descriptive adequacy requires a large set of complex, intricate and detailed statements in order to account for the properties of particular languages, explanatory adequacy requires a finite set of universal statements that can represent Universal Grammar in terms that are psychologically plausible. In particular, the goal of explanatory adequacy requires a small set of statements that are maximally general (in order to apply cross-linguistically) and maximally simple and economical (in order to account for the rapid acquisition of language, as well as for its creativity and the intuitions of its speakers).

A number of key developments in the Chomskyan model stand out as attempts to resolve this tension between the objectives of descriptive and explanatory adequacy. For example, the move away from the sets of constructions and construction-specific transformational rules to the single generalised transformational rule Move-Alpha (Chomsky 1980) represented a move towards explanatory adequacy. The development of the Principles and Parameters approach (Chomsky 1981) also brought generative grammar closer to resolving the tension between the requirements of descriptive and explanatory adequacy, by positing the existence of a universal set of principles that account for Universal Grammar, together with a finite set of options or parameters that account for cross-linguistic variation.

There are a number of current generative theories of language. These theories tend to focus on the directly 'measurable' structural aspects of language such as morphology, syntax and phonology, although some (notably Jackendoff's (e.g. 1983) theory of Conceptual Semantics) attempt to integrate theories of linguistic meaning into a formal generative framework. While all generative theories assume Universal Grammar as a common working hypothesis, they differ in terms of how they model the system. For example, some theories such as Head Driven Phrase Structure Grammar (HPSG) and Lexical Functional Grammar (LFG) place the burden of explanation on information stored in the lexicon, and assume only a single 'monostratal' level of syntactic representation.[1] Others, such as the Transformational Grammar model, place the burden of explanation on the syntax, and therefore assume a 'multistratal' system, where 'underlying' and 'surface' syntactic structures are linked by generalised derivational processes.

3.2.2 *The transformational model*

Central to the Chomskyan model is the grammatical transformation or displacement operation, which links two positions in a structure: the position in which an expression is interpreted, and the position to which that expression has 'moved' in order to satisfy other grammatical

---

[1] For HPSG, see Gazdar et al., (1985); Pollard & Sag (1994); Sag & Wasow (1999). For LFG, see Kaplan & Bresnan (1982); Bresnan (2001).

requirements. For example, in (4), the fronted question word *who* is
interpreted as the object of the verb *saw*. The position in which it is
interpreted is indicated by the underscore.

(4)   who did Bill say Ted saw__yesterday?

The Transformational Grammar model was first proposed by Chomsky in
the late 1950s, and has evolved through a number of historical stages into
models known as Transformational Generative Grammar, Standard Theory,
Extended Standard Theory, Government and Binding Theory, Principles
and Parameters Theory and, most recently, the Minimalist Program.[2]

Within the transformational framework, lexical items are stored in the
lexicon together with information about their phonological, semantic and
core syntactic properties (such as the argument structure or valency of
lexical verbs). Together with generalised syntactic principles, this information gives rise to syntactic structures (deep structures) in which the core
requirements of the lexical items are satisfied in accordance with syntactic
principles. These structures then undergo syntactic movement or transformation processes (for example, the process that derives an English-type
interrogative clause like (4) by raising a constituent from its thematic
position to clause-initial position), giving rise to surface structures. A
version of the model in (1) that incorporates a transformational syntax is
shown in (5). This corresponds to the model of transformational syntax
assumed within Government and Binding Theory and within Principles and
Parameters Theory.

The transformational model is open to a range of interpretations. At one
extreme, it can be interpreted as underlying a literal step-by-step process of
(unconscious) sentence construction in the mind of the speaker, where
syntactic trees are assembled and reassembled during the processing of each
sentence uttered. There is little evidence for this view – indeed, the
transformational model is not intended as a model of language processing,
but as a model of linguistic knowledge that interfaces with performance
systems. From this perspective, the syntactic transformation can be viewed
as a metaphor that attempts to capture similarities between related
constructions (for example, declarative and interrogative clauses) both
within and between languages, and attempts to model the aspects of human
cognition that underlie those similarities.

3.2.3 *X-bar syntax*

X-bar syntax is one approach to the statement of generalised syntactic
principles that was introduced into the transformational model during the

---

[2] See Chomsky (1957; 1965; 1970a; 1970b; 1973; 1977; 1980; 1981; 1982; 1986; 1993; 1995;
2000; 2001a; 2001b).

(5)

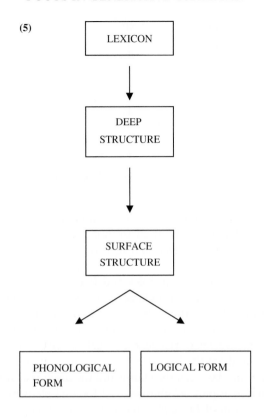

1970s, some version of which remains in the current model.[3] The X-bar model replaces category-specific phrase structure rules with a small set of category-neutral rules, where hierarchical relationships are universal but linear precedence relations are subject to cross-linguistic variation. The tree diagram in (6) represents the X-bar structure, where X^0 is the head and XP its phrase or 'maximal projection'. An important constraint on this structure is that it is (maximally) binary branching, a constraint that limits the types of possible structure and thus goes some way towards achieving explanatory adequacy.

The structure in (6) is used to model the relationships between heads, specifiers, complements and adjuncts not only within lexical phrasal categories such as Noun Phrase (NP) and Verb Phrase (VP), but also within functional categories such as Complementiser Phrase (CP), Determiner Phrase (DP) and the clause or Inflectional Phrase (IP), more recently referred to as Tense Phrase (TP). Indeed, the extension of the X-bar model to a range of functional categories was one of the defining features of the Principles and Parameters framework in the late 1980s and early 1990s. To this end, the fact

[3] See Chomsky (1970a); Jackendoff (1977).

(6)

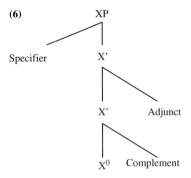

that the same basic structure is used to model lexical and functional categories entails that it can be used to model clauses as well as phrases, given the assumption that inflectional features are central to licensing the clause.

In current versions of the Principles and Parameters Minimalist model, the structural representation of a clause consists of three sub-domains: (1) the lexical layer, headed by the verb, which forms the predicational core of the clause; (2) the inflectional layer, headed by functional elements that license the clause (associated with features such as tense, aspect, mood, case and agreement); and (3) the left periphery or complementiser layer, which provides the interface between the clause and the discourse domain, hosting constituents such as topics, *wh*-phrases and focused elements.

In the 1980s version of Principles and Parameters theory, each layer was identified with a single syntactic phrase (VP, IP, CP); but this model turned out to be too restrictive to cover the whole range of newly discovered syntactic facts. Research in comparative syntax revealed that the IP and the CP domains might be more insightfully modelled in terms of sets of distinct functional projections. The evidence for the existence of such functional phrases and their relative ordering within the clause rests upon the distribution of adverbial elements and upon the patterning of tense, aspect, negation, complementisers and topic and focus morphology (see, e.g. Pollock 1989; Rizzi 1997; Cinque 1999). The diagram in (7) represents the model of clause structure that is assumed in this book. Since this book is mainly concerned with the syntax of focus, this model assumes an articulated left periphery, but does not assume an articulated verbal/inflectional layer. The motivation for this model is discussed with respect to the Hausa facts in Chapter 4 (§ 4.3).

3.2.4 *The Minimalist Program: Merge, Move and Agree*

More recently, the development of the Minimalist Program (Chomsky 1995 onwards) represents a move towards the objective of explanatory adequacy

(7)

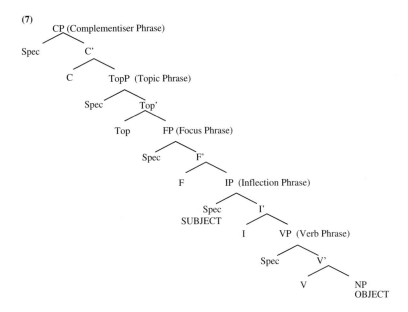

by reducing the grammar to two basic operations: Merge (structure building) and Move (displacement). The diagram in (8) represents the Minimalist model of the grammar.

An important difference between the Minimalist model and the model assumed within the Principles and Parameters framework concerns the elimination of Deep Structure and Surface Structure as distinct levels of syntactic representation.[4] Instead, a single syntactic component referred to by Chomsky as the Computational System derives syntactic structures from sets of lexical items (including both lexical and functional categories), and maps these structures onto two distinct interface levels: the level of Phonological Form (PF), which interfaces with the articulatory-perceptual performance system, and the level of semantic or Logical Form (LF), which interfaces with the conceptual-intentional performance system. In principle, the lexical items themselves, consisting of phonological, semantic and formal features, encode all the information required for the derivation, so that principles operating over the derivation remain maximally simple and general. This idea is captured by the Inclusiveness Condition (Chomsky

---

[4] A further difference between the Minimalist Model and the Principles and Parameters model concerns the Minimalist hypothesis of 'bare phrase structure' (Chomsky 1995). In essence, since only minimal (word-level) and maximal (phrase-level) units are recognisable within the computational system and at the interface, the intermediate (X-bar) levels of representation are redundant. Furthermore, the minimal/maximal status of constituents is not inherent but relational, depending on the structures in which they occur. For expository purposes, however, standard X-bar notation is retained throughout this book.

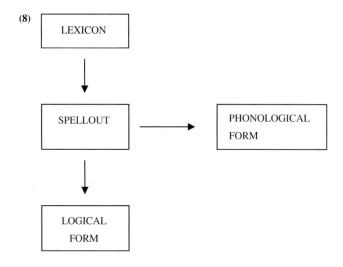

1995: 228), which reduces to a constraint upon introducing features into the derivation that are not present at the point of lexical selection. According to Chomsky (2000), the two basic structural operations occurring within the computational system, Merge and Move, are both driven by the feature-matching relation Agree. The Agree relation matches and then eliminates uninterpretable (non-semantic) morphosyntactic features, whose function is to drive the processes that build syntactic structure, but which cannot be interpreted at the semantic interface. The statement in the grammar that captures this idea is the principle of full interpretation (Chomsky 1995: 220), which states that all uninterpretable features must be eliminated from the derivation by the time it reaches the semantic interface. A derivation that fails to meet this requirement will result in an ill-formed structure.

  Merge is a basic structure-building operation that is driven largely by the thematic properties of the predicational item(s) within the set of lexical items. This operation assembles tree structures from pairs of syntactic objects. Within a phrase, Merge first creates the head–complement structure, and then merges the resulting structure with its specifier, finally combining the resulting phrase markers into larger structures. Merge is an asymmetric operation: if α and β merge, then either α or β must project to the phrasal level, and the head of the projection is the category that selects and projects. If α and β merge and α projects, then β is within the appropriate local configuration with α (either the specifier–head configuration or the sisterhood configuration) for the Agree relation to apply. This local configuration is illustrated in (9), in which α and β merge and α projects, so that α and β are sisters. In this configuration, which represents the head-complement relation, features such as the category selection features of a lexical verb can be satisfied under the Agree relation.

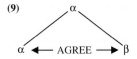

(9)

Any subsequent Merge operation applies at the root, as illustrated in (10) in which α and γ merge and α projects. In this configuration, γ is the specifier of α, and α and γ can enter Agree. This type of configuration represents the specifier–head relation, under which category selection features (among others) can also be satisfied.

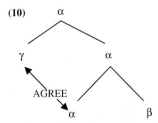

(10)

To provide a canonical example of how these rather abstract operations derive familiar structures, diagram (11) shows how, in the two steps illustrated in diagrams (9) and (10), a transitive verb has its category selection features satisfied as it becomes part of a structure representing the thematic core of a clause. The uninterpretable category selection features of the verb *play*, represented as [*u*N, *u*N], are matched and eliminated (indicated by strikeout) as the verb is merged in a structure with the nominal complement *guitar* and nominal specifier *Ted*. Subsequent Merge operations build functional structure that introduces properties such as agreement, tense, case and so on.

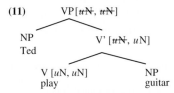

(11)

The operation Move is motivated by features on functional heads that are known as 'EPP' features because, like the position created for 'dummy' or expletive subjects by the Extended Projection Principle (Chomsky 1981), they result in the projection of specifier positions not determined by thematically driven structure building. Move targets specifier positions of 'core' functional categories such as CP, and IP. EPP features are uninterpretable or non-semantic, and, like other uninterpretable features, must therefore be eliminated by Agree in the course of the derivation. While some uninterpretable features are eliminated by Agree without Move (for example, category selection features are eliminated by Agree as soon as the thematic structure is built), uninterpretable EPP features are the formal mechanism for displacement, and are assigned to heads at the point of lexical selection only if they will (mechanically) give rise to a distinct interpretation at the semantic interface. As an example of this process, EPP features are the mechanism for operations such as *wh*-fronting, which raises a constituent to a position in the left periphery of the clause and thus licenses an interrogative interpretation.

Turning finally to cross-linguistic differences, an aspect of parametric variation that is particularly pertinent to the present study concerns the 'overt/covert' movement distinction that originated within the Principles and Parameters framework (Huang 1982; 1984). According to this perspective, the difference between '*wh*-movement' languages like English and '*wh*-in situ' languages like Chinese is accounted for in terms of the point in the derivation at which movement occurs. Overt movement takes place in the syntactic component (that is, before the derivation is transferred to the phonological component), and therefore has consequences both for word order and for interpretation. In contrast, covert movement takes place after the point of transfer to the phonological component, having consequences for the interpretation but not for the word order.[5] English and Chinese *wh*-constructions therefore share the same interpretation by virtue of having their *wh*-expressions in the appropriate scope-taking position at LF, but displacement of the *wh*-expression takes place 'later' in Chinese, leaving the surface word order unaffected.

This sketch of the theoretical framework assumed in this book is sufficient for the discussion that follows. For the most part, a rather simple Principles and Parameters-style representation of the Hausa facts will be adopted throughout this book; but aspects of the Minimalist framework that are central to a syntactic theory of focus, and are thus incorporated into the analysis, are elaborated below (§ 3.4).

---

[5] In more recent versions of the Minimalist framework, Spellout occurs cyclically by phase, so that there is no single 'moment' between pre- and post-Spellout for any given derivation. Chomsky (2001a) defines a phase as consisting of a functional head and the substantive XP it selects as a complement. Chomsky (2001b) defines vP and CP as strong phases (those eligible for Spellout) since these are both 'propositional' constructions. Despite cyclic Spellout, however, Chomsky (2001b: 9) states that Move can apply either before or after Transfer, the operation that passes the output of the syntactic computation to the phonological and semantic components. In this version of the model, cyclic Spellout occurs between Transfer and the phonological interface, while covert displacement occurs between Transfer and the semantic interface, hence the overt/covert distinction is maintained.

3.3 What is focus?

3.3.1 *Semantics and pragmatics*

Focus is one aspect of a linguistic phenomenon known as information structure (Halliday 1967) or information packaging (Chafe 1976a). These terms refer to ways in which a sentence may be structured, syntactically, morphologically or prosodically, to reflect pragmatic or discourse-related goals. A long-held view is that sentences are structured to reflect the distinction between 'old' information and 'new' information.[6] Focused constituents are often described as indicating 'new' information, and are contrasted with topics, which reflect 'old', 'given' or 'presupposed' information. Consider example (12), where underlining indicates topic:

(12) <u>that flatmate of yours</u>, he's a budding pop star

Lambrecht (1994: 325) defines topic 'as being the element which the proposition will be about or which serves to establish the temporal, spatial or instrumental framework within which the proposition holds'. Sentences of the type illustrated in (12) are traditionally divided into 'topic and comment' or 'theme and rheme', where topic/theme represent the 'old' or discourse-given information (*that flatmate of yours*), and comment/rheme contains new information about that topic (*he's a budding pop star*). Topicalisation in Hausa is discussed in Chapter 4 (§ 4.2.2).

As Lambrecht (1994) points out, the characterisation of focus in terms of 'new' information may be too simplistic. For example, a constituent may be simultaneously focused and reflect 'old' or 'given' information (a referent known to both hearer and speaker), as illustrated by (13) (Lambrecht 1994:211):

(13) Q: where did you go last night, to the movies or to the restaurant?
      A: we went to the **restaurant**

As Lambrecht suggests, what is 'new' about the information encoded by focus is not the introduction of new or unfamiliar referents into the discourse, but the relation between the referent of the focused constituent and the proposition in which it participates. Lambrecht, who views focus as a pragmatic relation, distinguishes topic and focus as follows:

> While the pragmatic relation between a topic and a proposition is assumed to be predictable or recoverable, the relation between the focus element and the proposition is assumed to unpredictable or non-recoverable for the addressee at the time of the utterance ... and thereby

---

[6] See e.g. Bolinger (1954); Halliday (1967); Chomsky (1970b); Kuno (1972); Chafe (1976a; 1976b); Jackendoff (1972), Clark & Haviland (1977); and discussion in Lambrecht (1994).

creates a new state of information in the mind of the addressee.
(Lambrecht 1994: 218)

The information encoded by focus can be subdivided into distinct types
depending on its semantic/pragmatic properties. Consider the following
examples.

(14) a. guess what? I've just seen Ted!
     b. Q: who did you see at work yesterday?
        A: I saw **Ted**
     c. Q: did you see Bill or Ted at work yesterday?
        A: I saw **Ted**
     d. Q: did you see Bill at work yesterday?
        A: no, it was **Ted** I saw, not Bill

Presentational focus, which is a type of new information focus, arises in
presentational or 'out of the blue' contexts like (14a). In an English example
like this, prosodic prominence falls on *Ted*, but the focus encompasses more
than this constituent, spreading to the predicate and arguably to the entire
proposition, which represents 'new' information. New information focus
also arises in discourse-linked contexts such as *wh*-question–answer pairs
(14b), where the focused constituent in the answer provides a value for the
variable introduced by the *wh*-phrase in the question. New information
focus foregrounds a particular constituent, but not to the exclusion of other
possibilities. For example, in (14a) and (14b), Ted is not necessarily the only
person seen by the speaker. Exhaustive listing focus, a term introduced by
Kuno (1972) and developed by Szabolcsi (1981a; 1983), specifies an
exhaustive set of which the proposition holds true, and excludes other
possibilities (14c).

Contrastive focus (14d) can be seen as a sub-case of exhaustive listing
focus, where the other members of the set are explicitly ruled out, either
within the utterance that contains the focus itself or by inference from the
discourse context.

Within the functional tradition, which places emphasis on the commu-
nicative functions of language, focus is viewed primarily as a pragmatic
phenomenon.[7] According to this perspective, the meaning and the form (i.e.
morphosyntactic and prosodic properties) of focus constructions cannot be
separated from the discourse goals that motivate them, so that any account of
focus must take into account the broader discourse context of the utterance,
the intentions of the speaker and so on. Within the formal tradition, which
attempts to model the meaning and form of a sentence independently of
discourse context, a formal semantic analysis is adopted, wherein focus
is generally viewed as a scope-taking operator. For example, Jackendoff

---

[7] See Halliday (1967); Kuno (1972); Dik (1981b); Firbas (1992); and discussion in Lambrecht
(1994).

(1972), among others, suggests that focus has the role of 'structuring' the proposition into presupposition (information shared by both speaker and hearer) and focus (information that the speaker assumes is not shared by the hearer). Consider the following examples (Rooth 1996: 275):

(15) a. John introduced **Bill** to Sue
     b. $\langle \lambda x$ [introduce (j,x,s)],b$\rangle$

(16) a. John introduced Bill to **Sue**
     b. $\langle \lambda y$ [introduce (j,b,y)],s$\rangle$

According to this perspective, the semantics of a sentence like the one in (15) consists of a presupposition *John introduced somebody to Sue*, where the variable x ('somebody') is assigned a value by the focused constituent, which represents the new information in the sentence (*Bill*). Equally, example (16) consists of the presupposition *John introduced Bill to somebody*, where the value of x ('somebody') is assigned by the focused constituent *Sue*. The scope-taking properties of focus are represented in the semantic structure by a lambda-operator.

Szabolcsi (1981a; 1983) proposes an analysis of focus within a Montague Grammar framework, wherein the focus operator has an exhaustive listing function: it 'operates on a set of contextually relevant entities present in the domain of discourse, and identifies all and only the elements of this set of which the predicate holds' (É. Kiss 1995a: 15). Within this approach, the semantics of the following Hungarian example in (17a) can be modelled as in (17b) (É. Kiss 1995a: 15):

(17) a. **János** kapott jelest
        John   got   A+
        '**John** got A+'
     b. For every x, x got A+ if and only if x = John

Rooth (1992; 1996) develops a theory known as 'alternative semantics' in which the focus operator has the function of generating a set of alternatives. Consider the following example (Rooth 1996: 276):

(18) Q: does Ede want tea or coffee?
     A: Ede wants **coffee**

The focus in the response to the question generates a set of alternatives of the form *Ede wants x* (here, *Ede wants tea*), against which the utterance is interpreted. However, as É. Kiss (1995a: 17) points out, Rooth's characterisation of focus does not capture exhaustivity. In other words, it does not entail that only the alternative identified by the focus is true; this aspect of the semantics of focus is introduced in his theory by explicit *only*.

A further widely adopted distinction is between broad focus and narrow focus, which is based on the semantic scope of prosodically marked focus.

Languages like English, which can mark focus primarily by prosodic means, have been the subject of much discussion within this perspective.[8] Example (19) illustrates broad focus in English. If prosodic prominence (marked by SMALL CAPITALS) falls on the final constituent, the whole sentence may be interpreted as focused, and is therefore licensed in a presentational context:

(19) guess what? Ted bought a new guitar with six STRINGS

If the prosodic prominence falls earlier in the sentence, the scope of focus becomes less broad. In example (20), the scope of focus corresponds to the bracketed constituent, the subject of the sentence:

(20) [a new guitar with six STRINGS] was in the shop window

Compare finally example (21), where the focus is narrower still:

(21) [a NEW guitar] with six strings was in the shop window

While this prosodic scope-based distinction between broad and narrow focus may appear to correlate with the semantic distinction between new information and exhaustive focus respectively, the correlation is not direct. For example, sentence-final prosodic prominence can result in a wide range of interpretations depending on discourse context, as the following examples illustrate. In each example, the scope of focus is marked by square brackets. Selkirk (1984) refers to this phenomenon as focus projection.

(22) a. Q: what's that noise?
          A: [Ted's playing his new GUITAR]
      b. Q: what's Ted doing?
          A: Ted's [playing his new GUITAR]
      c. Q: what's Ted playing?
          A: Ted's playing [his new GUITAR]
      d. Q: is Ted playing his tuba?
          A: no, Ted's playing his [new GUITAR]

Despite these differences between formal and functional approaches on the one hand and between different formal approaches on the other, what unites most theories of focus is the recognition of a broad distinction between (non-exhaustive) new information focus on the one hand and exhaustive/contrastive focus on the other, a distinction that will be further explored with respect to Hausa in Chapter 4.

3.3.2 Structural features and typology

From the examples in the preceding section, it is already clear that languages may realise focus by a range of structural means, which may be

---

[8] See Bolinger (1954; 1985); Selkirk (1984); Ladd (1996); Cruttenden (1997).

phonological (prosodic), morphological or syntactic, or some combination of these. Phonological realisation of focus may involve different phonological features depending on the language type. The term 'prosody' refers to suprasegmental sound features such as relative pitch, duration (length) and intensity (loudness). These features may combine to function at various levels within languages, affecting small units like syllables and words, or larger units like sentence-level utterances. Prosodic features are therefore involved in marking lexical and grammatical contrast at the word level, as well as in distinguishing grammatical clause types (e.g. declarative from interrogative) and in marking information structure properties at the sentence level.[9]

While languages cannot be strictly classified according to a strict tone/intonation dichotomy (§ 2.3.1), a more plausible typology divides languages into tone, pitch accent and stress accent languages. In a tone language like Hausa, pitch (relative highness or lowness of a speech sound) functions mainly at the word level to mark lexical or grammatical contrast. In a pitch accent language like Japanese, word meanings are also distinguished by pitch, but unlike in a tone language, the pitch of each syllable is dependent upon the others. With respect to stress accent languages like English, 'stress' refers to the relative prominence of a particular part of an utterance (either at the word or the sentence level) resulting from some combination of pitch, intensity and duration. The relationship between focus and prosody involves prosodic features that function at the sentence level, resulting in the relative prosodic prominence of a particular constituent.[10]

According to Harries-Delisle (1978), phonological strategies for the realisation of focus are common in the Indo-European languages, as well as in the Finno-Ugric and Bantu families (see Hyman 1999) and in Chinese. In English, for example, focus can be realised in situ (without syntactic reordering) by means of prosodic prominence. Indeed, this is the least restricted strategy in English; prosodic prominence can be used to mark any constituent within the clause, and can be used in a range of discourse contexts to encode distinct types of focus, as the examples in (13)–(22) above illustrate. Harries-Delisle (1978: 471) provides the following examples of a phonological strategy in the tone language Kihung'an (Bantu), where focus is marked by a final-syllable tone change from L to H:

(23) a. Kìpès   ka-swīm-in   kìt   zǒn   'neutral'
        Kipes   SUBJ.AGR-buy-PAST chair yesterday
        'Kipes bought a chair yesterday'

---

[9] In addition, prosodic features can mark 'affective' features (such as the emotion or attitude of the speaker), which will not be discussed here.

[10] Since the terms 'stress' and 'accent' (prominence due to pitch) are often used inconsistently in the literature, I follow Cruttenden (1997) in using the more neutral term 'prosodic prominence'.

     b.   Kìpès   ka-swīm-in   **kit**   zὸn   *object focus*
          Kipes   SUBJ.AGR-buy-PAST   chair   yesterday
          'Kipes bought **a chair** yesterday'
     c.   **Kìpes**   ka-swīm-in   kìt   zὸn   *subject focus*
          Kipes   SUBJ.AGR-buy-PAST   chair   yesterday
          '**Kipes** bought a chair yesterday'

While the phonological realisation of focus is a common strategy for focus marking, it does not always occur independently. For many languages that use morphological and syntactic means for focus marking, phonological marking often co-occurs with these strategies. While Lambrecht (1994: 225) describes the phonological strategy as 'the only device that occurs by itself', Harries-Delisle (1978: 421) claims that 'there are no languages that solely make use of phonological means to express contrastive emphasis'. Harries-Delisle (1978: 471) further claims that all languages that have this device also have additional means for marking focus, whereas some languages, including Vei (Niger-Congo), Amharic (Semitic) and Mohawk (Iroquoian), do not make use of phonological focus marking at all.

Morphological strategies for focus marking include focus particles (frequently related to non-verbal copulas) and 'special inflection' within the verbal-inflectional system. Languages with focus particles include many African languages (including Hausa, § 2.4.3), Malayo-Polynesian (Austronesian) languages, and Indian (Indo-Iranian) languages including Bengali, Hindi and Marathi. Examples (24)–(26) illustrate (Harries-Delisle 1978: 430-32). As these examples show, the presence of a focus particle may or may not co-occur with syntactic re-ordering.[11]

(24) a.   tia   anao   izahay   *Malagasy (Austronesian)*
         love   you   we   *'neutral'*
         'we love you'
     b.   **izahay** no tia   anao   *subject focus*
         we   FM   love   you
         '**we** love you'
(25) a.   maganda   ang   bata   *Tagalog (Austronesian)*
         beautiful   the   child   *'neutral'*
         'the child is beautiful'
     b.   **ang**   **bata**   ay   maganda   *subject focus*
         the   child   FM   beautiful
         '**the child** is beautiful'

---

[11] Since Harries-Delisle concentrates her investigation on 'contrastive emphasis', she labels constructions lacking this feature as 'neutral'. As Lambrecht (1994: 16-17) points out, however, 'there are no sentences without information structure': every sentence uttered contains some focus, given that it is uttered within a context that includes assumptions about what is known to the hearer. Lambrecht suggest that a 'pragmatically unmarked' sentence type is one that performs a wider range of discourse functions than its 'pragmatically marked' correlates.

(26) a. mi   tyana   pəyse   dein   *Marathi (Indo-Iranian)*
         I   them   money   give   *'neutral'*
         'I give them money'
     b. mi   **tyana**-ts   pəyse   dein   *indirect object focus*
         I   them-FM   money   give
         'I gave **them** money'

Languages that display 'special inflection' in focus constructions include Hausa (§ 2.3.2), Diola-Fogny (Niger-Congo), Telugu (Dravidian) Kikuyu (Bantu) and Kanuri (Nilo-Saharan) (Harries-Delisle 1978); Chamorro (Austronesian; Chung 1998); Palauan (Austronesian; Georgopoulos 1985;1991); Coptic (Ancient Egyptian; Reintges 2003a); and Makua (Bantu; Stucky 1979, cited in Croft 2003). The following examples illustrate:

(27) a. nĩn   gahaica   kĩrĩma   *Kikuyu*
         I   shall.climb hill   *'neutral'*
         kĩu   rũciũ   (Harries-Delisle 1978: 427)
         that tomorrow
         'I shall climb that hill tomorrow'
     b. nĩ   **kĩrĩma kĩu**   ngahaica   *object focus*
         FM(COP) hill   that   I.shall.climb
         rũciũ
         tomorrow
         'I shall climb **that hill** tomorrow'
(28) a. hín-sepété   áhó-han-á   *Makua*
         Sepete   SUB.TNS-forge-ASP   *'neutral'*
         níváka   (Stucky 1979,
         spear   in Croft 2003: 109)
         'Sepete forged a spear'
     b. hín-sepété   aa-han-ílé   *object focus*
         Sepete   SUB.TNS-forge-ASP
         nivaka
         spear
         'Sepete forged a **spear**'

Syntactic strategies for marking focus may include displacement of the focused constituent to a designated focus position, the use of a designated syntactic clause structure (clefting), or scrambling. Languages with a designated focus position are often described as discourse configurational (É. Kiss 1995a). The discourse configurational group can be further split according to where the designated focus position is. A common pattern is for the designated focus position to be clause-initial, as in Hausa (§ 2.4.3) and many other languages including Somali (Cushitic; Svolacchia et al. 1995; see also Saeed 1984; 1999) and Greek (Tsimpli 1995):

(29) a. **wiilal-kii** baa moos   cunayá   *Somali*
        boys-the FM banana eating   *subject focus*
        (Svolacchia et al. 1995: 68)
        'the boys are eating a banana'
     b. **moos**   baa wiil-kii cunayaa   *object focus*
        banana   FM boy-the eating
        'the boy is eating **a banana**'
(30) a. **to   vivlio** edhose i   Maria   *direct object focus*
        the.ACC book gave.3s the.NOM Maria   *Greek*
        sto   Yani   (Tsimpli 1995: 177–9)
        to.the.ACC Yani
        'Maria gave **the book** to Yani'
     b. **tis   Marias** edhosa to   vivlio   *indirect object focus*
        the.GEN Maria gave.1s the.ACC book
        'I gave the book **to Maria**'

The clause-initial position is not the only widely attested designated
focus position, however. Other common patterns include movement to a
position local to the verb. For example, the designated focus position is
a pre-verbal position in Basque (Ortiz de Urbina 1995) and in
Hungarian, where the clause-initial constituent is the topic (É. Kiss
1995b: 209):

(31) a. Évát   **János** várta a   mozi   *subject focus*
        Eve.ACC John waited the cinema *Hungarian*
        előtt   (É. Kiss 1995b: 209)
        in.front.of
        'Eve was waited for in front of the cinema by **John**'
     b. János   **Évát**   várta a   mozi   *object focus*
        John   Eve.ACC waited the cinema
        előtt
        in.front.of
        'John waited for **Eve** in front of the cinema'
     c. a   mozi   előtt   **János** várta   *subject focus*
        the cinema in.front.of John waited
        Évát
        Eve.ACC
        'in front of the cinema, **John** waited for Eve'

In certain Chadic languages, as in the Bantu language Aghem (Hyman
& Watters 1984), the designated focus position is the postverbal
position (Tuller 1992). In the VSO Chadic language Podoko, the
focus position is immediately adjacent to the verb, whereas in the
SVO Chadic language Kanakuru, the focus position follows the direct
object:

(32) a   təla   **də** ˠkwədəgə malə   sləɓə   *Podoko*
     INFL cook in kitchen   mother.my meat   (Jarvis 1981: 161)
     'my mother cooked the meat **in the kitchen'**

(33) are lowoi **jewoi**   la lusha   *Kanakuru*
     bury boy.the slave-the in bush   (Newman 1974,
     '**the slave** buried the boy in the bush'   in Tuller 1992:307)

Clefts are distinct from the focus fronting structures shown in (29) and (30) in that, while displacement to a designated clause-initial focus position does not create a biclausal structure, clefting does. The following English examples illustrate:

(34) a. **macadamia nuts**, they're called   (Lambrecht 1994: 225)
     b. it's **macadamia nuts** (that) she wants, not pecan nuts

While the structure in (34a) involves displacement to the clause-initial position, the structure remains monoclausal, containing a single lexical verb. The cleft structure in (34b), on the other hand, is biclausal, containing a copula verb that projects its own clausal structure in addition to that of the lower lexical verb contained within the relative clause. This distinction between monoclausal focus fronting structures and cleft structures is not a matter of consensus in the literature, however. The label 'cleft' is frequently applied to focus fronting structures, particularly those that contain some form of copula (a common focus strategy), regardless of whether the resulting structure is monoclausal or biclausal. Harries-Delisle, for example, defines clefts as follows:

> Cleft sentences … are equational sentences which establish an identity between a known or presupposed entity and a focused entity which represents the new information… The subject of a cleft sentence consists of a head noun like *the one* which is modified by a restrictive relative clause. The head noun is always a neutral noun like *the one, the man, the person, the he*, which is more closely defined by the relative clause. (Harries-Delisle 1978: 422)

Harries-Delisle (1978: 424) then states that 'the copula as well as the neutral head noun and/or the relative clause marker can be absent', thereby collapsing cleft structures and focus fronting structures into a single category, where the latter are viewed as 'underlying' clefts. This view is prevalent, particularly in the descriptive literature, and arises from the fact that cleft structures and focus fronting structures are often functionally equivalent, as well as the fact that focus fronting structures are sometimes historically related to clefts, given that focus particles often emerge from cleft sentence markers (§ 5.3). The issue of whether or not Hausa focus constructions should be described as clefts is examined in Chapter 4 (§ 4.3).

A striking observation relating to languages with designated focus positions concerns the position targeted by *wh*-phrases. It is extremely common for *wh*-phrases to target the designated focus position. This is attested in a wide range of languages including Somali (Cushitic), Chadic languages, Aghem (Bantu), Basque, Hungarian, Haida (Na-Dene), Omaha (Siouan), Quechua (Quechuan), Korean and Greek (É. Kiss 1995a: 23). Recall from Chapter 2 (§ 2.4.3) that Hausa shares this property. The extent to which a unified syntactic analysis can be developed for focus and *wh*-constructions in Hausa is explored in Chapter 4 (§ 4.4).

The final syntactic strategy for focus marking explored here is scrambling, a phenomenon common within the Romance languages, among others. Scrambling does not involve a designated focus position nor a designated clause structure, but rather a syntactic reordering process that, in some languages at least, is prosodically motivated (Zubizarreta 1998). In other words, the scrambled structure differs from the 'unmarked' structure in that constituents are displaced from their canonical positions in order to 'strand' the focused constituent in the default position for prosodic prominence within the clause. In Catalan, for example, the default position for prosodic prominence is at 'the righthand boundary of the core clause' (Vallduví 1995: 127), and scrambled constituents are either right- or left-detached. Detached constituents are linked to clitic resumptive pronouns within the core clause, and, in the case of right detachment, are separated from the core clause by a pause. The following examples show a subset of possible constructions that may arise from the 'base' word order in (35a) (Vallduví 1995: 127-8):[12]

(35) a. ficarem   el   ganivet   **al**   **calaix**
        we.will.put the knife   in.the   drawer
        'we'll put the knife **in the drawer**'

     b. hi$_i$-ficarem   **el   ganivet**, al   calaix$_i$
        LOC(RP)-we.will.put   the knife   in.the   drawer
        'we'll put **the knife** in the drawer'

     c. al   calaix$_i$ hi$_i$ ficarem   **el   ganivet**
        in.the   drawer   LOC(RP)   we.will.put   the knife
        'in the drawer we'll put **the knife**'

     d. el   ganivet$_i$ al   calaix$_i$ l$_i$-hi$_k$-**ficarem**
        the knife   in.the   drawer   OBJ(RP)-LOC(RP)-we.will.put
        'we will **put** the knife in the drawer'

A (non-exhaustive) typology of focus marking strategies is given in Table 3.1.[13] From this brief survey, it is clear that languages frequently, if not

---

[12] See Zubizarreta (1998) for a similar, but apparently more restricted, process in Spanish and Italian.

[13] Compiled from É Kiss (1995a); Lambrecht (1994); Croft (1991); Reintges (2003b); Tuller (1992); Rebuschi & Tuller (1999); Kihm (1999); Lecarme (1999); Ouhalla (1999).

Table 3.1 Typology of focus-marking strategies

Phonological	Morphological		Syntactic		
	FOCUS PARTICLE	SPECIAL INFLECTION	FOCUS MOVEMENT	CLEFTING	SCRAMBLING
English	Hausa	Hausa	Hausa	English	Catalan
Finnish	Malagasy	Diola Fogny	English	French	Spanish
Hungarian	Tagalog	Telugu	Somali	Arabic	Italian
Chinese	Bengali	Kanuri	Greek	Wolof	
Kihung'an	Hindi	Chamorro	Basque		
	Marathi	Palauan	Hungarian		
	Somali	Coptic	Podoko		
		Kikuyu	Kanakuru		
		Makua	Finnish		

always, have recourse to more than one means of structurally instantiating focus, and that these strategies may co-occur. Naturally, the question arises of whether there is any evidence for form–function mapping within focus systems between structural realisation of focus on the one hand and semantic/pragmatic focus type on the other. This issue is discussed further below (§ 3.4.3).

3.4 GENERATIVE THEORIES OF FOCUS

Various syntactic theories have been proposed to account for the morphosyntax of focus within the framework described above (§ 3.2). These theories can be broadly divided into those that place the burden of explanation on syntactic mechanisms (§ 3.4.1) and those that investigate properties of the phonological component in accounting for the morpho-syntax of focus (§ 3.4.2). In addition, there are also phonological theories that aim to account for the prosody–syntax interface but have less to say about the morphosyntax of focus independent of prosody (e.g. Selkirk 1984). The latter require an exploration of phonological theory that goes beyond the scope of the current volume, and will not be discussed here.[14]

3.4.1 Syntax-based theories

A number of theories of focus emerged within the Government and Binding framework and within the Principles and Parameters framework that relied upon the presence of a syntactic [+ FOCUS] feature as a mechanism for explaining the displacement properties of focus constructions. While the idea of a [+ FOCUS] feature has its roots in early generative theories of focus that attempted to explain stress assignment (e.g. Jackendoff 1972), the

---

[14] The relationship between prosody and focus in Hausa is the subject of ongoing research (Green, in preparation). See also Hartmann & Zimmermann (forthcoming, a).

status of the [+ FOCUS] feature in more recent theories is somewhat different, in that it is viewed as an abstract syntactic feature (analogous with the [+ *wh*] feature or with case features) that drives displacement in focus movement languages, resulting in an analysis of focus as a scope-taking operator. From this perspective, focus constructions are one type of operator-variable dependency (rather like *wh*-constructions), which involve a relation between an open position or 'gap' in the clause corresponding to the thematic position of the focused constituent (the variable) and the higher element (the extracted constituent, or operator) upon which the variable relies to be fully interpreted. Hence, the emphasis in such treatments is less on prosody and more on the morphosyntax and semantics of focus movement constructions.

Horvath (1986) was among the first to develop a theory of focus within a modern transformational framework. Horvath's analysis rested upon the presence of a syntactic feature [+ FOCUS]. She proposed that this feature occurred cross-linguistically in one of two ways (the 'Focus Parameter'): either [+ FOCUS] is freely assigned to any category within a given language, resulting in focus-in situ languages like English, or [+ FOCUS] is part of the feature matrix of some syntactic head to which a focused constituent must be local, deriving focus-movement languages like Hungarian. This analysis is reminiscent of structural case theory in the transformational framework, where a NP is only licensed if it stands in a local configuration with a case-assigning head. In Hungarian, for example, Horvath argued that the [+ FOCUS] feature was part of the feature matrix of the verb, since the Hungarian ex situ focus position is left adjacent to the verb.

As the Government and Binding framework gained ground in the mid-1980s, the extension of the X-bar structure to the clause (IP) and the left periphery of the clause (CP) gave rise to a number of analyses in which focus movement received a parallel syntactic analysis to *wh*-movement, targeting the SpecCP position. Such analyses include Ortiz de Urbina (1986) and Tuller (1986a). This soon became the standard transformational approach to focus fronting, given well-attested cross-linguistic parallels between focus fronting constructions and *wh*-movement constructions (§§ 2.4, 3.3.2).[15]

In an influential paper, Brody (1990) extended Horvath's (1986) proposals for Hungarian focus constructions, and proposed that the [+ FOCUS] feature is assigned within a designated functional projection: the focus phrase (FP). In Hungarian, focused constituents either move to the pre-verbal position (also the target of *wh*-phrases) or receive in situ focus (marked by prosodic prominence), which happens when the verb itself is in focus, or in the case of multiple focus constructions, where one focused constituent must move and the other remains in situ. In Brody's theory, the [+ FOCUS] feature is assigned freely to focused constituents in situ within the

---

[15] See Rebuschi & Tuller (1999: 3–13) for a more detailed history of this period.

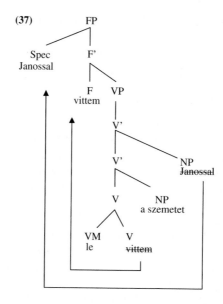

(37)

propositional part of the sentence (VP), but can also be assigned outside VP, by V, to moved focus phrases. Consider the following examples. Example (36a) represents the unmarked counterpart of (36b).

(36) a. le-vittem   a   szemetet Janossal
       down-took.1s the rubbish   John.with
       Hungarian (Brody 1990: 210)
       'I took down the rubbish with John'
    b. **Janossal** vittem-le   a   szemetet
       John.with took.1s-down the   rubbish
       'I took down the rubbish with **John**'
    c. * **Janossal** le-vittem   a   szemetet
       John-with   down-took.1s the   rubbish

As these examples demonstrate, the position of the verbal modifier *le* is left-adjacent to the verb in neutral sentences, but must occur right-adjacent to the verb in focus constructions. According to Brody, this is evidence that the verb raises in order to assign the [+ FOCUS] feature to the focused phrase under the conditions of government and adjacency. The verb targets the F position (head of FP), and the focused phrase is located in SpecFP. Brody's analysis of focus movement in Hungarian is illustrated in (37).

Brody proposes the following conditions, reminiscent of Rizzi's (1996) *Wh*-Criterion, which Horvath (1995) calls the Focus Criterion (Brody 1990: 208):

(38) a. At S-structure and LF the spec of an FP must contain
         a [+ FOCUS] phrase
      b. At LF all [+ FOCUS] phrases must be in an FP

Clause (38a) applies only to languages with focus movement, whereas
clause (38b) is universal. In Brody's (1990) theory, then, parametric
variation in focus constructions arises from the level at which the
requirements of the focus criterion are fulfilled.

A more recent proposal by É. Kiss (1998a) raises some interesting
questions for a transformational theory of focus. In this frequently cited
paper, É. Kiss adopts Brody's (1990) FP analysis and assumes that the
overt/covert movement distinction can be exploited as the mechanism for
explaining parametric variation with respect to focus movement. More
interesting is É. Kiss's proposal that 'identificational' focus (for our
purposes, exhaustive listing focus) is associated cross-linguistically, either
overtly or covertly, with focus movement to a scope-taking position,
whereas 'informational' (new information) focus is realised cross-linguistically as focus in situ. Essentially, É. Kiss's analysis predicts a partial form–
function mapping between structural realisation of focus on the one hand
and semantic focus type on the other: in situ focus may have a new
information interpretation, or it may have an exhaustive interpretation
resulting from 'covert' movement to a scope-taking position. In contrast, ex
situ focus is predicted to entail an exhaustive ('identificational') interpretation in all instances.

In addition to these empirical issues, a theoretical issue also arises here.
Given the Minimalist view of language as a perfectly economical system, it
is perhaps unexpected that languages should have more than one marked
structural means of achieving the same interpretive goal. If a language has
more than one focusing strategy, the question that arises is whether each of
these corresponds to a distinct interpretive goal, or whether interpretive
'decisions' are instead forced by pragmatic factors. It is clearly considerations of this nature that motivate approaches like the one developed by É.
Kiss (1998a). If it can be established for a given language that each distinct
focusing strategy results in a distinct interpretation, then the view of
language as a perfectly economical system receives some support. If, on the
other hand, the empirical facts turn out to be inconsistent with this
hypothesis, the conclusion follows that optionality exists in the syntax.
These questions have been explored for Hausa by Green & Jaggar (2003), a
discussion that is taken up in Chapter 4 (§ 4.6).

3.4.2 *Prosody-based theories*

A number of recent theories emphasise the role of the phonological
component in accounting for the syntactic properties of focus constructions,

approaches that reflect suggestions made by Chomsky (1995; 2000) that 'stylistic' operations such as focus movement might be relegated to the phonological component. For example, Reinhart (1993; 1995) proposes a theory of focus that relates structure and use by means of the notion of interface economy, which is distinct from derivational economy:

> The intuition behind interface economy is that in actual human practice, deriving sentences is not an activity motivated just by a compulsion to check features, but speakers use their innate tools to express ideas, or to reach other interface goals. When the computational system leaves room for optionality, maybe the choice of operations is directed at such kinds of goals. (Reinhart 1995: 47)

The idea behind Reinhart's theory is that 'marked' derivations involve a greater processing cost, which can only be offset by some interpretive benefit at the interpretive interface: global economy will only allow marked derivations if they achieve some interface goal that could not be achieved by a less costly derivation.

Reinhart illustrates this theory by examining the relationship between distinct strategies for marking focus: phonological strategies and syntactic strategies. Reinhart assumes the nuclear stress rule (NSR) of Chomsky & Halle (1968), more recently elaborated by Cinque (1993), wherein it is argued that there is a 'default' stress assignment rule that places prosodic prominence on the most deeply embedded constituent: the object, in English. As illustrated above in example (22), repeated here as (39), this can give rise to a range of contextually determined interpretations without recourse to any additional operations that mark focus structurally:

(39) a. Q: what's that noise?
        A: [Ted's playing his new GUITAR]
     b. Q: what's Ted doing?
        A: Ted's [playing his new GUITAR]
     c. Q: what's Ted playing?
        A: Ted's playing [his new GUITAR]
     d. Q: is Ted playing his tuba?
        A: no, Ted's playing his [new GUITAR]

As these examples illustrate, the NSR gives rise to interpretations where focus takes scope either over the whole clause, over the VP, or over sub-parts of the VP. However, the NSR does not license subject focus:

(40)   Q: is Bill playing his new guitar?
        A: #no, Ted's playing his new GUITAR
        A': no, TED's playing his new guitar

In order to focus the subject, prosodic prominence has to be relocated to that constituent. Cinque calls this the 'marked' focus rule, a costly process that involves 'deaccenting' (reversal of the NSR) followed by reassignment of prosodic prominence to the focused constituent.

Reinhart (1995) incorporates these ideas into her theory of interface economy, claiming that if a language can achieve focus on constituents not containing nuclear stress by some means other than Cinque's marked focus rule (by scrambling, for example) it will do so. Although various questions arise concerning the extent to which it is possible to define a 'marked' operation from a theory-internal perspective, it is nevertheless possible to offer the following intuitive explanation: PF operations, being 'closer to the surface', are strongly inclined towards generalisation (witness the consistency of prosodic processes), and strongly disinclined to allow exceptions. It follows from this perspective that syntactic operations such as scrambling are 'less costly' than PF operations, and a 'costly' operation will only be licensed where it results in a distinct interpretation, or in other words, corresponds to a distinct interface goal.

As Reinhart suggests, the features that derive such marked structures might be optionally introduced at the point of lexical selection, an approach that has been built into Chomsky's recent theory in terms of optional EPP features (§ 3.2.4). Reinhart does not rule out the presence of a syntactic [+ FOCUS] feature, but leaves open the question of whether focus assignment may take place at the PF interface.

Although Reinhart discusses scrambling, it is not clear what status focus movement has in her theory, nor the extent to which this widely attested syntactic operation may be considered 'costly'. As argued in Green & Jaggar (2003), focus movement might be considered an extremely costly operation, given that it involves not only displacement in the syntax but also, in many instances, relocation of prosodic prominence from its default position to the ex situ focused constituent. Yet in English, for example, the 'marked focus rule' is applied at least as freely as clefting, and both can result in exhaustive listing focus. While the predictions of Reinhart's theory for scrambling languages are clear, it is less clear what the predictions are for focus movement (including clefting) languages. Furthermore, it remains to be established whether this approach can be usefully extended to tone languages like Hausa.

Zubizarreta (1998) develops a theory that is similar in spirit to Reinhart's theory; indeed, an earlier version of Zubizarreta's theory appeared in 1994 and is frequently cited by Reinhart (1995). Zubizarreta argues that scrambling in Spanish is motivated by the objective of 'stranding' a constituent in nuclear stress position by scrambling other constituents to a higher position. In other words, the grammar resorts to operations in the syntax in order to satisfy a PF constraint. Zubizarreta calls this operation P-movement, distinct from 'M-movement' (syntactic operations that apply to satisfy morphological feature checking).

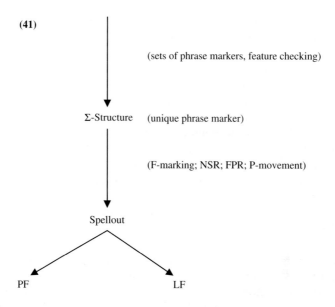

(41)

(sets of phrase markers, feature checking)

Σ-Structure   (unique phrase marker)

(F-marking; NSR; FPR; P-movement)

Spellout

PF   LF

Zubizarreta argues that the standard FP analysis is problematic, particularly with respect to the status of the [+ FOCUS] feature. She argues that this feature violates the inclusiveness principle (Chomsky 1995), which states that outputs of the system should consist of no more than lexical features. Focus is not an inherent lexical feature, nor is the prosodic prominence that accompanies it. Zubizarreta's solution is to weaken the Inclusiveness Principle to allow for the features [+ FOCUS] and [+ PROSODIC PROMINENCE] at the interface levels, given that focus operates over clause-level structures. Zubizarreta proposes a model of the grammar that incorporates a level 'Σ-Structure'. This is the level at which the derivation becomes a single (clause-level) structure (see (41)).[16]

Between Σ-Structure and Spellout, rules apply that map syntax onto prosody, such as the NSR and the matching of the focused constituent with prosodic prominence: the Focus Prominence rule or FPR. If the outputs of these two rules do not match, P-movement applies to rescue the derivation. P-movement raises the scrambled constituent to an adjoined position, deriving the correct word order and stranding the focused constituent in the default position for prosodic prominence. Like Reinhart's theory, Zubizarreta's theory of focus provides a persuasive analysis of the relationship between prosody and syntax in scrambling languages, but the predictions for focus movement languages are less clear.

---

[16] This diagram is a simplified version of Zubzarreta's (1998: 32) model, eliminating some further theoretical details.

Kidwai (1999) proposes a theory of focus that attempts to account for a wider range of structural focus strategies. Kidwai (1999: 223) considers the FP analysis 'ultimately descriptive', since it does not address the issue of why only some languages have the option of focus movement, and why those languages also have access to other structural devices for marking focus. In her theory, the [+ FOCUS] feature drives displacement, but this displacement takes place within the phonological component, under conditions of linear adjacency to a verbal projection. The [+ FOCUS] feature is checked by a verbal projection, Kidwai argues, on the basis that in many languages the focus position is local to the verbal projection. Like Horvath (1986) and Kenesei (1993), however, Kidwai (1999: 229) does not view [+ FOCUS] checking analogous to case checking, but suggests that it may be more closely associated with properties of TENSE (INFL), the position to which the verb raises, 'rather like mood, and choice of tense of aspect'.

Kidwai proposes that [+ FOCUS] is [+PF INTERPRETABLE], so that it can be licensed at any of the PF-internal levels: by PF-movement, by morphology, or by prosody. According to Kidwai, optionality follows from this analysis; movement is not forced, since the [+ PF INTERPRETABLE] [+FOCUS] feature can be spelled out in other ways. This is similar in spirit to Chomsky's (2001b: 16) statement that an uninterpretable feature 'must be transferred [to the phonological component] by transfer before it is eliminated, since it may have a phonetic reflex.' In Kidwai's model, [+ FOCUS] is interpreted in a subcomponent of PF: Domain Discourse (DD), rather than at LF. Kidwai therefore builds into the model a sharp semantic/pragmatic distinction. Kidwai's treatment of optionality is particularly appealing, but this theory leaves questions unanswered for languages in which the focus position is not local to VP, including Hausa, where there is no evidence for verb raising, and where non-verbal copular sentences also have a focus position (§§ 2.3, 5.2).

Finally, Szendröi (2001; 2003) proposes an economy-driven, prosody-based account of focus. In this analysis (in parts reminiscent of Zubizarreta's (1998) model), focus is always related to prosodic prominence, either as the result of the NSR, of movement to NSR position, of scrambling to strand a constituent in NSR position or of the relocation of main stress to a non-NSR position. In all cases, focus resulting from NSR is the unmarked or 'free' option; all other options are marked or 'costly', and what determines the 'option' chosen by a given language is the ranking of constraints within an Optimality Theory framework. Marked operations are only justified by interpretation at the interface (after Reinhart 1995).

Szendröi assumes an FP structure but, unlike Zubizarreta (1998) and Kidwai (1999), argues that there is no motivation for a [+ FOCUS] feature in the syntax at all, since focus is driven by prosodic prominence. Crucially,

Szendrői assumes that the interpretive interface can access both phonological and semantic interface levels, and follows Selkirk (1984) in assuming that main stress is not assigned to the syntactic structure, but to a prosodic structure that is related to the syntactic structure via mapping principles.

This analysis captures the Hungarian facts, because the designated focus position happens also to be the (left-peripheral) NSR position: in other words, the constituent is moved into the position where it can receive main stress by the NSR. In Optimality Theory terms, Szendrői argues that Hungarian prefers a syntactic operation over a prosodic one ('relocate main stress'), because prosody is 'ranked' higher than syntax, and therefore violations of syntax are preferred. For a language like English, on the other hand, syntax is ranked higher than prosody, so that a violation of prosody is preferred, hence the relocation of main stress for marked focus in English.

Szendrői does not discuss focus clefting or focus fronting in English, however. Given that such operations cannot be described as stress-driven, it is unclear how such constructions could be accounted for within this theory. Furthermore, as Szendrői acknowledges, it is not clear what the implications of her model are for tone languages, an issue that requires further investigation. It seems, therefore, that although Szendrői's stress-based analysis provides a persuasive explanation for certain phenomena, it may not provide the basis for a comprehensive theory of focus.

3.4.3 Model of focus assumed in the present study

As the preceding sections illustrate, there are a number of theories of focus arising from different interpretations of the current generative framework. These theories can be broadly divided into those that rely upon the presence of a syntactic [+ FOCUS] feature in explaining the syntax of focus and those that prioritise the prosodic features of focus constructions in building a theory of the syntax of focus. The issues of markedness and optionality are also recurring themes, as is the issue of the (in)dependence between the phonological and interpretive components of the grammar. This is a particularly challenging question for a strictly modular formal theory, given that focus is a phenomenon involving not only morphology and syntax, but also prosody, semantics and discourse goals. These caveats notwithstanding, this section outlines the theory of focus that will be assumed in the remainder of this study, which assumes a syntactic [+ FOCUS] feature and adopts Brody's (1990) focus phrase (FP) structure. Within this structure, the head F has a focus-EPP feature. This is not an inherent lexical feature, but is introduced into the derivation because it is the mechanism responsible for reaching an otherwise unavailable interpretation: it drives the movement process that gives rise to the marked structure that entails a focus interpretation.[17] As far as the syntactic component is concerned, this feature is uninterpretable and must therefore be eliminated as a consequence of the operation Agree. The Agree operation takes place within a local specifier–head configuration, in which the moved focus phrase in SpecFP and the head of the left-peripheral functional projection FP have a matching feature. While the [+ FOCUS] feature on the head of FP is uninterpretable, the matching feature on the focus phrase itself is interpretable, and survives to feed into the interpretive properties of the construction at LF. If movement takes place before the derivation is transferred to the phonological component, the result is overt displacement (ex situ focus). If movement takes place after the derivation is transferred to the phonological component, the result is covert displacement. In this case, the focused phrase is spelled out in situ, together with its phonological reflex.[18]

The structural analysis of focus constructions sketched here is illustrated in (42), which illustrates the focus fronting of an object NP. This analysis assumes the copy theory of movement. Within the Government and Binding/Principles and Parameters frameworks, each step of a movement operation left behind a trace: a derivational element with the interpretive properties of the moved constituent, but lacking phonetic content (Chomsky 1981; Rizzi 1990). The moved constituent and the trace together formed a chain, which linked the thematic position of the moved constituent to its surface position. Under the Minimalist Program, trace theory has been replaced by copy theory, according to which movement does not introduce a trace but leaves behind a identical copy of the moved constituent, with the result that structures formed by movement exhibit multiple copies of the moved element (Chomsky 1993; 1995; 2000). Typically, it is the higher copy that is pronounced, while lower copies are phonetically unrealised. This theoretical development was motivated by the

---

[17] According to Chomsky (2001a), while displacement operations may affect the semantics of the outcome, the displacement operations are not themselves *driven* by semantic features: 'a 'dumb' computational system shouldn't have access to considerations of that kind, typically involving discourse considerations and the like. These are best understood as properties of the resulting configuration' (Chomsky 2001a: 32). Related to this is the proposal that there may be 'optional' EPP features: these may be assigned to an item at the stage of lexical selection only if they result in an outcome that yields a distinct interpretation at the interface (Reinhart 1993 [1997]). Chomsky (2001b: 11) states that while Merge, the basic structure building operation, is associated with thematic structure, Move is 'motivated by non-theta-theoretic C-I conditions: scopal and discourse-related (informational) properties in particular'. According to this perspective, a given head is assigned an EPP feature 'only if that yields new scopal or discourse-related properties ... Informally, we can think of [EPP features] as having the 'function' of providing new interpretations; ... such functional accounts are eliminated in terms of mechanisms' (Chomsky 2001b: 11).

[18] The EPP feature analysis sketched here represents a simplified version of the analysis developed by Green & Reintges (2005b). No attempt is made here to address the Phase model developed by Chomsky (2001a; 2001b), in which head–head relations replace the specifier–head relation as the configuration under which the Agree relation applies.

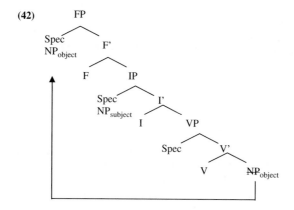

Inclusiveness Condition, according to which syntactic derivations are driven by features of the selected lexical items. As 'book-keeping' devices, traces were not included in the initial lexical array, but introduced into the syntactic representation as part of the movement operation. In contrast, the copy theory of movement does not introduce new elements into the derivation.[19] In (42), and throughout the book, unpronounced copies are indicated by strikeout.

Finally, it is worth emphasising that the theoretical discussion in the remainder of the book has little to say about the interaction between morphosyntax and prosody in Hausa focus constructions. Since the prosodic properties of Hausa focus constructions are not fully understood, the emphasis here is on developing an account of the morphosyntax, semantics and pragmatics of these constructions. However, certain restrictions on the focus marking strategies available to Hausa may be explained by the prosodic features of the language. Where relevant, hypotheses concerning the interaction between prosody and syntax in Hausa focus constructions are identified (§ 4.6). Although these hypotheses cannot be fully investigated here, they form the basis of ongoing research, and may subsequently motivate revisions to the model assumed here.[20]

---

[19] For further discussion of copy theory, see e.g. Brody (1995a); Groat & O'Neil (1996); Pesetsky (1997; 1998; 2000); Bobaljik (2002) et al.; and Reintges (2006).

[20] See Inkelas et al. (1987); Inkelas & Leben (1990); Hartmann & Zimmermann (forthcoming, a); Green (in preparation).

4

FOCUS CONSTRUCTIONS

4.1 INTRODUCTION

This chapter investigates focus in Hausa verbal clauses from both descriptive and theoretical perspectives. It begins by reviewing the descriptive properties of focus fronting constructions, a well-known feature of Hausa syntax (§ 4.2). Example (1) illustrates this construction. Observe that the left-peripheral focused constituent (the instrumental PP *dà sàndā* 'with a stick') is followed optionally by the focus marker (non-verbal copula) *nè* (with polar tone), and that the INFL word *sukà* appears in its focus form (**boldface** indicates the constituent in focus).

(1)   **dà**   **sàndā**   nè̀   sukà   dòkē   shì
       with   stick   FM.m   3PL.FOC.PF   beat   PRO.ms
       'they beat him **with a stick**'

The element *nē/cē/nē* (m/f/p/) functions as a copula in non-verbal clauses, where it also has a focus marking function (see Chapter 5). However, in this chapter I will argue against a biclausal cleft analysis of constructions like (1). Instead, this chapter explores a focus phrase (FP) analysis of Hausa focus fronting constructions, according to which the non-verbal copula is reanalysed as a grammaticalised focus marker that instantiates the head of the focus phrase, and focus fronted phrases occupy the specifier of FP (§ 4.3). Recall from Chapter 3 that this type of movement analysis treats focus constructions as operator-variable dependencies, which involve a relation between an open position or 'gap' in the clause corresponding to the thematic or base position of the focused constituent (the variable) and the extracted constituent (the operator) upon which the variable relies to be fully interpreted (§ 3.4).

The FP analysis developed in this chapter is evaluated against alternative analyses proposed in the literature, and is further explored in relation to the focus fronting of a range of phrasal and clausal constituents. The analysis is then extended to account for *wh*-fronting, a further type of operator-variable dependency that shares certain key characteristics with focus fronting constructions (§ 4.4). Example (2) illustrates a *wh*-fronting construction. Observe that this shares two morphosyntactic properties in common with the focus fronting example in (1), namely the left-peripheral position of the extracted *wh*-phrase *mè* 'what' and the presence of the focus form of the INFL word *sukà*.

(2) mề yârā sukà cê?
what children 3pl.FOC.PF say
'what did the children say?'

The FP analysis is also extended to provide a configurational account of the syntactic conditioning of 'special inflection' or relative/focus marking on INFL (Green & Reintges 2004; 2005a; 2005b; Reintges & Green 2004). It is argued that special inflection is the morphological reflex of the operator-variable dependency that characterises focus and *wh*-fronting constructions, which spells out an agreement relation between the functional heads of FP and IP (§ 4.5).

The last main section of the chapter discusses Hausa focus/*wh*-in-situ constructions (§ 4.6). While the facts concerning focus/*wh*-fronting in Hausa are generally well understood, the facts concerning focus/*wh*-in situ have only recently begun to be described (Jaggar 2001; 2006a; Green & Jaggar 2003). The question–answer pair in example (3) illustrates in situ new information focus in the answer, and example (4) illustrates *wh*-in situ. Observe that these examples are characterised by the fact that the focus/*wh*-phrase remains in its thematic or base position, and by the fact that the focus form of the INFL word is not licensed.

(3) Q: wànè kāyā kikà mântā?
which things 2fs.FOC.PF forget
'which things did you forget?'

A: nā (*na) mâncē **jàkātā dà hùlātā** *focus in situ*
1s.PF (*1s.FOC.PF) forget bag.of.1s and hat.of.1s
'I forgot **my bag and my hat**'

(4) sunà (*sukề) fitôwa dàgà inā? wh-*in situ*
3pl.IMPF (*3pl.FOC-IMPF) come.out.VN from where
'where are they coming out from?'

These data are discussed with respect to the analysis proposed in the earlier sections of the chapter, and the question of whether there is a form–function mapping between syntactic realisation of focus and semantic/pragmatic focus type is addressed. The findings of recent studies by Green & Jaggar (2003) and Jaggar (2006a) are discussed, which argue against a strict correlation between morphosyntactic strategy and interpretation, particularly where the distinction between new information focus and exhaustive/contrastive focus is concerned. Finally, the discussion in this section identifies some hypotheses concerning the relation between prosody and focus in Hausa, and indicates directions for future research in this area.

4.2 FOCUS FRONTING: DESCRIPTIVE FACTS

This section provides a detailed descriptive overview of focus fronting in Hausa, and compares and contrasts the morphosyntax of focus fronting

with topicalisation, a superficially similar construction that also involves
the placement of constituents in the left periphery of the clause. In addition,
the question of whether Hausa focus fronting constructions should be
described as clefts is addressed.

4.2.1 *Focus fronting*

In Hausa focus fronting constructions, focused constituents are preposed
to the left periphery of the clause and optionally followed by the non-
verbal copula *nē/cē/nē* (m/f/pl), which shows polar tone. Unlike some
Chadic languages, which have a designated postverbal focus position
(§ 6.2.1), Hausa has only a left-peripheral ex situ focus position, so that
fronting is the only displacement strategy available for marking focus in
this language. In most cases, focus fronting leaves a gap in the base
position of the extracted constituent, although extraction of verbal
constituents conditions the resumptive pro-verb *yi* 'do' (5f)–(5g), as does
extraction from prepositional and possessive constructions (7)–(9). A
further distinguishing feature of focus fronting constructions in Hausa is
'special inflection': the obligatory shift from the neutral to the focus form
of the inflection word. Jaggar (2001: 500 ff.) provides the following
representative examples of the types of constituent that can be focus
fronted. Example (5a) is provided for purposes of comparison, and
illustrates the unmarked SVO constituent order as well as the unmarked or
'general' form of the INFL word.

(5)   a. Mūsā   dà   Audù sun   zō   *'neutral' sentence*
         Musa   and   Audu 3pl.PF   come
         'Musa and Audu came'

      b. **Mūsā   dà   Audù** (nē) sukà   zō   *subject NP focus*
         Musa   and   Audu FM.pl 3pl.FOC.PF come
         '**Musa and Audu** came'

      c. **yârā**   (nè) mukà   ganī   *direct object NP*
         children FM.pl 1pl.FOC.PF see   *focus*
         'we saw **the children**'

      d. **Audù** (nē) ya   nūnà wà   gōnā   *indirect object NP*
         Audu FM.m 3ms.FOC.PF show IOM farm   *focus*
         'he showed the farm to **Audu**'

      e. **dà   sàndā** (nè) sukà   dòkē shì   *adjunct PP focus*
         with   stick   FM.m 3pl.FOC.PF beat 3ms.PRO
         'they beat him **with a stick**'

      f. **sàyen àbinci** (nè) sukà   yi   *VNP focus*
         buy.VN food   FM.m 3pl.FOC.PF do
         'they **bought food**'

g. **kashḕ su** (nḕ) akà yi   *VP focus*
  kill 3pl.PRO (FM.m) 4pl.FOC.PF do
  'they were **killed**'

h. yā yi ƙaryā nḕ   *IP (clausal) focus*
  3ms.PF do lie FM.m
  'he **did** lie'

i. **cêwař Bàlā yà řubùtà littāfìn nân**   *CP (clausal) focus*
  COMP Bala 3m.SBJ write book this
  nē ya kyàutu
  FM.m 3m.FOC.PF be.good
  '**that Bala should write this book** is good'

Observe that the subject focus example in (5b) shows the same SVO word order as the unmarked example in (5a). The question arises of whether cases of subject focus are best analysed as focus in situ or as 'string-vacuous' movement to a left-peripheral position.[1] In fact, there are two kinds of empirical evidence in favour of a movement analysis of subject focus constructions. First, the presence of special inflection is suggestive of movement, given that special inflection patterns with syntactic reordering in other types of focus fronting construction: observe that the remainder of the examples in (5) represent clear cases of syntactic reordering. The second piece of evidence concerns the optional presence of the focus-marking copula, which agrees in number and gender with the preceding constituent. As the examples in (5) illustrate, in declarative focus constructions, this focus-marking copula patterns with displacement to a clause-external position in the left periphery (see also Newman 2000: 189). In addition, further evidence for a movement analysis of object focus constructions is found in verbal-inflectional morphology. As example (6) illustrates, the stem-final vowel in 'grade 2' verbs signals the presence of a gap in the complement position (Newman 2000: 637–43; Jaggar 2001: 230–35). Compare the verb form *sàyi* 'buy' in (6a) with the alternating form *sàyā* in (6b) (§ 2.3.2).

(6) a. nā sàyi řìgā
      1s.PF buy dress
      'I bought a dress'

    b. **řìgā** cḕ na sàyā
      dress FM.f 1s.FOC.PF buy
      'I bought **a dress**'

Two strategies are available for focusing prepositional objects. The preposition can either be 'pied-piped', as in (5e), or stranded, as in (7) below. The latter strategy triggers the insertion of the resumptive pronoun

---

[1] See Clements et al. (1983); Chomsky (1986); Rizzi (1990); and, more recently, Agbayani (2000).

ita 'it' in the extraction site. Observe that if the whole PP is focus fronted, the focus marker appears in its default masculine form (5e).

(7) **sàndā** cè̃ sukà   dòkē shì   dà   ita
    stick FM.f 3pl.FOC.PF beat PRO.3ms with PRO.3fs
    'they beat him with a **stick**'

Similarly, the fronting of prepositional indirect objects can either pied-pipe the preposition (8a) or strand it (8b), where the latter strategy also conditions resumption.

(8) a. **gà mālàm** nē   na   mai   dà   littāfìn
        to teacher FM.m 1s.FOC.PF return PART book.DD
        'I returned the book **to the teacher**'
     b. **mālàm** nē   na   mai   dà   littāfìn gàrē shì
        teacher FM.m 1s.FOC.PF return PART book.DD to   RP.3ms
        'I returned the book to **the teacher**'

Possessives can be focused either by pied-piping the entire possessive NP (9a) or by fronting the possessor NP and stranding the possessed NP (9b). The latter strategy conditions the presence of a (cliticised) resumptive pronoun in the base position of the fronted possessor NP.

(9) a. **'yar̃**   **Audù** cè̃   na   àurā
        daughter.of Audu FM.m 1s.FOC.PF marry
        'I married **Audu's daughter**'
     b. **Audù** nē   na   àuri   'yar̃sà
        Audu FM.m 1s.FOC.PF marry daughter.of.3ms
        'I married **Audu's** daughter'

As the examples in (5) illustrate, the focus marker can occur clause-finally, marking focus on a main clause (5h) or an embedded clause (5i). In this case, the focus marker occurs in its default masculine form. The examples in (10) (Jaggar 1998: 226) illustrate that it is also possible for the clausal focus marker to occur to the left of (bracketed) VP adjuncts (10a) and (10b), or adverbial subordinate clauses (10c).

(10) a. gidan   fur̃sùnàn   Kìr̃ikìr̃i yā   ɓàcì,   ta   yàddà
        house.of prisoner.of Kirikiri 3ms.PF deteriorate via RELPRO
        har̃   fur̃sùnàn   sukàn yi barcī   nề   [kāmù-kāmù]
        even prisoners.DD 3pl.HAB do sleeping FM.m in.shifts
        'Kirikiri prison has deteriorated such that the prisoners sleep in shifts'
     b. wannàn làbār̃ĩ yanà̃   zuwà̃   mukù nē   [dàgà Sāshèn
        DEM.ms news 3ms.IMPF come.VN io.2pl FM.m from section
        Hausa na BBC]
        Hausa of BBC
        'this news is coming to you from the BBC Hausa Service'

c. nā   kirā   shì   wāwā   nè   [sabòdà   sākar̃cìn   dà
1s.PF call PRO.3ms fool FM.m because.of stupidity REL
yakè   yî]
3ms.FOC.IMPF do.VN
'I called him a fool because of the stupid things he does'

However, while speakers freely accept examples with a clause-final focus
marker, they reject declarative focus fronting constructions that also
contain a clause-final focus marker, such as (11).

(11) * dà   sàndā   (nè)   sukà   dòkē shì   nē
      with stick   FM.m   3pl.FOC.PF beat 3ms.PRO FM.m
      'they beat him **with a stick**'

Example (12a) shows that focus cannot be marked in situ by the focus
marker nē/cē/nē, although it is possible for focus in situ to co-occur with the
clausal focus marker (§ 4.6). Neither is multiple focus fronting possible
(12b):

(12) a. *zân   nūnà̃   wà   **Audù**   nē   gōnā
        FUT.1s show   IOM Audu   FM.m farm
        'I'll show the farm to **Audu**'
     b. *__Audù__ nē   **gōnā**   cè   zân   nūnà̃   wà
        Audu   FM.m farm   FM.f FUT.1s show   IOM
        'I'll show **the farm** to **Audu**'

As example (13) shows, the subjunctive (like the potential) is not licensed in
clauses with a focused constituent in the left periphery (§ 2.3.2).

(13) *munà̃   fātā   **sābuwar̃ mōtà̃** cē   yà   (Tuller 1986a: 70)
     1pl.IMPF hope new.of   car   FM.f 3ms.SUB
     sayà̃   manà
     buy   IO.PRO.1pl
     'we hope he buys **a new car** for us'

Tuller (1986a: 71–4, 108) and Jaggar (2001: 504) attribute this restriction
to a semantic incompatibility between modality and focus, an explanation
that can equally be applied to the potential future. Jaggar (2001: 201)
adopts a similar line of reasoning: 'the Potential is best analyzed, like the
Subjunctive, as a modal category ... semantically incompatible with focus
constructions'. This statement is based on the view that, as modal
(irrealis) categories, the subjunctive and potential future express uncertainty, doubt or probability, whereas focus expresses 'semantic
specificity' (Jaggar 2001: 62). As Tuller (1986a: 70) points out, this
restriction only applies to extraction to the local left periphery. Long-
distance extraction from a subjunctive clause is licensed, as illustrated by
example (14).

(14) **sābuwař mōtà** cē mukè̄   yîn   fātā yà   sayà manà
     new.of car   FM.f 1pl.FOC.IMPF do.VN hope 3ms.SUB buy IO.PRO.1pl
     'we hope he buys **a new car** for us'

As Green & Reintges (2004; 2005a; 2005b) observe, a challenge to the
semantic account proposed by Tuller (1986a) and by Jaggar (2001; 2006a) is
offered by the fact that the focus perfective can occur in open conditional
constructions, which also express epistemic modality. Consider example
(15).

(15) in   kin/kikà   kintsā̀   zā mù tàfi
     if/when 2fs.PF/2fs.FOC.PF be.ready FUT 1pl go
     'if/when you're ready, we'll go'

Finally, Hartmann & Zimmermann (forthcoming, a: 18) observe that
there are cases in which only a sub-part of the focused constituent is
fronted. For example, a question like 'What happened?' might be expected
to elicit a response in which the predicate or indeed the entire clause is
focused. The following example illustrates an exchange in which only the
subject is focus fronted in response to this question.

(16) Q: mè̄   ya   fàru?   (HB: 4.03)[2]
        what 3ms.FOC.PF   happen
        'what happened?'
     A: ɓàrā̀yī nè̄   sukà   yi   mîn   sātā̀!
        thieves FM.pl 3pl.FOC.PF do   IO.1s theft
        '**thieves** have stolen from me!'

4.2.2 *Focus versus topic*

Focus fronting and topic constructions in Hausa are superficially similar,
since both are marked information structure constructions that are
characterised by the placement of a constituent in the left periphery of
the clause. However, in addition to their distinct discourse functions
(§ 3.3.1), the two construction types are also distinguished by a number of
morphosyntactic and prosodic features. Focus fronting and topic constructions differ in four main respects. First, a topic may be followed by a
modal/adverbial particle (§ 2.3.6), but not by the non-verbal copula nē̄/cē̄/
nē̄. Secondly, the focus form of INFL does not occur in topic structures.
Thirdly, while focus fronting is characterised by gapping, the topic may be
coreferential with a resumptive pronoun (RP) in the comment clause,
although example (17a) shows that this generalisation does not hold for

---

[2] This example is taken from *Hausar Baka* 'Spoken Hausa' (HB) (Randell et al. 1998), a five-
hour collection of video recordings of spontaneous discourse edited and transcribed for the
purposes of language teaching.

subject topics. Finally, there is also a characteristic break in intonation after the topic, represented by the comma in the following examples.[3] Jaggar (2001: 541–2) provides the following examples, which can be compared with some of those in (5):

(17) a. yāròn   dai,   yā   kai   wà   Mūsā   kuɗī   *subject NP topic*
    boy.DD PART 3ms.PF take IOM Musa   money
    'as for the boy, he took the money to Musa'

  b. kuɗī   dai,   yāròn   yā   kai   wà   Mūsā   *direct object*
    money PART boy.DD 3ms.PF take IOM Musa   *NP topic*
    sū
    3pl.RP
    'as for the money, the boy took it to Musa'

  c. Mūsā   dai,   yāròn   yā   kai   masà   *indirect object*
    Musa PART boy.DD 3ms.PF take 3ms.IO.RP   *NP topic*
    kuɗī
    money
    'as for Musa, the boy took him the money'

  d. sàyen   àbinci   kò̃,   zā   sù   yi   (shì)   *VNP topic*
    buy.VN food   PART FUT 3pl do   3ms.RP
    'as for buying food, they'll do (it)'

  e. kai   wà   Mūsā   kuɗī   dai,   yāròn   yā   *VP topic*
    take IOM Musa   money PART boy.DD 3m.PF
    yi   (shì)
    do   3ms.RP
    'as for taking the money to Musa, the boy did (it)'

As Tuller (1986a) and Junaidu (1987; 1990) argue, topicalisation and left dislocation (usually characterised by a resumptive pronoun) are not distinct in Hausa, given that the resumptive pronoun is optional and no functional difference is conveyed by its presence/absence. Indeed, Tuller (1986a) argues that, since Hausa is a pro-drop language, the resumptive pronoun is obligatory in all cases but may be phonetically unrealised (although where objects are concerned, only in the case of non-human referents).

Both Tuller (1986a) and Junaidu (1987; 1990) take the view that topics are base-generated in the clause-initial position, rather than being linked to clause-internal positions by displacement. This view is largely based on the fact that topic constructions permit resumptive pronouns. Further evidence

---

[3] According to Jaggar (2001: 538) the topic 'is external to the clause proper and is typically segregated from the comment by a prosodic … pause'. Jaggar (2001: 540) further mentions 'several other prosodic correlates to the operation (all of which require further investigation). Firstly, sentence downdrift is normally suspended and the comment initiates a new downdrift pattern appropriate to the sentence type. Secondly, with some speakers a topic-final short vowel undergoes prepausal lengthening.'

in support of this view is the fact that multiple topics are possible, but multiple focus fronting is not (cf. example (12b)):

(18) Mūsā   kò,   Mar̃sandî kàm,   yā   sayar̃
     Musa   part   Mercedes   PART   3m.PF   sell
     'as for Musa, concerning the Mercedes, he's sold (it)'

The base-generation account of topics in Hausa is further supported by the fact that the language allows not only multiple topics but also multiple modal/adverbial particles co-occurring with a single topic NP (Junaidu 1990). It is therefore difficult to see how constructions like (18) and (19) could be accounted for by a movement analysis in which topic phrases raise to the specifier position of a left-peripheral functional topic head that is lexically realised by the modal/adverbial particle (Rizzi 1997).

(19) Audù   fa   dai   kàm,   yanà̀   sadakà̀   kōyàushē
     Audu   PART   PART   PART   3ms.IMPF give.alms always
     'as for Audu, well, he definitely, decidedly, indeed gives out alms always'

As example (20) illustrates, in clauses where topic and focus co-occur, the topic precedes the focus:[4]

(20) fur̃sunōnī   kàm, **sōjōjì**   nè̀   sukà   tsarè̀ su
     prisoners   PART soldiers   FM.pl   3pl.FOC.PF jail   3pl.RP
     'as for the prisoners, **the soldiers** jailed them'

Further evidence in favour of a base-generation account for Hausa topic constructions is the fact that, unlike focus fronting constructions, they do not show subjacency effects. The following examples illustrate this fact with respect to Ross's (1967) '*wh*-island constraint': while extraction of a focus phrase from an embedded question results in an ungrammatical sentence (21a), the corresponding topic construction is perfectly grammatical (21b):

---

[4] Although the statement that topics must precede focus phrases is generally supported in the literature, Yalwa (1995) claims that in some dialects it is possible to find the focus phrase preceding the topic (Yalwa 1995: 449):

(i) **biyàn**   **hàr̃ājì** nē   Tankò   fa   ya   kàmātà   yà   yi
    paying.of   tax   FM.m Tanko   TOP   3ms.FOC.PF be.fitting   3ms.SUB do
    'it is **paying taxes**, as for Tanko, (that) it is fitting that he should do'

Recall from Chapter 2, however, that what is glossed here as 'TOP' occurs freely as an adverbial/modal particle, which entails the possibility the constituent *Tankò* occupies subject position rather than topic position in example (i). Yalwa does not describe the prosodic properties of the construction, information that would reveal the most accurate analysis.

(21) a. *Àli (nè) mukà san wà zâi (Tuller 1986a:
      Ali FM.m 1pl.FOC.PF know who FUT. 3ms 55 [my gloss])
      àurā
      marry
      'we know who **Ali** will marry'

    b. Àli, mun san wà zâi àurā / àurē tà
      Ali 1pl.PF know who FUT. 3ms marry / marry 3fs.RP
      'Ali, we know who (he) will marry'

Finally, note the following example of a 'contrastive topic' (Yalwa 1995: 429, [my gloss]). It is clear from examples like (22) that when topic phrase and the focus phrase are coreferential, the topic 'inherits' focus.

(22) hàrājìn dai, **shī** nè ya kàmātà Tankò
     tax.DD PART PRO.3ms FM.m 3ms.FOC.PF be.fitting Tanko
     yà biyā
     3ms.SUB pay
     'as for the taxes, **they** are what it is desirable for Tanko to pay'

In this example, the resumptive pronoun *shī*, which links to the topic NP *hàrājìn* 'the taxes', is in the focus position, having raised from the complement position of the verb *biyā* 'pay'.

4.2.3 *Focus fronting versus clefting*

Given the evidence in favour of a movement analysis of focus fronting constructions (§ 4.2.1), the question that naturally arises is whether such constructions are best analysed as cases of focus fronting or clefting: in other words, whether the resulting structure is monoclausal or biclausal. Recall from Chapter 3 (§ 3.3.2) that focus fronting constructions and clefts are not always clearly distinguished in the descriptive literature, which follows from the fact that the two construction types are structurally and functionally similar, both involving displacement of a constituent to a marked focus position. However, there are important structural differences between focus fronting constructions and cleft constructions. Clefts are usually defined as biclausal constructions, in which the clefted (focused) constituent is introduced by a copula in the higher clause, and modified by a lower clause. The lower clause resembles a relative clause in that it is introduced by a relative pronoun or a complementiser, and contains a 'gap' corresponding to the clefted constituent.[5] In languages like English, which do not tolerate null subjects in main clauses, the cleft also contains an expletive subject pronoun like *it*:

(23) it was **Ted** who/that bought a guitar

---

[5] See Schachter (1973); Heggie (1993); Lambrecht (2001); Doetjes et al. (2003).

Focus fronting constructions, on the other hand, are monoclausal structures in which the focused constituent is moved to the left periphery of the clause:

(24) **macadamia nuts**, they're called   (Lambrecht 1994: 225)

The distinction between focus fronting and clefting is more obvious in English than in some languages, partly because the English copula is a lexical verb. It follows that examples like (23) necessitate a biclausal structure, given that each lexical verb entails its own clause, while examples like (24) more closely resemble other monoclausal structures like topic constructions or *wh*-questions, where a left peripheral constituent is linked to a clause-internal position either by gapping or resumption, but no additional structure is motivated.

For languages like Hausa, on the other hand, the analysis of focus constructions as either focus fronting constructions or as clefts is less straightforward. Indeed, Hausa focus constructions resemble clefts not only in their discourse function but also in that they contain a copula. An analysis of Hausa focus constructions as clefts is developed by McConvell (1973), who rejects a monoclausal focus fronting analysis (Schachter 1966) in favour of a biclausal clefting analysis in which Hausa focus constructions are derived from pseudocleft constructions. This analysis is based on functional and syntactic similarities between cleft sentences in English and focus constructions in Hausa. McConvell (1973: 30–31) provides the descriptive schema of clefts in (25a), with (25b) an example of a cleft sentence in English. A descriptive schema of the 'underlying' pseudocleft construction is provided in (26a), illustrated by the English example in (26b).

(25) a. *it–be–*focus–relative clause (introduced by a *wh*-word or *that*)
     b. it was eggs which/that they bought
(26) a. relative clause introduced by a *wh*-word – be–focus
     d. what they bought was eggs

McConvell's analysis is representative of the 1970s-style transformational analysis of clefts, according to which the cleft is derived from the pseudocleft by rightward extraposition of the relative clause followed by insertion of the expletive subject *it* (Akmajian 1970). McConvell adopts a 'focus raising' version of this analysis (Emonds 1969). According to this analysis the unmarked declarative clause (e.g. *They bought eggs*) is embedded in the subject position of the main clause headed by the copula *be*. This construction is first transformed into a pseudocleft by a process of 'focus raising', which raises the focused constituent (*eggs*) from the embedded clause rightwards to a focus position adjacent to the copula. A process of 'relativisation' then fills the base position of the focus-raised constituent with a *wh*-word, deriving the pseudocleft (26). Finally, a process of (rightward) 'cleft extraposition' of the relative clause, followed by expletive insertion, derives the cleft construction.

Example (27) illustrates the Hausa pseudocleft construction. Like its English counterpart, this is a copular sentence in which two NPs are equated, one of which consists of a headless or free relative clause:

(27) a. waddà   nakè   sô   **Kànde** cè   *pseudocleft*
        RELPRO.fs 1s.FOC.IMPF love.VN Kande FM.f
        'the one I love is **Kande**'

     b. **Kànde** cè   waddà   nakè   sô   *reverse pseudocleft*
        Kande FM.f RELPRO.fs 1s.FOC.IMPF love.VN
        '**Kande** is the one I love'

McConvell (1973: 59) favours this clefting analysis for Hausa focus constructions on the basis that 'it provides an immediate explanation for the fact that the clause in focus-emphatic sentences behaves so much like a relative clause'. Indeed, according to McConvell (1973: 188) 'Despite the absence of the initial relative marker ... *dà* the "clause" in focus-emphatic sentences shares many characteristics with relative clauses ... the clause in [a] focus-emphatic [sentence] shares the characteristics of a relative clause because it is a type of relative clause.' McConvell advances two main arguments for this position: first, the presence of special inflection in both relative clauses and focus constructions, and secondly, the fact that both relative clauses and focus constructions are operator-variable (gapping) constructions. In essence, then, McConvell's analysis of Hausa focus constructions treats these as 'conclealed clefts' in the sense that they are viewed as underlyingly biclausal and derived from constructions that contain embedded relative clause structure.

Although Hausa focus constructions do share some important morphosyntactic characteristics with relative clauses (§ 2.4), a pattern that receives an explanation from the fact that both are types of operator-variable construction, focus fronting constructions do not tolerate relative pronouns or relative complementisers. This fact casts serious doubt on the clefting analysis. In addition, recall that the copula in Hausa focus constructions is optional, a fact that further calls into question the clefting analysis. As Tuller points out, there are no grounds for viewing focus constructions with the non-verbal copula as distinct from those without:

> The 'cleft-like structure'... is syntactically identical to focus fronting...The only difference between the two is the presence of an overt focus-marker (isomorphic with the copula, a point to which we return below) [... the 'cleft-like structure'] does not represent a separate syntactic construction and it is possible to speak of focus fronting as encompassing [...] both. (Tuller 1986a:54)

In further support of the view that these constructions are monoclausal, Tuller (1986a: 57–8) also considers phonological evidence that examines the intonational pattern of downdrift in the sentence (a progressive lowering of pitch over the utterance), and demonstrates that while downdrift is interrupted in topic structures, it is uninterrupted in focus structures. As Tuller points out, this suggests that focus fronted phrases target the left periphery of the clause from which they are extracted. Therefore, the position adopted in this book is that Hausa ex situ focus constructions are most insightfully analysed as monoclausal focus fronting constructions.[6] Given the parallels between focus fronting and *wh*-fronting, this analysis also carries over straightforwardly to *wh*-fronting constructions, which are best analysed as monoclausal *wh*-fronting constructions rather than *wh*-clefts, despite the optional presence of the copula (§ 4.4). Of course, the rejection of the clefting analysis raises questions about the role and status of the non-verbal copula in Hausa focus fronting constructions. In the next section, an analysis is developed that treats the non-verbal copula as a grammaticalised focus marker.

4.3 FOCUS FRONTING: THE FP ANALYSIS

This section develops an analysis of Hausa focus fronting constructions as monoclausal structures in which the non-verbal copula is analysed as a grammaticalised focus marker that instantiates the head of the left-peripheral functional projection FP (focus phrase) (§ 4.3.1). The empirical evidence in support of this analysis is evaluated (§ 4.3.2), followed by an investigation of the theoretical arguments in favour of this analysis (§ 4.3.3).

---

[6] It is worth observing that there is an alternative focus construction in Hausa that contains two INFL (TAM) morphemes and might therefore (arguably) be analysed as a biclausal construction.

(i) a. **watā̀   shidà** kḕ   nan   nakḕ   r̃ubū̀tà takàr̃dar̃   nàn
         month six   FOC.IMPF there   1s.FOC.IMPF   write   paper.of   here
         'it's **six months** I've been writing this paper (for)'
     b. an   r̃ubū̀tà takàr̃dar̃ nàn   yâu   **shèkarà̀   hàmsin** kḕ   nan
         4pl.PF write   paper.of here today year   50   FOC.IMPF there
         'it's **fifty years** since this paper was written'

Example (ia) contains a focus-fronted NP followed by focus imperfective TAM marker *kḕ* (unmarked for person/number/gender) and the deictic adverbial *nan* 'there'. Example (ib) illustrates that the same expression can occur clause-finally. This type of construction tends to be restricted to temporal expressions (Jaggar 2001: 511). The structure of these examples is not pursued here, but Russell Schuh (p.c.) suggests that they are most insightfully analysed as monoclausal constructions, like those with *nḕ/cḕ/nē*, given that the expression *kḕ nan* functions synchronically as a copula, and indeed shares similar historical origins as the copula *nḕ/cḕ/nē*. See Chapter 5 (§ 5.3) for some historical discussion.

4.3.1 *Proposal*

Recall from Chapter 3 (§ 3.4) that the transformational analysis built upon a syntactic [+FOCUS] feature, and embedded within the focus phrase (FP) structure proposed by Brody (1990), has received much cross-linguistic support in the literature. The proposal advanced here is that the FP structure also provides the basis of an empirically and theoretically sound analysis of Hausa focus fronting constructions. In this section, the clause structure of Hausa is mapped out, with particular attention to the structure of the left periphery. The relative ordering of complementiser, topic phrases and focus phrases reveals that focus fronting targets a single focus projection that is located below the force-indicating complementiser node and above the inflectional domain.

Since subordinating complementisers precede embedded focus fronting constructions, the position targeted by focus fronting cannot be the specifier of the complementiser phrase (28).

(28) mutằnên sun   tsayằ cêwā **Kànde** cề   sukề   sô
     men.DD 3PL.PF insist COMP Kande FM.f 3pl.FOC.IMPF love.VN
     'the men insisted that it is **Kande** they love'

Hausa also allows embedded topicalisation where a left-dislocated topic appears following a subordinating complementiser (29).

(29) mutằnên sun   tsayằ cêwā Kànde kùwa sunằ   sônta
     men.DD 3pl.PF insist COMP Kande PART 3pl. IMPF love.VN.of.3fs
     'the men insisted that, as for Kande, they love her'

While topics and focus fronted phrases may co-occur within the left periphery, the topic precedes the focus phrase (30a). The reverse order, in which a focus fronted phrases precedes a left-dislocated topic, yields ungrammatical results (30b).

(30) a. ɓàrāwòn kùwa, **Audù** nē   ya   kashề shi
        thief.DD PART   Audu FM.m 3MS.FOC.PF kill PRO.3ms
        'as for the thief, it was **Audu** who killed him'
     b. ***Audù** nē,   ɓàrāwòn kùwa, ya   kashề shi
        Audu FM.m thief.DD PART 3ms.FOC.PF kill PRO.3ms
        'it was **Audu**, as for the thief, who killed him'

Given the word order facts illustrated by examples (28)–(30), the hierarchical organisation shown in (31) of the Hausa clause is assumed. For the purposes of developing an analysis of Hausa focus contructions, this structure exploits proposals in the literature relating to an articulated left periphery (§ 3.2.3), but does not assume an articulated inflectional layer. Yusuf (1991) has explored the split INFL hypothesis for Hausa, arguing that the adoption of this framework might be motivated by the fact that Hausa

(31)
```
              C'
           ／＼
          C    FP
             ／＼
        TOPIC    FP
              ／＼
           Spec    F'
        FOCUSED XP ／＼
              F      IP
            nē/cē  ／＼
               Spec    I'
             (subject)／＼
                  I      VP
              INFL[+FOC] ／＼
                     Spec    V'
                          ／＼
                         V    NP
                            (object)
```

INFL is often (although not always) made up of distinct subject agreement and TAM morphemes (§ 2.3.2). For example, Yusuf proposes that the INFL projection is split into Agreement Phrase and Aspect Phrase in the case of perfective and imperfective INFL, whereas future INFL involves Agreement Phrase and Tense Phrase, where the Tense head raises to left-adjoin to the Agreement head in order to derive the ordering of morphemes within the future paradigm (recall Table 2.1). While an articulated inflectional layer might plausibly account for the morphological complexity of Hausa INFL, there is no evidence that the verb raises to INFL in this language. Recall from Chapter 2 that there is no TAM morphology on the Hausa verb (§ 2.3.2), and that adverbial/modal particles can occur between INFL and the verb (§ 2.3.6). In addition, as Tuller (1986a) points out, the INFL complex in Hausa does not display clitic features such as tonal polarity with the verb. For these reasons, there seems little empirical motivation for introducing this largely redundant additional level of complexity into the model of Hausa clause structure. Neither is an articulated VP layer assumed here, but see below (§ 4.3.3).[7]

In developing a syntactic analysis of Hausa focus fronting constructions, the main proposal advanced in this section is that the focused constituent is raised from its canonical position (e.g. subject or object position within the

---

[7] In the literature, the articulated functional projection approach has been extended to the VP domain, which is conceptualised as consisting of several layers in which the arguments of the verb are licensed by distinct verbal heads. The external argument that surfaces as the clausal subject is introduced by a 'light verb' *v* that takes a VP complement. The internal argument that surfaces as the direct object in active transitive clauses is located in the specifier position of the VP complement. Double object constructions involve yet another verbal layer. See Larson (1988a); Hale & Keyser (1993); Marantz (1997); and Doron (2003).

IP clause structure) to the specifier of the FP position, hence its realisation at the left periphery of the clause. The (optional) non-verbal copula *nē/cē/nē* is analysed as a grammaticalised focus marker (FM) which instantiates the head of FP. This displacement process also triggers 'special inflection' (the focus/relative form of the inflection word) in the clause whose left periphery contains the focused constituent (§ 4.5). Recall that topics precede focused constituents in the left periphery of the clause, and that topics pattern differently from focus phrases in that they do not observe constraints on extraction, show a preference for resumption, and may be followed by multiple adverbial particles. These facts suggests an analysis in which topics are adjoined to FP rather than occupying the specifier position of a left-peripheral topic phrase. For this reason, topics are represented in the present analysis as adjuncts (31).

4.3.2 *Empirical evidence*

This rather simple syntactic analysis of Hausa focus fronting constructions has a number of empirical motivations. In addition to providing an explanation for the left-peripheral exsitu focus position in Hausa, the FP structure also enables a principled account of the (optional) presence of the non-verbal copula in focus fronting constructions: this element is reanalysed as a focus marker, the realisation of the functional head of FP. Furthermore, this structure also correctly predicts that multiple focus fronting is not possible in Hausa, given the assumption that there is only one left-peripheral position in which a focused phrase can be licensed: the specifier of (a single) FP. This prediction is borne out by examples like (12b), repeated here as (32):

(32) **Audù* nē **gōnā** cè zân nūnà̄ wà
Audu FM.m farm FM.m FUT.1s show IOM
'I'll show **the farm** to **Audu**'

In addition, this analysis correctly predicts that a constituent cannot be focused in situ by *nē/cē/nē*, since in its function as a focus marker, this element occurs only as the head of FP, a left-peripheral functional projection. Recall example (12a), repeated here as (33) (see also § 4.6 for further discussion):

(33) **zân* nūnà̄ wà **Audù** nē gōnā
FUT.1s show IOM Audu FM.m farm
'I'll show the farm to **Audu**'

A further empirical advantage of the FP analysis is that it accounts for the fact that focus fronting targets a projection in the left periphery of the clause that is distinct from the complementiser phrase (CP). Recall that this is demonstrated by examples like (28). Finally, the gender and number

agreement that holds between *nē/cē/nē* and the element in the specifier of
FP provides further empirical support for the analysis developed here, since
the local specifier–head relationship is the canonical configuration under
which such agreement relations hold in the Principles and Parameters
model.

The FP analysis accounts straightforwardly for the focus fronting of a
range of constituents. Recall that in addition to noun phrases and
prepositional phrases, Hausa also allows the focus fronting of verbal
noun phrases (VNP) and verb phrases (VP) (§ 4.2.1.).[8] Examples (5f) and
(5g) are repeated in (34):

(34) a. **sàyen àbinci** nè̀   sukà   yi   *VNP focus*
        buy.VN food   FM.m   3pl.FOC.PF do
        'they **bought food**'

   b. **kashè̀ su**   nè̀   akà   yi   *VP focus*
        kill   3pl.PRO FM.m 4plFOC.PF do
        they **killed**'

Observe that the verbal noun/verb pied-pipes its direct object, a
requirement that might be explained by the case relation between the
head and its complement. Recall that this case relation is often spelled out
by means of the genitive linker on the verbal noun, as illustrated by example
(35).[9]

(35) **tàmbayàr̃tà**   mukà   yi
      ask.VN.of.3fs 1pl.FOC.PF do
      'we **asked** her'

As Tuller (1986a) points out, VNP/VP fronting obeys the same movement
constraints as NP fronting (recall example (21)), which further supports the
extension of the movement analysis to these constructions. Example (36)
illustrates the *wh*-island constraint: the focused phrase cannot be extracted
from an embedded question.

---

[8] Jaggar (2001), after Newman (2000), describes the form of the verb that occurs in examples
like (34b), together with its object(s), as the 'infinitive phrase'. This term is applied by
Newman to V plus its object(s) (VP) when the VP occurs in the same range of contexts as the
verbal noun (e.g. after imperfective INFL, as subject, or as complement of another verb). As
Jaggar (2001: 288) points out, apart from its distribution the 'infinitive' VP is identical to any
other VP consisting of V plus its object(s); crucially, it is not morphologically distinct.

[9] Tuller (1992), in her discussion of postverbal focus in Chadic, argues that the order V–FOC–
DO (found in Western Bade and Podoko) is possible due to the case-transmitting properties
of the chain: when V raises it may strand its direct object due to the ability of its trace to
transmit case. Tuller argues that in languages displaying V–DO–FOC order (Tangale,
Kanakuru, Ngizim), the chain cannot transmit case, hence the direct object cannot be
stranded (§ 4.8.1). A version of this account may explain why Hausa VNP/VP fronting
cannot strand the direct object either.

(36) *kaɽàntà **Kùɽ'ānì** Àli   ya   cè   (Tuller 1986a: 432)
     read   Koran   Ali 3ms.FOC.PF say
     wà   yakè   yî
     who 3ms.FOC.IMPF do.VN
     '**reading the Koran** Ali said who does'

Recall that main and embedded clauses can also be focused in Hausa
(§ 4.2.1). Examples (5h) and (5i) are repeated in (37):

(37) a. yā   yi ƙaryā nè   *IP focus*
         3ms.PF do lie   FM.m
         'he **did** lie'
     b. **cêwaɽ Bàlā yà   ɽubùtà littāfìn**   *CP focus*
         COMP Bala 3m.SUB write   book.DD
         nân nē ya   kyàutu
         this   FM.m 3m.FOC.PF be.good
         '**that Bala should write this book** is good.'

These examples differ from those discussed previously in that they involve
clausal focus (Jaggar 2001: 508–10). In example (37a) the main clause is in
focus, whereas in (37b) an embedded clause is in focus. Since example (37b)
involves the displacement of an embedded clause, it is consistent with the
patterns observed thus far: a constituent is displaced to the left periphery, the
focus marker occurs to the right of the displaced constituent, and the main
clause INFL is in the focus form. Observe, however, that example (37a), as an
instance of main clause focus, might at first glance call into question the
movement analysis, given that this analysis entails that the whole clause (IP)
is displaced to its own left periphery. However, a number of rather striking
facts suggest a displacement analysis. First, observe that INFL does not occur
in its focus form in (37a). When INFL is part of the moved constituent itself, it
is not in the correct configuration to appear in the focus form. In other
words, the focus form of INFL only occurs within a clause from which a
constituent has been extracted. Secondly, observe that the focus marker
occurs in its (default) masculine form in (37a), despite the fact that it is
immediately preceded by a feminine noun, ƙaryā. Recall that this agreement
pattern is also evident in the case of displaced preposition phrases (5e). Since
the focus marker agrees with its left-adjacent consituent, its appearance in
the default masculine form is consistent with the view that the left-adjacent
constituent is the clause. Thirdly, this analysis also explains the fact that
while speakers freely accept examples of clausal focus with a clause-final
focus marker, they reject declarative focus fronting constructions that also
contain a clause-final focus marker. Example (11) is repeated here as (38).

(38) * **dà sàndā** (nè) sukà   dòkē shì   nē
       with stick   FM.m 3pl.FOC.PF beat 3ms.PRO FM.m
       'they beat him **with a stick**'

This pattern is consistent with the claim that the presence of clause-final *nē* in examples like those in (37) indicates a displacement structure: under the analysis developed here, examples like (38) represent cases of multiple focus fronting.[10]

Finally, recall that 'clause-final' *nē* can precede VP adjuncts. Example (10) (Jaggar 1998: 226) is repeated here as (39). These examples suggest either that the fronted clause can strand the VP-adjoined adjunct or embedded subordinate clause in situ, or that the VP adjunct/embedded clause can be extraposed from the fronted clasual constituent. The structure of these examples is not further explored here.

(39) a. gidan   fuȓsùnàn   Kìȓiƙìȓi yā   ɓàci,   ta
       house.of prisoner.of Kirikiri 3ms.PF   deteriorate via
       yàddà haȓ fuȓsùnàn   sukàn   yi barcī nè   kāmù-kāmù
       RELPRO even prisoners.DD 3pl.HAB do sleeping FM.m in.shifts
       'Kirikiri prison has deteriorated such that the prisoners sleep in shifts'

    b. wannàn làbāȓì yanà   zuwà   mukù nē dàgà Sāshèn
       DEM.ms news   3ms.IMPF come.VN   IO.2pl FM.m from section
       Hausa   na   BBC
       Hausa   of   BBC
       'this news is coming to you from the BBC Hausa Service'

    c. nā   kirā shì   wāwā nè   sabòdà   sākaȓcìn   dà
       1s.PF call PRO.3ms fool FM.m because.of stupidity REL
       yakè   yî
       3ms.FOC.IMPF   do.VN
       'I called him a fool because of the stupid things he does'

The analysis developed in this chapter is suggested by Tuller's (1986a; 1986b) analysis, although it differs in a number of important ways. In her comprehensive GB survey of Hausa, Tuller (1986a) proposes that focus fronting is a subtype of *wh*-movement, wherein focus fronted constituents are raised to [Spec CP]. Tuller assumes a *wh*-movement analysis on the basis of the parallels between focus and *wh*-fronting in Hausa, and the fact that these obey the same movement constraints, as she illustrates with examples like (21) and (36). The syntactic parallels between focus and *wh*-fronting are addressed in more detail below (§ 4.4).

Tuller's analysis contains a number of important insights. The analysis addresses the syntactic parallels between focus-fronting and *wh*-fronting constructions not only in terms of syntactic position and locality constraints over extraction, but also with respect to the syntactic conditioning of relative/focus marking on INFL, a point that is also taken up in more detail below (§ 4.5). Furthermore, Tuller (1986a: 54) describes *nē/cē/nē* in focus fronting

---

[10] See below (§ 4.4) for a discussion of an alternative function associated with clause-final *nē*.

constructions as a 'focus marker … isomorphic with the copula'. Although Tuller's implication is that these are distinct (historically related) categories, this description suggests the FP analysis (see also McConvell 1973).

By incorporating Tuller's insights into an FP analysis, a number of unexplained empirical facts receive an explanation. For example, unlike the FP analysis, Tuller's CP analysis provides no explanation for the presence of *nē/cē/nē* in focus fronting constructions; this element appears attached to the focused element in [Spec CP], but no account is provided for the appearance of *nē/cē/nē* in the syntactic structure. Furthermore, recall that examples like (28) provide empirical evidence that focus fronting targets a projection distinct from CP, which in this case dominates FP. This type of data receives no explanation under an analysis wherein focus movement targets the specifier of CP. Finally, and perhaps most importantly, the CP analysis developed by Tuller fails to provide insights into the relationship between *nē/cē/nē* as it occurs in focus fronting constructions and *nē/cē/nē* as it occurs in copular sentences, a connection that provides further support for the reanalysis of *nē/cē/nē* as a (synchronic) focus marker. This idea is explored in Chapter 5.

4.3.3 *Theoretical issues*

This section briefly addresses the theoretical details of the proposal outlined above. In particular, the discussion focuses on the mechanism responsible for the displacement of focus phrases to the left periphery, constraints that hold over this displacement operation, and the question of which element of the chain created by displacement is phonetically realised. With respect to the mechanism that drives focus fronting, and recalling the discussion of the syntax of focus within recent versions of the Principles and Parameters/Minimalist approach (§ 3.4.3), the theory of Hausa focus fronting assumed here can be summarised as follows. The optional focus marker *nē/cē/nē* instantiates the head of the left-peripheral functional projection FP. The head F has an (optional) uninterpretable focus-EPP feature, which is eliminated by the matching feature on the focus phrase XP under the Move operation, which brings the focused phrase and the focus marker into the correct local configuration for the Agree relation to hold: the specifier–head configuration.

(40)

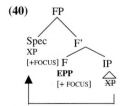

Recall Tuller's observation that Hausa focus fronting constructions are subject to locality constraints on displacement, as illustrated by examples like (21) and (36). In Principles and Parameters terms, island constraints on *wh*-type movement are accounted for by the subjacency condition (Ross 1967; Chomsky 1973 and subsequent work), which states that a displaced constituent may not cross more than one bounding node in a single 'step'.[11] The nodes that function as bounding nodes may be subject to parametric variation. In English, for example, bounding nodes are NP and IP. This generalisation explains the various island constraints observed by Ross (1967), such as the *wh*-island constraint (41a), where a constituent cannot be extracted from an embedded question, and the complex NP constraint (41b), where a constituent cannot be extracted from a clause embedded within a noun phrase:

(41) a. *[$_{CP}$ what did [$_{IP}$ Ted wonder [$_{CP}$ who [$_{IP}$ ~~who~~ saw ~~what~~]]]]
      b. *[$_{CP}$ who did [$_{IP}$ Ted deny [$_{NP}$ the fact [$_{CP}$ ~~who~~ that [$_{IP}$ Bill saw ~~who~~]]]]]

As discussed above, focus fronting in Hausa is subject to the subjacency constraint (Tuller 1986a: 55). Compare the following examples. The ungrammaticality of example (42b) illustrates the fact that an embedded focus fronting construction creates an 'island' in the same way as an embedded *wh*-question. The extraction of the NP *yârā* 'children' to the embedded FP derives a grammatical construction (42a), but the NP *ƙwai* 'eggs' cannot then be extracted out of the embedded clause.

(42) a. Yūsùf   yā   cè   [$_{FP}$ **yârā**   nè [$_{IP}$ ~~yârā~~   sukà
          Yusuf   3ms.PF   say children FM.pl   3pl.FOC.PF
          sàyi   ƙwai]]
          buy   eggs
          'Yusuf said **the children** bought eggs'
      b. *[$_{FP}$ **ƙwai** nè   [$_{IP}$ Yūsùf   ya   cè   [$_{FP}$ **yârā**   nè
             eggs   FM.pl   Yusuf   3ms.FOC.PF   say children FM.pl
          [$_{IP}$ ~~yârā~~   sukà   sàyā   ~~ƙwai~~]
                 3pl.FOC.PF   buy
          'it was **eggs** that Yusuf said **the children** bought'

As has often been observed in the literature on constraints on extraction, the existence of island constraints suggests that displacement must apply locally, which in turn suggests that cases of 'long-distance' focus fronting are derived by a series of local displacement operations (for recent discussion, see Fanselow & Mahajan 2000; Felser 2004). As long as there

---

[11] In Minimalist terms, the subjacency condition is captured by the PHASE IMPENETRABILITY CONDITION (Chomsky 2000), which states that only the left edge of an embedded phase is 'visible' to a head outside that phase. A phase consists of a functional XP and the YP it selects as its complement. It follows from this condition that movement must be local and successive cyclic, applying at each step within a single phase.

are no intervening constituents in any specifier of FP along the path of movement, apparent long-distance extraction is licensed (43).

(43) [FP ƙwai nè   [IP Yūsùf ya   cè [FP ƙ̶w̶a̶i̶ [IP yârā
      eggs FM.pl   Yusuf 3ms.FOC.PF say   children
      sun   sàyā   ƙ̶w̶a̶i̶]]]]
      3pl.PF   buy
      'Yusuf said the children bought **eggs** at market'

In this example, the focused phrase *ƙwai* raises from object position to embedded [Spec FP] position, and subsequently to the matrix [Spec FP] position. The ungrammaticality of example (42b) thus follows from the fact that the embedded [Spec FP] position is already occupied by another focused phrase, *yârā*, so that *ƙwai* cannot raise to this position. This causes movement to be blocked.

Recall next the restriction on local extraction from subjunctive clauses that was illustrated by examples (13) and (14), repeated here in (44).

(44) a. *munà   fātā   **sābuwar̃ mōtà** cē   (Tuller 1986a: 70)
          1pl.IMPF hope   new.of   car   FM.f
          yà   sayà   manà
          3ms.SUB   buy   IO.PRO.1pl
          'we hope he buys **a new car** for us'

      b. **sābuwar̃ mōtà** cē   mukè   yin   fātā   yà   sayà
          new.of   car   FM.f 1pl.FOC.IMPF do.VN hope 3ms.SUB buy
          manà
          IO.PRO.1pl
          'we hope he buys **a new car** for us'

As these examples show, extraction of a focused phrase to the local (embedded) left periphery of a subjunctive clause is not licensed (44a), but long-distance extraction out of a subjunctive clause to the left periphery of a higher non-subjunctive clause is licensed (44b). While Tuller (1986a: 71–4; 108) and Jaggar (2001: 504) attribute this restriction to a semantic incompatibility between modality and focus, the analysis developed by Green & Reintges (2005a; 2005b) draws upon proposals made by McDaniel (1989: 573–5) and Dayal (1991), and treats the subjunctive as a 'defective' tense category (like the infinitive in other languages) that lacks an articulated left periphery. According to this perspective, since there is no focus layer above the root clause (the IP), it follows that there is no designated scope position for focused phrases to move to. In order to be interpreted, the embedded focused phrase has to move to the matrix clause. An analysis along these lines may explain why long-distance extraction from subjunctive clauses is forced, as well as accounting for the incompatibility between subunctive inflection and focus/relative aspect marking (§ 2.3.2).

Turning finally to the properties of the chain created by movement, recall that overt movement operations of the type that derives Hausa focus fronting constructions can be accounted for by assuming that movement occurs prior to the point at which the derivation is transferred to the phonological component. According to the copy theory of movement, extraction does not leave a trace but an exact copy of the displaced constituent, which forms a chain with the displaced constituent (§ 3.4.3). The chain enables the pair of copies to satisfy various syntactic requirements in relation to both/all the positions related to the chain. The canonical pattern is that the higher copy is spelled out or phonetically realised, while the lower copy is left unpronounced. This accounts for the typical pattern in Hausa focus fronting constructions, in which movement leaves an unpronounced copy (gap) in the base position of the extracted constituent.[12] However, a point of theoretical interest arises in relation to resumption strategies in Hausa focus fronting constructions. Recall that extraction of V(N)P constituents conditions the presence of the resumptive 'pro-verb' *yi* 'do/make' (45).[13]

(45) **tsarè fuȓsùnàn** nē   akà   yi (bà harȓbȇ shi   ba)
      jail   prisoner.DD FM.m 4pl.FOC.PF do NEG shoot 3ms.PRO NEG
      'the prisoner was **jailed** (not shot)'

Recall further that Hausa INFL is a free morpheme (§ 2.3.2). This is demonstrated by the fact that it is possible to find adverbial/modal particles occurring between INFL and the verb (Parsons 1981; Tuller 1986a).

---

[12] Not only does copy theory provide a theoretically elegant model of displacement, but as Reintges (2005: 2–4) observes, it also accounts for a broader range of empirical facts than trace theory, according to which it is always the head of the chain that is pronounced. For example, some languages can spell out every copy of an extracted phrase along the path of movement (i), while Reintges argues that Coptic Egyptian spells out the lower copy (§ 6.2.4). See Reintges (2002; 2003a); Reintges et al. (2006); Reintges & Green (2004); Green & Reintges (2004; 2005a; 2005b); Fanselow & Mahajan (2000); Felser (2004); Groat & O'Neil (1996); Pesetsky (1997; 1998; 2000); Bobaljik (2002); Nunes (1995; 2004).

(i) German (Reintges 2005: 3, adapted from Fanselow & Mahajan 2000: 219)
     wen   denkst   du   wen   sie   meint wen   Harald   liebt?
     who.ACC think.2s you.NOM who.ACC she.NOM believes who.ACC Harald.NOM love.3s
     'who do you think that she believes that Harald loves?'

[13] The verb *yi* has independent lexical function, occurring with 'activity nouns', as in (ic). In addition, this verb can occur in its nominalised form as part of the complement of aspectual verbs such as *gamà* 'stop' or *fàrà* 'start'(ib).

(i) a. yā   yi   aikin
         3ms.PF do   work.DD
         'he did the work'
     b. yàushè zâi   gamà (yîn) aikȋ?
         when   FUT.3ms stop do.VN working
         'when will he stop working?'

(46) sunằ   dai   yî   nē   kawài
     3pl.IMPF PART do.VN FM.m only
     'they are just doing (it)'

As example (47) shows, it is also possible to find these particles intervening between INFL and pro-verb *yi* in VNP focus constructions:

(47) **sàyen** **àbinci** nè̀   yârā   sukà   mā yi
     buy.VN food FM.m children 3pl.FOC.PF PART do
     'the children did indeed **buy food**'

Despite the fact that both INFL and *yi* are free morphemes, it seems that INFL usually requires an overt complement, although resumption is optional in imperfective clauses:

(48) **sayaȓ dà** **mōtōcī** yakè̀   (yî)   yànzu
     sell PART car.pl 3ms.FOC.IMPF (do.VN) now
     'he's **selling cars** now'

The optionality of *yi* in constructions headed by imperfect INFL might be explained by the nominalised status of *yî* (verbal noun) in such constructions, which follows from the fact that imperfect INFL does not select VP as its complement, only nominalised VNP or non-verbal complements (§ 2.3.2). A similar pattern, which demonstrates the optionality of nominalised *yî*, is observed by Jaggar (2001: 430) in what he describes as 'phrasal verb' constructions where *yi* is followed by an 'activity' noun. While *yi* is generally obligatory in such constructions (49a), it is optional in the imperfect (49b), where it occurs in its nominalised form:

(49) a. zân   yi   sallà̀
         FUT.1s do prayer
         'I'm going to pray'
     b. yāròn yanà̀   (yîn)   barcī
         boy.DD 3ms.IMPF (do.VN.of) sleeping
         'the boy is sleeping'

Recall further that extraction from within prepositional and possessive constructions also conditions resumption. Examples (5e) and (7) are repeated here in (50), and example (9) is repeated as (51).

(50) a. **dà** **sàndā** (nè̀) sukà   dòkē shì   *pied-piping*
         with stick FM.m 3pl.FOC.PF beat 3ms.PRO
         'they beat him **with a stick**'
     b. **sàndā** cè̀ sukà   dòkē shì   dà   ita   *preposition*
         stick FM.f 3pl.FOC.PF beat PRO.3ms with PRO.3fs *stranding*
         'they beat him with a **stick**'

(51) a. **'yaȓ**   **Audù** cē   na   àurā
     daughter.of Audu FM.m 1s.FOC.PF marry
     'I married **Audu's daughter**'

   b. **Audù** nē   na   àuri   'yaȓsà
     Audu FM.m 1s.FOC.PF marry daughter.of.3MS
     'I married **Audu's** daughter'

Tuller (1986a: 437) analyses the pro-verb *yi* as a spellout of the VP/VNP trace, an analysis that might in principle be extended to other cases of resumption in Hausa focus fronting constructions. However, there are a number of theoretical problems with this analysis. First, assuming the copy theory of movement outlined above, the lower member (foot) of the chain must be an exact copy of the displaced constituent, which discounts both pro-verbs and pronouns as as members of the chain created by movement. Secondly, regardless of whether the copy theory of movement is adopted, if resumptive elements are analysed as the spellout of the foot of the chain the question arises of what prevents both/all members of a chain being spelled out in all Hausa focus fronting constructions.[14]

An alternative analysis developed by Green (1997) adopts a VP shell structure and analyses *yi* as the spellout of the 'light verb' in Hausa.

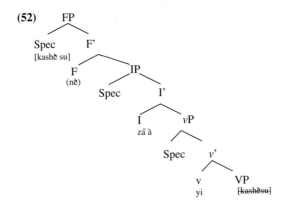

(52)

---

[14] Nunes (1995; 2004) argues that under a copy theory of movement, traces as copies must be subject to Kayne's (1994) Linear Correspondence Axiom (LCA), which states that linear order follows from a precedence relation established on the basis of asymmetric C-command, so that A precedes B in linear order if A asymmetrically C-commands B. If both members of a chain are spelled out, no linear order can be established according to the LCA, and the derivation fails. If only one member of the chain is pronounced the issue does not arise, since the LCA only orders elements that are phonetically realised. However, questions arise for languages that do license the spellout of multiple copies (see n. 12 above). Reintges (2005) adopts a late insertion view of Distributed Morphology (Halle & Marantz 1993; Marantz 1997) and argues that spellout and linearisation operations are post-syntactic, determined by parameter setting and language-specific morphosyntactic constraints.

However, this analysis also encounters problems: if *yi* is the spellout of the light verb, it is not clear what prevents it from being spelled out in the absence of focus fronting of the VP/VNP. While constructions like (49), where *yi* takes a nominalised complement, are grammatical and may provide some plausibility for the analysis in (52), examples like (53) are not grammatical. In other words, where *yi* occurs in its non-resumptive function, its complement must be nominal.

(53) *zā à   yi   kashè   su
      FUT 4pl do kill   3pl.PRO
      'they will be killed'

Finally, while the VP shell analysis may be worth exploring in developing an account of resumption in V(N)P focus fronting, questions remain concerning resumption in prepositional and nominal possessive constructions (50, 51). This issue is not pursued further here.

4.4 *WH*-FRONTING

It is well known that *wh*-fronting constructions and focus fronting constructions share core syntactic properties in Hausa, as in many other languages. Indeed, since the 1970s considerable attention has been paid to the syntactic similarities between such apparently diverse construction types as relative clauses, constituent questions and focus structures. What these sentence types have in common is that they are most insightfully analysed as operator–variable constructions: they all involve an open position or variable that is assigned an interpretation by a scope-taking operator. As discussed in Chapter 3, in the transformational generative framework, the operator–variable relation has been described as the outcome of a movement operation that links two or more positions in the syntactic structure (see Chomsky (1977) and much subsequent research). This approach has been fruitfully explored in the analysis of Hausa focus fronting constructions that was developed in the previous section. In this section, the similarities between focus fronting and *wh*-fronting in Hausa are explored with a view to establishing the extent to which a unified FP analysis can be motivated. Consider the following set of representative examples. Example (54a) illustrates an unmarked declarative for purposes of comparison.

(54) a. Audù yā   sàyi baƙař   mōtà jiyà   *declarative*
         Audu 3MS.PF buy black.of car   yesterday *sentence*
         'Audu bought a black car yesterday'
     b. su-wằnē (nè)   sukà   sàyi baƙař   *subject*
         3pl-who (FM.pl) 3pl.FOC.PF buy black.of   wh-*question*
         mōtà?
         car
         'who bought a black car?'

c.   wànè   littāfì   (nē)   Kànde   ta   *direct object*
    which   book   FM.m   Kande   3fs.FOC.PF   wh-*question*
    sàyā?
    buy
    'which book did Kande buy?'

d.   gà   wằ   ka   mai   dà   *indirect object*
    to   who(ms)   2ms.FOC.PF   return   with   wh-*question*
    littāfìn?
    book.DD
    'to whom did you return the book?'

e.   wằ   ka   mai   dà   *indirect object*
    who(ms)   2ms.FOC.PF   return   with   wh-*question*
    littāfìn   gàrē   shì?
    book.DD   to   PRO.3ms
    'whom did you return the book to (him)?'

f.   inā   (nè)   sukà   jē?   *adverbial* wh-
    where   (FM.m)   3pl.FOC.PF   go   *question (locative)*
    'where have they gone?'

g.   yàushē (nè)   sukè   zuwằ?   *adverbial* wh-
    when   (FM.m)   3pl.FOC.PF come   *question (temporal)*
    'when is it they are coming?'

h.   ta   yằyằ   (nē)   kukà   *adverbial* wh-
    by.means.of   how   (FM.m)   2pl.FOC.PF   *question (manner)*
    sằmi   kuɗîn?
    find   money.DD
    'how did you find the money?'

i.   'yaȓ   wằ   ka   àurā?   *possessive*
    daughter.of   who   2ms.FOC.PF   marry   wh-*question*
    'whose daughter did you marry?'

j.   wằ ka   àuri   'yaȓsà?   *possessive*
    who   2ms.FOC.PF marry   daughter.of.3ms   wh-*question*
    'whose daughter did you marry?'

The obvious similarity between the two construction types is that *wh*-fronted phrases are displaced to the same left periphery position as focus fronted phrases. This is demonstrated by the fact that the fronted *wh*-phrase can be followed (optionally) by the focus marker. It is also striking that the *wh*-expressions *wằ/su-wằ* 'who (s/pl)' and *mè* 'what' have alternative gender-marked forms that incorporate the (polar tone) focus marker. For example, *wằ/su-wằ* 'who (s/pl)' alternate with *wằnē/wằcē/su-wằnē* (m/f/pl) and *mè* 'what' alternates with *mènē/mècē* (m/f), although the feminine form is rare. While the unmarked forms of these expressions do not license the presence of the focus marker (54d,e,i,j), these gender-marked forms require the presence of the focus marker, resulting in what Hausa linguists describe as the repeat copula construction. Although it is a monoclausal construction, the repeat copula construction has the impact of a *wh*-cleft in English (e.g. *Who was it that died? What was it that happened?*). The following examples illustrate (the unmarked examples (55a) and (56a) are provided for comparison):

(55) a. wằ   ya   mutù?
      who 3ms.FOC.PF   die
      'who died?'

    b. wằnē   nề   ya   mutù?
      who.m FM.m 3ms.FOC.PF die
      'who (m) died?'

    c. wằcē   cề   ta   mutù?
      who.f FM.f 3fs.FOC.PF die
      'who (f) died?'

    d. su-wằnē nề   sukà   mutù?
      who.pl FM.pl 3pl.FOC.PF die
      'who (pl) died?'

(56) a. mề   ya   fằru?
      what 3ms.FOC.PF happen
      'what happened?'

    b. mềnē   nề   ya   fằru?
      what.m FM.m 3ms.FOC.PF happen
      'what (m) happened?'

Other *wh*-expressions with incorporated variants of the focus marker are the determiners *wànè/wàcè/wàdànnè* 'which (m/f/pl)' and the pronouns *wànnē/wàccē/wàdànnē* 'which one(s) (m/f/pl)'.[15]

As a comparison of the examples in (54) with the focus fronting examples above will verify (§ 4.2.1), the syntax of focus fronting runs parallel to the syntax of *wh*-fronting in Hausa, which suggests that a movement analysis can also be straightforwardly extended to *wh*-fronting. The arguments in favour of a 'string vacuous' movement analysis of subject *wh*-questions holds equally for *wh*-extraction as it does for focus fronting. In particular, it is the presence of the focus form of the inflection word and the optional presence of the focus marker in subject *wh*-questions like (54b) and (55,56) that motivate this analysis. Observe further that the extraction of a *wh*-phrase from the complement position of a 'grade 2' verb is registered in the morphology of the verb (54c). As with focus fronting, two strategies are available for questioning prepositional objects. The preposition can either be 'pied-piped', as in (54d), or stranded, as in (54e). The latter strategy triggers the insertion of the resumptive pronoun *shì* 'him' in the extraction

---

[15] The *wh*-expressions containing incorporated variants of the copula are treated here as grammaticalised forms that do not result (synchronically) from an FP projection, although as *wh*-expressions they participate in FP structures.

site. Hausa does not have a possessive question word 'whose'. Instead, the language relies on a construction in which the interrogative pronoun *wà* 'who' occurs in the postnominal position of a possessive noun phrase. As shown by the contrast between (54i) and (54j), in *wh*-possessives either the entire possessive NP is pied-piped (this is the only option for subjects) or the questioned possessor noun is extracted out of the *wh*-possessive, with a resumptive pronoun left behind in the original position.

In addition, *wh*-fronting obeys the same locality constraints as focus fronting. Example (57) shows that extraction from an embedded question (*wh*-island) results in ungrammaticality:

(57) *mè   Kànde   ta   san   wà   ya   sàyā?
       what   Kande   3fs.FOC.PF know   who   3ms.FOC.PF   buy
       'what did Kande know who bought?'

As with focus fronting, it is not possible to prepose multiple *wh*-phrases:

(58) *su-wà   mè   sukà   sàyā?
       who.pl   what   3pl.FOC.PF   buy
       'who what bought?'

Neither is it possible to simultaneously focus front and *wh*-front constituents within a single clause (59a), although the corresponding topic construction is grammatical (59b).

(59) a. *yârā   mè   sukà   sàyā?
           children what   3pl.FOC.PF   buy
           'what did **the children** buy?'
      b. yârā   (dai), mè   sukà   sàyā?
          children (PART)   what   3pl.FOC.PF   buy
          '(as for) the children, what did they buy?'

Given these well-known parallels between *wh*-fronting and focus fronting, it is straightforward to extend the FP analysis to *wh*-fronting. The arguments presented above against CP as the target of focus fronting in Hausa also apply to *wh*-fronting (§ 4.3.3). For example, an overt complementiser may precede an embedded *wh*-phrase, suggesting a projection in addition to and below CP as the target of *wh*-fronting:

(60) zân   tàmbàyē sù   kō   wànē nè   sukà   gayà̀ wà làbā̀rì
       FUT.1s ask   3pl.PRO COMP   who FM.m 3pl.FOC.PF   tell IOM news
       'I'll ask them who they told the news to'

It is well known that it is the selectional properties of the main clause verb that license embedded questions. As Green & Reintges (2005b) observe, the Hausa verb *tàmbayà̀* 'ask' selects an interrogative complement, which results in an indirect question interpretation (61a). This restriction is reflected in the selection of the complementiser: the interrogative complementiser *kō* 'whether' is optionally selected by this verb (61a), while the declarative complementiser *cêwā* 'that' gives rise to an ungrammatical sentence (61b). Observe that the embedded inflection word occurs in the focus form because the embedded question contains a *wh*-fronted phrase in its left periphery.

(61) a. Kànde tā   tàmbàyē nì (kō)   mè na   sàyā à kàsuwā
      Kande 3fs.PF ask   1s (COMP) what 1s.FOC.PF buy at market
      'Kande asked me what I bought at market'

     b. *Kànde tā   tàmbàyē nì cêwā mè   na   sàyā à kàsuwā
      Kande 3fs.PF ask   1s COMP what 1s.FOC.PF buy at market
      'Kande asked me what I bought at market'

In contrast, the Hausa verb *yi tsàmmānì* 'think' selects a declarative complement.[16] As a consequence, this verb does not license embedded questions (62a), although main-clause questions are well-formed (62b). As shown by the grammaticality contrast between (62b) and (62c), this verb only licenses the declarative complementiser *cêwā*.

(62) a. *Kànde tanà   tsàmmānin wà ya   sàyi littāfìn   à
      Kande 3fs.IMPF thinking.of who 3ms.FOC.PF buy book.DD at
      kàsuwā
      market
      'Kande thinks who bought the book at market'

     b. wà Kànde takè   tsàmmānin cêwā yā   sàyi
      who Kande 3FS.FOC.IMPF thinking.of COMP 3MS.PF buy
      littāfìn à   kàsuwā?
      book.DD at   market
      'who does Kande think (that) bought the book at market?'

     c. *wà Kànde takè   tsàmmānin kō   yā   sàyi
      who Kande 3fs.FOC.IMPF thinking.of COMP 3ms.PF buy
      littāfìn à   kàsuwā?
      book.DD at   market
      'who does Kande think (whether) bought the book at market?'

Unlike *tàmbayà* 'ask' and *yi tsàmmānì* 'think', the Hausa verb *sanì* 'know' licenses both declarative complements and interrogative complements. It follows that both direct questions (63a) and indirect questions (63b) are well-formed, as long as the appropriate complementiser is selected: the selection of *kō* is ungrammatical in direct questions (63c), as is the selection of *cêwā* in indirect questions (63d).

---

[16] The Hausa verb *yi tsàmmānì* 'think' is what Jaggar (2001: 430) describes as a 'phrasal verb', consisting of the verb *yi* 'do' followed by an activity noun. In imperfective constructions like (62), which require the nominalised form of the verb that follows the inflection word (§ 2.3.2), the nominalised form of *yi* (*yîn* 'do.vn.of') is usually omitted, in which case the imperfective inflection word is followed directly by the activity (verbal) noun.

(63) a. wằ   Kànde ta   san   (cêwā) yā   sàyi littāfìn
      who   Kande 3fs.foc.pf know (comp) 3ms.pf buy   book.dd
      à   kằsuwā
      at   market
      'who does Kande know (that) (he) bought the book at market?'

   b. Kànde tā   san   kō   wằ   ya   sàyi littāfìn
      Kande 3fs.pf   know   comp who   3ms.foc.pf buy book.dd
      à   kằsuwā
      at   market
      'Kande knows who bought the book at market'

   c. *wằ Kànde ta   san   kō   yā   sàyi littāfìn
      who Kande 3fs.foc.pf know comp 3ms.pf buy   book.dd
      à   kằsuwā
      at   market
      'who does Kande know whether (he) bought the book at market?'

   d. *Kànde tā   san   cêwā   wằ   ya   sàyi littāfìn
      Kande 3fs.pf   know   comp   who   3ms.foc.pf buy book.dd
      à   kằsuwā
      at   market
      'Kande knows that who bought the book at market'

As with focus phrases (44), a wh-phrase cannot be extracted to the left periphery of a subjunctive (or potential future) clause (64a), although long-distance extraction from a subjunctive clause to the left periphery of a finite clause is licensed (64b).[17]

(64) a. *nā   cê   mề   yà   yi   Tuller (1986: 69)
      1s.pf say   what 3ms.sub do
      'I said what he should do'

   b. wàcè   yārinyằ kakề   sô   kà   àurā?
      which.f   girl   2ms.foc.impf want.vn 2ms.sub marry
      'which girl do you want to marry?'

Finally, recall that the focus marker can occur clause-finally, but that speakers reject examples of focus fronting that also contain a clause-final focus marker. Examples (5h) and (11) are repeated here in (65). Recall that examples like (65a) were analysed as clausal focus, and the FP analysis was extended to such cases on the basis of the ungrammaticality of examples like (65b), which suggest that clausal focus is blocked if the clause already contains a focus fronted constituent (§ 4.3.2).

---

[17] Extraction from an embedded subjunctive clause is particularly common in cases of constructions headed by 'complement-taking expressions' that select a subjunctive clausal complement, e.g., dōlè nē 'it is necessary that...'. See Newman (2000: 104–5) for further examples.

(65) a. yā   yi   ƙaryā   nè
         3ms.PF   do   lie   FM.m
         'he **did** lie'

   b. * dà   sàndā   (nè)   sukà   dòkē   shì   nē
       with   stick   (FM.m)   3pl.FOC.PF beat   3ms.PRO   FM.m
       'they beat him **with a stick**'

However, a different pattern obtains with the clause-final copula in *wh*-fronting constructions. Constructions such as those exemplified in (66) are freely accepted by speakers, suggesting that the clause-final non-verbal copula performs a distinct function from focus marking in these constructions. Example (66b) shows that the clause-final copula must occur in its default masculine form, as in the case of clausal focus, but the function of the clause-final copula in these constructions is perhaps most accurately described in terms of a tag question. In the examples in (66), the semantic contribution of the clause-final copula is not reflected in the translations, but the copula is glossed as COP rather than FM to indicate that it does not function as a focus marker in these constructions. This issue is not pursued here, but see Newman (2000: 500, 546–7) and Jaggar (2001: 524).

(66) a. kā   sàyi   mōtà   nē?   yes-no *question*
         2ms.PF   buy   car   COP.m
         'did you buy a car?'

   b. *kā   sàyi   mōtà   cē?   yes-no *question*
       2ms.PF   buy   car   COP.f
       'did you buy a car?'

   c. su-wằnē nè   sukà   sàyi mōtà   *subject* wh-*question*
       who.pl   FM.pl   3pl.FOC.PF buy car
       nē?
       COP.m
       'who (pl) bought a car?'

   d. mềnē   nè   sukà   sàyā   à   *direct object*
       what.m FM.m   3pl.FOC.PF buy   at   wh-*question*
       kàsuwā nè?
       market COP.m
       'what did they buy at market?'

   e. inā   sukà   jē   nè?   *adverbial* wh-*question*
       where   3pl.FOC.PF go   COP.m
       'where did they go'

   f. 'yar̃   wằnē   nè   ka   *possessive* wh-*question*
       daughter.of who.m FM.m 2ms.FOC.PF
       àurā   nè?
       marry   COP.m
       'whose daughter did you marry?'

g. mḕ Kànde takḕ   tsàmmānìn (kō)   *long-distance*
   what Kande 3fs.FOC.IMPF think.VN.of (COMP)   wh-*extraction*
   Audù yā sàyā à   kằsuwā   nḕ?
   Audu 3ms.PF buy at   market   COP.m
   'what does Kande think Audu bought at market?'

4.5 SPECIAL INFLECTION

Recall from Chapter 3 (§ 3.3.2) that a number of related and unrelated
languages from around the world display distinctive inflectional morphology in relative clauses, focus constructions and wh-constructions. The term
'special inflection' is used here as an umbrella term for a phenomenon that
has received a number of different labels in the literature, including 'wh-
agreement' and 'operator-C agreement' (Chamorro [Austronesian]; Chung
1998); 'second tenses' (Coptic [Ancient Egyptian]; Reintges 2002) and the
traditional term 'relative aspect' applied to Hausa special inflection, which
Jaggar (2001) calls the 'focus' form of INFL, the term that is adopted in the
present study. What these languages share in common is that special
inflection tends to group together the same range of operator–variable
constructions. See Hyman & Watters (1984), Haïk (1990), Watanabe (1996)
and Chung (1998) for representative studies.[18] However, while in some
languages special inflection co-occurs with displacement of a constituent, in
other languages special inflection co-occurs with focus/wh-in situ. Further
potential differences between languages displaying special inflection
concern the head upon which the special inflection is marked, and the
single versus multiple occurrence of special inflection in the clause. Reintges
et al. (2006) identify a set of parameters of variation including the location,
recursiveness and syntactic distribution of special inflection. In this section,
the descriptive facts concerning special inflection in Hausa are presented in
the context of this cross-linguistic typology of special inflection (Green &
Reintges 2004; 2005a; 2005b; Reintges & Green 2004).

4.5.1 *Special inflection in Hausa: descriptive facts*

According to Reintges et al.'s (2006) LOCATION parameter, special inflection
is restricted to verbs, inflectional heads or functional heads in the left
periphery of the clause (Zaenen 1983). In Chamorro, for example, a VSO
language, special inflection is marked on the verb (wh-agreement) as well
as on complementisers (operator-C agreement) in relative clauses,
wh-questions and focus constructions. According to Chung (1998),
wh-agreement registers the case of the variable (gap) created by wh-

---

[18] See also Chapter 5 (§ 5.3) for an overview of Schuh's (2000) hypothesis concerning the
historical origins of special inflection and the Hausa non-verbal copula.

movement, while operator-C agreement indicates the categorial features and the thematic content of the operator (extracted constituent) in the specifier position of C. Compare the simple declarative clause in (67a), in which the clause-initial verb appears in its neutral form, with the constituent questions in (67b–d), where the *wh*-interrogative phrase has moved overtly to the left of the verb. In (67b), the nominative case of the moved *wh*-subject is flagged by the *wh*-agreement morpheme -*um*-, while the objective case of the *wh*-object is registered by the *wh*-agreement morpheme -*in*- plus possessor agreement -*nña* in (67c). In (67d), the complementiser *ni* is in a local (specifier–head) relationship with the left-adjacent *wh*-phrase *manu* 'where' and registers both its nominal features and its locative semantics. Observe that *wh*-agreement has no surface realisation in (67d). Special inflectional morphology is indicated by boldface in example (67). (Chung does not gloss the particle *si*, which precedes proper names.)

(67) a. ha-fa'gasi si Juan i   kareta.   *Chamorro*
         AGR-wash   Juan the car   (Chung 1998: 236, 58)
         'Juan washed the car.'   *neutral declarative clause*
     b. hayi **fum**a'gasi   i   kareta?   wh-*agreement (*wh-*subject)*
         who WH(SUBJ).wash the car
         'who washed the car?'
     c. hafa   **fin**a'gsése-**nña**   wh-*agreement (*wh-*object)*
         what   WH(OBJ).wash.PROG-AGR
         si   Henry pära hagu?
               Henry for   you
         'what is Henry washing for you?'
     d. manu **ni**   mañ-ásaga siha?   *operator-C*
         where WH.COMP AGR.live.PROG they   *agreement* (wh-*adverb)*
         'where are you living?'

Hausa special inflection is marked on the inflectional head, but recall from Chapter 2 that this morphological alternation between 'general' and 'focus' forms is restricted to perfective and imperfective INFL (§ 2.3.2). The habitual, future and allative forms show no morphological alternation between 'general' and 'focus' forms but may occur in both focus and non-focus contexts. Example (68) illustrates this point with respect to future INFL.

(68) a. zâi   gamà   aikìn   gòbe
         FUT.3ms finish work.DD   tomorrow
         'he'll finish the work tomorrow.'
     b. wằ   zâi   shìga rìjìyar̃ nàn?
         who FUT.3ms enter well   this
         'who will enter this well?'

While the rhetorical form of INFL is restricted to focus/*wh*-constructions, the subjunctive and potential forms are not licensed in focus/*wh*-constructions (recall the discussion of examples (44) and (64) above). The Hausa pattern corresponds broadly to the two types of special inflection in Chamorro. Thus, Hausa special inflection is on a par with Chamorro 'wh-agreement', the difference being that while Chamorro inflectional morphology is affixed to the verb, Hausa inflectional morphology forms an independent free morpheme. Equally, the focus-marking copula can be related to Chamorro 'operator-C agreement' in the sense that it is a left-peripheral functional head that also registers the presence of an operator-variable dependency.

Reintges et al.'s (2006) recursiveness parameter states that in cases of long-distance movement, in which the extracted constituent crosses one or more clause boundaries, special inflectional morphology may be recursive (it surfaces on every designated head in the path of movement), or non-recursive (it surfaces only on the highest designated head in the path of movement). For example, wh-agreement in Chamorro surfaces on every verb in the path of long-distance extraction (69a), while operator-C agreement appears only on the highest complementiser (69b). The intermediate positions of the extracted constituents are not shown in (69). Special inflectional morphology is marked in boldface.

(69) a. hayi **sin**angane-nña   si Juan   *Chamorro*
         who WH(OBJ).say.to-AGR   Juan   (Chung 1998: 211)
         malago'-ña   pära **u**-bisita ~~hayi~~?
         WH(OBL).want.AGR FUT   WH(OBJ).AGR-visit
         'who did Juan tell (us) that he wants to visit?'

     b. amanu **na**   ha-tagu'   *Chamorro*
         where WH.COMP.   WH(OBJ).AGR-order (Reintges et al. 2006)
         si Dolore   i   lahi-ña pära u-tohgi?
         Dolores the son-AGR FUT   AGR-stand
         'where did Dolores tell her son that he should stand?'

Unlike Chomorro special inflection, Hausa special inflection is non-recursive: it occurs only in the clause whose left periphery contains the extracted constituent. Example (70) illustrates long-distance subject extraction; the extracted constituent receives matrix scope and the construction is interpreted as a direct question. Special inflection surfaces only on the highest designated functional head, while the general form occurs in the lower clause. This inflection pattern also holds for long-distance object/adjunct extraction.[19]

---

[19] Tuller (1986a: 120) observes that while this generalisation holds for most Hausa speakers, some speakers permit special inflection to surface on every inflectional head in the path of movement. (This appears to represent a case of dialect variation, since most speakers of Standard (Kano) Hausa do not produce such constructions; but Tuller is not precise about the relevant dialect(s).)

(i) mè   sukà   cê   yârā   sun/sukà   sàyā?   (Tuller 1986a: 120)
     what 3PL.FOC.PF say children 3PL.PF/3PL.FOC.PF buy
     'what did they say the children bought?'

(70) wàcè   yārinyằ ka   cề   tā   ràsu?
     which.f girl   2MS.FOC.PF say 3FS.PF die
     'which girl did you say had died?'

Compare example (71), where the *wh*-phrase undergoes partial movement
to the embedded [Spec FP]. In this construction, the extracted constituent
receives embedded scope and the construction is interpreted as an indirect
question (§ 4.4). Special inflection surfaces in the lower clause.

(71) zân   tàmbàyē sù   kō   wằnē nề   sukà   gayằ
     FUT.1S ASK   3PL.PRO COMP who FM.m 3PL.FOC.PF tell
     wà làbārì̃
     IOM story
     'I'll ask them who they told the news to'

Turning finally to Reintges et al.'s (2006) distribution parameter, this
relates to the class of constructions in which special inflection is found.
Special inflection prototypically flags classic *wh*-constructions (relative
clauses, *wh*-questions and focus constructions), but in some languages
special inflection shows a wider distribution, extending to temporal adverbial
clauses, conditionals, secondary predicates and narrative uses (Hyman &
Watters 1984; Haïk 1990). In Modern Irish, for example, special inflection
has a relatively broad syntactic distribution. A salient feature of Irish *wh*-
constructions is the presence of the alternating complementiser particles *aL*
(the 'direct relative particle' of traditional grammars) and *aN* (the 'indirect
relative particle'). When *wh*-movement leaves a gap in the base position, the
COMP-particle *aL* must be selected (72a). However, when *wh*-constructions
contain a resumptive pronoun, this conditons the complementiser allomorph
aN instead (72b) (McCloskey 1979; 1990; 2001).[20] Example (72) illustrates
this pattern in the Modern Irish relative clause. Special inflectional
morphology is marked with boldface in examples (72) and (73).

(72) a. an ghirseach **a**   ghoid na   *Modern Irish*
        the girl   COMP.*aL* stole the   (McCloskey 2001: 67)
        síogaí   ~~an ghirseach~~
        fairies
        'the girl that the fairies stole away'
     b. [an ghirseach]$_i$ **ar**   ghoid na   síogaí [í]$_i$
        the girl   COMP.*aN* stole the   fairies her
        'the girl that the fairies stole away'

---

[20] According to McCloskey (1990: 206), the phonological and morphological distinction
between the alternating complementisers is sometimes not reflected in the phonological
shape of the complementiser itself, but rather in the initial phonological mutation induced
on the following sentence element (typically a verb). The abbreviations *aL* and *aN* reflect the
fact that the former complementiser induces lenition on the adjacent verb, whereas the latter
induces nasalisation on the initial segment of a following verb.

The complementiser form *aL* patterns with a special form of verbal inflection in present and future tenses, which McCloskey (2001) calls the wh-form. This special inflectional morphology has a broad syntactic distribution, appearing in all clause types in which the complementiser *aL* must be selected. These include not only relative clauses (73a) and *wh*-questions (73b), but also various types of temporal subclause (73c).

(73) a. an chéad amhrán eile   **a**   *Modern Irish*
       the first song   other COMP.*aL* (McCloskey 2001: 72)
       bheas   agann
       be.FUT.WH at.us
       'the next song we'll have'

   b. cá   huair **a**   **thiocfas**   tú   'na bhaile?
      what time COMP.*aL* come.FUT.WH you   home
      'when will you come home?'

   c. nuair **a**   **bíos**   daoine tinn
      when COMP.*aL* be.PRES.HAB.WH people sick
      'when people are sick'

Like Modern Irish, Hausa represents an instance of the broader distribution of special inflection. In addition to its presence in focus/*wh*-fronting constructions and in conditional clauses (15), Hausa special inflection also occurs (a) in relative clauses, (b) in various types of temporal adjunct clause and (c) in foregrounded chains of events in narrative discourse. The remainder of this section provides a descriptive overview of the distribution of special inflection in these three contexts.

As mentioned in Chapter 2, relative clauses can be grouped together with focus/*wh*-fronting constructions in Hausa on the basis of certain shared morphosyntactic properties, of which special inflection is one (§ 2.4.1). The relevant examples are repeated here. Example (74a) shows a restrictive relative clause with a definite head noun and the relativiser *dà*. Example (74b) shows a restrictive relative clause with a head noun unmarked for definiteness and the full high-low tone relative pronoun *wandà*.[21] Example (74c) shows a restrictive relative clause with a specific indefinite head noun and the relativiser *dà*, and (74d) the same construction with the full relative pronoun. Example (74e) shows that the relative pronoun may also substitute for the head noun.

(74) a. [yāròn dà   sukà   dōkā] yanà   asibitì
        boy.DD REL 3pl.FOC.PF beat   3ms.IMPF hospital
        'the boy that they beat up is in hospital'

   b. [yārò̃ wandà   sukà   dōkā] yanà   asibitì
      boy RELPRO(m) 3pl.FOC.PF beat   3ms.IMPF hospital
      'the boy that they beat up is in hospital'

---

[21] As Jaggar (2001: 528) points out, nouns may be interpreted as definite despite the absence of the definite determiner. Examples (74a) and (74b) are therefore potentially equivalent, although (74a) is the more natural construction.

c. [wani   yārə̀ dà kḕ   nan à lōkàcîn] yā   ga
   SID(m) boy REL FOC.IMPF there at time.DD 3ms.PF see
   kōmē
   everything
   'a boy who was there at the time saw everything'

d. [wani   yārə̀ wandà   kḕ   nan à lōkàcîn] yā
   SID(m) boy RELPRO(m) FOC.IMPF there at time.DD 3ms.PF
   ga kōmē
   see everything
   'a boy who was there at the time saw everything'

e. waɗàndà   sukà   mutù...
   RELPRO(pl) 3pl.FOC.PF die
   'those who died...'

Example (75) shows a non-restrictive relative clause, which is characterised by pause intonation and by the full form of the relative pronoun. In addition, some speakers prefer an all-low tone relative pronoun in non-restrictive relative clauses, and some speakers also find the non-focus form of INFL acceptable in this construction (Jaggar 1998; 2001):

(75) ɗālìbân,   waɗàndà /wàɗàndà sukà/sun   gamà aikìnsù,
     students.DD RELPRO(pl)   3pl.FOC.PF/3pl.PF finish work.of.3pl
     duk sun   tàfi
     all 3pl.PF go
     'the students, who have finished their work, have all gone'

Like focus/*wh*-fronting constructions, relative clauses are operator–variable constructions that show a dependency between an operator (the relative pronoun) and a gap inside the clause. This accounts for the presence of special inflection in relative clauses. Despite these morphosyntactic similarities, relative clauses are functionally rather dissimilar to focus/*wh*-constructions, although Jaggar (2001: 531) suggests that what focus/*wh*-fronting and restrictive relative clauses have in common from a semantic perspective is that 'the identification of the leftshifted element is highly constrained, i.e. it is uniquely restricted/defined/specified'. Jaggar (2001: 538) further suggests that it is this absence of this semantic feature that accounts for the acceptability (for some speakers) of non-focus form of INFL in non-restrictive relatives. Beyond pointing out the morphosyntactic similarities between relative clauses and focus/*wh*-constructions, no attempt is made here to provide a syntactic analysis of relative clauses. For a transformational analysis of Hausa relative clauses, see Tuller (1986a: 52–3, 80–86).[22]

---

[22] The fact that the relativiser *dà* is homophonous with the complementiser *dà* suggests a CP analysis to Tuller (1986a), wherein the CP that post-modifies the head noun is headed by *dà*, and hosts in [Spec CP] the *wan-* morpheme that raises from within the relative clause.

In Hausa, special inflection also occurs in various types of temporal adjunct clause. The presence of special inflection in these constructions can be accounted for on the basis that these temporal subclauses have relative clause syntax, where the nominal *lōkàcîn* 'the time' functions as the head that is modified by the relative clause. For further discussion, see Bagari (1976), Tuller (1986a: 112–16), Jaggar (2001: 606–8; 2006b).

(76) lōkàcîn   dà   mukà   ganshì   yanà   zàune   bàkin   hanyà
       time.DD   COMP 1pl.FOC.PF see.3ms 3ms.IMPF sit.STAT side.of road
       'when we saw him, he was sitting by the side of the road'

Finally, recall from Chapter 2 that the focus perfective also occurs in narrative sequences. A recent account of this phenomenon is provided by Jaggar (2006b), who argues that the focus perfective is motivated by the same discourse function both in narrative and in focus/*wh*-constructions:

> My core claim is that the use of the 'Focus Perfective' in fronted focus/ *wh*-constructions and the pivotal foregrounded portions of past-time narratives is a function and diagnostic of the fact that they all supply the most communicatively PROMINENT and focal NEW information and so achieve the same DISCOURSE-PRAGMATIC goals ... The psychological focus of attention is therefore syntactically signalled (grammaticalized) by the special focus tense-aspect. (Jaggar 2006b: 8)

In particular, Jaggar (2006b: 9) argues that 'prominent foregrounded event-clauses carrying the story-line require the Focus/Narrative Perfective, but less salient background clauses occur with the General Perfective'. In addition to describing the syntactic contexts in which focus and general perfective are required (the former in focus/*wh*-fronting constructions and relative clauses, and the latter in declarative clauses, *yes/no* questions and topic constructions), Jaggar examines the properties of narrative discourse that condition the interaction of focus and general perfective forms.[23] Although both focus and general perfective forms are conditioned by temporal anteriority, the focus perfective has the function of highlighting or foregrounding a new event or a series of events in a narrative sequence, against the context provided by the preceding discourse. Consider the following examples taken from a 'brush with death' narrative (Jaggar 2006b: 22–3):

---

[23] Jaggar (2006b:15) also presents a brief discussion of the distribution of general and focus forms in subordinate adverbial clauses, observing: 'Although the form–function correlations are typically complex rather than one-to-one, the distribution of the two sets in subordinate environments is basically consistent with the pervasive structural–semantic correlation that the primary (deictic) use of the Focus/Narrative Perfective is to signal realis, single-occurrence events which are anterior to the utterance time ... When these conditions do not apply, the default General Perfective occurs'. For example, the general perfective occurs in counterfactual clauses.

(77) na   būɗè, tô darē <u>yā</u>   <u>fārà yî</u>,   sai   ƙarfèn
1s.foc.pf open well night 3ms.pf start do.vn then metal.of
tayà   ya   kaɽcè tītì
tyre   3ms.foc.pf scrape road
'I opened [the door], well night-time <u>had arrived</u>, then the metal rim
of the tyre scraped on the road'

(78) na   kāsà   mā   būɗè ƙōfà sabò dà <u>nā   giggìcē</u>,
1s.foc.pf be.unable even   open door because 1s.pf panic
duk <u>nā   zàtā</u> duk <u>sun rìgā sun mutù</u>   Na   būɗè ....
all <u>1s.pf think</u> all   3pl.pf do.already 3pl.pf die 1s.foc.pf open
'I couldn't even open the door because <u>I'd panicked</u>, <u>I thought</u> that
<u>they had all died</u> already. I opened...'

The underlined portions of these texts occur in the general perfective, and
relate to background information, which is anterior to the reference time
and relates either to the physical or temporal background (77), or to the
speaker's 'causal evaluation' of the main event described (78) (Jaggar
2006b: 23). In contrast, the foregrounded events being described occur in
the focus perfective. Jaggar provides a range of similar examples, in which
the general perfective is used to describe 'flashbacks' or explanations of the
main sequence of events being described. In contrast to the focus perfective,
the focus imperfective only occurs in narratives when syntactically
conditioned (e.g. in focus or *wh*-fronting constructions or in relative
clauses).[24]

4.5.2 *Special inflection in Hausa: theoretical issues*

This section presents a summary of the analysis of Hausa special inflection
developed by Green & Reintges (2005b). Recall that the Principles and
Parameters/Minimalist analysis of focus/*wh*-fronting proposed earlier in
the chapter derives focus/*wh*-fronting constructions by raising the focus/
wh-phrase to the specifier of FP, an operation that is driven by the need to
eliminate nonsemantic or uninterpretable focus/*wh*-features on the
functional head, while the displaced phrase itself retains its semantic
focus/*wh*-features. Green & Reintges extend this analysis to account for
special inflection by assuming a direct relationship between the force-
indicating C head, the F head and the infl head in Hausa.[25] A plausible

---

[24] See Abdoulaye (2004) for an alternative account. Abdoulaye suggests that relative or focus
perfective has grammaticalised a meaning of punctual past tense (or 'preterite' in Newman's
(2000) terms), and this innovation accounts for its extension to new contexts, including
narrative and conditional clauses.

[25] Tuller (1986a:108) also proposes an analysis of special inflection as the result of an operator-
variable configuration, but one that is based on the matching of a [+/−definite] feature,
where nonrelative forms, including the subjunctive, are [−definite] and relative/focus forms
are [+ definite].

assumption, given the well-known selectional properties of subordinating complementisers, is that the focus head inherits its uninterpretable feature from the immediately dominating head C (Chomsky 2001b: 9). Indeed, the selectional properties of dedicated declarative and interrogative subordinating complementisers provide evidence for the relationship between C and F (§ 4.4). Green & Reintges further assume that F and INFL are in a syntactic agreement relation of feature sharing (Chomsky 2000; 2001a), which results in the special inflection located in INFL. According to this perspective, special inflection represents the spellout or morphological realisation of the features inherited by INFL from F (Rizzi 1996; Chomsky 2001b).[26] Although INFL does not raise to F in Hausa, there is nevertheless compelling evidence of the agreement relation between these two heads. First, the fact that relative aspect marking is obligatory when a constituent moves to the specifier of FP provides strong support for the existence of this relationship. Secondly, the prohibition against relative aspect marking in subjunctive clauses suggests that special inflection on INFL is contingent upon the presence of F as the functional head that drives the displacement operation. Finally, there is also evidence that the agreement relation may extend from INFL to the V head, given the morphology of Hausa 'grade 2' verbs (§2.3.2), which flag the presence of an unpronounced copy of the extracted phrase (recall example (6)). Green & Reintges further observe that Hausa subject questions with partitive *wh*-phrases provide direct evidence for movement of the *wh*-subject from the specifier of IP to the specifier of FP, because the partitive phrase itself can be stranded in the specifier of IP (79) (adapted from Newman 2000: 494). The tree diagram in (80) illustrates the derivation of a (partitive) subject *wh*-question. In the tree diagrams (80) and (82), the agreement relation between heads is represented by dotted arrows, while syntactic displacement is represented by unbroken arrows.

(79) wàccē   cè̄   dàgà cikin-sù   ta   kashè̄ shi?
      which.one.f FM.F from among-3pl 2fs.FOC.PF kill PRO.3ms
      'which of them killed him?'

Consider the direct object *wh*-question in (81). Assuming that direct objects in Hausa are case-licensed in situ in the complement position of the lexical verb, there is no case-motivated reason for the raising of *wh*-objects within IP. Green & Reintges therefore assume that the direct object *wh*-phrase moves direcly from its base position to the specifier of FP, and that this direct movement is made possible by the fact that all the functional heads along the path of movement are connected within a feature-sharing

---

[26] As pointed by Chomsky (2001b: 13), successive-cyclic *wh*-movement may have morphological effects surfacing 'sometimes in C (where we would expect it), but commonly in the agreement system headed by T (where we would not). That makes sense if C-T are really functioning as a unit in inducing agreement.'

relationship, creating the extended domain within which movement is possible (81).[27]

(80)

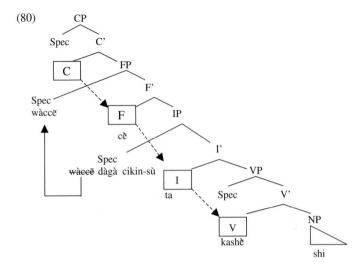

(81) mề yârā sukà cê?
what children 3pl.FOC.PF say
'what did the children say?'

Of course, the analysis proposed by Green & Reintges accounts only for the syntactic conditioning of special inflection. Recall from the previous section that the focus perfective form is also used to signal foregrounded or new information in narrative contexts, a discourse phenomenon that Jaggar (2006b) attributes to the morphosyntactic 'signalling' or 'grammaticalisation' of the focus of speaker/hearer attention. A formal account of this phenomenon, which unifies the narrative use of special inflection with its occurrence in focus/wh-fronting constructions and in relative clauses, entails the presence of an operator-variable dependency in which the operator is null. This issue is not pursued here, but see Tuller (1986a: 117) for a sketch of an analysis along these lines, in which the narrative use of special inflection is related to the presence of a null focus operator that specifies the clause.

---

[27] This analysis departs from Chomsky's (2001a) Derivation by Phase model, according to which wh-movement proceeds successive-cyclically through different derivational domains or PHASES, including the verb phrase with full argument structure and the CP. Phases are domains that are eligible for phonological realisation, which means that a constituent has to target the left edge of each phase in order to undergo subsequent movement. Green & Reintges (2005b) argue that there is no evidence for autonomous cyclic domains in Hausa. Instead, the TP-VP field and the left periphery function as a single domain for syntactic derivation.

(82)

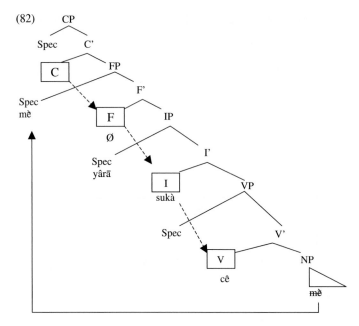

4.6 Focus/*wh*-in situ

Until recently, Hausa was described as a language in which focus constructions and *wh*-interrogatives could only be formed by fronting the relevant constituent to clause-initial position. The generalisation to emerge from the facts discussed in this section is that Hausa clearly permits focus/*wh*-in situ, but unlike focus/*wh*-fronting constructions, the parallels between focus and *wh*-constructions break down in the in situ case. For some speakers, *wh*-in situ (argument) questions are unacceptable unless they function as echo questions. By contrast, focus in situ is the preferred strategy for presentational focus, and is generally acceptable as new information focus. Focus in situ is also attested in exhaustive/contrastive contexts. These facts were first explicitly discussed by Jaggar (2001), and have been further investigated by Green & Jaggar (2003), Jaggar (2006a), Hartmann & Zimmermann (forthcoming, a) and Green & Reintges (2005b).[28] This section

---

[28] Although Newman (2000) does not explicitly describe Hausa as a language that allows *wh*-in situ, he does provide examples of adverbial *wh*-in situ (Newman 2000: 496):

(i) a.   sunà   fitôwā   dàgà   inā?
          3pl.IMPF come.out.VN from   where
          'where are they coming out from?

     b.   yā   tàfi   yàushē?
          3ms.PF   go   when
          'when did he go?'

Newman (2000: 496) states that 'although fronting is the norm, adverbial Q[uestion]-words can remain in regular declarative sentence position with only a slightly strengthened nuance. With normal word order, the general rather than the Rel TAM is used.'

presents a representative body of data illustrating *wh*-in situ (§ 4.6.1) and
focus in situ (§ 4.6.2), as well as exploring whether functional distinctions can
be established between the ex situ and in situ focus strategies (§ 4.6.3). There
follows a discussion of multiple focus/*wh*-constructions (§ 4.6.4). Finally,
focus/*wh*-in situ constructions are discussed in the light of the FP analysis of
Hausa focus/*wh*-constructions developed in this chapter (§ 4.6.5). Since
research into Hausa focus/*wh*-in situ is at a relatively early stage, sources are
provided for all data given in this section.

4.6.1 Wh-*in situ: descriptive facts*

There is considerable inter-speaker variation in Hausa with respect to the
acceptability of *wh*-in situ. This variation does not appear to be conditioned
by dialect differences, since judgements vary from one speaker to another
from the same dialect area. However, all speakers accept *wh*-in situ as echo
questions. Echo questions, as the term suggests, echo a preceding utterance
and indicate either that the hearer has misheard part of the utterance
(functioning as a request for repetition) or disbelief or surprise about some
part of the previous speaker's utterance. It follows that echo questions are
functionally distinct from genuine *wh*-questions. In many languages, echo
questions are also exempt from the syntactic requirements that govern
genuine *wh*-questions (see Huddleston & Pullum (2002: 886–90). In Hausa,
echo *wh*-questions surface as *wh*-in situ constructions, in which the INFL
word assumes the general form. The *wh*-movement strategy is not available
for echo question formation. Example (83) illustrates an echo question.
Since these are not morphosyntactically distinct from genuine *wh*-in situ
questions, context determines the echo versus genuine *wh*-interpretation.

(83) kin   ga   wằ   à   kằsuwā?   (Jaggar 2001: 523)
     2fs.PF see who at   market
     'you saw *who* in the market?'

In addition, all speakers accept *wh*-in situ in non-verbal locative and
possessive constructions of the kind illustrated in (84).

(84) a. sunằ   inā   yànzu?   (Jaggar 2001: 522)
        3pl.IMPF where   now
        'where are they now?'
     b. kunằ   dà   mề?   (Newman 2000: 494)
        2ms.PF   with   what
        'what do you have?'

The third point of consensus among speakers concerns the ungrammaticality
of *wh*-subjects in situ. Examples like (85) are uniformly rejected by native
speakers. Observe that the INFL word occurs in the general (non-focus) form
in this example. It is this property that renders the sentence ungrammatical.

Given that special inflection (the focus form of INFL) patterns together with
extraction, example (85) must be analysed as *wh*-in situ.[29]

(85) *su-wằ   sun   zō?   (Jaggar 2006a: (10))
      who (pl) 3pl.PF come
      'who (pl) came?'

A final point of consensus concerns the ungrammaticality of embedded *wh*-
in situ questions, which are rejected by all speakers, regardless of whether
they contain *wh*-arguments or *wh*-adjuncts (86).

(86) a. *Kànde tanằ   tsàmmānìn nā jē ìnā   (Green & Reintges
         Kande 3fs.IMPF think   1s.PF gowhere   2005b: ex. 40)
         'where does Kande think I went?'
     b. *Kànde tanằ   tsàmmānìn nā ga wằ   à kằsuwā
         Kande 3fs.IMPF think.VN.of 1s.PF see who at market
         'who does Kande think I saw at market?'
     c. *Kànde tanằ   tsàmmānìn nā sàyi littāfìn kàmař
         Kande 3fs.IMPF think.VN.of 1s.PF buy book.DD for
         nawà   à kằsuwā
         how.much   at market
         'how much does Kande think I bought the book for at market?'

For those speakers who accept *wh*-in situ, there is some evidence of an
argument–adjunct asymmetry, where *wh*-adjunct questions like those in
(87) are more widely acceptable in situ than *wh*-arguments.

(87) a. sunằ   fitôwā   dàgà ìnā ?   (Newman 2000: 496)
         3pl.IMPF come.out.VN from where
         'where are they coming out from?'
     b. yā   tàfi yàushē?   (Newman 2000: 496)
         3ms.PF go   when
         'when did he go?'
     c. nā   gayằ makà sàu   nawà?   (Jaggar 2001: 523)
         1s.PF tell 2ms.IO time how.many
         'how many times have I told you?'

However, Green & Reintges (2005b) observe that *wh*-object questions are
accepted by some speakers in contexts that introduce a strong presupposition, for example where a set of discourse referents has been introduced and
this set is narrowed down by the question. Chang (1995) describes this type
of question as 'detail-seeking'. Upper-case A and B indicate a dialogue pair.

[29] The fact that speakers reject all subject *wh*-constructions with general perfective/imperfective
forms suggests that the restriction on subject focus/*wh*-in situ may have been extended to
echo questions, although a study of spontaneous discourse may prove otherwise. It is worth
observing that Newman (2000: 494) only provides examples of object echo questions, and
Jaggar's (2001: 523) single example of a subject echo question has future inflection.

(88) A. duk   mun   ga   mutằnên can   (Jaggar 2006a: ex. 5)
        all   1pl.PF see   people.DD there
        'we saw all the people there'
     B. kun   ga   wằ   dà   wằ?
        2pl.PF see   who   and   who
        'who (pl) did you see?'
(89) A. jiyà   nē   dà   na   ci   àbinci sai   na   mâncē
        yesterday FM.m when 1s.FOC.PF eat food then 1s.FOC.PF forget
        kāyānā
        things.1s
        'it was yesterday when I'd eaten I forgot my things'
     B: kin   mântà   wànè   kāyā?   (Jaggar 2006a: ex. 8)
        2fs.PF forget   which   things
        'which things did you forget?'

In contexts that introduce a weaker presupposition, *wh*-in situ objects are
degraded. For example, in the following exchange speaker A and speaker B
are looking in a shop window, but A's utterance does not strongly
presuppose that B intends to purchase anything.

(90) A. dừbi   wàdàncân tufāfī   màsu kyâu!   (Green & Reintges
        look.at DEM.PL   clothes POSS beauty 2005b: ex. 44)
        'look at those beautiful clothes!'
     B. *kinằ   sôn   mề?
        2fs.IMPF want.VN.of what
        'what do you want?'

Neither are *wh*-in situ object questions acceptable when used as paraphrases
of alternative questions, despite the fact that this context involves a strong
presupposition. In the following exchange, A and B know that there are two
men who want to marry Aisha. A and B discuss the situation, then B
wonders, hoping that A may know the answer:

(91) A. Mūsā   dà   Audù dukà   sunằ   (Green & Reintges
        Musa   and   Audu both   3pl.IMPF   2005b: ex. 45)
        sôn   Aishà,
        love.VN.of   Aisha
        sunằ   kuma sô   sù   àurē   tà
        3pl.IMPF and want.VN 3pl.SUB marry PRO.3fs
        'Musa and Audu both love Aisha, and they want to marry her'
     B. *Aishà   zā   tà   àuri   wằ?
        Aisha   FUT   3fs   marry   who
        'who will Aisha marry?'

Finally, Green & Reintges (2005b) observe that even non-argument *wh*-in
situ questions like those in (87) are degraded when the *wh*-adjunct is
preceded by a quantificational expression (92), or by negation (93). These

intervention effects provide further evidence for the restricted nature of *wh*-in situ in Hausa.

(92)　*kōwànè　yārò̀　yā　　　zō　　dàgà　inā?　　(Green & Reintges
　　　　each　　　boy　3ms.PF　come　from　where　　2005b: ex. 46)
　　　'where does each boy come from?'

(93)　A.　nā　jē　kō'　inā,　yâu!　Nā　jē　jāmi'à̄r,　　nā　jē
　　　　　1s.PF　go　every　where　today　1s.PF　go　university.DD　1s.PF　go
　　　　　kàsuwā,　nā　　kuma　jē　　asìbitì...
　　　　　market　1s.PF　and　　go　　hospital
　　　　　'I've been everywhere today! I've been to the University, I've
　　　　　been to market, and I've been to hospital...'

　　　B.　*bà　kà　　jē　inā　ba?　　　　　　　(Green & Reintges
　　　　　NEG　2ms.PF　go　where　NEG　　　　　2005b: ex. 47)
　　　　　'where haven't you been?'

4.6.2 *Focus in situ: descriptive facts*

The parallelism observed between Hausa focus and *wh*-constructions in the canonical fronting strategy begins to break down in the more marked in situ strategy. Hausa focus in situ is considerably more widespread than *wh*-in situ (Jaggar 2001; 2006a; Green & Jaggar 2003). For example, while in situ subject *wh*-questions are never licensed, Hausa requires in situ subject focus in presentational focus contexts (94a). Presentational focus is a subtype of new information focus where a new discourse referent is introduced 'out of the blue' (Rochemont 1986). In other words, presentational focus is not 'discourse-bound' in the sense that it is interpreted in the context of preceding discourse. Instead, presentational focus shifts attention to a new referent or topic of conversation (§ 3.3.1). Example (94b) illustrates presentational object focus. The presentational focus interpretation is made explicit by the clause-initial interjection *àlbishìr̃inkà* 'guess what' (lit: 'your good news').[30]

(94)　a.　àlbishìr̃inkà?　　**Bàƙîn**　sun　isō!　　(Green & Jaggar
　　　　　good news.of.2MS　guests.DD　3pl.PF　arrive　2003: 211)
　　　　　'guess what? **The guests** have arrived!'

　　　b.　àlbishìr̃inkà?　　Mun　ga　　**yārònkà!**
　　　　　good.news.of.2ms　1pl.PF　see　son.of.2ms
　　　　　'guess what? We saw **your son!**'

---

[30] Of course, even in an out-of-the-blue context there may be certain aspects of shared knowledge between speaker and hearer that affect information structure. Constructions like those in (94) could therefore involve presentational focus on the NP referents, on the predicate or on the whole proposition. It may be that a study of the prosodic properties of such utterances together with their context of utterance casts light on this issue (Green, in preparation).

As example (95) shows, focus fronting is not licensed in a presentational context. The symbol # indicates a construction that is not acceptable in the given context, rather than an ungrammatical construction. The fact that presentational focus can only be encoded in situ explains in part why focus in situ is considerably more widespread than *wh*-in situ in Hausa.

(95) # àlbishìr̃inkà,   **far̃ar̃**   **mōtà** (cē)   mukà   sàyā
       good news.of.2ms white.of car   (FM.f) 1pl.FOC.PF buy
       'guess what? We bought **a white car**'

In expressing information that is not construable from the previous context, presentational focus differs systematically from the new information focus that 'answers' the *wh*-phrase (provides a value for the variable) in a preceding question. Recall that question–answer pairs provide a standard diagnostic for new information focus. Example (96) shows that subjects are not licensed in situ in this type of new information context, while example (97) shows that objects can receive new information focus in situ. In this respect, subjects contrast with presentational subjects in situ, and with objects in situ across the board.

(96) Q: su-wằ   sukà   tàfi Amìr̃kà?   (Green & Jaggar
          3pl-who   3PL.FOC.PF go   America   2003: 197–8)
          'who (pl) went to America?'

      A: *su* Audù dà Mūsā sukaæ   taæfi   *in situ subject NI focus*
          3pl Audu and Musa 3pl.FOC.PF   go
          '**Audu and Musa** went'

      A': *su Audù dà Mūsā sun   taæfi
          3pl Audu and Musa 3pl.PF   go
          '**Audu and Musa** went'

(97) Q: wànè   kāyā   kikà   mântā?   (Green & Jaggar
          which   things   2fs.FOC.PF forget   2003: 197)
          'which things did you forget?'

      A: nā   mâncē **jàkātā** **dà** **hùlātā**   *in situ direct object*
          1s.PF forget bag.of.1s   and   hat.of.1s   *NI focus*
          'I forgot **my bag and my hat**'

Example (98) illustrates that the in situ focus strategy can also be used to encode contrastive focus. As expected, Hausa contrastively focused subjects are not licensed in situ in such contexts (4.6.3).

(98) dằ nā   sanì dằ nā   zằɓi **Tankò**,   (Jaggar 2006a: ex. 41)
      if 1s.PF know then 1s.PF vote Tanko
      bằ Mūsā ba
      NEG Musa NEG
      'if I'd known, I would have voted for **Tanko**, not Musa'

As Newman (2000) points out, exhaustive focus in situ (although he does not use this term) can also be licensed by the focus-sensitive particle *sai* 'only'.

(99) bā mà   sôn   kōmē   sai **kuɗī**   (Newman 2000: 190)
     NEG 1PL.IMPF want.vn.of anything only money
     'we don't want anything except **money**'

4.6.3 *Exploring a form–function correlation*

As the examples in the preceding section indicate, Hausa in situ focus appears to be licensed in both new information and exhaustive/constrastive contexts. Given the existence of two syntactic strategies for marking focus (ex situ and in situ focus), and given the existence of two broad categories of focus (new information and exhaustive/constrastive focus), the question of whether there is a form–function correlation between syntactic strategy and semantic focus type immediately arises. Some researchers (notably É. Kiss 1998a) have claimed that in certain languages each type of focus is signalled by a distinct morphosyntactic strategy (§ 3.4.1). According to Jaggar (2001: 494–498), both ex situ and in situ focus constructions in Hausa are compatible with new information and with exhaustive/contrastive focus. In order to investigate É. Kiss's (1998a) hypothesis for Hausa in detail, Green & Jaggar (2003) examined in situ and ex situ focus constructions in a range of discourse contexts in order to establish whether any such form-function correlation could be claimed.[31] The generalisation to emerge from this study was consistent with Jaggar's (2001) description: Green & Jaggar found no evidence in Hausa for a systematic correlation between the in situ/ex situ focus construction on the one hand and the interpretation of that construction in terms of new information or constrastive/exhaustive focus on the other. Instead, the interpretation of a focus construction in terms of either new information or exhaustive–constrastive focus is determined by discourse-pragmatic factors. The findings of this study are also consistent with a more recent study carried out by Jaggar (2006a), which includes a greater proportion of data collected from naturalistic discourse (see also Hartmann & Zimmermann forthcoming, a).[32]

---

[31] É. Kiss (1998a) discusses a number of semantic tests aimed at distinguishing between new information and exhaustive focus, which Green & Jaggar (2003a) applied to both ex-situ and in situ Hausa focus constructions. The findings, which were inconsistent, did not uphold a strict correlation between syntactic focus strategy and semantic focus type. These semantic tests are not discussed here, but see Green & Jaggar (2003a: 191–3; 199–201) for details.

[32] Both Jaggar (2006a) and Hartmann & Zimmermann (forthcoming, a) rely in part on data taken from *Hausar Baka* 'Spoken Hausa' (HB) (Randell et al. 1998), a five-hour collection of video recordings of spontaneous discourse edited and transcribed for the purposes of language teaching.

The first descriptive generalisation to emerge from these recent studies is that, with the exception of subjects (96), a wide range of constituent types can occur as in situ new information focus. In addition to examples (96) and (97), examples (100–104) provide a representative set of examples of new information (NI) in situ focus. These data are given in question–answer pairs (where upper-case A and B denote speakers in a conversational exchange). This discourse context reveals the type of focus. Recall, for example, that question–answer pairs are a standard diagnostic for new information focus: where a constituent in the answer provides a value for the variable corresponding to the *wh*-phrase in the question, that consituent is identified as new information focus (§ 3.3.1).

(100) Q: wǎ   kikà   nūnǎ   wà   hōtunàn?   (Jaggar p.c.)
         who   2fs.foc.pf show iom   photo.pl.dd
         'who did you show the photos to?'

      A: nā   nūnǎ   wà   **iyàyēnā**   *in situ indirect*
         1s.pf show   iom   parent.pl.1s   *object NI focus*
         'I showed (them) to **my parents**'

(101) Q: ìnā   kòfī?   (Jaggar 2001: 497)
         where coffee
         'where's the coffee?'

      A: yanǎ   **can   cikin kwabǎ**   *in situ locative*
         3ms.impf there   in   cupboard   *predicate NI focus*
         'it's **there in the cupboard**'

(102) Q: dà   mề   dà   mề   kakè   (Jaggar 2001: 497)
         and   what and   what 2ms.foc.impf
         dà   shī?
         with 3ms.pro
         'what have you got?'

      A: inằ   dà   **fensiř dà   kuma bīřò**   *in situ possessive*
         1s.impf with pencil and   also biro   *NI focus*
         'I have **a pencil and a biro**'

(103) Q: karfề   nawà   zā   kà   dāwō?   (Jaggar 2006a:
         o'clock how.many fut 2ms   return   ex. 32)
         'what time will you return?'

      A: zân   dāwō   **dà   karfề   biyu**   *in situ adverbial*
         fut.1s return   at   o'clock two   *NI focus*
         'I'll return **at 2 o'clock**'

(104) Q: mề   ya   fằru   gà   'yan-tāwāyèn? (Jaggar 2001: 497)
         what 2ms.foc.pf happen to rebel.pl.dd
         'what happened to the rebels?'

      A: **an   ɗaurề**   su   *in situ V(P)*
         4.pl   imprison   3pl.pro   *NI focus*
         'they were **imprisoned**'

However, the second descriptive generalisation to emerge is that new information focus is not limited to the in-situ strategy. Examples (105) and (106) illustrate that focus-fronted constituents can also provide a value for the *wh*-phrase in question–answer pairs.

(105) Q: su-wằnē nề   sukà   fằrà   zuwằ watằ? (Jaggar 2001: 494)
         3pl-who FM.pl 3pl.FOC.PF be.first go.VN moon
         'who got to the Moon first?'

    A: **Amiřkāwā** nề   sukà   fằrà   zuwằ   *ex situ subject*
         Americans FM.pl 3pl.FOC.PF be.first go.VN   *NI focus*
         '**The Americans** got there first'

(106) Q: wằ   kukà   ganī à   kằsuwā?   (Jaggar 2001: 494)
         who 2pl.FOC.PF see at   market
         'who did you see at market?'

    A: **yārònkà** (nē)   mukà   ganī   *ex situ object*
         boy.of.2m (FM.m) 1pl.FOC.PF see   *NI focus*
         'we saw **your boy**'

Thirdly, recall from examples (98) and (99) that, with the exception of subjects, in situ focus is also licensed in exhaustive listing (EL)/ constrastive contexts. Example (107) illustrates the ungrammaticality of subject focus in situ in a contrastive context. The exhaustive/contrastive interpretation is made explicit by the context, where some aspect of the utterance is explicitly contrasted with some other aspect of the same utterance, or where the second speaker's utterance explicitly contradicts or corrects some aspect of the first speaker's utterance in a conversational exchange.

(107) A: *'yan-sàndā sun   gānō   gāwař   (Jaggar 2006a: ex. 49)
         police   3pl.PF discover body.of
         mamàcîn?
         dead.man.DD
         'did the police discover the dead man's body?'

    B: *ā'ằ, *'yā'yan   **mamàcîn** sun   gānō   shì
         no children.of dead.man.DD 3pl.PF discover PRO.3ms
         'no, **the dead man's children** discovered him'

    B': ā'ằ, 'yā'yan   **mamàcîn** sukà   gānō   shì
         no children.of dead.man.DD 3pl.PF discover PRO.3ms
         'no, **the dead man's children** discovered him'

Example (108) illustrates contrastive object focus in situ. Observe that this example illustrates the grammaticality of the clause-final focus marker in focus in situ constructions. While the analysis developed in this chapter entails that examples like (108) are analysed as clausal focus (§ 4.3), it is clear from the context that the direct object is also in focus, raising the possibility that in situ focus can occur in addition to (or within) clausal focus.[33]

(108) A: kā   aikà   dà   takàr̃dâr̃?   (Green & Jaggar 2003: 196)
        2ms.PF send   with   paper.DD
        'did you send the paper?'

     B: ā'à, nā   aikà   dà   **littāfìn** nē,   bà̀   takàr̃dâr̃ ba
        no 1s.PF   send   with   book.DD   FM.m NEG paper.DD NEG
        'no, I sent **the book**, not the paper'

Further examples of exhaustive/contrastive focus in situ are provided in (109–111).

(109) Q: kòfī   zā   kà   shā?   Jaggar (2006a: (38)
         coffee FUT 2ms   drink
         'will you drink coffee?'

      A: ā'à, zân   shā **shāyì**   *in situ direct object*
         no   FUT.1s drink tea   *EL focus*
         'no, I'll drink **tea**'

(110) Q: kā   gayà̀   wà   Audù   làbār̃ìn?   (Jaggar 2006a: ex. 45)
         2ms.PF tell   IOM Audu   news.DD
         'did you tell Audu the news?'

      A: ā'à, nā   dai gayà̀   wà **Kànde**   *in situ indirect*
         no 1s.PF PART tell   IOM Kande   *object EL focus*
         'no, I actually told (it) to **Kande**'

(111) Q: yārònkà   yanà̀   Amìr̃kà   kō?   (Jaggar 2006a: ex. 51)
         boy.of.2ms 3ms.IMPF America   Q
         'your son's in America, isn't he?'

      A: ā'à, bā   yà̀ **Amìr̃kà**, yanà̀   **Ingìlà**
         no   NEG 3ms.IMPF America   3ms.IMPF England
         in situ locative predicate EL focus
         'no, he's not in **America**, he's in **England**'

---

[33] With respect to the generalisation that focus in situ cannot be marked by *nē/cē/nē*, and with respect to the co-occurrence of focus in situ and clausal focus, consider the following example from Hartmann & Zimmermann (forthcoming: ex. 17):
(i) a. wà̀cē   cè   Ìbrahìm   ya   bai wà kuɗī?
        who.f FM.f Ibrahim   3ms.FOC.PF give IOM money
        'who did Ibrahim give the money to?'
     b. Ìbrahìm   yā   bai wà **tsōhuwarsà** nē   kuɗī
        Ibrahim   3ms.PF   give IOM mother   FM.m money
        'Ibrahim gave the money to **his mother**'
Variation in speaker judgements notwithstanding, this is an apparent counterexample to the generalisation that focus in situ cannot be marked by the focus marker (cf. example (12a)), since the indirect object is in focus and the focus marker precedes the direct object. Observe, however, that the focus marker occurs in the default masculine form, despite the fact that the focused indirect object *tsōhuwarsà* 'mother' is a feminine noun. In this respect, the focus marker patterns like the clausal focus marker, despite the fact that it is not in clause-final position. Further research into the distribution of the focus marker in such examples is required.

Finally, examples (112) and (113) illustrate that exhaustive/contrastive focus can also be expressed by the ex situ construction (the unmarked strategy).

(112) Q: **tsōhuwar̃sà**   cē   ta   mutù?   (Jaggar 2001: 495)
          mother.of.3ms FM.f 3fs.FOC.PF die
          'was it **his mother** who died?'

     A: ā' à, **màtar̃sà**   cē   ta   mutù   *ex situ subject*
          no   wife.of.3ms FM.f 3fs.FOC.PF die   *EL focus*
          (bà   tsōhuwar̃sà   ba)
          NEG mother.of.3ms NEG
          'no, it was **his wife** who died
          (not his mother)'

(113) Q: kun   sàyi bakar̃   mōtà?   (Jaggar 2001: 495)
          2pl.PF buy black.of car
          'did you buy a black car?'

     A: ā'à, **farar̃**   **mōtà** (cē)   mukà   *ex situ direct object*
          no   white.of car   (FM.f) 1pl.FOC.PF   *EL focus*
          sàyā (bà   bakā   ba)
          buy NEG black NEG
          'no, we bought a **white car**
          (not a black one)'

As these examples show, the interpretation of a focused constituent as either new information or exhaustive/contrastive appears to be determined not by the morphosyntax but by the discourse context. As Jaggar (2006a: 11) points out, a more extensive corpus study is required in order to establish the relative frequency of the in situ versus the ex situ focus strategy. It may be that such a study would also reveal a preference for a particular strategy in a particular context, despite the fact that both strategies are attested in new information and contrastive/exhaustive contexts.[34] Green & Jaggar (2003) also found that the presence/absence of the focus marker in focus fronting constructions does not alter the type of focus, only its 'impact': native speakers describe it as 'adding emphasis'. The focus marker might therefore be described as fully optional in this construction.[35]

A further question that arose in Green & Jaggar's study relates to the prosodic properties of focus in situ constructions. Green & Jaggar (2003:

---

[34] Hartmann & Zimmermann (forthcoming, a) have carried out a pilot study on the *Hausar Baka* corpus, and argue that new information focus is more frequently expressed by the in-situ strategy, while contrastive focus is more frequently expressed by the ex-situ strategy.

[35] In contrast, Hartmann & Zimmermann (forthcoming, a: 3) state in a footnote that the focus marker indicates exhaustivity, referring to a forthcoming paper for supporting evidence. This hypothesis was stated by Green (1997: 29), but Green & Jaggar (2003) found no evidence to support the hypothesis.

205–7) hypothesise that prosodic prominence may underlie the restriction of focus/*wh*-in situ to non-subjects: if prosodic prominence is associated with the most deeply embedded constituent by default, as in English (Cinque 1993; Reinhart 1995; Zubizarreta 1998), only postverbal constituents can be focused in their base position without the need for a marked prosodic operation. A related question concerns whether the default prosodic properties of the focus in situ construction license either broad or narrow focus interpretations (§ 3.3). See Green & Jaggar (2003: 198; 205) and Jaggar (2006a: 13). These issues await further research (Green, in preparation).[36]

While Green & Jaggar's study attempts to answer an important empirical question concerning whether any functional distinction can be established between the in situ and ex situ strategies, the study also addresses the theoretical issue of interface economy: the idea that the existence of two morphosyntactic strategies for marking focus might be explained by distinct interface goals (in other words, a distinct interpretation for each strategy) (§ 3.4). Recall, for example, that É. Kiss's (1998a) theory of focus predicts a partial form–function mapping between structural realisation of focus on the one hand and semantic focus type on the other: in situ focus may have a new information interpretation, or it may have an exhaustive interpretation resulting from 'covert' movement to a scope-taking position. In contrast, ex situ focus is predicted to entail an exhaustive ('identificational') interpretation across the board (§ 3.4.1). Of course, the existence of exhaustive/ contrastive focus in situ in Hausa can be assimilated to Kiss's hypothesis if a covert movement analysis is assumed (§ 4.6.5). However, the fact that Hausa licenses focus fronting in new information contexts is perhaps the most unexpected fact, given the cross-linguistic tendency for the displacement strategy to pattern with exhaustive focus, at least in those languages with an alternative in situ focus strategy.

The consequences of these empirical findings for the theoretical issues of optionality and economy are striking. Not only is the existence of two focus strategies unexpected under assumptions of global derivational economy in the sense that the 'computational' derivational system is driven towards the single most economical derivation (Chomsky 1991), but the facts described

---

[36] A pilot study by Hartmann & Zimmermann (forthcoming, a) suggests that there are no prosodic differences between broad and narrow focus interpretations of the same construction. Hartmann & Zimmermann asked speakers to read 16 question–answer pairs, where the scope of focus in the answer is determined by the preceding question (§ 3.3). For example, the question *What happened?* places the entire response clause (IP) in focus, while the question *What did Halima do?* places the VP in focus, and the question *What did Halima cut?* places the object in focus (Hartmann & Zimmermann, forthcoming, a: 27). The fact that these different focus scope readings are not prosodically distinguished is consistent with Green & Jaggar's hypothesis that the default prosodic properties of the clause license a range of focus interpretations excluding narrow focus on the subject; but since Hartmann & Zimmermann's study does not compare question–answer pairs with unmarked declaratives in order to establish the default prosodic pattern, it does not fully address this hypothesis.

here are also unexpected under assumptions of interface economy (Reinhart 1993; 1995; Chomsky 2001a; 2001b): in Hausa, in situ and ex situ focus do not serve distinct interpretive goals. If the two morphosyntactic focus strategies in Hausa are not distinct in terms of interface goals, neither can they be distinct in terms of their underlying derivational features. In other words, there is no basis for proposing the existence of distinct [NEW INFORMATION FOCUS] and [EXHAUSTIVE FOCUS] features that drive the derivation in different directions. This entails a case of true derivational optionality: a choice between overt or covert movement (§ 4.6.5).

In sum, these findings suggest that the interpretation of focus is underdetermined by core syntax. Instead, it is the discourse context that determines which focus interpretation is selected from the range of options provided by the syntax. Setting aside theory-internal considerations, this conclusion is not unexpected: the coexistence of functionally non-distinct or minimally distinct linguistic units and constructions is the norm rather than the exception in language, given variation in dialect, register and style, as well as patterns of language contact and borrowing, and processes of language change. It remains for future research to establish fully the extent to which the two Hausa focus strategies are interchangeable in different contexts of use.

4.6.4 *Multiple focus*/wh-*constructions*

Given that both ex situ and in situ focus/*wh*- are attested in Hausa, the question of whether a simple clause may simultaneously contain both an ex situ and an in situ focus/*wh*-phrase naturally arises. First, an empirical issue arises with respect to the grammaticality of non-echo multiple *wh*-questions, in which one *wh*-phrase is fronted and the other remains in situ. According to Tuller (1986a: 129), Green (1997) and more recently Hartmann (2006) and Hartmann & Zimmermann (forthcoming, a), Hausa allows non-echo multiple *wh*-constructions of the English type, which which both the ex situ and the in situ *wh*-phrase receive a genuine *wh*-interpretation. It follows that these constructions should admit the pair-list response (e.g. *Audu bought a pen, Kande bought a book and Musa bought a gown*) and the single pair response (e.g. *Kande bought a book*) that characterise multiple *wh*-questions in English-type languages. However, as Newman (2000: 494) has pointed out, 'wằ ya sàyi mề? "Who bought what?" is not semantically comparable to the corresponding English sentence, but rather carries the connotation, "What did you say who bought?" with echo focus on "What?." Green & Reintges (2005a; 2005b) also found that the echo interpretation of the in situ *wh*-phrase in multiple questions was consistently confirmed by their Hausa informants, who judged multiple questions as ungrammatical on a true interrogative reading of the in situ *wh*-phrase (114).

(114) wằ   ya   sàyi   mề   Newman (2000: 494)
      who   3MS.FOC.PF   buy   what
      *'who bought what?'   *interrogative reading*
      'who bought WHAT?!'   *echo reading*

Green & Reintges (2005b) also found that informants rejected non-echo multiple *wh*-questions with three *wh*-expressions. Significantly, only the left-peripheral *wh*-phrase receives a genuine interrogative interpretation, while both in situ *wh*-phrases are licensed only with an echo interpretation. In other words, it seems that multiple *wh*-questions in Hausa neither admit the pair-list response nor the single pair response that characterise multiple *wh*-questions in languages like English. Therefore, Green & Reintges propose an analysis of Hausa multiple *wh*-questions with one genuine and one or more echo *wh*-phrase(s) as instances of what Comorovski (1996) calls second-order questions: questions that function as responses to questions, where the echo marks the misheard or unexpected part of the preceding question.[37]

Unlike in English-type languages, then, only the fronted *wh*-phrase in Hausa multiple *wh*-questions receives a genuine *wh*-interpretation. It follows that the mechanism that brings about the pair-list interpretation in English-type languages is not available for Hausa. Green & Reintges assume that this is due to the fact that there is only one scope position that licenses the genuine question interpretation of *wh*-phrases: the specifier position of the left-peripheral focus phrase. If this position is occupied, extraction of the lower *wh*-phrase is blocked, which explains the absence of a genuine interrogative interpretation of the in-situ *wh*-phrase. This analysis predicts that a left-peripheral focus phrase should also block a genuine question interpretation for a *wh*-in situ phrase, a prediction that is borne out by the empirical evidence. As shown by example (115), *wh*-in situ questions with a fronted focus phrase are only acceptable (albeit marginally) with an echo reading of the in situ *wh*-phrase.

(115) Yūsùf   yā   cê   **Audù**   **dà**   **Mūsā**   *interrogative*
      Yusuf   3ms.PF   say   Audu   and   Musa   *reading of*
      nề   sukà   sàyi   mề   à   kằsuwā   wh-*in situ phrase*
      FM.pl   3pl.FOC.PF   buy   what   at   market

---

[37] The following discourse illustrates a second order question, where subscript indicates an inaudible element that corresponds to the request-for-repetition echo in the response (cf. also Bošković 2002: 370).

   (i)   a.   Where did Ted put $_{\text{the plectrum}}$?
        b.   Where did Ted put WHAT?
        c.   (I said) where did Ted put the plectrum.

*'Yusuf said what **Audu and Musa**   *echo reading of the*
bought at market'   wh-*in situ phrase*
?'Yusuf said that it was **Audu and Musa**   (Green & Reintges
who bought WHAT at   market?!'   2005b: ex. 79)

To explain the unavailabiliy of the genuine interrogative reading of wh-in situ phrases in focus fronting contexts like (115), it could be argued that Hausa wh-phrases are required to be in focus. According to this perspective, if some other constituent is in focus, the out-of-focus status of the wh-phrase yields an ungrammatical result. However, Green & Reintges (2005b) argue that this view can be refuted on two main grounds. First, the received wisdom that non-echo wh-phrases are inherent focus expressions has been disputed in the literature (see Erteschik-Shir 1986). Secondly, as example (116) shows, Hausa does permit a combination of ex situ focus and in situ focus within a single clause. Green & Jaggar found that speakers accepted these multiple focus constructions in contexts where the two focused constituents are explicitly contrastive (contra Green 1997: 115).

(116) Q: kun   ga   màtātā   à   makaɽantā   kō?   (Green & Jaggar
         2pl.PF see wife.of.1s at   school   Q   2003: 198)
         'you saw my wife at school didn't you?'
      A: à'à **yàrònkà** (nē)   mukà   ganī à **kàsuwā**
         no   boy.of.2m   (FM.m) 1pl.FOC.PF see at market
         'no, we saw **your boy** at **market**'

The fact that multiple focus constructions of this type are acceptable suggests that Hausa has a genuine in situ focus position, which is available for presentational, new information and contrastive focus. This contrast between focus in situ and wh-in situ is consistent with the fact that focus in situ is more widely available across the board in Hausa than wh-in situ.

4.6.5 *Extending the FP analysis*

As Green & Reintges (2005b) point out, although wh-in situ has marginal status in Hausa, where licensed, a covert movement analysis provides a feasible account of its properties. In other words, the analysis developed earlier in the chapter to account for wh-fronting (§ 4.3; §4.4) can be extended to wh-in situ, with the difference being that the displacement operation takes place after the syntactic derivation is transferred to the phonological component (§ 3.2.4). The result is that the wh-phrase is pronounced in situ, but receives the interpretation that results from its presence in the wh-scope taking position in the interpretive component (LF).

To begin with, this account accommodates the prohibition against special inflection (the focus form of INFL) in these constructions: since wh-movement takes place after the point of transfer to the phonological component, it is to be expected that it does not feed overt morphology. Secondly, the argument–adjunct asymmetry described above (§ 4.6.1) also receives an explanation under an LF movement analysis. It has been proposed for Mandarin Chinese *wh*-in situ questions that only *wh*-adverbials, as genuine operators, are licensed to move to their scope position at LF, while *wh*-arguments do not have operator status. For most Hausa speakers, the preference for non-arguments in *wh*-in situ constructions suggests an analysis along similar lines: only *wh*-adjuncts are licensed to raise at LF. Unlike Chinese, Hausa lacks a true *wh*-in situ licensing strategy for arguments.[38]

The third type of evidence in favour of an LF movement analysis of Hausa *wh*-in situ comes from the intervention effects that were described above (recall examples (92) and (93)). These intervention effects indicate that LF movement of the *wh*-phrase to its scope position is blocked by an intervening scope-taking element, such as a quantifier or negation marker (Beck & Kim 1997; Pesetsky 2000).

Recall finally that an in situ *wh*-phrase is only licensed to receive an echo interpretation in constructions that contain an ex situ focus/*wh*-phrase in the left periphery of the clause (§ 4.6.4). Earlier LF movement analyses of multiple *wh*-questions like *Who bought what?* in English proposed that, while the left-peripheral *wh*-phrase *who* moves to its scope position in the overt syntax, the in situ *wh*-phrase *what* also raises and adjoins to the *wh*-scope position at LF (Higginbotham & May 1981; Pesetsky 1987). As a result, the English multiple *wh*-question is licensed to receive a pair-list reading, requiring an answer in which individuals and objects bought are matched in pairs (e.g. *Ted bought a plectrum, Mary bought a trumpet, Bill bought a guitar strap*). See Kuno & Robinson (1972), Pesetsky (1987; 2000), Dayal (2002), Aoun & Li (2003) for representative views. Green & Reintges (2005b) argue that the fact that Hausa in situ *wh*-phrases can only receive an echo interpretation in such constructions is due to the fact that there is only one scope position that licenses the genuine question interpretation of *wh*-phrases: the specifier position of the left-peripheral focus phrase. If this position is occupied, extraction of the lower *wh*-phrase is blocked both in the overt syntax and at LF.

The question that remains is whether LF movement is also available for Hausa focus in situ. Recall that multiple-focus constructions are possible (§ 4.6.4), suggesting that Hausa has a genuine in situ focus position that is available for presentational, new information and contrastive focus. Green

---

[38] An alternative to the LF movement analysis has been developed by Reinhart (1998) and Tsai (1999), according to which *wh*-in situ phrases can be unselectively bound by a null question operator. However, only *wh*-arguments, which contain a nominal head, can function as variables, while *wh*-adverbs, due to the lack of such a nominal head, cannot be interpreted via unselective binding. The non-movement analysis does not accommodate the clear preference for non-argument *wh*-in situ in Hausa, suggesting that unselective binding is not the relevant licensing mechanism.

& Reintges (2005b) argue that their analysis also accommodates the echo reading of *wh*-in situ expressions, assuming with Erteschik-Shir (1986), Artstein (2002) and various others that echo *wh*-phrases are focus constituents. However, LF movement must be excluded for echo *wh*-in situ phrases on the basis that if such phrases were able to raise at LF, they should license a genuine *wh*-intepretation in the same way that non-echo *wh*-in situ phrases do. In addition, an LF movement analysis is also unfeasible for presentational focus, which lacks operator status and is therefore prohibited from raising to the left periphery in the overt syntax. Due to their operator characteristics, new information and constrastive focus in situ would in principle be eligible for LF movement (Surányi 2002). However, since echo and presentational focus are interpretable in situ, it is at least possible that the same discourse-driven interpretive mechanisms are also applicable to new information and contrastive focus in situ. This question is left open here.

4.7 CONCLUSIONS

This chapter began with a description of Hausa focus fronting construc-tions (§ 4.2). A single constituent can be focus fronted per clause, optionally followed by the non-verbal focus marking copula, a process that typically requires gapping rather than resumption in the base position of the displaced constituent. In addition, focus fronting requires special inflection (the 'relative' or 'focus' form of INFL) in the clause whose left periphery hosts the extracted focus phrase. In each of these respects, focus fronting is morphosyntactically distinct from topicalisation, which licenses multiple topic phrases to occur in the left periphery, co-occurs with modal/adverbial particles rather than the focus copula, does not license special inflection and typically patterns with resumption rather than gapping. It was also established that Hausa focus fronting constructions are not best described as clefts, but are monoclausal constructions containing a single lexical verb and a non-verbal focus-marking copula.

A syntactic analysis of focus fronting was developed, according to which the focused constituent is displaced to the specifier position of the left-peripheral functional projection, the focus phrase (FP), a process that is motivated in the current Chomskyan framework by the requirement to match and eliminate non-semantic features (§ 4.3). It was shown that this rather simple syntactic analysis provides an account of the features of the focus construction, in particular the restriction to a single focus-fronted phrase per clause and the presence of the focus-marking copula, which is reanalysed as a focus marker that instantiates the head of the focus phrase. The focus fronting construction was then compared with the *wh*-fronting construction (§ 4.4). The syntactic parallels between the two construction types entail that the FP analysis can be straightforwardly extended to *wh*-fronting.

The phenomenon of special inflection was discussed at some length (§ 4.5). The morphological alternation between 'general' and 'focus' forms is restricted to perfective and imperfective INFL, and the focus form is conditioned by the presence of an extracted focus/*wh*-phrase in the left periphery of the clause. Although habitual, future and allative forms show no morphological alternation between 'general' and 'focus' forms, they may occur both in focus and non-focus contexts, unlike the rhetorical, which is restricted to focus contexts, and the subjunctive and potential, which are not licensed in focus contexts. An analysis developed by Green & Reintges (2005b) was discussed, according to which special inflection surfaces as the morphological realisation of agreement features between functional heads.

Finally, focus/*wh*-in situ constructions were discussed (§ 4.6). While all speakers accept *wh*-in situ with echo interpretation, genuine interrogative *wh*-in situ appears to have relatively marginal status, and there is considerable inter-speaker variation. However, while *wh*-subjects in situ are uniformly rejected, there is evidence of an argument–adjunct asymmetry, with non-argument *wh*-phrases in situ more widely attested than arguments. In contrast, focus in situ appears to be more widespread in Hausa, and a number of recent studies suggest that, like its ex situ counterpart, the in situ construction licenses both new information and exhaustive/contrastive focus interpretations.

These findings suggest that the interpretation of focus is underspecified by the syntax in Hausa. Instead, it is the discourse context that determines which focus interpretation is selected from the range of options provided by the syntax. However, presentational focus cannot be expressed by the ex situ construction. Multiple focus/*wh*-constructions (with one in situ and one ex situ phrase) were found to be acceptable only where they contain two contrastively focused constituents, or where the *wh*-in situ phrase receives an echo interpretation.

Finally, focus/*wh*-in situ was discussed in the light of the syntactic analysis of focus/*wh*-fronting proposed earlier in the chapter. The fact that in situ *wh*-phrases are only licensed to receive an echo interpretation in multiple *wh*-constructions suggests that the genuine *wh*-interrogation interpretation is linked to extraction, either in the overt syntax or covertly. In contrast, echo questions and presentational focus constructions are thought to lack movement altogether, hence their distinct morphosyntactic/functional properties. Finally, the fact that multiple contrastively focused constituents are possible within a single clause raises the question of whether Hausa focus in situ is best analysed, like *wh*-in situ, as a case of covert movement, or whether focus phrases can be interpreted in situ. Further research into the prosodic properties of Hausa focus constructions is required, which is expected to cast light on some of the questions raised but left unanswered in this chapter (Green, in preparation).

5

COPULAR CONSTRUCTIONS

5.1 INTRODUCTION

In the previous chapter, the Hausa non-verbal copula *nē/cē/nē* (m/f/pl) was analysed as a grammaticalised focus marker, which occurs optionally in monoclausal focus/*wh*-fronting constructions (1). According to the analysis developed in the previous chapter, the non-verbal copula instantiates the head of the left-peripheral functional projection (focus phrase), with focus/*wh*-fronted constituents occupying its left-adjacent specifier position.

(1) a. **yârā** (nè) mukà ganī   *direct object NP focus*
children FM.pl 1pl.FOC.PF see
'we saw **the children**'

    b. wànè littāfì (nē) Kànde ta   *direct object NP*
which book FM.m Kande 3fs.FOC.PF   *wh-question*
sàyā?
buy
'which book did Kande buy?'

This chapter explores the other major context in which *nē/cē/nē* occurs: the non-verbal copular clause. This construction is illustrated in (2). Example (2a) illustrates a specificational (equative) copular sentence, in which two referring expressions are equated. Example (2b) illustrates a predicational copular sentence, in which the predicate (here, the adjective phrase *dōguwā* 'tall') is not a referring expression, but simply predicates some property of the subject *Aishà*. As indicated by boldface, the constituent left-adjacent to the non-verbal copula is in focus.

(2) a. Aishà **màtātā** cè   *specificational (equative)*
Aisha wife.1s FM.f
'Aisha is **my wife**'

    b. Aishà **dōguwā** cè   *predicational*
Aisha tall.f FM.f
'Aisha is **tall**'

The main empirical question addressed in the present chapter is whether the reanalysis of *nē/cē/nē* as a grammaticalised focus marker in focus/*wh*-fronting constructions (1) is upheld by its function in the non-verbal clause (2). The empirical claim made in this chapter is that despite the fact that the non-verbal copula shows a less grammaticalised status in the non-verbal clause in the sense that its presence is required to attribute clausal status to a subject-predicate structure that lacks verbal-inflectional properties, there is also evidence in the non-verbal clause of its evolving function as a focus marker. This accounts for the fact that there is a designated focus position both in canonical and non-canonical copular clauses. The main theoretical question addressed in this chapter is whether the focus phrase (FP) analysis developed in the previous chapter can be extended to account for the properties of this construction type. The theoretical claim made in this chapter is that the FP structure provides a simple account of these constructions which accurately captures both their morphosyntactic properties and their information packaging properties.

This chapter begins with a description of the properties of the Hausa non-verbal copular clause, sets out the descriptive distinction between specificational and predicational copular sentences, and provides a descriptive overview of the morphosyntactic properties of each type in Hausa (§ 5.2). This section also describes both canonical and non-canonical (marked) non-verbal copular clause structures, and describes the information packaging properties of these constructions. The second main section of the chapter explores the historical evidence for the analysis of the copula as an evolving focus marker (§ 5.3). This section examines the evidence presented by Schuh (1983a) for the claim that the Hausa non-verbal copula *nē/cē/nē* emerged via a process of grammaticalisation from pronominal elements as topic–comment structures evolved into subject-predicate structures (Li & Thompson 1977), and argues that this element is undergoing a continuing process of grammaticalisation from copula to focus marker. The last main section of the chapter addresses the question of how the syntactic analysis developed for focus/*wh*-fronting constructions in the previous chapter can be extended to account for the properties of non-verbal copular sentences (§ 5.4). This section first sets out the clause structure that is proposed to account for non-verbal copular clauses, and then looks in further detail at the properties of these constructions in order to establish the extent to which the FP structure provides an explanatory account of the properties of the construction. This section also sets the present analysis within a broader theoretical context by looking at other analyses that have been proposed in the literature, both for Hausa and for similar constructions in other languages.

5.2 NON-VERBAL COPULAR SENTENCES: THE DATA

This section provides a description of the morphosyntactic features of non-verbal copular clauses in Hausa. The section begins with a comparison of verbal and non-verbal copular clauses, and establishes the word order and agreement properties of the canonical non-verbal copular clause (§ 5.2.1).

This section also compares the basic non-verbal copular clause with the pseudocleft, a type of copular construction that contains additional embedded (relative clause) structure. The next section introduces Declerck's (1988) descriptive classification of copular clauses, which enables the partition of this clause type into two major categories: specificational and predicational copular sentences (§ 5.2.2). The morphosyntactic properties of specificational and predicational copular clauses in Hausa are then established, together with a discussion of their canonical and non-canonical word order permutations, which are related to information structure (§ 5.2.3–4).

5.2.1 *Morphosyntactic features*

Copular sentences in Hausa fall into two main categories: those with a verbal copula and those with a non-verbal copula. Jaggar (2001: 428) describes copular verbs in Hausa, such as *kōmà* 'become' (3). These verbs take a subject complement: the complement of the verb corefers with or describes the subject of the sentence.[1]

(3) ruwā   zâi   kōmà   ƙànƙarā
     water FUT.3ms become   ice
     'the water will turn into ice'

Further examples include *zama* 'become', *kasàncē* 'become, turn out', *rikìdē* 'change into', and *zaunà* 'remain'. These copular verbs are distinct from the non-verbal copula in Hausa in two main ways. First, these verbs have semantic content, and therefore fall into the category of quasi-copulas. Secondly, like all verbs in Hausa (§ 2.3.2), these quasi-copular verbs lack inflectional features and must therefore co-occur with the INFL word, for example *zâi* in example (3).

In contrast, the non-verbal copular clause is formed with the non-verbal focus marking copula *nē* (m/pl)/*cē* (f), sometimes referred to in the descriptive literature as the 'stabilizer' (see Newman 2000 and Schuh 2000). Unlike the copular verb, the non-verbal copula is marked for gender and number. Although the non-verbal copula is not marked for tense or aspect, it does not license the presence of the INFL word.[2] Instead, the tense–aspect properties of the utterance are determined by context (Newman 2000: 60). For example, in the absence of contextual temporal information the copular sentence in (4) is interpreted as true of the present time (the default case).

---

[1] In the modern Chomskyan tradition, the relationship between the subject and the subject complement is accounted for under the analysis of copular verbs as raising or unaccusative verbs. See e.g. Stowell (1978); Burzio (1986); Levin & Rappaport Hovav (1995); as well as discussion in § 5.4.3.

[2] See § 5.4.3 for a discussion of relativisation out of non-verbal copular clauses, a construction that licenses the co-occurrence of the non-verbal copula with the 'pro-relative' imperfective INFL (TAM) word.

(4)   Audù   **bāwà**   nē
      Audu   slave   FM.m
      'Audu is a **slave**'

In contrast, the examples in (5) illustrate the contribution of temporal adverbials to the interpretation of non-verbal copular sentences.

(5)   a.   Audù **ɗālìbī**   nè̀   lōkàcîn dà na   gan shì   bằra
           Audu student FM.m time.DD REL 1s.FOC.PF see PRO.3ms last.year
           'Audu was a **student** when I saw him last year'
      b.   yànzu Audù   **likità**   nē
           now   Audu   doctor   FM.m
           'now Audu's a **doctor**'
      c.   bàɗi   wàr̃hakà   fa,   nī   **likità**   nē
           next.year at.this.time PART PRO.1s doctor FM.m
           'by this time next year I'll be a **doctor**'

As the examples in (4) and (5) demonstrate, the copula shows polar tone: it takes on the opposing tone to the final tone of the preceding expression. Non-verbal copular constructions in Hausa may be formed with a nominal predicate (6a) or an adjectival predicate (6b). Recall from Chapter 2 (§ 2.3.3) that non-verbal clauses with a locative/prepositional predicate are formed with the imperfective TAM rather than the non-verbal copula (7) (see discussion in § 5.4.3).

(6)   a.   Audù **ɗālìbī**   nè̀
           Audu student.m FM.m
           'Audu is a **student**'
      b.   Audù **dōgō**   nè̀
           Audu tall.m   FM.m
           'Audu is **tall**'
(7)   kāyā   sunà̀   cikin   mōtà
      goods 3pl.IMPF inside car
      'the stuff is in the car'

Examples (4–6) represent the canonical or unmarked word order for a non-verbal copular sentence: SUBJECT–PREDICATE–NON-VERBAL COPULA. Within this configuration, number and gender agreement holds between subject, adjectival predicate and non-verbal copula nē/cē/nē. Nominal predicates with distinct masculine/feminine/plural forms also agree with the subject and the non-verbal copula (e.g. ɗālìbī 'student' (m)/ ɗālìbā 'student' (f)/ ɗālìbai 'students' (pl)). According to some descriptions, in cases where the gender of subject and predicate nominal differ, some speakers prefer the non-verbal copula to agree with the subject (8), although contrastive predicate focus presents an exception to this generalisation, where either form of the copula is acceptable (9) (see Newman 2000: 162–3; Jaggar 2001: 457–9; Curnow 2000).[3]

(8) [wannàn màganà]$_f$ [**shìr̃mē**]$_m$ cè
this.f matter nonsense.m FM.f
'this matter is **nonsense**'

(9) [aikìn Mūsā]$_m$ [**sāƙà**]$_f$ nē/cē (bà ƙīrà ba)
work.of Musa weaving FM.m/FM.f NEG smithing NEG
'Musa's work is **weaving** (not smithing)'

This agreement pattern is also evident in pseudoclefts. Recall from Chapter 4 (§ 4.2.3) that pseudoclefts are a type of copular construction in which two (nominal) constituents are linked by the copula, one of which typically consists of a headless or free relative clause representing the presupposition, and the other of which is in focus (10).

(10) a. waddà nakè sô **Kànde** cè   *pseudocleft*
RELPRO.fs 1s.FOC.IMPF love.VN Kande FM.f
'the one I love is **Kande**'

b. **Kànde** cè waddà nakè sô   *reverse pseudocleft*
Kande FM.f RELPRO.fs 1s.FOC.IMPF love.VN
'**Kande** is the one I love'

Examples like (10a) correspond most closely to this standard definition of pseudoclefts, which are sometimes also described as *wh*-clefts, in that the subject-initial constituent is a (*wh*-related) relative pronoun (§ 2.4.1). The relative pronoun agrees with the pre-copular nominal head in this type of construction, so the issue of agreement mismatch does not arise. However, compare example (11), in which the subject is headed by the masculine substantive noun *àbîn* 'the thing', which is modified by the relative clause. The copula agrees with the left-adjacent (focused) feminine noun *shìnkāfā* 'rice' (11a) or *àlāwà* 'halva' (11b), rather than the masculine noun *àbîn* that heads the subject.[4]

---

[3] Agreement patterns in examples like (8) and (9) present an interesting issue for further research. According to Russell Schuh (p.c.), choices over the gender of the copula are not a matter of speaker variation, but are determined by which constituent is in focus. Schuh cites an unpublished paper presented by Ismail Junaidu at the 1995 Hausa Language and Literature Conference (Kano).

[4] Both Newman (2000: 194–5) and Jaggar (2001: 507–8) analyse constructions like (10)–(12) as pseudoclefts. Declerck (1988: 71) also extends the term pseudocleft/*wh*-cleft to English constructions like those in (i), in which the subject does not begin with a *wh*-expression, on the basis that the *wh*-expressions *how* and *who* cannot begin a pseudocleft, but have to be replaced by *the way (that)* and *the one who*, respectively (ii).
    (i) a. the way she spoke was amusing
         b. the one who spoke was John
    (ii) a. ?how she spoke was amusing
         b. *who spoke was John

(11) a. [àbîn   dà takè   bùkātà]_m [shìnkāfā]_f cè   *pseudocleft*
     thing.DD REL 3fs.FOC.IMPF need.VN rice   FM.f
     'what she needs is **rice**'

  b. [àbîn   dà nakè   sô]_m   [àlāwà]_f cē   *pseudocleft*
     thing.DD REL 1s.FOC.IMPF love.VN halva   FM.f
     'what I love is **halva**'

The examples in (12) illustrate the reverse pseudocleft constructions
corresponding to those in (11).

(12) a. [shìnkāfā]_f cè   [àbîn   dà takè   *reverse pseudocleft*
     rice   FM.f thing.DD REL 3fs.FOC.IMPF
     [bùkātà]_m
     need.VN
     '**rice** is what she needs'

  b. [àlāwà]_f cē   [àbîn   dà nakè   *reverse pseudocleft*
     halva   FM.f thing.DD REL 1s.FOC.IMPF
     sô]_m
     love.VN
     '**halva** is what I love'

Unlike the majority of the Chadic languages, where subject and nominal
or adjectival predicate may simply be juxtaposed in order to form a non-
verbal sentence, the presence of the Hausa copula *nē/cē/nē* is usually
obligatory in this type of construction. However, there are some common
exceptions to this generalisation, for example in 'name' sentences (13a),
where the non-verbal copula is not licensed, and in expressions relating to
days of the week (13b) and numerals (13c), where the non-verbal copula is
optional (see Jaggar 2001: 460–61).

(13) a. sūnānā   Bàlā
     name.of.1s Bala
     'my name is Bala'

  b. yâu   Jumma'à (cē)
     today Friday   FM.f
     'today is Friday'

  c. ɗàlìbanmù   gōmà   (nē) bana
     student.pl.of.1pl ten   FM.pl this.year
     'we have ten students this year' (lit. 'our students are ten
     this year')

The fact that the non-verbal copula is generally obligatory suggests that it is
required in order to attribute clausal status to a subject-predicate structure
that lacks verbal-inflectional properties.

Finally, recall that Hausa is a pro-drop (null subject) language, where a
subject can be omitted if its referent can be recovered from the discourse

context (§ 2.3.5). The following examples illustrate that this is also a feature of non-verbal copular sentences.

(14) a. **Bàhaushè**   nē
       Hausa.man   FM.m
       'he's/it's **a Hausa man**'
    b. **Ƙàramā**cè
       small.f   FM.f
       'it's **small**'
    c. **nī**   nè
       PRO.1s   FM.m
       'it's **me**'

5.2.2 *Specification and predication: descriptive terminology*

Copular sentences can be divided into various subtypes according to their grammatical and semantic/pragmatic properties. This section establishes some terminology for describing subtypes of copular sentences, based on the typology proposed by Declerck (1988), who divides [NP *be* NP] sentences into two main categories: specificational and predicational Declerck's typology draws on a rich and detailed literature on copular constructions of various kinds.[5] Although these categories can be distinguished on the basis of their semantics, discourse function and grammatical features, it is nevertheless possible for a single sentence to be ambiguous between a predicational and a specificational reading, depending on the context in which it occurs.

The defining semantic function of a specificational sentence is that it specifies a value for a variable. Consider example (15).

(15) Q: who is the bank robber?   *specificational*
     A: the bank robber is **John Thomas**   (Declerck 1988: 47)

In example (15), the specificational sentence *The bank robber is John Thomas* provides an answer to a question of the form *Who is NP?* This is a characteristic function of specificational sentences, which are discourse-

---

[5] Declerck traces the terms 'specificational' and 'predicational' back to Akmajian (1979). See also Higgins (1973 [1979]). As Declerck (1988: 23–3) points out, the term 'specificational' corresponds roughly to a number of alternative terms that are also widely used in the literature, including 'identifying' (e.g. Dik 1980; Gundel 1977), 'identificational' (e.g. Kuno & Wongkhomthong 1981; Quirk et al. 1985), 'equative' (e.g. Halliday 1967; Huddleston 1971; Kahn 1973) and 'equational' (e.g. Harries-Delisle 1978; Bolinger 1972b). An even broader set of terms has been applied to sentences of the predicational type, including 'attributive' (e.g. Gundel 1977), 'ascriptive' (e.g. Kahn 1973), 'property-assigning' (e.g. Dik 1980), 'characterizational' (e.g. Kuno & Wongkhomthong 1981; Quirk et al. 1985), 'classifying' (e.g. Erades 1949), 'intensive' (e.g. Halliday 1967), and 'non-equational' (e.g. Harries-Delisle 1978). Declerck's typology is not restricted to simple copular sentences of the type discussed here, but is also applied to clefts and pseudoclefts.

linked in the sense that they provide an answer either to an explicit question or to a question that is felt to be implicit in the discourse context. In example (15), the specificational sentence brings with it a presupposition, or old information: *the bank robber*. It follows that the NP that introduces the variable tends to be definite (Declerck 1988: 19). This old information introduces a variable for which the post-copular NP in (15) provides a value: *John Thomas*. The value NP therefore introduces new information, and is the focus of the sentence. Indeed, Declerck (1988: 24) argues that affirmative specificational sentences are characterised by a contrastive/exhaustive interpretation of the value NP.

English specificational sentences have two characteristic syntactic properties. First, a specificational sentence can be paraphrased by an *it*-cleft (Declerck 1988: 10), where the value NP is the clefted constituent (16).

(16) it's **John Thomas** who's the bank robber

Secondly, specificational sentences are reversible, a property that follows from the fact that both NPs are referring expressions, although the NP that introduces the variable is only 'weakly' referring: it refers to an individual, but does not identify that individual (Declerck 1988: 47). As a referring expression, the value NP tends to be but need not be definite. Compare example (15) with example (17).

(17) Q: who is the bank robber?   *specificational*
       A: **John Thomas** is the bank robber   (Declerck 1998: 40)

It follows that there is no fixed relative order between the NP that introduces the variable (*the bank robber*) and the value NP (*John Thomas*), since in the context given in (17), *John Thomas* remains the value NP despite its pre-copular position.[6]

The fact that specificational [NP *be* NP] sentences are reversible means that it is not a straightforward matter to determine which NP is the underlying subject, an issue that has received much attention in the literature (§ 5.4.3). Declerck favours the value NP as the underlying subject, on the basis of the fact that it provides a value corresponding to the focus (*wh*-phrase) that is the subject in the corresponding question:

(18) Q: who is the thief?   (Declerck 1998: 44)
       A: **Bill** is the thief

---

[6] Declerck points out that the value NP, as the focus of the sentence, carries nuclear stress. In example (15), the nuclear stress on *John Thomas* corresponds to the default, since nuclear stress in English is marked on the most deeply embedded constituent. Example (17), therefore, shows a marked assignment of nuclear stress on the subject NP. See Cinque (1993) and references cited there.

In addition to simple copular sentence of the type illustrated in (15)–(18), clefts and (typically) pseudoclefts are also types of specificational sentence, in the sense that they contain a relative clause structure expressing the presupposition, which contains a variable, and a focused constituent that provides a value for that variable (19).[7]

> (19) a. it was **John** who opened the door *cleft* (Declerck 1988: 8)
>   b. what I got was **a book**   *pseudocleft* (Declerck 1998: 6)

In contrast to a specificational sentence, a predicational sentence, rather than specifying a value for a variable, simply predicates some property of the subject:

> (20) John is a good student   *predicational*   (Declerck 1998: 55)

Unlike specificational sentences, predicational sentences are not necessarily discourse-linked. It follows that they are licensed in out-of-the-blue contexts. A further important semantic characteristic of a predicational sentence is that, while the subject NP is a referring expression, and therefore tends to be definite unless generic (Declerck 1988: 61), the property NP is not a referring expression, whether it is indefinite (21a) or definite (21b).

> (21) a. John is a good man   *predicational* (Declerck 1988: 57)
>   b. John is the acme of courtesy

A characteristic syntactic restriction follows from the fact that the property NP is not a referring expression: predicational copular sentences are not reversible:[8]

> (22) a. *a good student is John   (adapted from Declerck 1998: 62)
>   b. *the acme of courtesy is John

Neither can the property NP be clefted (in Standard English):

> (23) a. *it is a good student that John is
>   b. *it is the acme of courtesy that John is

In these respects, the property NP patterns with predicate APs, which can also appear in post-copular position in predicational copular sentences. Indeed, Declerck observes that the property NP shows a number of adjectival characteristics. Among others, the property NP may be gradable

---

[7] Although pseudoclefts are typically specificational, examples like (i) illustrate that this construction can also be predicational:
   (i)   what Henry sells is expensive (Declerck 1988: 71)
[8] As Declerck (1988: 62) points out, reversibility should not be confused with preposing. In a reversible copular sentence (e.g. *Tony Blair is the Prime Minister/the Prime Minister is Tony Blair*), the pre-copular NP is interpreted as the superficial subject. This is not the case for preposed/inverted NPs (e.g. *a teacher John is*).

(24a), it may be used without the indefinite article (24b), it licenses the same anaphoric pro-form as an AP (24c), and it may occur in small clauses (functioning as object complement, in traditional terms) (24d):

(24) a. John is <u>a better teacher</u> than you   (Declerck 1998: 65)
      b. Tom is <u>captain</u> of the cricket team   (Fodor 1976: 118,
                                              in Declerck 1988: 66)
      c. they all say Bill is <u>a fool</u>, and <u>that</u> he is   (Declerck 1988: 66)
      d. I thought Bill <u>a good linguist</u>   (Declerck 1988: 68)

Although predicational sentences are not necessarily discourse-linked, observe that in response to the question in (25), the predicational example in (20) becomes specificational, because it acquires discourse-linked status. Although the question requires predicational information in the response (*a good student*), this information is presented specificationally in that it supplies a value for the variable (*what John is*) (Declerck 1988: 56).

(25) Q: what is it that John is?   *specificational*
      A: John is a good student   (Declerck 1998: 56)

In this type of example, therefore, the properties of predication and specification 'overlap'. Although the NP *a good student* is the value NP, the fact that it is also the property NP means that it cannot be clefted (23). Table 5.1 summarises the properties of specificational and predicational sentences.

In addition to the major classification into specificational and predicational sentences, Declerck identifies some further types of [NP *be* NP] sentence, one of which is the descriptionally identifying sentence:[9]

(26) Q: who is that man?
      A: that man is John's brother   (Declerck 1998: 95)
(27) Q: who's Bill Smith?
      A: Bill Smith is a friend of mine   (Declerck 1988: 100)

According to Declerck, sentences of this type are not specificational because the subject NP is already fully referential. Subjects of these sentences are typically either deictic NPs, names or descriptions, which ensure full reference. Although this type of sentence introduces new information, the

---

[9] Declerck's fourth type is the identity statement, which is usually classified within the specificational type. Declerck argues that the semantics of specification are not the same as identity ('is the same entity as'):

   (i)   the Morning Star is the Evening Star   (Declerck 1988: 110)

Declerck's fifth type is the definition:

   (ii)   a pyramid is what the Egyptians built to bury their pharaohs in (Declerck 1988: 70):

These differ from specificational sentences semantically, and cannot be clefted. Definitions also differ from predicational sentences in that their main semantic function is to provide a definition, which is not the case for predicational sentences, even if these provide characteristics or attributes of the subject.

Table 5.1 Properties of specificational and predicational sentences

Specificational sentence	Predicational sentence
specifies a value for a variable: Q: *who is the bank robber?* A: *the bank robber is John Thomas*	predicates some property of subject: *John Thomas is a bank robber*
discourse-linked; tends not to occur 'out of the blue'	not necessarily discourse-linked; may occur 'out of the blue'
subject (variable) NP tends to be definite	subject NP tends to be definite, unless generic
value NP is a referring expression; often but not always definite	property NP is not a referring expression, whether definite or indefinite
value NP can be clefted: *it's John Thomas who's the bank robber*	property NP cannot be clefted: **it's a bank robber who's John Thomas*
is reversible: *the bank robber is John Thomas John Thomas is the bank robber*	is not reversible: *John Thomas is a bank robber *a bank robber is John Thomas*

constituent corresponding to the new information cannot be clefted, unlike in specificational sentences.

(28) a. *it is John's brother that that man is   (adapted from
      b. *it's a friend of mine that Bill Smith is   Declerck 1998: 108)

Neither are descriptionally identifying sentences reversible:

(29) Q: who is that man?
      A: *John's brother is that man
(30) Q: who is Bill Smith?
      A: *a friend of mine is Bill Smith

5.2.3 *Predicational copular sentences in Hausa*

Predicational copular constructions in Hausa are non-verbal sentences containing subject nominal, predicate (property) nominal (31a) or adjectival phrase (31b), and the non-verbal focus-marking copula (FM). The canonical constituent order for the predicational copular construction, exemplified in (31), is SUBJECT–PREDICATE–FM.

(31) a. Kànde **ɗālìbā**   cè   *predicational*
          Kande student.f   FM.f
          'Kande is a **student**'

b. Kànde **dōguwā** cè   *predicational*
   Kande tall.f   FM.f
   'Kande is **tall**'

As indicated by the boldface, the predicate nominal or adjectival phrase,
left-adjacent to the copula, is in focus. If these sentences are uttered 'out of
the blue', the focus is presentational. However, example (32) shows that in
response to the *wh*-question *Who is Audu?* the property NP *mahàucī*, which
also has a specificational function in this discourse context, is interpreted as
new information focus. In a similar way, in response to an utterance
asserting that Audu has some other profession, the constituent *mahàucī* in
(33) is interpreted as a type of exhaustive listing focus (corrective or
contrastive focus). These examples illustrate that the type of focus is
contextually determined.

(32) Q: wằnē   nè   Audù?
        who.m   FM.m   Audu
        'who is Audu?'
     A: Audù   **mahàucī** nè   *new information focus*
        Audu   butcher   FM.m
        'Audu is a **butcher**'
(33) Q: Audù   **manòmī** nè,   kō?
        Audu   farmer   FM.m   Q
        'Audu is a **farmer**, isn't he?
     A: ā'à, Audù **mahàucī** nè   *exhaustive listing focus*
        no Audu   butcher   FM.m
        'no, Audu is a **butcher**'

The following exchanges further illustrate the canonical construction in new
information and contrastive contexts (Jaggar 2001: 506).

(34) Q: mềnē nè   aikìnkà?
        what FM.m   work.of.2ms
        'what is your job?'
     A: nī   **mālàmī** nè   *new information focus*
        PRO.1s teacher   FM.m
        'I'm a **teacher**'
(35) Q: wannàn **wuƙā** cè?
        this   knife FM.f
        'is this a **knife**?'
     A: ā'à wannàn **cōkàlī** nè   *exhaustive/*
        no   this;   spoon   FM.m   *contrastive focus*
        (bằ wuƙā   ba)
        NEG knife   NEG
        'no, this is a **spoon** (not a knife)'

Recall from Chapter 2 (§ 2.3.4) that in Hausa, a bare NP can be interpreted as definite or indefinite, depending on context. It follows that the definite determiner (DD) -`n/ -`r̃/-`n (m/f/pl) can therefore be described as optional in some contexts. For example, observe that the 'discourse-old' NP tayà 'tyre' is not marked with the definite determiner in example (36) (Jaggar 2001: 317).

(36) dà   mukà   jāwō   tà   mukà   canjà   tayà
     when   1pl.FOC.PF pull.out 3fs.PRO 1pl.FOC.PF change tyre
     'when we pulled it (the car) out, we changed the tyre'

Despite the optionality of the definite determiner in certain contexts, the unacceptablilty of example (37) illustrates the preference for the subject of a predicational copular sentence to be definite:

(37) #mùtûm ɗālìbī   nề
     man   student.m   FM.m
     'a man is a **student**'

As in many languages, an indefinite subject is licensed only with a generic reading, which is illustrated by example (38) (Jaggar, p.c.).

(38) yārồ   dai   yārồ nē
     boy   PART   boy   FM.m
     'boys will be boys' (lit. 'as for a boy, (he) is a boy')

In contrast, the property NP tends to be indefinite in this construction.

Although the canonical word order for predicational copular sentences is SUBJECT–PREDICATE–FM, a number of other constituent order possibilities are also possible, which reflect distinct information packaging options. The non-canonical structure of a predicational copular sentence may be either PREDICATE–FM–SUBJECT (focus on the predicate/property NP/AP), as shown by example (39), or SUBJECT–FM–PREDICATE (focus on the subject), as shown by example (40):

(39) a. **ɗālìbī**   nề   Audù (bằ likità ba (nề))   *predicational*
        student.m FM.m Audu NEG doctor NEG FM.m
        'Audu is a **student** (not a doctor)'
     b. **dōgō**   nề   Audù (bằ gàjērē ba   (nề))
        tall.m   FM.m Audu NEG short.m NEG FM.m
        'Audu is **tall**, (not short)'

(40) a. **Audù** nē   ɗālìbī   (bằ Bàlā ba)   *predicational*
        Audu   FM.m student.m   NEG Bala NEG
        '**Audu** is a student (not Bala)'
     b. **Audù** nē   dōgō   (bằ Bàlā ba)
        Audu   FM.m tall.m   NEG Bala NEG
        '**Audu** is tall, not (Bala)'

These examples illustrate that Hausa, unlike English, allows either the
subject or the property NP/AP to become the focus of a marked syntactic
construction that involves the fronting of a focused constituent (the
monoclausal focus fronting construction in Hausa as opposed to the
biclausal cleft in English). However, like predicational copular sentences in
English, this construction is not reversible. In this respect, the non-referring
property NP patterns together with the AP.

(41) a. *ɗālìbī   **Audù** nē
        student.m   Audu   FM.m
        'a student is **Audu**'
     b. *dōgō **Audù** nē
        tall.m Audu FM.m
        'tall is **Audu**'

Example (42a) shows that the subject NP can be topicalised. Indeed, this
construction may be preferred to constructions like (6a), where the subject
is nominal rather than pronominal (Newman 2000: 166). Recall from
Chapter 4 (§ 4.2.2) that topic structures are typically characterised by pause
intonation. In contrast, the property NP/AP cannot be topicalised (42b,
42c), a restriction that can be explained by the non-referring status of this
constituent.[10]

(42) a. Audù (dai),   **ɗālìbī**   nē   *predicational*
        Audu (PART) student.m FM.m
        '(as for) Audu, (he) is a **student**'
     b. *ɗālìbī   (dai),   **Audù** nē
        student.m (PART) Audu FM.m
        '(as for) a student, (he) is **Audu**'
     c. *dōgō, **Audù** nē
        tall.m Audu FM.m
        'tall, **Audu** is'

Finally, example (43) shows that either the subject (43a) or the property NP
(43b) may be (indeed, usually is) null in a predicational copular sentence, as
long as the meaning can be recovered from context.

(43) a. Q: wànē nè̀   Audù?
            who.m FM.m Audu
            'who is Audu?'
        A: **ɗālìbī**   nè̀   *predicational*
            student.m FM.m
            '(he) is a **student**'

---

[10] In Green (1997), examples like (42b) and (42c) were described as grammatical, but further
investigation reveals a strong preference for a definite NP in the topic position.

b. Q: wằnē   nề   dằrāktằ   à   nân?
   who.m FM.m director at here
   'who is director here?'

A: **Audù** nē   *predicational*
   Audu FM.m
   '**Audu** is/it's **Audu**'

5.2.4 *Specificational/equative copular sentences in Hausa*

Although a bare NP can be interpreted as definite or indefinite, depending on context, two definite NPs (such as NP plus DD, or proper name) are required to form a specificational (equative) copular sentence in Hausa (44). It follows that this type of construction is discourse-linked, and, like its English counterpart, provides the answer to an explicit or implicit question rather than being licensed to occur 'out of the blue'. As example (44) shows, an adjective like *dōgō* 'tall' may acquire nominal status in Hausa through affixation of the definite determiner.

(44) Audù **dōgôn** nē   *specificational*
     Audu tall.m.DD FM.m
     'Audu is **the tall one**'

In keeping with Declerck's typology of English copular sentences, what distinguishes this type of copular sentence syntactically from the predicational copular sentence is the property of reversibility: since both NPs are referring expressions, they may occur in either order in the canonical NP–NP–FM construction without a topic pause (cf. examples (41) and (42)):

(45) a. Audù **ɓàrāwòn** nē   *specificational*
        Audu thief.DD   FM.m
        'Audu is **the thief**'
     b. ɓàrāwòn **Audù** nē   *specificational*
        thief.DD Audu   FM.m
        'the thief is **Audu**'

However, in Hausa, unlike in English, descriptionally identifying sentences (such as examples (46)–(49) below) pattern together with specificational sentences in their syntactic behaviour. For this reason, the term 'equative' is used here as a cover-term for both types of copular sentence in Hausa. The examples in (46) show the canonical structure of the equative copular sentence (NP–NP–FM), where the NPs may occur in either order, and the NP left adjacent to the copula is in focus.

(46) a. mùtumìn cân **likitànā** nề   *equative (descriptionally*
        man.of there doctor.of.1s FM.m   *identifying)*
        'that man is **my doctor**'

b. likitằnā   **mùtumìn cân**   nē
   doctor.of.1s   man.of   there FM.m
   'my doctor is **that man**'

The non-canonical structure of an equative copular sentence is NP–FM–NP, as
shown by the examples in (47), where either NP can occur in the pre-
copular focus position:

(47) a. **mùtumìn cân**   nē   likitằnā   *equative*
        man.of   there FM.m doctor.of.1s
        (bà̀   mùtumìn   nân   ba)
        NEG man.of   here NEG
        '**that man** is my doctor' (not this man)
     b. **likitằnā**   nè̀   mùtumìn cân   (bà̀   àbōkīnā   ba)
        doctor.of.1s FM.m man.of   there NEG   friend.of.1s NEG
        '**my doctor** is that man' (not my friend)

Example (48) shows that either NP can be topicalised in an equative
copular sentence (cf. example (42)):

(48) a. mùtumìn   cân   (dai),   **likitằnā**   *equative*
        man.of   there   (PART) doctor.of.1s
        nè̀   (bà̀ àbōkīnā   ba   nè̀)
        FM.m NEG friend.of.1s   NEG FM.m
        '(as for) that man, (he) is **my doctor**' (not my friend)
     b. likitằnā   (dai),   **mùtumìn cân**   *equative*
        doctor.of.1s (PART) man.of   there
        nē   (bà̀   mùtumìn   nân   ba)
        FM.m NEG man.of   here NEG
        '(as for) my doctor, (he) is **that man**' (not this man)

Finally, example (49) shows that either NP can be null in an equative
copular sentence:

(49) a. **mùtumìn cân**   nē   *equative*
        man.of   there FM.m
        '(he) is **that man over there**'
     b. **likitằnā**   nè̀   *equative*
        doctor.of.1s FM.m
        '(he) is **my doctor**'

As the description of the data in this section suggests, there is a designated
focus position in Hausa non-verbal copular constructions. The constituent
left-adjacent to *nē/cē/nè* is in focus, and the type of focus associated with
the constituent left-adjacent to *nē/cē/nè* is contextually determined. These
data therefore suggest that the non-verbal copula functions (synchronically)
as a focus marker not only in constructions involving focus/*wh*-fronting in
verbal clauses (Chapter 4) but also in non-verbal clauses. Of course, the

marked or non-canonical word order in these constructions can be straightforwardly explained in terms of focus fronting in the non-verbal copular construction, but the placement of focus in the unmarked or canonical non-verbal copular construction suggests that the non-verbal copula is evolving a focus-marking function across the board, a fact that raises some interesting questions not only in relation to a syntactic analysis of these constructions (§ 5.4) but also in relation to the historical development of the Hausa non-verbal copula (§ 5.3).

5.3 THE EVOLUTION OF NĒ/CĒ/NĒ

Given that the synchronic data suggest that the non-verbal copula in Hausa functions as a focus marker, questions naturally arise concerning the historical origins of this morpheme. It is well known that copular morphemes often develop from demonstratives (Li & Thompson 1977). It is also common for copulas, as cleft sentence markers, to evolve into focus markers (Heine & Reh 1984; Harris & Campbell 1995). These processes of change are instances of grammaticalisation, a process whereby lexical (open-class) expressions acquire grammatical (closed-class) functions, or existing grammatical expressions acquire further grammatical functions. Grammaticalisation is described as unidirectional and cyclic (Croft 2003: 253): lexical (open-class) expressions evolve into grammatical (closed-class) expressions via the process of grammaticalisation (a process of change that does not occur in the opposite direction), and may eventually leave the language via a process of loss. Grammaticalisation is characterised by correlated changes in both the form and the meaning/function of a linguistic expression. The form change typically involves processes such as

Table 5.2 Common grammaticalisation patterns (adapted from Croft 2003: 254)

---

content verb > auxiliary > tense-aspect-mood affix
verb > adposition
noun > adposition
adposition > case affix
adposition > subordinator
emphatic personal pronoun > clitic pronoun > agreement affix
cleft sentence marker > focus marker
noun > classifier
verb > classifier
demonstrative > article > gender/noun class marker
demonstrative or article > complementiser or relativiser
numeral 'one' > indefinite article
numerals 'two' or 'three' > dual/paucal/plural affix
collective noun > plural affix
demonstrative > copula
positional verb > copula

---

phonological reduction and morphological cliticisation, and is accompanied by meaning/function change that is usually described in terms of semantic bleaching or attenuation. This process of change often results in layering: the coexistence of related meanings/functions, each of which has emerged at a different point along the grammaticalisation path. Table 5.2 illustrates some common grammaticalisation patterns (Croft 2003: 254).

Li & Thompson (1977: 419) argue that one mechanism for the emergence of copular morphemes results from the 'reanalysis of a topic–comment construction', a process of change that they suggest is widely attested cross-linguistically. This reanalysis is represented schematically in (50) (adapted from Li & Thompson 1977: 427).

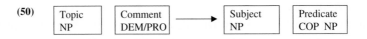

(50)

Topic	Comment		Subject	Predicate
NP	DEM/PRO	⟶	NP	COP NP

As this diagram illustrates, Li & Thompson suggest that when a topic-comment clause structure is reanalysed as a subject–predicate clause structure, the topic NP is reanalysed as a subject NP, and the resumptive demonstrative pronoun in the comment clause is reanalysed as a copula in the predicate. They illustrate this process with the following Chinese examples.

(51) a. *Archaic Chinese (5th century BC)* (Li & Thompson 1977: 423)
    qíong   yù jiàn,   shì rén   *topic-comment*
    poverty and debasement this people
    zhǐ   sǔo   wù   yě
    GEN   NOMIN dislike DECL
    'poverty and debasement, that is what people dislike'
   b. *Modern Mandarin* (Li & Thompson 1977: 422)
    nèi-ge rén shì xuéshēng   *subject-predicate*
    that-CL man be   student
    'that man is a student'

Example (51a) shows that the element *shì* functions as an anaphoric demonstrative (resumptive pronoun) in the Archaic Chinese topic–comment construction. In the Modern Mandarin subject–predicate construction in (51b), the same element has been reanalysed as a copula, because the subject NP is clause-internal and does not require resumption. Schuh (1983a) suggests that the Hausa copula may have developed along the lines suggested by Li & Thompson (see Parsons 1961; Schachter 1966; Rufa'i 1977: 306–11):

I am unaware of any previous account of Hausa *nē/cē* which explicitly links these morphemes with the Hausa demonstrative or pronominal system, but such a link is obvious, at least from a historical point of view. For example, the *n-* of *nē* corresponds to the masculine singular and the plural marker of previous reference [DD], whereas the *c-* of *cē* corresponds to the feminine *-r̃* in the same function ... the set of formatives *n* (m. sg.), *t* (f. sg.), *n* (pl.) in the determiner and pronominal system is an ancient pattern reconstructable from proto-Afroasiatic (Greenberg 1960) ... Despite this historical link, ... *nē/cē* have been entirely grammaticalized as copulas and have no deictic or anaphoric function. (Schuh 1983a: 312–13; macrons and italics added)

The feminine /t/, a widespread Afroasiatic feature, appears throughout the pronominal and agreement system in Hausa (e.g. third person singular independent pronoun *ita*, bound pronoun *-tà*, indirect object pronoun *matà*, and third person feminine singular INFL (TAM) morphemes *tā* (perfective), *tanà* (imperfective)). The consonant pattern that marks number and gender in the Hausa non-verbal copula *nē/cē/nē* (m/f/pl) is also identical to that found in the Hausa genitive linker *na/ta/na* (m/f/pl) (Newman (2000: 545). Schuh (1983b: 183) argues that the genitive linker has also evolved from the definite determiner. In Standard/Eastern Hausa, a palatalisation process changes the feminine marker /t/ into the palatal-alveolar /tʃ/ (represented in standard Hausa orthography as *c*) before front vowels, hence the form of the feminine singular copula *cē*. Western dialects preserve the /t/ in the feminine copula *tā* (see example (53)). The same feminine marker /t/ is realised as /r̃/ in its definite determiner function (e.g. *mōtà* 'car' → *mōtà-r̃* 'the car') as a result of a phonological process known as Klingenheben's Law, which weakens syllable-final obstruents.[11] Examples (52) and (53) illustrate the copula forms in both Eastern (Kano) Hausa and Western (Sokoto) Hausa (Schuh 2000: 1 (my glosses):

(52) a. Mūsā **d̃ālìbī** nè   *masculine copula: Eastern Hausa*
        Musa   student.m FM.m
        'Musa is **a student**'

     b. Mūsā **d̃ālìbī** nà̀   *masculine copula: Western Hausa*
        Musa   student.m FM.m
        'Musa is **a student**'

(53) a. Hàdīzà **d̃ālìbā** cè̀   *feminine copula: Eastern Hausa*
        Hadiza   student.f FM.f
        'Hadiza is **a student**'

     b. Hàdīzà **d̃ālìbā** tà̀   *feminine copula: Western Hausa*
        Hadiza   student.f FM.f
        'Hadiza is **a student**'

As Schuh (1983a) points out, the fact that *nē/cē/nē* follow the predicate in unmarked copular constructions requires an explanation, given that

---

[11] For details of how Klingenheben's law applies to Hausa, see Newman (2000: 230–4).

subject–predicate order is the unmarked pattern in Hausa. If the copula originated as a (subject) resumptive pronoun, as Li & Thompson's (1977) hypothesis predicts, it is expected to precede rather than follow the predicate. In a more recent paper, Schuh (2000) develops this historical analysis, and argues that the copula may have developed from the demonstrative pronoun as a result of the doubling of the original demonstrative in *wh*-constructions, which became cliticised to the question word. As a consequence, the doubled *nē/cē/nē* was reanalysed as a copula. This hypothesised path of development (illustrated with modern forms) is represented schematically in (54) (adapted from Schuh 2000: 3).

(54)

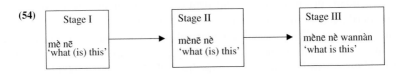

As this diagram suggests, the copula was originally a demonstrative subject pronoun, which occurs in the Stage I construction in clause-final position as a result of the *wh*-fronting of the predicate. At Stage II, the demonstrative pronoun is incorporated into the *wh*-expression, and the requirement for a subject pronoun results in the doubling of the demonstrative pronoun. At Stage III, the reanalysis of *nē/cē/nē* as a copula entails that if an overt demonstrative subject pronoun is required, the demonstrative *wannàn* is inserted. Schuh suggests that the Hausa copula *nē/cē/nē* spread from this type of *wh*-construction to other non-verbal clauses. The advantage of this analysis is that it explains the post-predicate position of the copula in unmarked non-verbal clauses: its original position was post-predicate because of the *wh*-fronting of the predicate. This hypothesis also provides an explanation for the doubling of the copula morphology (the 'repeat copula') in certain *wh*-constructions (§ 4.4).[12] Schuh (2000) further suggests

---

[12] Schuh (2000) also argues that special inflection (§ 4.6) has evolved from deictic determiners. Consider the non-verbal clause in example (i), in which the TAM part of the INFL word occurs without the person/number/gender morpheme. In this case, the vowel of the TAM marker is surface long.

(i) **halinsà**   kè   nan
     character.of.3ms   FOC.IMPF   there
     'that's just **his character**'

According to Schuh (2000: 5), examples like (i) 'represent the original use of *kè* ... as a copula in non-verbal sentences. Its function as a relative TAM marker in verbal sentences is the innovative extension ... Like the *nē/cē* ~ *nā/tā* copula, the *kè* copula has its origin in the determiner system, although unlike *nē/cē* ~ *nā/tā*, which represent a recent innovation within Hausa, *kè* with copula function must have been inherited as such from the language ancestral to Hausa. Proto-Chadic had a **k* determiner base ... which probably originally functioned as a gender neutral marker of definiteness.'

that this analysis accounts for the absence of the copula in constructions like (13), since constructions with name or number predicates would not have contained referential demonstratives.

Schuh's analysis accounts for the evolution of the non-verbal copula from the pronominal system. The hypothesis advanced here is that the copula is grammaticalising further into a focus marker, a process of evolution that is still underway, hence the layering in the function of the copula. While the non-verbal copula appears as a fully grammaticalised focus marker in focus/*wh*-fronting constructions, it retains a copular function in the non-verbal clause, but its focus-marking properties are also evident from the fact that there is a designated focus position in non-verbal copular clauses. The diagram in (55) represents this path of evolution.

(55)

The evolution of designated focus markers from copulas is widely attested in the grammaticalisation literature. For example, Heine & Reh (1984) argue that focus particles in many African languages emerge from copulas as a result of the grammaticalisation of biclausal cleft constructions into monoclausal focus constructions. In a similar vein, Heine & Kuteva (2002: 11) describe a cross-linguistic grammaticalisation chain DEMONSTRATIVE > (PERSONAL PRONOUN) > COPULA > FOCUS MARKER, which corresponds to the path of grammaticalisation hypothesised here for the Hausa copular focus marker (55). Drubig (2003) also adopts a version of this analysis, and suggests that the evolution of monoclausal focus operator constructions from biclausal cleft constructions may also be evident in the remnants of other properties of the biclausal cleft in the monoclausal focus construction. Although this discussion is not pursued here, it is worth observing that special inflection that characterises Hausa focus/*wh*-constructions is also a property of relative clauses, a feature that has been analysed from a synchronic perspective as the morphological reflex of the operator–variable construction (§ 4.5). For further discussion of the evolution of focus markers from copulas, see Harris & Campbell (1995), Lambrecht (2001) and Schwarz (2004), among others.

5.4 EXTENDING THE FP ANALYSIS

As indicated above (§ 5.2), there is a designated focus position in Hausa non-verbal copular constructions: the constituent left-adjacent to *nē/cē/nē* is focused, a generalisation that also holds true of focus/*wh*-fronting in verbal clauses. It is therefore justified on both empirical and theoretical grounds to explore a unified analysis for both focus/*wh*-fronting and non-verbal copular constructions. Indeed, the analysis outlined in Chapter 4 can be straightforwardly extended to non-verbal copular constructions. This section outlines the proposed analysis of Hausa non-verbal copular constructions (§ 5.4.1), followed by a more detailed discussion of the empirical evidence for this approach (§ 5.4.2), and a discussion of the theoretical issues arising from this analysis (§ 5.4.3).

5.4.1 *Proposal*

In this section, the analysis of *nē/cē/nē* as a focus marker is extended to non-verbal copular sentences in Hausa. Example (56) represents the canonical word order for a predicational copular sentence. The proposed structure for this sentence is shown in (57).

(56) Audù   **ɗālìbī**   nè   *predicational*
      Audu   student.m   FM.m
      'Audu is a **student**'

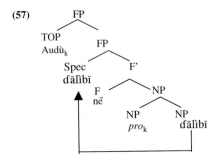

The analysis in (57) holds that copular sentences consist of a predicational/equative lexical core (a small clause headed by the NP or AP predicate) dominated by the functional projection FP. When, as in (56), it is the predicate that is focused, this constituent raises from the small clause to the focus position: the specifier of the focus phrase (FP). Of course, the fact that the subject of the canonical copular clause precedes the focused predicate entails an analysis in which the subject occupies a position higher in the structure than the (left-peripheral) focus position. The analysis proposed here posits that the subject of this type of copular clause occupies the topic position. Recall that evidence from verbal clauses in Hausa shows that topics precede focused constituents in the left periphery of the clause (§ 4.3). Furthermore, recall that topics pattern differently from focus phrases in that they do not observe constraints on extraction, show a preference for resumption, and may be followed by multiple adverbial particles. These facts suggest an analysis in which topics are adjoined to FP rather than occupying the specifier position of a left-peripheral topic phrase. For this reason, topics are represented in the present analysis as adjuncts, although little of relevance to the present analysis hinges on this decision. If this left-peripheral clause structure is extended to non-verbal clauses, it suggests that the 'subject' NP in a construction like (56) occupies the topic-adjoined position, coreferential with a null resumptive pronoun in the small clause. This analysis predicts that only an NP with topic-like qualities is expected to occur as 'subject' of a canonical copular sentence, a hypothesis that is addressed in detail in the next section.

Of course, the alternative to analysing the canonical non-verbal copular clause as a construction derived by movement is to treat this as a case of focus/wh-in situ, a possibility worth exploring given the fact that focus/wh-in situ is attested in verbal clauses (§ 4.6). For example, Jaggar (2001: 522) describes the examples in (58) as cases of wh-in situ because they show the canonical copula-final structure (the marked counterparts are shown in brackets):

(58) a. shī   wằnē nề   (cf. *wằnē nề shī*)
       PRO.3ms who FM.m
       'who is he?'

    b. wannàn mềnē nề   (cf. *mềnē nề wannàn*)
       this   what   FM.m
       'what is this?'

    c. fàrāshìn wannàn nawà   nē (cf. *nawà nē fàrāshìn wannàn*)
       price.of this   how.much FM.m
       'how much is the price of this?'

Equally, example (59a) could be described as a case of focus in situ, and (59b) as its ex situ counterpart.

(59) a. nī   **mālàmī** nề
       PRO.1s teacher FM.m
       'I'm a **teacher**'

    b. **mālàmī** nề   nī
       teacher FM.m PRO.1s
       'I'm a **teacher**'

While this position is tenable from a descriptive perspective, particularly since it recognises the distinction between the canonical and non-canonical copular constructions, it is inadequate from a theoretical perspective, since it fails to account for the fact that the focus/wh-phrase is in the same (left-adjacent) configuration with the focus-marking copula as in the non-canonical case, a pattern that requires explanation.

Consider next the non-canonical predicational copular sentences shown in (39) and (40), repeated here as (60) and and (61). Recall that these illustrate predicate focus and subject focus, respectively.

(60) a. **ɗālìbī** nè̀ Audù (bà̀ likità ba (nè̀))   *predicational*
       student.m FM.m Audu NEG doctor NEG FM.m
       'Audu is a **student** (not a doctor)'

   b. **dōgō** nè̀ Audù (bà̀ gà̀jērē ba (nè̀))
       tall.m FM.m Audù NEG short.m NEG FM.m
       'Audu is **tall**, (not short)'

(61) a. **Audù** nē ɗālìbī (bà̀ Bàlā ba)   *predicational*
       Audu FM.m student.m NEG Bala NEG
       '**Audu** is a student (not Bala)'

   b. **Audù** nē dōgō (bà̀ Bàlā ba)
       Audu FM.m tall.m NEG Bala NEG
       '**Audu** is tall (not Bala)'

The proposed structures for (60) (predicate focus) and (61) (subject focus) are shown in (62) and (63), respectively:

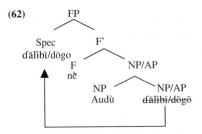

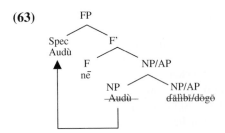

In the structure in (62), the predicate occupies the clause-initial focus position left-adjacent to *nē*. In this case, the predicate raises from its base position in the small clause, and the subject remains in situ in the small clause subject position. In the structure in (63), the subject raises to the clause-initial focus position, while the predicate remains in situ.

Consider next example (42a), repeated here as (64). The structure of this example, in which the constituent *Audù* is a topic, also follows straightforwardly from the analysis proposed here. According to this analysis, predicational copular sentences in which the topicalised subject is followed by a topic pause involve the same structure as canonical predicational copular sentences (57), a claim that is addressed in detail in the next section.

(64) Audù, **ɗālìbī** nè   *predicational*
   Audu student.m FM.m
   'as for Audu, (he) is a **student**'

Finally, consider the examples in (43), repeated here as (65).

(65) a. Q: wằnē nè Audù?
     who.m FM.m Audu
     'who is Audu?'
   A: **ɗālìbī** nè   *predicational*
     student.m FM.m
     '(he) is a **student**'
  b. Q: wằnē nè dằřaktà à nân?
     who.m FM.m director at here
     'who is director here?'
   A: **Audù** nē   *predicational*
     Audu FM.m
     '**Audu** is'

The structure of these sentences also follows from the FP analysis. In (65a), assuming the canonical sentence as the underlying structure, the subject is null and the predicate is in focus. Examples like (65b) are licensed in contexts where the predicate is contextually determined. Consider example (66) (Jaggar 2001: 505), where upper-case A and B indicate a dialogue pair:

(66) A: **Audù** nē dằřaktà   *predicational*
   Audu FM.m director
   '**Audu** is director'
  B: ā'à, **ita** cè   *predicational*
   no PRO.3fs FM.f
   'no, **she** is'

Assuming that (66B) mirrors the non-canonical structure in (66A), the elided predicate nominal *dằřaktà* occupies its base position, but is not pronounced because it can be retrieved from discourse context.

Consider next the equative copular sentences shown in examples (44)–(49). As these examples show, the focus properties of equative copular sentences in Hausa mirror those of predicational copular sentences: the canonical order is NP NP FM and the marked structure is either NP₁ FM NP₂ or NP₂ FM NP₁, where either of the definite NPs can occur in the pre-copular focus position. Therefore, the syntactic structures proposed in this section for the marked and unmarked predicational copular sentences can also be applied to the equative cases. However, it is less straightforward to determine whether the structure of the small clause is the same in predicational and equative copular sentences. Recall that the canonical predicational copular sentence was argued to involve a topic subject and predicate raising (57). There are two options for the analysis of canonical (NP NP FM) equative sentences. The first is to assume that one NP is 'subject' and the other is 'syntactic predicate' (i.e. the head of the small clause). According to this analysis, the structure of (46a), repeated here as (67), mirrors that of the canonical predicational sentence: the 'syntactic predicate' raises and the 'subject' occupies topic-adjoined position (68).

(67) mùtumìn cân **likitànā**   nè   *equative*
     man.of there doctor.of.1s FM.m
     'that man is **my doctor**'

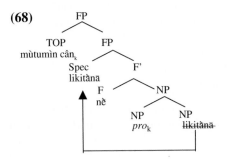

Assuming the same underlying structure for (46b), repeated here as (69), where the NP *likitànā* is treated as the underlying 'syntactic predicate', the resulting structure is as shown in (70).

(69) likitànā   **mùtumìn cân** nē   *equative*
     doctor-of-1s man.of   there FM.m
     'my doctor is **that man over there**'

As indicated by (70), this analysis accords the underling 'syntactic predicate' topic status, which entails a coreferential null pronominal in the predicate position of the small clause. The second option is to assume that (69) has a distinct underlying structure from (67), wherein the positions of the NPs in the small clause are reversed. According to this analysis, (69)

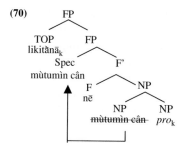

involves a topic subject and 'syntactic predicate' raising, just like (67). There is little to choose between these two options, – an unsurprising conclusion given the nature of equative sentences. Both analyses suggest that a null pronoun, coreferential with the topic, occupies a position in the small clause. Given that topics permit resumption in Hausa, observe that this analysis predicts that a resumptive pronoun might alternate with a null pronoun in the small clause, a prediction that is addressed in the next section. Recall that the optionality of resumptive object pronouns in Hausa topic constructions can be explained by the pro-drop properties of the language (§ 2.3.5).

The remainder of the equative sentences can be accounted for straightforwardly according to the proposal outlined in this section. The non-canonical equative sentences in (47) involve raising of either NP_1 'subject' or NP_2 'syntactic predicate' to the focus position, and the topic–pause examples in (48) mirror the structure of the canonical equative sentences. Finally, the examples in (49) can also be accounted for by the structures proposed here, given an appropriate context that licenses the discourse-given NP (either subject or predicate) to be null.

5.4.2 *Empirical evidence*

Having set out the basic structure assumed for non-verbal copular clauses in the previous section, this section addresses the empirical evidence for extending the FP analysis to these constructions, looking in more detail at their properties and at how these properties reflect upon the predictions identified in the previous section. Three main empirical issues are addressed in this section. First, it is argued that the presence of a designated focus position left-adjacent to the focus-marking copula in non-verbal copular clauses provides compelling motivation for the extension of the focus phrase (FP) analysis to these constructions. This discussion also addresses the issue of gender agreement between the focus-marking copula and the subject/predicate of the clause, for which a configurational account is proposed. Secondly, it is argued that the subject of the canonical copular clause shows properties of a topic, providing support for an analysis of these constructions that is built around the left-peripheral topic/focus layer of clause structure (§3.2.3). Finally, it is argued that non-verbal copular clauses show evidence of displacement, thereby providing support for an analysis of these constructions as derived by movement of a focused constituent to left-peripheral operator position.

Copular sentences have a designated focus position

The most striking empirical evidence for the extension of the FP analysis to non-verbal copular sentences in Hausa relates to the focus properties of those sentences. As the examples in previous sections indicate, the structure of these sentences is such that the consituent left adjacent to the focus-marking copula is interpreted as the focus of the sentence, whether this is presentational, new information or exhaustive/contrastive focus. It follows that this construction allows considerable flexibility in terms of constituent order. Of course, the question that arises is why this construction should be syntactically marked for focus as a default, given that other sentence types in Hausa can be syntactically unmarked for focus.[13] From the perspective of the analysis developed here, the answer lies in the fact that the copula *nē/cē/nē* is a (grammaticalised/grammaticalising) focus marker (§ 5.3). In other words, this analysis posits that the focus interpretation associated with this construction relates to the properties of the copula. Recall the path of grammaticalisation represented in (55), and the fact that the process

---

[13] It is worth observing, for example, that an alternative non-verbal construction formed with the associative particle *dà* (lit. 'with') does not license a tag that provides explicit contrast with the predicate, which shows that this construction type does not license an exhaustive/constrastive focus interpretation:

   (i)   dōgō dà   shī   (# bằ gàjērē ba   (nề))
        tall   with PRO.3ms NEG short NEG (FM.m)
        'he's tall, (he's) not short'

Newman (2000: 162) describes these constructions as 'colloquial Kano speech ... not accepted by all speakers. They are definitely marked as compared with the straightforward HAVE sentences; but the exact semantic/pragmatic nuances are far from clear.' Example (ii) illustrates the canonical 'have' construction, which is formed with the imperfective INFL (TAM). This type of construction was briefly discussed in Chapter 2 (§ 2.3.3):

   (ii) tanằ   dà   sābuwar munduwā
        3fs.IMPF with new.of bracelet
        'she has a new bracelet' (lit. 'she is with a new bracelet')

Focus fronting is possible in the *dà* construction, however. Consider the following examples.

   (iii) a. **kařimcì** nē   dà   shī
           generosity FM.m with PRO.3ms
           'he's **generous** alright'
       b. **littāfì** nē dà   shī   (à hannunsà)
           book FM.m with PRO.3ms at hand.3ms
           'he has a **book** (in his hand)' (lit. 'a book is with him (in his hand)')

of grammaticalisation often results in layering, where a given element displays some 'overlap' between its older and newer functions. While the function of *nē/cē/nē* in verbal focus/*wh*-fronting constructions represents its 'more grammaticalised' role in the language (as a focus marker), its function in the non-verbal copular sentence represents its 'less grammaticalised' role: the copula licenses predication and equation in the non-verbal clause, in the sense that it attributes clausal status to a subject–predicate structure that lacks verbal-inflectional properties. The fact that the non-verbal copula has also evolved a focus-marking function in Hausa explains why the non-verbal clause has a designated focus postion by default. Furthermore, the evolving function of *nē/cē/nē* from copula to focus marker may go some way towards explaining the absence of this element in non-verbal constructions expressing inalienable possession (§ 5.2.1).

There is also a clear relationship between the existence of a designated focus position and the agreement properties of the non-verbal copular clause. Observe that Schuh's (1983a) historical analysis explains why the focus-marking copula shows gender/number agreement: it has its roots in the Proto-Afroasiatic determiner system, which shows a gender/number agreement pattern that is evident throughout the wider language family (see Chapter 6). From the perspective of the (synchronic) analysis developed here, the agreement properties of the non-verbal copular construction receive a configurational account: the focus marking copula typically agrees in gender and number with the constituent in its left-adjacent specifier position.[14] This analysis can also be straightforwardly extended to pseudoclefts where the contituent left-adjacent to the focus marking copula is also in focus (recall examples (10)–(12)).

Topic prominence and subject prominence in Hausa

The extension of the FP analysis from focus/*wh*-fronting in verbal clauses to non-verbal copular sentences entails that all constructions of this type involve displacement of the focused constituent to the designated focus position. This account accurately predicts not only the constituent orders that are attested in this type of construction but also their information packaging properties. However, this analysis makes one striking claim that requires further empirical support: that the 'subject' of a canonical copular sentence occupies the topic position (57). Recall that the theory-internal motivation for this claim follows from the fact that the topic position precedes the focus position in Hausa verbal clauses: if the same left-

---

[14] Of course, the fact that counterexamples to this generalisation are attested (recall examples (8) and (9)) raises questions about whether agreement is licensed in the left periphery or in some 'deeper' layer of clause structure. See below for further discussion (§ 5.4.3).

peripheral clause structure is assumed for non-verbal clauses as for verbal clauses, any constituent preceding the focus position is a topic.

In order to investigate the empirical basis for adopting this analysis, it is worth reviewing the status of subject prominence and topic prominence in Hausa. In their well-known (1976) paper, Li & Thompson argue that languages may fall into one of four typological categories with respect to the organisation of the clause:

1. subject-prominent languages;
2. topic-prominent languages;
3. languages that are both subject-prominent and topic-prominent;
4. languages that are neither, since the two have merged.

Although most languages have both types of construction, Li & Thompson argue that languages can be classified according to which type of construction best represents the 'basic' or unmarked clause type in the language. Table 5.3 summarises the properties that identify subject-prominence and topic-prominence. Li & Thompson also argue that these typological differences reduce to the stage that a language is at with respect to the grammaticalisation of topics into subjects, a view that is consistent with their (1977) theory concerning the emergence of copulas (§ 5.3). According to this perspective, 'Subjects are essentially grammaticalized topics' (Li & Thompson 1976: 484).

Table 5.3 Subject prominence and topic prominence (Li & Thompson 1976)

Subject prominent (SP)	Topic prominent (TP)
basic sentence type has subject–predicate structure	basic sentence type has topic–comment structure
surface coding on subject (position, morphology)	surface coding on topic (position, morphology)
subject is an argument of the verb (clause-internal)	topic is not an argument of the verb (clause-external)
subject agrees with verb	topic does not agree with verb
subject takes precedence in controlling anaphors (e.g., reflexives)	topic takes precedence in controlling anaphors (e.g., reflexives)
the SP language has dummy subjects	the TP language lacks dummy subjects
the passive construction is widespread in SP languages	the passive construction is either absent or marginal in TP languages
the 'double subject' construction is absent or marginal in SP languages	the 'double subject' construction is widespread in TP languages

Although Hausa is a pro-drop (null subject) language, there are grounds for describing subject–predicate structure as basic in the verbal clause. Recall that there is surface coding on the nominal subject, in terms both of its pre-verbal position and of its agreement with the INFL word (§ 2.3.2). However, the topic–comment structure is also very common in Hausa, and topics do not agree with the verb in terms of person, number or gender, unless they are linked to the subject. There is also surface coding on the topic, which is marked by its left-peripheral position, by the topic pause and by the optional presence of adverbial particles that emphasise its separation from the clause (§ 4.2.2).[15]

Hausa shows subject prominence in that subjects bind reflexives in verbal clauses (71a). Reflexives do not occur in non-verbal copular sentences.[16] Example (71b) shows that a null subject can bind the reflexive pronoun complement (Jaggar 1997). It follows that the generalisation that reflexives are bound by the subject can be maintained even where the subject is null, and preceded by a (coreferential) topic (71c):

(71) a. yārinyàr̃   tā   cùci   kântà
        girl.DD   3fs.PF   harm   REFL.3fs
        'the girl harmed herself'

     b. kun   cùci   kânkù
        2pl.PF harm   REFL.2pl
        'you harmed yourselves'

     c. yārinyàr̃ kàm,   tā   cùci   kântà
        girl.DD PART   3fs.PF   harm   REFL.3fs
        'as for the girl, she harmed herself'

As a pro-drop language, Hausa has no 'dummy' subject pronouns. For example, 'weather sentences' are formed with the impersonal ('4th person') TAM:

(72) an   sōmà yîn   ruwā
     4.PF   begin do.VN.of   water
     'it's begun to rain'

---

[15] Hausa also allows a right-peripheral 'afterthought' or right-dislocation construction (see Newman 2000: 49):
   (i) yā   kàmātà   Tànî tà   biyā shì,   hàr̃ājìn fa
       3ms.PF   be.fitting Tani 3fs.SUB pay   PRO.3ms tax.DD   PART
       'it is fitting that Tani should pay it, the tax'

[16] This generalisation applies to bound reflexive pronouns occurring in the predicate position (ia). 'Emphatic reflexives', which occur in apposition to the subject NP, are licensed in non-verbal copular constructions (ib):
   (i) a. *Kànde kântà   cē
          Kande REFL.3fs FM.f
          'Kande is herself'
       b. Kànde ita   kântà   ɗālìbā   cè
          Kande PRO.3fs   REFL.3fs student.f FM.f
          'Kande herself is a student'

The agentless passive can be expressed in Hausa by a grade 7 verb, which is a derived intransitive verb form that can take a patient subject (Jaggar 1988). Compare the following examples (Newman 2000: 665). Observe that the patient subject in (73b) agrees with the INFL word.[17]

(73) a. sun   wāsà   wuƙā   (grade 1 transitive *wāsà*)
        3pl.PF sharpen knife
        'they sharpened the knife'
    b. wuƙā tā   wàsu   (grade 7 intransitive *wàsu*)
        knife 3fs.PF sharpen
        'the knife was fully sharpened'

Finally, Hausa lacks the 'double subject construction' found in some East Asian languages, although constructions in which a topic is followed by a subject are common in Hausa. However, the topic only co-occurs with a subject pronoun when the latter is in focus (74b), otherwise the subject is null (74c).

(74) a. Kànde, Audù yā   rìgā   yā   àurē   tà
        Kande Audu 3ms.PF do.already 3ms.PF marry PRO.3fs
        'as for Kande, Audu has already married her'
    b. yāròn dai, **shī** (nè) ya   kai wà Mūsā kuɗī
        boy.DD PART PRO.3ms FM.m 3ms.FOC.PF take IOM Musa money
        'as for the boy, **he** took the money to Musa'
    c. yāròn dai, yā   kai wà Mūsā kuɗī
        boy.DD PART 3ms.PF take IOM Musa money
        'as for the boy, he took the money to Musa'

As these examples reveal, the independent pronoun cannot occur as the unmarked subject in verbal clauses, which has to be expressed either by a null subject or by a lexical NP. If the independent pronoun occurs in clause-initial position, it is either in focus (75a, 75b) or the topic of the clause (75c, 75d):

(75) a. **shī**   nè   ya   fàɗi haƙà   *subject focus*
        PRO.3ms FM.m 3ms.FOC.PF say this
        '**he** said this'
    b. **sū**   nè   ya   ganī   *object focus*
        PRO.3pl FM.pl 3ms.FOC.PF see
        'he saw **them**'

---

[17] Some grade 7 verbs take experiencer rather than patient subjects, which warns against treating the grade 7 verb as a straightforward passivised verb (see Jaggar 2001: 265). The equivalent of an agentless passive canalso be expressed by a construction containing the impersonal TAM (Newman 2000: 271):
    (i) an   kāmà ɓàrāwòn
        4.PF catch thief.DD
        'the thief has been caught' (lit. 'one has caught the thief')
According to Schuh (p.c.), the Hausa grade 7 verb form might be more accurately described as marking middle voice.

c. shī   (kàm),   yā   fàɗi hakà   *subject topic*
PRO.3ms PART 3ms.PF say this
'as for him, he said this'

d. sū   (kàm),   yā   gan sù   *object topic*
PRO.3pl PART 3ms.PF see PRO.3pl
'as for them, he saw them'

As (75c) shows, a 'subject topic' prohibits resumption in verbal clauses, but it is worth observing that subject topics require the full form of the INFL word (including the person agreement morpheme), e.g., *yanà* (3ms.IMPF) rather than Ø-*nà* (IMPF). The 'object topic' permits resumption (§ 4.2.2), as illustrated by example (75d).

This construction is also widespread in non-verbal clauses. Although subject pro-drop is licensed in non-verbal copular sentences, the presence of a subject pronoun is less marked in this type of construction, perhaps because the non-verbal copula does not carry person features. Compare the following examples. The construction illustrated by the (optional) presence of the independent pronoun in (76a) might be described as a 'double topic' construction, according to the analysis developed here.[18]

(76) a. Audù, (shī)   **fùr̃ôfēsà**   nē
Audu PRO.3ms professor FM.m
'As for Audu, he's a **professor**'

b. Audù, **fùr̃ôfēsà** nē   (shī)
Audu professor FM.m PRO.3ms
'As for Audu, he's a **professor**'

c. Audu, **shī**   nè   fùr̃ôfēsà
Audu PRO.3ms FM.m professor
'As for Audu, **he** is a professor'

In sum, according to Li & Thompson's typology, Hausa shows properties of both subject prominence and topic prominence. However, there are some striking differences between verbal clauses and non-verbal copular clauses. In particular, the absence of person features on the non-verbal copula entails that independent pronouns can function as less marked subjects. Furthermore, the surface coding (in terms of linear order) emphasises discourse configurationality (topic and focus) above subject–predicate

---

[18] Newman (2000: 162) distinguishes between topic pronouns and 'pleonastic independent pronouns', which add 'a degree of prominence':

(i) a. Sāni shī   mùtûm nē
    Sani PRO.3ms man   FM.m
    'Sani (he) is truly a man (i.e. is a truly decent person)'

    b. mutànên sū   wāwàyē nè
       men.DD PRO.3pl fools   FM.pl
       'the people (they) are fools indeed'

This type of construction lacks the pause intonation and the modal/adverbial particle that are characteristic of a topic construction.

structure in this type of construction. For example, observe that subject (*shī*) and predicate (*fùřòfēsa*) are reversed in (76b).

The fact that Hausa licenses null subjects can be explained by the presence of subject agreement morphemes within the INFL word (§ 2.3.2). Although there is evidence to suggest that these morphemes are historically incorporated pronominals (§ 5.3), the consensus in the descriptive literature that these morphemes are best described (synchronically) as agreement morphemes (despite the fact that they are often described as 'subject agreement pronouns') emerges from the fact that these morphemes can co-occur with a clause-internal subject (see Tuller 1986a: 91; Newman 2000: 564–7; Jaggar 2001: 415–16). However, the fact that Hausa is a null subject language entails that the presence of an overt subject is only required when the referent of that constituent is marked as discourse-prominent in some way, either because it is the topic, because it cannot be retrieved from context (presentational/new information focus), or because it stands in a relationship of exhaustive/contrastive focus with some other discourse-linked informa-tion. This pattern is most evident in the distribution of independent pronouns in verbal clauses. There are sound reasons, therefore, for describing Hausa subject and topic as points on a continuum rather than sharply distinct categories, a position that is consistent with historical analyses (Li & Thompson 1976; Schuh 1983b): subject agreement morphemes are gramma-ticalised subject pronouns, and subjects are grammaticalised topics.[19]

A number of properties displayed by the initial NP in canonical (NP NP FM) non-verbal copular sentences provide support for the topic–subject analysis in (57). Firstly, this noun phrase has to be definite (unless generic), a generalisation that is borne out by the unacceptability of example (37), repeated here as (77). The requirement for topics to be definite relates to the fact that they refer to identifiable entities, relating to discourse-old or given information (Chafe 1976b).

(77) #mùtûm   **ɗālìbī**   nè
      man   student.m   FM.m
      'a man is a **student**'

Observe that this requirement also explains why predicational copular sentences are not reversible. Example (41a) is repeated here as (78). In this type of construction, the predicate nominal is an indefinite noun phrase and cannot therefore occupy a position restricted to definite (referring and identifiable) noun phrases.

(78) *ɗālìbī   **Audù**   nē
      student.m Audu   FM.m
      'a student is **Audu**'

---

[19] See also Comrie (1988: 277), who describes topic and subject as 'endpoints of a chain of intermediate degrees of syntacticization'

Secondly, the initial NP in the canonical NP–NP–FM clause cannot be independently negated by means of consituent negation. The fact that topics cannot be negated follows from the fact that the function of a topic is to 'limit the applicability of the main predication to a certain restricted domain' (Chafe 1976b: 50), a function that is semantically incompatible with constituent negation.

(79) *bằ   mùtumìn ba   ɗālìbī   nè
     NEG   man.DD   NEG   student.m FM.m
     'not the man is a **student**'

According to the FP analysis, the ungrammaticality of example (79) follows from the fact that the NP *ɗālìbī* occupies the sole focus position in the clause. It is well known that constituent negation patterns together with focus. Consider the following examples:

(80) a. bằ **Audù** nē   dằřaktằ   NEG NP FM NP **NEG**
        NEG Audu   FM.m director
        ba (**Mūsā** nè)
        NEG Musa   FM.m
        '**Audu**'s not the director (**Musa** is)'
     b. bằ **Audù** ba nè   dằřaktằ   NEG NP **NEG** FM NP
        NEG Audu   NEG FM.m director
        Mūsā nè
        Mūsā FM.m
        '**Audu**'s not the director (**Musa** is)'

Example (80) shows that negation of the subject gives rise to the marked construction NP–FM–NP, where the negation morphemes either surround the clause as a whole (80a), or the subject NP (80b). According to Jaggar (2001: 498–9), the two constructions are synonymous. Compare (80) with (81):

(81) a. Audù bằ **malàmī** nè   ba   NP **NEG** NP FM **NEG**
        Audu NEG teacher   FM.m NEG
        (**likità** nē)
        doctor FM.m
        '**Audu**'s not a **teacher** (he's a **doctor**)' NP **NEG** NP **NEG** FM
     b. Audù bằ **malàmī** ba nè
        Audu NEG teacher   NEG FM.m
        (**likità** nē)
        doctor FM.m
        '**Audu**'s not a **teacher** (he's a **doctor**)'

The examples in (81) show that negation of the predicate maintains the canonical NP–NP–FM structure, because this construction places the predicate in focus. In this case, the two negation morphemes surround either the predicate

and the focus marker together (81a) or just the predicate NP (81b). According
to Jaggar (2001: 507), these constructions are also synonymous.

Thirdly, recall that an analysis like (57), in which constituents preceding
the focus position are treated as topics, posits a null pronoun in the small
clause that links the topic to its thematic or predicate nominal position. The
fact that topics generally permit resumption in Hausa predicts that this null
pronominal should be able to alternate with an overt resumptive pronoun.
Example (82) illustrates a clear case of a topic (observe that *Sābo* is
separated from the clause by a topic pause) that is coreferential not with a
null pronominal (*pro*) in the small clause, but with a phonetically realised
pronoun *shī* (Jaggar 2001: 539).

(82) Sābo, ai   **fùr̃ôfēsà** nē   shī
     Sabo PART professor   FM.m   PRO.3ms
     'Sabo, well he's a **professor**'

As the examples in (83) show, this pattern is also attested for that the
subject of the unmarked copular sentence. Jaggar (2001: 506) describes this
resumption strategy as follows: 'The … predicate noun or adjective can also
be futher emphasised by repreating the subject with an independent
pronoun in clause-final position.' Observe that *yārinyàtā* and *Audù* are
described as 'subject' in these examples because they are not separated from
the clause by a topic pause (see Newman (2000: 162) for further examples).

(83) a. yārinyàtā **dōguwā** cè   ita   (bà gàjēriyā ba)
        girl.1s   tall.f   FM.f PRO.3fs NEG short.f   NEG
        'my girlfriend is **tall** (not short)'
     b. Audù **dàr̃aktà** nē   shī   (bà ciyàmân ba)
        Audu director   FM.m PRO.3ms NEG chairman NEG
        'Audu is the **director** (not the chairman)'

The parallels between (82) and (83) in terms of resumption provide further
empirical support for the position that the 'subject' of the canonical copular
sentence occupies topic position, despite the fact that it lacks the pause
intonation that typifies topics in Hausa (§ 4.2.2). The examples in both (82)
and (83) therefore correspond to the structure that was given in (57), the
difference being that the topic is coreferential with an overt independent
pronoun in the subject position of the small clause, rather than a null
pronominal. In sum, there is considerable empirical support for an analysis
in which the constituent preceding the focus position is analysed as a topic.
As the discussion later in this chapter and in the next chapter will show, this
proposal is also consonant with other proposals that have been made in the
literature.[20]

---

[20] See the discussion of Basilico's (2003) analysis of English copular constructions in § 5.4.3
and Shlonsky's (2000a) analysis of Hebrew copular constructions in § 6.3.4.

Evidence of displacement

The FP analysis proposed in the previous subsection entails that all non-verbal copular constructions are derived by displacement. The empirical evidence in favour of this position relates to restrictions on multiple focus constructions and extraction restrictions. First, it is not possible to place the subject of canonical NP NP FM copular sentences in focus, as illustrated by the ungrammaticality of example (84):

(84) *mùtumìn nē ɗālìbī nè̄
     man.DD FM.m student.m FM.m
     'the man is **a student'**

The ungrammaticality of this example is explained on the same basis as the ungrammaticality of example (79). The restriction on multiple left-peripheral foci in Hausa means that there is only one designated left-peripheral focus position in the clause. According to the FP analysis, this position is occupied by the predicate in the canonical copular sentence: the NP *ɗālìbī* in example (84).

Secondly, as Tuller (1986a) observes, it is not possible to *wh*-front the subject of the canonical NP–NP–FM copular clause:

(85) *wā̀ sarkī nè̄ à gàrin nàn?   (Tuller 1986a:187)
     who emir FM.m in town.of here
     'who is the emir in this town?'

This restriction on extraction also follows from the FP analysis because a simplex copular clause only has a single focus position, and this position is always filled by the constituent left-adjacent to *nē/cē*. In other words, example (85) is ungrammatical because it represents an attempt to *wh*-raise the NP *wā̀* into the focus position already occupied by the NP *sarkī*. This unlicensed displacement is represented by the dotted arrow in (86).

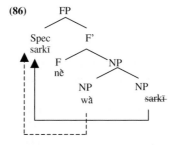

Compare example (87). According to the analysis developed here, this
example is grammatical because a single NP *wằnē* 'who' is *wh*-extracted to
the focus position, while the NP *sarkī* remains in its base position. The
structure for this example is shown in (88).

(87) wằnē   nề   sarkī à   gàrin   nàn?   (Tuller 1986a:188)
     who.m   FM.m emir   in   town.of here
     'who is the emir in this town?'

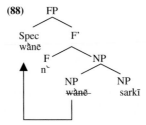

A similar explanation holds in the case of copular 'complement-taking
expressions', which select a subjunctive (irrealis) embedded clausal
complement, indicated by square brackets (89). Observe that if an NP is
focus fronted from within the clausal complement, the focus shifts from the
predicate adjective *dōlè* 'necessary' to that NP (89b). Example (89c) shows
that multiple foci are not possible in this construction (Newman 2000: 165).

(89) a. **dōlè**   nē   [Audù yà   àuri   Bintà]
        necessary   FM.m Audu   3ms.SUB marry   Binta
        'it is **necessary** for Audu to marry Binta'
     b. **Audù** nē dōlè   [Audù yà   àuri   Bintà]
        Audu   FM.m necessary 3ms.SUB marry Binta
        'it is necessary for **Audu** to marry Binta'
     c. *Audù nē   dōlè   nē   [Audù yà   àuri   Bintà]
        Audu   FM.m necessary FM.m 3ms.SUB marry Binta
        'it is **necessary** for **Audu** to marry Binta'

These data suggest a structure in which the adjective *dōlè* selects a clausal
(IP) complement. In (89a), *dōlè* raises to the focus position, as shown in
(90). In (89b), *Audù* raises to the focus position, as shown in (91). The fact
that multiple foci are not permitted (89c) suggests that this construction
only has a single focus position (that is, the clausal (IP) complement is not
dominated by its own FP).

Perhaps unexpectedly, this restriction does not appear to hold in the case
of negated complement-taking expressions (92a), nor in the case of *wh*-
extraction (92b) (Newman 2000: 165, 104). These constructions therefore

appear to fall outside the generalisations that hold for most Hausa focus/
wh-constructions.[21]

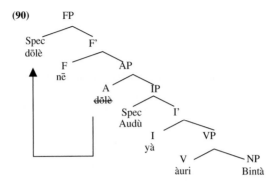

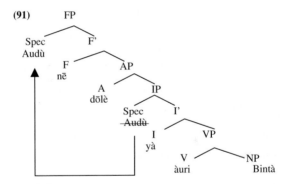

(92) a. **Audù** nē   bà̀   dōlè   ba   nè̀ yà   àuri   Bintà
        Audu FM.m   NEG necessary NEG FM.m 3ms.SUB marry Binta
        'it is not necessary for **Audu** to marry Binta'

     b. dàgà wā̀nḕ nè̀ dōlè   (nḕ) mù   kàr̃6i kuɗin
        from who   FM.m necessary FM.m 1pl.SUB take   money.of
        hàr̃ājìn?
        tax.DD
        'from whom must we take the tax money?'

Finally, recall that focus/*wh*-fronting in embedded verbal clauses gives rise
to island effects (§ 4.3). In other words, if a constituent is extracted to the
embedded focus position, it is not possible to extract another constituent

---

[21] Russell Schuh (p.c.) suggests that the examples in (92) may not be universally acceptable.

from the embedded clause and raise it to the matrix focus position. This is
illustrated by the ungrammaticality of example (93).

(93) *Àli (nè)   mukà   san   (Tuller 1986a: 55; my gloss)
     Ali FM.m   1pl.FOC.PF know
     [wà A̶l̶i̶   zâi   àurā w̶à̶]
     who   FUT. 3ms   marry
     'we know who **Ali** will marry'

The extension of the FP analysis to non-verbal copular constructions predicts
that there should also be a restriction on extraction from embedded non-
verbal copular clauses, given the premise that non-verbal copular clauses are
derived by displacement of a consituent to the left-peripheral focus position.
However, as example (94) illustrates, this prediction is not borne out.

(94) wà   sukà   cê   [sarkī nè   (Tuller 1986a: 187)
     who   3pl.FOC.PF say emir   FM.m
     w̶à̶   s̶a̶r̶k̶ī̶ à   gàrin nàn]?
     in   town.of   here
     'who did they say the emir is in this town?'

Perhaps related is the fact is that long-distance (successive cyclic) extraction
is not licensed in non-verbal copular sentences, as illustrated by example
(95), which is ungrammatical with or without *nè* in the embedded clause.

(95) *w̶à̶(̶n̶ē̶)̶(nè)   sukà   cê [w̶à̶(̶n̶ē̶)̶ (nè) [w̶à̶(̶n̶ē̶)̶ sarkī   à
     who(m)(FM.m) 3pl.FOC.PF say   (FM.m)   emir   in
     gàrin   nàn]]?
     town.of here
     'who did they say is the emir in this town?'

In this example, the predicate NP *sarkī* remains in its base position in the
small clause, and the NP *wà(nē)* 'who (m)' raises first to the embedded focus
position (left-adjacent to *nè*) and then to the matrix focus position. Recall
that long-distance (successive cyclic) extraction is licensed in verbal
sentences (§ 4.3.3).

As Tuller (1986a: 185) observes, the copula is a clitic, which entails that it
requires a phonologically overt consituent to attach to. While the focus
marking copula is optional in verbal clauses, it is required to license
predication or equation in non-verbal clauses, but cannot be stranded due
to its clitic status. This explains why successive cyclic extraction is not
licensed in non-verbal copular sentences like (95), in which the copula is
stranded without an overt constituent in its specifier position.

This explanation might also be extended to account for the absence of
island constraints in non-verbal copular sentences. Example (94) would not
be grammatical without the focus-marking copula in the embedded clause
because there would not be an embedded clause without it, but neither can

it be stranded without an overt constituent in its specifier. In other words, the function of the non-verbal copula in licensing predication or equation in non-verbal clauses, together with its clitic status, takes precedence over constraints on extraction. The fact that the parallels between the verbal and non-verbal FP constructions diverge in this respect can therefore be explained by the 'less grammaticalised' status of the focus-marking copula in non-verbal clauses.

In sum, although some questions remain, there is considerable empirical evidence in favour of extending the FP analysis to Hausa non-verbal copular constructions, given that the FP analysis provides an explanatory account not only of the information packaging properties of these constructions but also of their syntactic properties.[22]

5.4.3 *Theoretical issues*

In this section, the analysis of Hausa non-verbal copular sentences developed in this chapter is set within its broader theoretical context, and its advantages are evaluated against alternative proposals in the literature relating to the structure of copular sentences both in Hausa and in other languages.

The IP analysis

Recall that Tuller (1986a) develops an analysis of focus fronting in Hausa that entails movement of the focused constituent to the specifier position of the left-peripheral complementiser phrase (CP) (§ 4.3). Tuller does not, however, link *nē/cē/nē* in copular constructions to those in focus fronting constructions, beyond stating that they are 'isomorphic' and historically may have been focus markers (Tuller 1986a: 54, 188). Tuller analyses *nē/cē/ nē* in copular constructions as a 'defective' form of INFL, drawing support for this analysis from the claim that *nē/cē/nē* and imperfective INFL are in complementary distribution with respect to the category of their comple- ments (Tuller 1986a: 184–5):[23]

(96) a. Ā'ìshā tanà   kaɽàntà   ƙùr'ānī   *VNP complement*
        Aisha 3fs.IMPF read.VN   Koran
        'Aisha is reading the Koran'
    b. yârā   sunà   cikin   kàntī   *PP complement*
        children 3pl.IMPF inside.of shop
        'the children are inside the shop'

---

[22] An investigation of the prosodic properties of canonical and marked copular constructions is expected to reveal the extent to which the FP analysis provides the most explanatory account of these constructions (Green, in preparation).

[23] Tuller's analysis is similar in spirit to Doron's (1986) analysis of the Hebrew pronominal copula (§ 6.3.4).

   c. Ā'ìshā   **mālàmā**   cè   *NP complement*
      Aisha   teacher.f   FM.f
      'Aisha is a **teacher**'
   d. littāfìn   **sābō**   nè   *AP complement*
      book.DD   new.m   FM.m
      'the book is **new**'

Tuller attributes the clause-final position of $n\bar{e}/c\bar{e}/n\bar{e}$ to its clitic status, of which polar tone is indicative. Tuller describes $n\bar{e}/c\bar{e}/n\bar{e}$ as a 'defective' INFL because it has gender marking but no tense/aspect/mood or person features, and suggests that it is generated under INFL, where it assigns a thematic role to the complement predicational AP/NP, and undergoes affix-hopping to cliticise to this element. The proposed structure is shown in (97) (adapted from Tuller 1986a: 385)

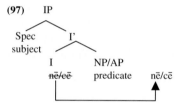

The advantage of this analysis is that it explains why the imperfective INFL word is not generally licensed to co-occur in a non-verbal clause with the non-verbal copula. However, there are a number of problems with this analysis. First, imperfective INFL and the non-verbal copula are not in strictly complementary distribution. Although Tuller describes imperfective INFL as licensing VP complements, it is only licensed to take a nominalised VNP complement (Jaggar 2001: 168–72). In addition, recall from Chapter 2 (§ 2.3.3) that the imperfective INFL is also licensed to occur with NP complements, in addition to its co-occurrence with the stative deverbal adverbial.[24]

  (98) a. Bintà   tanà̀   dà   mōtà   *possessive PP*
        Binta   3fs.IMPF   with   car
        'Binta has a car'
      b. Bintà   tanà̀   gidā   *locative NP*
        Binta   3fs.IMPF   house
        'Binta is at home'

---

[24] The deverbal adverbial stative in example (98c) is derived from the verb by the substitution of the final vowel with the suffix -*e*, and all low tones to the left of the suffix. See Jaggar (2001: 651–6).

  c. Bintà tanằ   zàune   kân kujềrā   *stative deverbal AdvP*
     Binta 3fs.IMPF sit.STAT on chair
     'Binta is sat on a chair'

  d. Bintà tanằ   mālàmā   à lōkàcîn   *'equational-like' NP*
     Binta 3fs.IMPF teacher(f) at time.DD
     'Binta was a teacher at the time'

As example (99) illustrates, it is also possible for the imperfective INFL (TAM) to take an adjectival complement, although as Jaggar (2001: 473) observes, the constructions in which imperfective INFL takes a nominal or adjectival complement are 'syntactically much more restricted than the widespread copula-linked constructions'.

(99) à lōkàcîn tanằ   ƙàramī
     at time.DD 3fs.IMPF small
     'at the time she was small'

Thus, while the imperfective INFL licenses a relatively wide range of categories as its complement, it cannot take a verbal complement. The non-verbal copula shows a narrower distribution, being licensed in Standard Hausa to occur only with NP and AP predicates. Like the imperfective INFL, it does not license a verbal predicate, but neither does it license a VNP complement. It is also worth observing that although the non-verbal copula is restricted to NP and AP predicates in Standard Hausa, Tuller (1986a: 219–20) points out that speakers of northern (e.g. Niger Hausa) dialects prefer the non-verbal copula over the imperfective INFL with PP predicates expressing permanent states:

(100)a. Kanồ à ƙasan   Nàjēr̃iyà nē   (Tuller 1986a: 219)
       Kano at land.of Nigeria FM.m
       'Kano is in Nigeria'

    b. gidansù   à wani kwar̃ì mài fāɗī   nề (Tuller 1986a: 220)
       house.of.3pl at SID   valley POSS width FM.m
       'their house is in a wide valley'

Finally, there is one striking exception to the generalisation that that the non-verbal copula and INFL do not co-occur in non-verbal clauses. Despite the constraints on extraction from copular sentences that were described earlier in this section, as Tuller (1986a) observes, relativisation from a simplex non-verbal copular sentence is licensed. According to Tuller, the non-verbal copula *nē/cē/nē* is not licensed to occur in this construction, which conditions in its place the presence of what Jaggar (2001: 532) calls the 'pro-relative' TAM *yakè*. Jaggar (2001: 532) describes the pro-relative TAM as a 'dummy element'. Observe that the TAM morpheme in this element *kè* has the short vowel that characterises the focus imperfective TAM form that occurs with non-verbal complements (§ 2.3.3).

(101) mùtumìn dà yakè   sarkī   (Tuller 1986a: 189)
man.DD   REL PRO.REL emir
'the man that is emir... '

However, the following examples show that relativisation is licensed in *nē/cē/nē* constructions (Jaggar 2001: 532–3).

(102) a. habà, yāròn dà shī   ɗan-sakandàr̃è   nē?
       INTER boy.DD REL PRO.3ms son.of-secondary.school FM.m
       'come on, a boy who's a secondary school student?'
     b. diyyàr̃   dà ita   cē mafi yawà   à tār̃īhì
       compensation REL PRO.3fs FM.f most amount in history
       'the compensation which is the most in history'

Verbal relative clauses in Hausa tend not to contain resumptive pronouns, at least for subject relatives (Jaggar 2001: 533). Observe, however, that the examples in (102) contain independent pronouns inside the non-verbal relative clause, coreferential with the head noun. Although Tuller (1986a: 188–9) suggests that the pro-relative TAM substitutes for the non-verbal copula *nē/cē* in cases of relativisation, the following examples show that the pro-relative TAM may co-occur with the non-verbal copula, which shows number/gender agreement with the subject and/or predicate of the copular clause. The pro-relative TAM may or may not show agreement with the head noun. Compare (103b) with (103c) (Jaggar 2001: 462).

(103) a. habà, yāròn dà yakè   shī
       INTER boy.DD REL PRO.REL.3ms PRO.3ms
       ɗan-sakandàr̃è   nē?
       son.of-secondary.school   FM.m
       'come on, a boy who's a secondary school student?'
     b. yârân   dà yakè   'yan   mahàutā nè
       boys.DD REL PRO.REL.3ms children.of butchers FM.pl
       'boys who are children of butchers'
     c. yârân   dà sukè   'yan   mahàutā nè
       boys.DD REL PRO.REL.3pl children.of butchers FM.pl
       'boys who are children of butchers'
     d. shī   dà yakè   bà Mùsùlmī ba
       PRO.3ms REL PRO.REL.3ms NEG Muslim   NEG
       'he who is not a Muslim'
     e. yārinyàr̃ dà yakè/takè   'yar̃   mahàucī cē
       girl.DD   REL PRO.REL.3ms/3fs daughter.of butcher FM.f
       'a girl who is a butcher's daughter'

To recapitulate, there are three possible constructions that relativise out of non-verbal clauses: one in which the pro-relative TAM substitutes for the non-verbal copula (104a), one in which the non-verbal copula occurs without the pro-relative TAM (104b), and one in which the pro-relative TAM and the non-verbal copula co-occur (104c). Although resumption is usually dispreferred in subject relatives, it is preferred in the latter two construction types.

(104) a. yāròn   dà   yakè   ɗan-sakandàr̃ḕ
      boy.DD   REL   PRO.REL   son.of-secondary.school
      'a boy who's a secondary school student'

    b. yāròn   dà   shī   ɗan-sakandàr̃ḕ   nē
      boy.DD   REL   PRO.3ms   son.of-secondary.school   FM.m
      'a boy who's a secondary school student'

    c. yāròn   dà   yakè   shī   ɗan-sakandàr̃ḕ   nē
      boy.DD   REL   PRO.REL   PRO.3ms   son.of-secondary.school   FM.m
      'a boy who's a secondary school student'

The structure of these examples is not discussed here, since no analysis of relative clauses is proposed in this book. However, the existence of non-verbal constructions such as these in which an INFL word co-occurs with the non-verbal copula casts further doubt on Tuller's analysis of the non-verbal copula as a form of INFL.

Although the imperfective INFL and the non-verbal copula do not occur in strictly complementary distribution, the fact that both occur in non-verbal clauses suggests that they share an overlapping role in terms of licensing predication, a fact that explains Tuller's approach in treating both as types of INFL. However, the fact that neither the imperfective INFL nor the non-verbal copula is licensed to co-occur with a VP predicate suggests the alternative perspective: the imperfective INFL is more like a non-verbal copula in its distribution than the non-verbal copula is like a form of INFL. These comments notwithstanding, the most striking differences between the imperfective INFL and the non-verbal copula in terms of distribution are that that only the former licenses VNP and PP predicates, while the latter does not. As Tuller (1986a: 184) points out, the Hausa non-verbal copula is restricted to [+ N] complements.[25] In traditional terms, while the Hausa non-verbal copula may occur with a subject predicative complement, it may not occur with an adverbial complement. It is worth observing that Hausa falls within the most common typological pattern in this regard (§ 6.3.1). Some suggestions are made later in this section regarding this restriction on predication (Basilico 2003).

Finally, Tuller's analysis also overlooks a striking empirical fact, namely that there is a designated focus position in the Hausa non-verbal copular

---

[25] In the Chomskyan tradition, the major categories noun, verb, adjective and preposition have been argued to represent combinations of the two basic category features [+/− N] and [+/− V], according to which nouns are [+ N, −V], verbs are [−N, + V], adjectives are [+ N, + V] and prepositions are [−N, −V]. These feature matrices represent an attempt to generalise over the distributional properties of the major categories. See Chomsky (1965).

construction, a fact that is suggestive of a unified (or at least partially unified) analysis of the non-verbal copula in both non-verbal and verbal (focus/*wh*) constructions. In sum, the grounds for analysing the non-verbal copula as a type of INFL are minimal in comparison to the grounds for analysing it as a copular focus marker that also licenses predication and equation in non-verbal clauses.

However, the question that naturally arises as this juncture is whether there are grounds for incorporating an inflectional layer into the analysis of non-verbal copular clauses in addition to the focus layer. In particular, questions arise concerning case and agreement in the non-verbal clause, properties that are typically associated with the IP (TP) layer in the Chomskyan framework (§ 3.2.3). First, null arguments are generally thought to be licensed by rich inflectional properties of the verbal-inflectional complex that allow their content to be recovered. It is not clear what licenses the recovery of null pronominal elements in the small clause in the absence of an inflectional layer (recall (57), for example). Secondly, recall that subject (nominative) case licensing is usually characterised in terms of raising to the specifier of IP (TP) (§ 3.2.3). From this perspective, it is not clear how nominal elements stranded in the small clause are case-licensed (recall (62), for example). Finally, recall example (8), which shows that the non-verbal copula may agree in number and gender with the subject/topic of the canonical NP–NP–FM construction. Agreement is also a feature typically associated with the inflectional layer. Although the typical pattern in spoken Hausa is for agreement to occur between the non-verbal copula and its left-adjacent focused constituent (see Curnow 2000), the fact that examples like (8) are attested nevertheless requires explanation.

One possible solution to these theoretical concerns is to incorporate an inflectional layer into the structure of the non-verbal copular clause. Consider the structure shown in (105).

(105)

FP

TOP   FP

Spec   F'

F'   IP

Spec   I'

I   NP

NP   NP/AP

In this structure, the small clause that represents the thematic (subject–predicate) core of the non-verbal clause is dominated by an inflectional layer, which in turn is dominated by the left-peripheral focus projection. The incorporation of this additional structure provides a partial solution to the issues raised above. First, if the null pronominal subject in (57) raised to the specifier of IP, it would be in the canonical position for subject agreement features to be realised, in principle enabling the recovery of its person/number/gender properties. Secondly, if the small clause subject *Audù* raised to the specifier of IP in (62), it would be in the canonical position for the licensing of nominative case. A similar line of reasoning might account for examples like (8), given the assumption that the clause-initial topic-subject is coreferential with a pronominal element in the specifier of IP, together with the assumption that there is a head–agreement relation along the lines of the analysis developed in the previous chapter to account for special inflection (§ 4.5). Given both assumptions, the agreement between the non-verbal copula and the clause-initial topic-subject might be mediated by the link between the head F and the INFL head, so that specifier–head agreement between INFL and the (null) pronominal in its specifier is spelled out (for some speakers) on the F head.

An analysis along the lines of the one sketched in (105) relies primarily on theory-internal rather than empirical motivations. The fact that Hausa non-verbal copular sentences lack independent tense/aspect/mood (TAM) properties mediates against the inclusion of an IP (or TP) layer in the structure, not only because of the absence of overt TAM morphology but also because of the absence of semantic TAM features that might plausibly license nominative case. The alternative to the analysis in (105) is to assume that null pronominals are licensed in non-verbal clauses by their anaphoric link either to the clause-external topic or to referents mentioned earlier in the discourse, and that case is licensed inside the small clause. This issue is left open here.

The predicate raising analysis

At this juncture, it is useful to broaden the discussion by setting the present analysis of Hausa non-verbal copular sentences within a wider theoretical context. There are a a number of well-known proposals concerning the underlying structure of copular sentences in various languages, which can be grouped together as types of predicate raising analyses (e.g. Heggie 1988; 1992; Moro 1990; 1997). Predicate raising analyses share the assumption that both predicative and equative (specificational) copular sentences are derived from a small clause subject–predicate structure from which either subject or predicate is raised (the latter case deriving inverse equative sentences). However, different versions of the predicate raising analysis posit different functional projections above the small clause, and may differ with respect to whether the displacement operation that derives copular sentences targets an argument (A) position or a non-argument (A') position. The FP analysis of Hausa non-verbal copular sentences is essentially a version of the predicate raising analysis. Because the FP analysis entails that Hausa copular sentences are derived by movement of the focused constituent to a non-argument position, as well as the presence of a topic subject in canonical NP–NP–FM copular sentences, the diagnostics that reveal A' movement in other languages might also be expected to apply to the Hausa case.

In her well-known Ph.D. dissertation, Heggie (1988) adopts Stowell's (1978) proposal that the English copula *be* is a raising verb that takes a small clause complement: a subject–predicate structure that lacks tense, aspect or mood properties. Heggie (1992) provides a summary of the analysis, according to which copular sentences have the structure shown in (106).

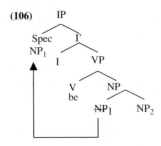

(106)

Heggie (1992: 06) states that the 'subject–predicate configuration' represented by the small clause (NP) adjunction structure underlies both 'identity' and 'equative' copular sentences (both specificational, in Declerck's terms), in addition to predicational copular sentences. In order to derive the [NP *be* NP] order, NP_1 raises to the specifier of IP, a displacement that is motivated by case-licensing of the subject NP in this position. Of course, the inclusion of an inflectional layer and a VP is uncontroversial in the English case, since the English copula is a verb and therefore participates in case and agreement relations in the same way as other verbs do in the language.

As Heggie points out, this analysis is uncontroversial for predicational copular sentences, but requires justification for equative (specificational) copular sentences. Heggie provides a number of arguments in support of the view that NP_2 is also a predicate in equative sentences, among them the fact that NP_2 cannot be clefted (107c), which shows that it is not an argument, despite the fact that it may be a referring expression.[26]

---

[26] Observe that Heggie's equative sentence in (107a) would be classified as descriptionally identifying in Declerck's typology (cf. examples (26) and (27) above).

(107) a. that man over there is Ronald Reagan   (Heggie 1992: 110)
      b. it's that man over there that is Ronald Reagan
      c. *it's Ronald Reagan that that man over there is

Heggie adopts a relative clause-type analysis for cleft constructions, which are derived by raising a null operator to the embedded specifier of CP. The null operator relies upon the clefted NP for identification. According to this analysis, (107c) is ungrammatical because it represents an attempt to raise a constituent (as null operator) that originates in predicate position at deep structure. Because this constituent is a theta role assigner rather than a theta role receiver, it cannot corefer with the clefted NP, and this gives rise to an ungrammatical sentence.

Heggie further observes that neither NP can be clefted in inverse equative constructions, as illustrated by example (108).

(108) a. Ronald Reagan is that man over there   (Heggie 1992:110)
      b. *it's Ronald Reagan that is that man over there
      c. *it's that man over there that Ronald Reagan is

According to Heggie's analysis, inverse equatives like (108a) are derived by raising NP₂ (the predicate) to the specifier of CP, which triggers the raising of the verb in the INFL position to C, stranding the underlying NP₁ in clause-final position (109).

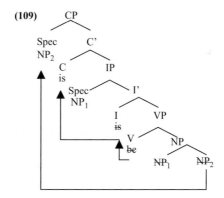

The movement of NP₂ to the specifier of CP creates an island from which no further extraction is licensed (because the specifier of CP is filled), hence the ungrammaticality of examples (108b) and (108c). In sum, Heggie's analysis derives predicational and canonical equative sentences by raising NP₁ to the specifier of IP (106), while inverse equatives also involve the subsequent raising of NP₂ to the spedifier of CP (109).

Like Heggie, Heycock (1992) also adopts a predicate raising analysis of inverse copular constructions, according to which the small clause subject remains in situ and the small clause predicate raises to the specifier of IP.[27] According to this view, both the canonical copular sentence in (110a) and the inverse copular sentence in (110b) are derived from the same underlying structure, represented in (110c), in which 'e' represents the empty SpecIP position (Heycock 1992: 99).[28]

(110) a. the Prime Minister is the real problem   *canonical*
      b. the real problem is the Prime Minister   *inverse*
      c. [IP e [VP is [NP [NP the Prime Minister] [NP the real problem]]]]

Heycock (1992: 99) proposes (111) as the structure for an inverse sentence like (110b):

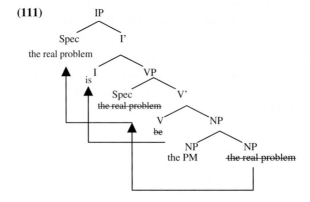

Note that this analysis assumes that *the Prime Minister* is the underlying subject. The fact that the predicate raises first to the specifier of VP and then to the specifier of IP defines this as an instance of A-movement. In this

---

[27] Heycock draws no clear distinction between predicational and specificational/equational copular sentences, although, as Declerck (1998) observes, only sentences of the latter type are reversible (§ 5.2.2).

[28] Heycock (1994: 224–5) observes that while either NP can be focused (prosodically prominent) in the canonical copular construction (i), only the postcopular NP can be focused in the inverse construction (ii):

(i) a.   A: was the culprit John or Bill?
          B: **John** was the culprit   *canonical*
     b.   A: was John the culprit or the victim?
          B: John was the **culprit**   *canonical*
(ii) a.   A: was the culprit John or Bill?
          B: the culprit was **John**   *inverse*
     b.   A: was John the culprit or the victim?
          B: *the **culprit** was John   *inverse*

respect Heycock's analysis of inverse copular sentences departs from Heggie's, since Heggie argues that the pre-copular NP in an inverse equative occupies the specifier of CP, a non-argument position. Heycock's position receives support from the fact that this movement can feed further A-movement, for example if the same NP goes on to raise to subject position of a raising verb like *seem* as in (112) (Heycock 1992: 99).

(112)   the real problem seems to be the Prime Minister

The grammaticality of examples like (112) supports Heycock's analysis because movement from a non-argument position (like the specifier of CP) to an argument position (like the specifier of IP) is ruled out as 'improper movement' on the basis that the head of a case-marked (A') chain cannot move into a case position (specifier of IP). In addition, Heycock (1992: 101) points out a number of additional problems with Heggie's claim that NP_2 raises to the specifier of CP in inverse equatives.

First, the CP analysis incorrectly predicts that inverse equatives should not occur as embedded clauses selected by a complementiser (113a). Secondly, the CP analysis incorrectly predicts that inverse equatives should not be selected by 'exceptional case marking' (ECM) verbs like *believe*, which license accusative case on the embedded subject (113b). Thirdly, the CP analysis also incorrectly predicts that inverse equatives should not allow (further) subject–auxiliary inversion, because this operation has already applied in order to derive the inverse equative (113c).[29]

(113)a. people are speculating about whether the cause of the problem is the Prime Minister
      b. I believe the cause of the problem to be the Prime Minister
      c. was the cause of the problem the Prime Minister?

The FP analysis proposed in this chapter to account for Hausa non-verbal copular sentences is essentially a version of the predicate raising analysis in the sense that a single underlying small clause structure is proposed, from which either NP_1 'subject' or NP_2 'predicate' (in the case of equatives) can be extracted to the focus position. The most striking difference between the FP analysis and the analyses of English copular sentences reviewed in this section is that the Hausa analysis posits extraction to FP instead of either CP or IP. The reasons for rejecting a CP analysis in favour of an FP analysis of focus fronting were addressed in Chapter 4 (§ 4.3), arguments

---

[29] More recently, while Moro (1997; 2000) maintains the predicate raising analysis, Heycock and Kroch (1999) posit distinct underlying structures for predicational and equative sentences. They argue that inverse copular sentences are a subtype of equatives, since they pattern with equatives in relation to extraction, and that predicational and equative sentences might therefore distinguished in syntactic structure by distinct types of small clause. The equative small clause is argued to involve the projection of a null functional head, which the predicational small clause lacks.

that apply equally to non-verbal copular sentences. As discussed above, the absence of an IP layer in the FP analysis of Hausa non-verbal copular sentences can be motivated on the basis that these constructions lack tense/aspect/mood (TAM) features, as well as by the rejection of Tuller's (1986a) proposal that the Hausa non-verbal copula is a defective form of INFL. Despite these differences, extraction to the specifier of FP is extraction to a non-argument position, which entails that Hausa non-verbal copular constructions should show properties of A' movement. Furthermore, canonical NP NP FM constructions involve subjects in topic position under the present analysis, also a non-argument position.

A number of Heycock's diagnostics (113) do not apply in the Hausa case. For example, Hausa lacks infinitival clauses and therefore lacks ECM constructions (113b).[30] In addition, Hausa lacks subject–auxiliary inversion (113c). Furthermore, the fact that focus/*wh*-fronting constructions can be embedded under a complementiser was one of the motivations for rejecting a CP analysis in favour of the FP analysis, an argument that applies equally to non-verbal copular sentences. Examples (114a) and (114c) show embedded canonical NP NP FM equative copular sentences, and examples (114b) and (114d) their marked NP FM NP counterparts.

(114) a. Kànde tanà   tsàmmānì̀ cêwā Aishà **'yar̃**   **mahàucī** cè
      Kande 3fs.IMPF think.VN   that Aisha daughter.of butcher FM.f
      'Kande thinks that Aisha is **the butcher's daughter**'

   b. Kànde tanà   tsàmmānì̀ cêwā **Aishà** cè 'yar̃   mahàucī
      Kande 3fs.IMPF think.VN   that Aisha FM.f daughter.of butcher
      'Kande thinks that **Aisha** is the butcher's daughter'

   c. Kànde tanà   tsàmmānì̀ cêwā 'yar̃   mahàucī **Aishà** cè
      Kande 3fs.IMPF think.VN   that daughter.of butcher Aisha FM.f
      'Kande thinks that the butcher's daughter is **Aisha**'

   d. Kànde tanà   tsàmmānì̀ cêwā **'yar̃**   **mahàucī** cè Aishà
      Kande 3fs.IMPF think.VN   that daughter.of butcher FM.f Aisha
      'Kande thinks that **the butcher's daughter** is Aisha'

It remains to consider raising constructions in Hausa. According to Tuller (1986a), although Hausa has what may be described as raising predicates in the sense that they have a non-thematic subject (115a), it does not for the most part have raising constructions, as the ungrammaticality of examples (115b) and (115c) demonstrates. According to Tuller, this restriction relates to the absence of infinitival clauses in Hausa: the embedded subject is case-licensed in the embedded clause, therefore raising is blocked.

---

[30] As Tuller (1986a: 27) points out, the subjunctive clause, which performs the functions of the English embedded infinitival clause, licenses nominative case. See also Jaggar (2001: 187).

(115)a. yā   kàmātà   Aishà tà   (Tuller 1986a: 17)
         3ms.PF be.necessary Aisha 3fs.SUB
         gamà   aikìntà
         finish work.of.3fs
         'it is necessary for Aisha to finish her work'
     b. *Aishà tà   gamà aikìntà   yā   (Tuller 1986a: 17)
         Aisha 3fs.SUB finish work.of.3fs 3ms.PF
         kàmātà
         be.necessary
         'that Aisha finish her work is necessary'
     c. *Aishà tā   kàmātà   tà   gamà aikìntà
         Aisha 3fs.PF be.necessary 3fs.SUB finish work.of.3fs
         'Aisha must finish her work'

Non-verbal copular sentences allow raising, albeit marginally. Consider the
following examples (adapted fromTuller 1986a: 190).[31]

(116)a. yā   kasàncē Kànde 'yaȓ   **mahàucī** cè̀
         3ms.PF happen Kande daughter.of butcher FM.f
         'it happens that Kande is **the butcher's daughter**'
     b. Kànde tā   kasàncē 'yaȓ   **mahàucī** cè̀
         Kande 3fs.PF happen daughter.of butcher FM.f
         'Kande happens to be **the butcher's daughter**'
(117)a. yā   kasàncē 'yaȓ   mahàucī   **Kànde** cè̀
         3ms.PF happen daughter.of butcher   Kande FM.f
         'it happens that the butcher's daughter is **Kande**'
     b. 'yaȓ   mahàucī tā   kasàncē **Kànde** cè̀
         daughter.of butcher 3fs.PF happen Kande FM.f
         'the butcher's daughter happens to be **Kande**'

As the grammaticality of the examples in (116) and (117) demonstrates, this
raising process is optional. Unlike raising in English, it cannot therefore be
driven by case licensing. Observe however that in both (116b) and (117b) it
is not the focused constituent that raises, but the topic subject. This follows
from the fact that it is only by occupying the position left-adjacent to the
non-verbal copula that a constituent is marked as focused. A constituent
cannot therefore be extracted from that position without losing its focus

---

[31] Tuller (1986a: 190–91) claims that her analysis of *nē/cē/nē* as a cliticising INFL explains why
raising of the subject of a copular clause is possible: because *nē/cē/nē* cliticisation takes place
at surface structure, the embedded subject has no governor in the lower clause, but is
governed within the matrix clause. The embedded subject is therefore permitted to raise to
the matrix IP, where its trace is still bound and governed within the matrix clause (the
governing category). It is worth making explicit that examples like (89) do not involve
raising in the sense intended here (raising to subject), since theses examples involve raising to
the focus position.

interpretation, which rules out the analysis in which, for example, (117b) is derived from (116a), with focus remaining on *'yar mahàucī*.

This being so, the question of raising from the embedded specifier of FP to the matrix specifier of IP does not arise, but the analysis entails that a noun phrase can raise from embedded topic–subject position to matrix subject position, a proposal that is consistent with a recent analysis of small clauses developed by Basilico (2003). Basilico's discussion rests on the differences between adjectival and verbal small clauses in English, illustrated by (118a) and (118b), respectively. The small clause is indicated by square brackets.

(118) a. we consider [the guard intelligent]   (Basilico 2003: 1)
      b. we saw [the guard leave]

The subject of the adjectival small clause can raise to matrix subject position of both passivised verbs (119a) and raising verbs (119b).

(119) a. the prisoner is considered [~~the prisoner~~   (Basilico 2003: 2)
         intelligent]
      b. the prisoner seems [~~the prisoner~~ intelligent]

In contrast, the subject of the verbal small clause cannot raise in either case:

(120) a. *the prisoner was seen [~~the prisoner~~ leave]   (Basilico 2003: 2)
      b. *the prisoner seems [~~the prisoner~~ leave every day at noon]

According to Basilico, the syntactic differences between adjectival and verbal small clauses relate to the fact that each type of small clause involves a different type of predication: adjectival clauses involve categorical predication, which means that the subject is 'singled out' as topic, and the predicate provides information about that subject. Nominal small clauses involve the same kind of predication, and also allow raising:

(121) a. we consider [the governor a fool]   (Basilico 2003: 4)
      b. the governor is considered [~~the governor~~ a fool]

In contrast, verbal small clauses involve thetic predication: the subject is not singled out as a topic, but is introduced as a participant in the event described by the predicate. In this case, both subject and predicate provide new information.[32]

Basilico points out that while individual-level predicates involve categorical predication, stage-level predicates involve thetic predication. The differences between individual and stage-level predication has been explored by Diesing (1992), among others, and relates to the relative permanence or otherwise of the property/event expressed by the predicate.

---

[32] See Basilico (2003: 3) for sources on categorical versus thetic predication.

While individual-level predicates typically express permanent properties like *intelligent*, stage-level predicates typically express temprorary properties or events, for example eventive predicates like *leave* (see Basilico 2003: 24, n. 13). As Diesing (1992) observes, bare plural subjects of individual level/categorical predicates receive a generic interpretation:

(122) the guard considers [prisoners intelligent]   (Basilico 2003: 4)

In contrast, bare plural subjects of stage level/thetic predicates receive an existential intepretation:

(123) the guard saw [prisoners leave]   (Basilico 2003: 4)

Diesing (1992) argues that these semantic differences relate to the syntactic position of the subject. She argues that individual level subjects are VP-external, occupying the surface subject position, and do not therefore permit sub-extraction. The constraint on sub-extraction from subjects is known as the subject constraint (see Kayne 1984; Stowell 1991). Consider example (124), in which the *wh*-phrase *who* cannot be extracted from within the small clause subject:

(124) *who did you find [[a photograph of ~~who~~]   (Basilico 2003: 5)
       rather unattractive]?

In contrast, Diesing (1992) argues that stage-level subjects are VP-internal. Because they do not occupy surface subject position, the Subject Constraint does not apply. In example (125), the *wh*-phrase *which planet* is extracted from within the small clause subject:

(125) which planet did you see [a picture of   (Basilico 2003: 5)
      ~~which planet~~ appear on your computer screen]?

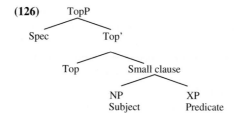

Basilico proposes that the predicational core of the small clause is dominated by a topic phrase (TopP). This structure is shown in (126). Basilico extends Diesing's insights concerning the structural position of the subject to the small clause structure by proposing that the subject of the adjectival/nominal small clause raises to the specifier of the topic phrase (hence the categorical predication). This structure is shown in (127).

(127)

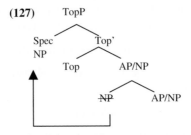

In contrast, Basilico argues that the subject of the verbal small clause remains in situ, as shown in (128). In this case, the specifier of TopP is occupied by a null pronominal (*pro*), which represents the stage topic in the sense of Erteschik-Shir (1997): a topic that singles out the time and place of the event described, rather than one of its participants.

(128)

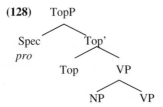

According to Basilico's analysis, the subject of the adjectival complement can then be extracted from the specifier of TopP to the matrix subject position of raising/passive verbs, while the subject of the verbal small clause cannot. This follows from the fact that the null pronominal cannot be extracted to a case position (because a null argument cannot check case), and the small clause subject cannot be extracted 'across' the specifier of TopP, under locality constraints on movement.[33]

Of course, the English small clause structures discussed by Basilico differ from the Hausa small clause structure under consideration, given that English small clauses are either selected by a matrix verb like *consider* or *want*, or occur as the complement of the copular (raising) verb *be*, while the Hausa small clause that is posited as the complement of F occurs as the complement

---

[33] Basilico (2003: 17 [fn. 12]) states that the Topic Phrase that dominates the small clause must be distinct from the Topic Phrase that hosts left-dislocated topics, since the latter is not expected to host a null argument.

of a non-verbal category. As the examples in (116) and (117) illustrate, however, the non-verbal copular clause may occur as an embedded clause in Hausa, and its topic subject may undergo (optional) raising. The proposal that the subject of the canonical NP–NP–FM clause is in topic position also receives some support from Basilico's observation that nominal and adjectival small clauses involve categorical/individual level predication. This observation may also go some way towards explaining why the Hausa non-verbal copular construction may not occur with PP or VNP predicates, given that preposition phrases and deverbal nouns have a tendency to express thetic/stage level (e.g. temporary/eventive) predication. Furthermore, Tuller's (1986a: 219–20) observation that Niger Hausa speakers prefer the non-verbal copular construction over the imperfective TAM construction for PP predicates expressing permanent states might also receive an explanation along these lines (100). This discussion is not pursued further here, but this may prove a fruitful direction for future research, with the following caveats in mind:

> While individual-level predicates must participate in a categorical predication, it is not the case that every categorical predication involves an individual-level predicate. For example, Lambrecht (1994) gives examples of thetic/categorical pairs that involve what would be considered a stage-level predicate ... Also, while stage-level predicates typically express temporary properties, not all predicates expressing temporary properties are stage-level predicates. For example, Diesing (1992) shows that certain adjectives expressing temporary psychological states are individual-level predicates. Thus, the adjectes *angry, nervous*, and *cheerful*, while expressing temporary states, fail to appear in *there*-insertion sentences and require their subjects to be generic. É. Kiss (1998[b]) also notes that there are certain predicates expressing temporary states that behave more like individual-level predicates, in that their subjects are generic. (Basilico 2003: 24)

Finally, the version of the predicate raising analysis developed in this chapter for Hausa receives further support from the fact that Hausa equatives pattern as predicted with respect to the extraction asymmetries that have been noted by various researchers. For example, Heycock (1992) cites Moro's (1990) observation that subextraction from the post-copular NP (129b) is felicitous in the case of the canonical copular sentence (129a), where the extracted NP originates in the small clause predicate position (Heycock 1992: 108).

(129) a. the photograph of the president may have been the cause of the riot
    b. [what] do you think [the photograph of the president may have been the cause of ~~what~~]?

In contrast, sub-extraction from the post-copular NP in inverse copular sentences gives rise to an ungrammatical sentence. In this case, the extracted NP originates in small clause subject position, since (130a) is derived by raising the predicate NP *the cause of the riot* and stranding the subject NP *the photograph of the president* in the small clause (Heycock 1992: 108).

(130) a. the cause of the riot may have been the photograph of the president
b. *[what] do you think [the cause of the riot may have been the photograph of ~~what~~]?

Heycock (1992) argues that these extraction asymmetries can be explained by the predicate raising analysis, since it entails that subject and predicate originate in different positions within the small clause, and extraction from subjects is prohibited by the Subject Condition. Now compare the following Hausa examples:

(131) a. hòton   shùgàbā   nè   dàlīlìn   fādùwaȓsà   *'canonical'*
photo.of president FM.m reason.of downfall.of.3ms
'the photo of the president was the cause of his downfall'
b. mè̀ kikè̀   tsàmmānì̀ hòton   shùgàbā   nè   dàlīlì(n)
what 2fs.FOC.IMPF think.VN photo.of president FM.m reason.(of)
~~mè̀~~
what
'what do you think the photo of the president was the cause of?'
(132) a. dàlīlìn   bòȓên   nē   hòton   shùgàbā   *'inverse'*
reason.of riot.DD FM.m photo.of president
'the cause of the riot was the photo of the president'
b. *wà̀ kikè̀   tsàmmānì̀ dàlīlìn   bòȓên   nē   hòtō(n)
what 2fs.FOC.IMPF think.VN reason.of riot.DD FM.m photo.(of)
~~wà̀~~?
who
'who do you think the cause of the riot was the photo (of)?'

Example (131a) is 'canonical' in the sense that the small clause subject *hòton shùgàbā* 'the photo of the president' precedes the small clause predicate *dàlīlìn fādùwaȓsà* 'the cause of his downfall', although it shows the marked NP FP NP structure in which the small clause subject *hòton shùgàbā* has raised to the specifier of FP, stranding the predicate in the small clause.

In example (131b), therefore, the *wh*-phrase *mè̀* 'what' is extracted from the small clause predicate, and the result is grammatical. In the 'inverse' example (132a), the small clause predicate *dàlīlìn bòȓên* 'the cause of the riot' has raised to the specifier of FP, stranding the subject *hòton shùgàbā* in the small clause. Observe that extraction from within the small clause subject is ungrammatical (132b). Although further research is required to establish whether these asymmetries occur systematically in Hausa, these data suggest that Hausa patterns like English in that sub-extraction from the small clause predicate is licensed, but sub-extraction from the small clause subject is not.[34]

PredP analysis

Another type of analyis that has been proposed in the recent literature on copular clauses posits a designated functional projection that dominates the thematic core of the clause: the predicate phrase (PredP) (see Bowers 1993; Svenonius 1994). For example, in their discussion of Scottish Gaelic copular sentences, Adger & Ramchand (2003) propose an analysis wherein the copular sentence consists of a 'predicational core' mediated by (PredP), the head of which takes only lexical projections as its complement: NP, VP, AP, PP. This claim is central to Adger & Ramchand's analysis. Crucially, an indefinite NP in Scottish Gaelic has no determiner, and is treated by Adger & Ramchand as NP. Definite NPs, on the other hand, are preceded by a definite determiner, and are therefore analysed as determiner phrases (DPs). In the structure adopted by Adger & Ramchand, PredP is dominated by tense phrase (TP). This structure is illustrated in (133) (adapted from Adger & Ramchand 2003: 326).

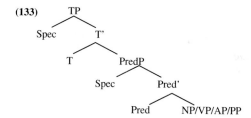

Adger & Ramchand argue that this structure underlies three distinct types of copular construction in Scottish Gaelic, a VSO language, where VSO order is derived from underlying SVO order by raising of the verb to the head of the inflection/tense phrase:

---

[34] Further research is also required to establish whether there is evidence of extraction asymmetries between VP-internal and surface (SpecIP) subject positions. This issue does not arise in relation to copular constructions per se, since these constructions neither license VP predicates nor (arguably) involve an INFL projection, although examples like (131) and (132) may prove revealing.

(134) dh'òl   Calum ~~dh'òl~~ an   (Adger & Ramchand 2003: 329)
      drink-PAST Calum   the
      t-uisge.beatha
      whiskey
      'Calum drank the whiskey'

An alternative to raising the main verb is to insert the verb *bith* 'be', which is known as the 'substantive auxiliary' and gives rise to a substantive auxiliary construction:

(135) bha   Calum ag òl   *substantive auxiliary construction*
      be-PAST Calum ASP drinking   (Adger & Ramchand 2003: 330)
      uisge.beatha
      whiskey
      'Calum was drinking the whiskey'

This type of construction can also take AP and PP in predicate positions:

(136) a. tha   Calum faiceallach   *substantive auxiliary construction*
         be-PRS Calum careful   (Adger & Ramchand 2003: 330)
         'Calum is (being) careful'
      b. tha   Calum anns a'bhuth   *substantive auxiliary construction*
         be-PRS Calum in   the.shop   (Adger & Ramchand 2003: 330)
         'Calum is in the shop'

However, a simple NP predicate is not licensed, but has to be accompanied by a form of the preposition *ann* 'in':

(137) a. *tha   Calum tidsear   (Adger & Ramchand 2003: 332)
         be.PRS Calum teacher
         'Calum is a teacher'
      b. tha   Calum 'na thidsear   *substantive auxiliary construction*
         be.PRS Calum in.3s teacher   Adger & Ramchand (2003: 332)
         'Calum is a teacher'

Neither is a DP (noun phrase with overt definite determiner) licensed in predicate position, with or without the preposition inserted:

(138) a. *tha   Calum an tidsear   (Adger & Ramchand 2003: 333)
         be.PRS Calum the teacher
         'Calum is the teacher'
      b. *tha   Calum anns an tidsear (Adger & Ramchand 2003: 334)
         be.PRS Calum in   the teacher
         'Calum is the teacher'

The structure of the substantive auxiliary construction is shown in (139) (adapted from Adger & Ramchand (2003: 331)). The Pred head hosts aspectual features when the complement of Pred is VP, as in example (135).

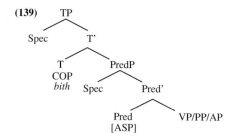

A second type of copular sentence in Scottish Gaelic is the inverted copular construction. These show the constituent order COP XP (predicate) DP (subject), and are formed with the 'defective' clitic copula verb, so-called because, unlike the 'substantive auxiliary' copula *bith* which inflects for four tenses, the defective copula only has two forms: *is* (present) and *bu* (past, future or conditional). The inverted copular construction can take either AP, PP or NP predicate, as illustrated by (140a–c), respectively. Like the substantive auxiliary construction, the inverted copular construction cannot take a DP predicate (140d).[35] Neither is it possible to form a sentence with the defective copula where subject precedes predicate (140e).

(140)a. is   mòr an   duine sin   *inverted copular constructions*
         COP.PRS big that man   (Adger & Ramchand 2003: 334)
         'that man is big'

---

[35] Adger & Ramchand present a range of data to demonstrate the restriction on DP occurring as a complement of Pred, and develop an analysis based on Zamparelli's (2000) claim that there are three distinct 'layers' within the DP: the Strong DP (SDP), which includes determiners and results in a referential expression (ia); the Predicational DP (PDP), which results in an expression that can occur in the same position as a predicational AP (iib); and the Kind DP (KIP), which denotes an 'atomic property' (iiic) (Adger & Ramchand 2003: 344):

(i) a. the dog is barking
     b. Fido is a dog
     c. Fido is a friendly kind of dog

According to Adger & Ramchand, Scottish Gaelic DPs headed by the definite determiner can only be SDPs, and are therefore restricted to appearing in non-predicational positions. Bare NPs, on the other hand, are KIPs (property denoting), and can occur as the complement of Pred. For English, Adger & Ramchand claim that the copula *be* is lexical, and can select either a property denoting XP (AP, PP or KIP), or a referential SDP. Furthermore, they claim that only SDPs (referential expressions) can be raised in English (raising to TP for case reasons). This claim is based on the observation that only an identificational reading is possible in English inverse copular sentences (Adger & Ramchand 2003: 30):

(i) a. [$_{SDP}$ What you are talking about] is [$_{SDP/KIP}$ garbage]
     b. [$_{SDP/*KIP}$ garbage] is [$_{SDP}$ what you are talking about]

Since *garbage* in example (ib) can only be interpreted as referential, Adger & Ramchand conclude that raising in English copular sentences is restricted to SDPs, thereby rejecting the predicate raising analysis and assuming a null Pred head.

  b. is   le   Calum an cù   (Adger & Ramchand 2003: 335)
     COP.PRS with Calum the dog
     'the dog belongs to Calum'
  c. is   tidsear Calum   (Adger & Ramchand 2003: 335)
     COP.PRS teacher Calum
     'Calum is a teacher'
  d. *is   an tidsear Calum   (Adger & Ramchand 2003: 337)
     COP.PRS the teacher Calum
     'Calum is the teacher'
  e. *is   an   duine sin mòr   (Adger & Ramchand 2003: 335)
     COP.PRS that man   big
     'that man is big'

Furthermore, bare existential subject NPs are not licensed in this
construction:

(141)*is   mòr duine   (Adger & Ramchand 2003: 338)
     COP.PRS big   man
     'a man is big'

The structure of the inverted copular construction is shown in (142)
(adapted from Adger & Ramchand 2003: 351). Adger & Ramchand argue
that the defective copula *is* instantiates the head of PredP, and derive the
inverted COP–XP–DP order by raising Pred' (containing the clitic copula and
its complement host, the predicate XP) to the specifier of TP, stranding the
subject DP in the specifier of PredP.

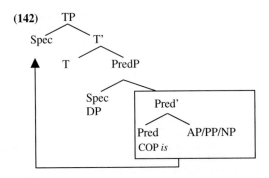

The third type of Scottish Gaelic copular construction is the augmented
copular construction. This construction is also formed with the 'defective'
copula, followed by a 'pronominal augment' (a third person masculine
singular pronoun), followed by subject DP and predicate DP:

(143) 's   e   Calum an tidsear   *augmented copular construction*
      COP.PRS3ms Calum the teacher   (Adger & Ramchand 2003: 339)
      'Calum is the teacher'

In an augmented copular construction like (143), the subject DP receives main stress and is interpreted as presentational or new information focus, depending on context. This stress placement is marked, given the fact that the default position for nuclear stress in Scottish Gaelic, as in English, is on the rightmost constituent. The structure proposed by Adger & Ramchand for the augmented copular construction is shown in (144) (adapted from Adger & Ramchand (2003: 352)).

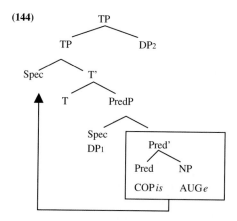

Adger and Ramchand argue that the pronominal augment is the complement of the copula in Pred, and derive the clause-initial position of these two constituents by raising Pred' to SpecTP. Adger & Ramchand (2003: 352) argue that DP$_2$ is a right-adjoined element that identifies the 'contextually given individual' denoted by the pronominal augment, which explains why DP$_2$ has to be definite in this type of copular construction. Because DP$_2$ corresponds to old/given information it is destressed, so focus shifts to DP$_1$, hence the marked information structure properties of this construction.[36]

    It is worth exploring whether the PredP analysis proposed by Adger and Ramchand (2003) can account for Hausa non-verbal copular sentences: the question that arises is whether the relationship of predication between the small clause subject and predicate would be better characterised by the inclusion of the PredP structure. Given the fact that Hausa non-verbal copular sentences have a designated focus position but lack tense/aspect/

---

[36] Adger & Ramchand are not specific about the position to which DP$_2$ is adjoined. On the assumption that it is adjoined at the root, as shown in (144), it resembles a topic/afterthought, which is consistent with its semantic properties.

mood features, FP remains the functional projection dominating the
structure (145).

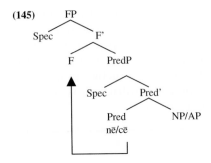

The structure in (145), in which *nē/cē/nē* originates as the head of PredP
and raises to the head of FP, has the advantage of capturing the 'dual
function' of *nē/cē/nē* in non-verbal sentences: it both licenses predication
and marks focus on its left-adjacent constituent. Observe that the canonical
NP–NP–FM structure can be derived by raising the focused constituent to the
specifier of FP and by positing a topic-adjoined position for the subject NP.
Equally, the marked NP–FM–NP construction can be derived by raising the
focused constituent to the specifier of FP, and by stranding the non-focused
constituent in PredP. Essentially, then, the PredP structure might substitute
for the small clause structure assumed thus far as the complement of FP.
Observe, however, that there is no restriction in Hausa on definite NPs
(DPs) occurring in predicate position (i.e. as the complement of Pred).
Furthermore, the structure in (145) suggests the possibility of copular
sentences without a designated focus position: a PredP structure from
which nothing need be displaced, given that Hausa non-verbal copular
sentences involve no overt inflectional (TAM) morphology and thus
(arguably) no case-licensing inflectional projection (IP/TP). Having
sketched out a possible analysis along these lines, this issue is left open here.

5.4.4 *Summary*

To conclude this section, there is substantial evidence to suggest that the
properties of copular sentences in Hausa are most insightfully analysed in
terms of an FP structure. Not only does this analysis capture the focus
properties of these constructions, but there is also evidence to substantiate
the claim that the 'subject' of canonical copular sentences occupies topic
position. The non-verbal copula *nē/cē/nē* consistently performs a focus

function, and instantiates the head of FP. In addition, the non-verbal copula licenses predication and equation in non-verbal clauses, in the sense that its presence is required to attribute clausal status to a subject–predicate structure that lacks verbal-inflectional properties. The FP analysis enables a unified account of the two apparently disparate contexts in which the focusmarking copula is found: focus/*wh*-fronting in verbal clauses, and non-verbal copular constructions.

5.5 CONCLUSIONS

A number of conclusions, both descriptive and theoretical, can be drawn from the discussion in this chapter. In terms of descriptive conclusions, it has been shown that the Hausa non-verbal copula *nē/cē/nē* is most insightfully analysed as a grammaticalised (or grammaticalising) focus marker. According to this perspective, *nē/cē/nē* evolved from pronominal elements into a copula (Li & Thompson 1977; (Schuh 1983a), and is in the process of evolving via its function in focus/*wh*-fronting constructions into a fully grammaticalised focus marker. While the non-verbal copula is required to license predication and equation, and in this respect shows a 'less grammaticalised' status in the non-verbal clause than it does in monoclausal focus/*wh*-fronting constructions, there is also evidence in the non-verbal clause of the evolving function of *nē/cē/nē* as a focus marker. Both predicational and equative copular sentences in Hausa permit a range of constituent order permutations that are unified by the fact that focus falls on the constituent left-adjacent to the copula. In other words, these constructions contain a dedicated focus position, both in their canonical and non-canonical forms.

In terms of theoretical conclusions, an analysis wherein *nē/cē/nē* is treated as the head of the left-peripheral functional projection FP accurately captures the attested word order permutations in the non-verbal copular clause, characterises the information packaging properties of the construction, and provides an account of constraints on extraction. The account developed here is essentially a predicate raising analysis of copular constructions; modifications to the analysis that incorporate additional functional layers (inflectional and predicational) in addition to the focus layer were also sketched but left open. In sum, the FP analysis has been shown to provide a simple and accurate account of *nē/cē/nē* as a focus marker in both the major contexts in which it occurs: in focus/*wh*-fronting constructions and in the non-verbal copular clause.

6

A CROSS-LINGUISTIC PERSPECTIVE

6.1 INTRODUCTION

In this chapter, Hausa focus/*wh*-constructions (§ 6.2) and non-verbal copular constructions (§ 6.3) are set within a broader cross-linguistic context. In the tradition of within-family comparison, the discussion in this chapter is limited to Afroasiatic languages, with a particular emphasis on Chadic. Focus/*wh*-constructions in Modern Standard Arabic, Modern Hebrew and Coptic Egyptian are also briefly discussed. Of course, the syntactic features of the focus/*wh*-constructions described here are by no means restricted to the Afroasiatic family, but form part of a typology of universal features that distinguish this class of constructions cross-linguistically. The second main section of the chapter compares and contrasts the Hausa non-verbal copular clause with its counterparts in a range of other Afroasiatic languages. This section begins with a discussion of Pustet's (2003) cross-linguistic typology of copular clauses, which sets out the most common patterns attested in the world's languages. This section then presents a survey of non-verbal clauses in selected Chadic languages, as well as some discussion of similar constructions in Arabic dialects, in Hebrew and in Coptic Egyptian. The picture that emerges from this discussion is that while Hausa is relatively unusual in the respect that copulas are rather uncommon in the Chadic family, there are striking similarities between Hausa and its more distant Afroasiatic relatives with respect to the properties of non-verbal copulas and the structures in which they participate.

The objectives of this chapter are primarily descriptive: to set the Hausa facts within their typological context, and to provide a glimpse of the patterns of variation and similarity that exist in focus/*wh*-constructions and non-verbal clauses within the Afroasiatic family. Of course, an exhaustive description of focus/*wh*-constructions and non-verbal clauses in the languages discussed here is beyond the scope of a single book. The descriptions presented here should therefore be seen as a 'snapshot' rather than a full picture of the facts in each language. Furthermore, no attempt is made to extend the analysis of the Hausa facts developed in this book to the languages discussed here, although where theoretical analyses have been proposed, these are discussed, and the relevant section is divided into 'descriptive facts' followed by 'theoretical issues'. Finally, it is worth emphasising that descriptions of only a small subset of Chadic languages are available, and many of these are rather brief grammatical sketches. Every attempt has been made to present the facts as accurately as possible given available descriptions, but the presentation is necessarily rather superficial. Future research is likely to motivate revisions to existing descriptions, and to fill in many gaps in the data.

6.2 FOCUS CONSTRUCTIONS

This section explores focus and *wh*-constructions in a selection of Chadic languages and in a small number of other Afriasiatic languages, with a view to establishing the extent to which the Hausa facts are mirrored in related languages, as well as providing a sense of the patterns of variation that exist.

The section begins with a descriptive survey of focus/*wh*-constructions in 11 Chadic languages, from which it emerges that the Chadic family illustrates a wide range of syntactic focus/*wh*-positions, including in situ, postverbal, clause-initial and clause-final positions. There follows a discussion of the theoretical analysis of postverbal focus in Chadic developed by Tuller (1992), and a brief discussion of the limitations of the focus phrase (FP) analysis in accounting for these facts (§ 6.2.1). The next subsection explores focus/*wh*-constructions in Standard Arabic and a subset of the spoken dialects. Standard Arabic shares a number of properties in common with Hausa in relation to the syntax of focus, although the two languages differ with respect to the distribution of focus marking particles. There also appears to be a stronger case for drawing a functional distinction between in situ and ex situ focus in Standard Arabic than in Hausa. There follows a discussion of focus in Modern Hebrew, which shares some properties with Hausa in terms of the formal features that mark information structure and distinguish declarative and inter-rogative clauses (§ 6.2.3). Like Hausa, Hebrew has a *wh*-fronting strategy. There is also evidence that Hebrew has access to a focus raising operation similar to the Hausa focus fronting operation. However, this does not result in clause-initial focus in Hebrew, but in a focus position local to the verb. In addition, Hebrew has a cleft construction, although this is restricted to subjects, Finally, while both Hebrew and Hausa have a VP fronting strategy that shows characteristics of movement, the Hebrew case is essentially a topic construction.

The final subsection discusses focus and *wh*-constructions in Coptic Egyptian (§ 6.2.4). Like Hausa, this language allows both in situ and ex situ monoclausal focus/*wh*-constructions, although the in situ pattern is the most frequently attested strategy in the Coptic corpus, and the biclausal cleft is also frequently attested. Unlike Hausa, special inflection patterns together with the in situ strategy in Coptic. There follows a discussion of the comparative analysis of special inflection in Hausa and Coptic Egyptian developed by Green & Reintges (2003; 2004; 2005a; 2005b) and Reintges & Green (2004).

6.2.1 *Chadic*

Descriptive facts

In this section, a brief survey of focus/*wh*-constructions in 11 Chadic languages is presented. Five of these languages belong, like Hausa, to the West A branch of the Chadic family, four to the West B branch, and two to the Biu-Mandara branch. This small subset of Chadic languages provides a representative illustration of the range of syntactic strategies for marking focus/*wh*-constructions in Chadic. According to Schuh (2003), only a minority of SVO Chadic languages prepose all *wh*-phrases to the left periphery of the clause (Hausa is typically described as belonging to this minority), although this is a typical feature of the VSO Chadic languages, including Gude (Biu-Mandara). A representative set of Gude examples is provided in (1). The final *ā* morpheme in examples (1b) and (1c) is an interrogative particle (Q).

Gude (Biu-Mandara A; VSO)

(1)   a.   kə 'ush Rābi ɗâfna   *Gude unmarked declarative*
         PF   cook Rabi mush   (Schuh 2003: 58)
         'Rabi cooked mush'

      b.   wù 'ùshi   ɗafə̂n ā   *Gude subject* wh-*question*
         who cooked mush Q   (Schuh 2003: 58)
         'who cooked this mush?'

      c.   mì   'ush   Rābi ā   *Gude object* wh-*question*
         what cooked Rabi Q   (Schuh 2003: 58)
         'what did Rabi cook?'

Podoko (Biu-Mandara A; VSO)

In Podoko, another VSO Chadic language belonging to the Biu-Mandara A branch, the focus/*wh*-position is immediately after the verb (Jarvis 1981). This applies both to subjects (which appear in situ in their usual postverbal position) and to non-subjects.

(2)   a.   a   təla   wa   sləɓə na?   *Podoko subject* wh-*question*
         ASP cook who meat Q   (Jarvis 1981: 160)
         'who cooked the meat?'

      b.   a   təla   **mala**   *Podoko subject focus*
         ASP cook mother.my   (Jarvis 1981: 160)
         'my mother cooked it'

(3) a. a təla tawə ndi na?   *Podoko object* wh-*question*
         ASP cook what one Q   (Jarvis 1981: 160)
         'what did one cook?'
     b. a təla **sləɓə** ndi   *Podoko object focus*
         ASP cook meat one   (Jarvis 1981: 130)
         'one cooked **meat**'

According to Schuh, the majority of SVO Chadic languages have wh-in situ. Some of these languages, however, while leaving non-subject wh-phrases in situ, postpose subject wh-phrases (as well as subject focus phrases) to a postverbal position, such as Bole (West A). This strategy, which is restricted to certain West Chadic languages, is illustrated by the Bole examples in (4).

Bole (West A; SVO)

(4) a. Bamoi kàppū mòrɗo   *Bole unmarked declarative*
         Bamoi planted millet   (Schuh & Gimba, forthcoming)[1]
         'Bamoi planted millet'
     b. kàppū mòrɗo lò   *Bole subject* wh-*question*
         planted millet who   (Schuh 2003: 59)
         'who planted millet?'
     c. Bamoi kàppū lè   *Bole object* wh-*question*
         Bamoi planted what   (Schuh 2003: 59)
         'what did Bamoi plant?'
     d. kàppū mòrɗo **Bamoi** *Bole subject focus*
         planted millet Bamoi   (Schuh & Gimba, forthcoming)[2]
         '**Bamoi** planted millet'

As example (4c) demonstrates, object wh-phrases appear in their canonical postverbal position. According to Schuh (2005: 26), object focus in Bole patterns like the unmarked declarative construction in (4a), with non-subjects occurring in situ.

Schuh and Gimba (forthcoming.) also observe that a 'clefting particle' (CP) *ye* precedes questioned subjects (5a) or focused subjects (5b) in Bole (optionally in verbal sentences, obligatorily in non-verbal sentences). Schuh (2005) also provides an example of this construction that involves object wh-question (5c). Of course, this raises the question of whether the object focus/wh-phrase really occurs in situ, or in some designated postverbal focus position (see French 2004).

---

[1] This example is taken from p. 1 of Schuh & Gimba's (un-numbered) draft chapter entitled 'The syntax of simplex verbal clauses'.
[2] This example is taken from p. 4 of Schuh & Gimba's (un-numbered) draft chapter entitled 'Subjects'.

(5) a. à   òna   saɗikà ye   *Bole clefting particle*
         IMPF give-FUT   alms   CP   (Schuh & Gimba, forthcoming)[3]
         mìl   lò?
         all   who
         'who all will give alms?'

     b. à   òna   saɗikà ye **mi'y'yà**
         IMPF give-FUT   alms   CP people
         '**the people** will give alms.'

     c. Bamoi kàppū   (ye) lè   *Bole clefting particle*
         Bamoi plant.PF CP   what   (Schuh 2005: 28)
         nzòno
         yesterday
         'what did Bamoi plant yesterday?'

The Bole clefting particle is not a copula. Non-verbal clauses are typically formed by simple juxtaposition of subject and predicate in Bole (§ 6.3.2).[4]

Pero (West A; SVO)

Frajzyngier (1989) describes focus and *wh*-constructions in the SVO Chadic language Pero (West A), which displays a similar *wh*-strategy to Bole, in that subjects can be postposed to clause-final position (6a), while objects remain in the postverbal position (6b). However, Frajzyngier also describes an alternative strategy, in which subject *wh*-expressions remain in the clause-intial position preceded by the interrogative clitic *aC-* (6c).

(6) a. tà-rímbò kòkkó-mò nón   *Pero subject* wh-*question*
         FUT-build road-this who   (Frajzyngier 1989: 218)
         'who will build this road?'

     b. cì-tá-cí-nì   *Pero object* wh-*question*
         2f-FUT-eat-what   (Frajzyngier 1989: 219)
         'what are you going to eat?'

     c. àn-nón mén-jì   àp-áanì   *Pero subject* wh-*question*
         Q-who   want-HAB open-VN   (Frajzyngier 1989: 218)
         'who wants to open?'

---

[3] These examples are taken from p. 4 of Schuh & Gimba's (un-numbered) draft chapter entitled 'Subjects'. The Bole 'clefting particle' is not a copula; in Bole, copular sentences are formed by simple juxtaposition of subject and predicate (§ 6.3.2).

[4] According to Schuh (2005) the Bole clefting particle *ye* is related to the definite determiner, which has evolved from the morpheme *i that appears in all the Bole-Tangale languages. There is no evidence that this particle has ever evolved a copular function in Bole, given the absence of a copula in Proto (West) Chadic (Russell Schuh, p.c.). Citing Schlenker (2004), Schuh (2005: 25) relates the function of this particle in focus/*wh*-constructions to its function as a clause-level marker of conditionality: 'an expression marked by a definite article (or demonstrative) refers to an *entity* that is most salient to the domain of discourse, whereas a conditional clause refers to a *world* that is most salient to the domain of the consequent clause.'

Frajzyngier does not provide any examples of *wh*-objects in the clause-initial position, with the exception of the alternative *wh*-construction shown in example (7), which according to Frajzyngier is restricted to patient arguments. This construction resembles a cleft or pseudocleft in that the *wh*-object occurs in the clause-initial position (preceded by the interrogative morpheme *aC*-), and the predicate takes the form of a relative clause:

(7) àl-láwò círè   cí-nì   tà-máj-áanì   *Pero object* wh-*question*
    Q-boy   which REL-1s FUT-ask-VN   (Frajzyngier 1989: 222)
    'which boy shall I ask?'

Frajzyngier (1989: 226) states that focus in Pero is marked by a departure from the canonical declarative word order. Nominal subjects, which occur clause-initially in the unmarked declarative clause, are focused by postposing to postverbal position, where it follows the direct object (8a). First and second person pronominal subjects can also be focused by means of this strategy (8b). Observe that the position of the focused second person pronoun in (8b) suggests that Pero has a postverbal rather than clause-final focus position; the alternative is to assume extraposition of the adjunct phrase (Russell Schuh, p.c.).

(8) a. ɗíg-kò   mìnáa-mo   **tàttáa-nò**   *Pero subject focus*
       build-PF house-this father-1s   (Frajzyngier 1989: 227)
       'it was **my father** who built this house'
    b. páttó-kò móɗɗ-ì   **ci** tà   *Pero subject focus*
       pour.PF   millet.DD 2f into   (Frajzyngier 1989: 228)
       ɓúndù-í
       granary-DD.Q
       'did **you** pour the millet into the granary?'

According to Frajzyngier, constituents that do not occur clause-initially in the unmarked declarative clause (i.e. non-subjects) are typically focused by movement to clause-initial position. Consider example (9), in which the subject is also postposed:[5]

(9) **cándè** céɓ-ínà   Múusà   *Pero object focus*
    yam   plant-VENT Musa   (Frajzyngier 1989: 229)
    'Musa planted **yam**'

Frajzyngier also describes a construction that he calls 'counter-presuppositional'. This construction 'has one primary function, and that is to negate what the speaker thinks is the belief of the hearer' (Frajzyngier 1989: 232).

---

[5] In fact, Frajzyngier (1989: 229) describes examples like (9) as grammatical but 'exceptional' because they do not occur in his running texts. It seems that most of the examples of preposed objects provided by Frajzyngier are in fact topic constructions, which raises the question of whether Pero does in fact front focus/*wh*-objects, or whether it is more like Bole in leaving these in the post-verbal position.

In other words, this *X, not Y* construction expresses constrastive focus. Rather like example (7), this construction resembles a cleft or pseudo cleft in that the focused constituent is moved to the left periphery of the clause (preceded by the focus marker *iC*), and is followed by the relative marker *ci*. According to Frajzyngier (1989: 204) the focus marker *iC* occurs as a copula in certain nominal sentences, although Russell Schuh (p.c.) expresses some doubt about the analysis of *iC* as a copula, since the canonical non-verbal clause in Pero is formed by simple juxtaposition of subject and predicate (§ 6.3.2). It follows that the morpheme *iC* may be best analysed as a focus marker that accompanies preposed (clause-intial) focus phrases.[6]

(10) a. íc-**cínù** cì-wè-n-ée-tò   *Pero subject focus*
      FM-3pl   REL-see-VENT-OBJ-PRO   (Frajzyngier 1989: 232)
      à-mínù-m
      neg-1pl-NEG
      'it is **they** who saw her, not we'

    b. ij-**júrà**   cì-púndú-kò   *Pero object focus*
      FM-peanuts   REL-cook-PF   (Frajzyngier 1989: 233)
      à-cándè-m
      NEG-yam-NEG
      'it is **peanuts** that she cooked, not yam'

Tangale (West A; Bole-Tangale; SVO)

Tuller (1992) describes focus and *wh*-constructions in the SVO Chadic language Tangale, which belongs to the Bole-Tangale subgroup of the West A branch. This language also displays postverbal focus, where the focus position is after the direct object rather than directly after the verb. Tuller (1992) only provides examples of *wh*-questions, but states that 'answers to these *wh*-questions have the exact same structure.' (p. 306). In other words, the syntax of declarative focus constructions mirrors that of *wh*-interrogatives.

(11) a. wa   patʊ   ayaba   nuŋ ta   *Tangale subject* wh-*question*
      FUT   buy   bananas   who at   (Tuller 1992: 307)
      luumo dooji
      market tomorrow
      'who will buy bananas at the market tomorrow?'

    b. ʊnʊgʊ naŋ   ti   lɔwei   *Tangale object* wh-*question*
      give   what   to   child   (Tuller 1992: 307)
      'what did she give to the child?'

Despite the fact that direct object focus/*wh*-phrases appear to be in situ, Tuller cites evidence from Kenstowicz (1985) concerning the phonological (sandhi)

---

[6] Russell Schuh (p.c.) also informs me that he is not aware of any equivalent morpheme in the Bole-Tangale languages.

phenomena final vowel deletion and tone delinking. While these sandhi processes apply between the verb and its direct object, they do not apply when the direct object is in focus, suggesting that this is a case of string-vacuous movement to a designated focus position. Tuller observes that complex direct objects (e.g. where the head noun is modified by a relative clause) may or may not be 'split' by the focus/*wh*-phrase, which may therefore occur directly after the head noun (12a) or after the whole complex direct object (12b).

(12) a. shag [wamunjaanan] nɔŋ [nam   *Tangale*
        ate food.REL   who REL   (Tuller 1992: 310)
        Aisha ɗikɔ]
        Aisha prepared
        'who ate the food that Aisha prepared?'

     b. shag [wamunjaanam Aisha   *Tangale*
        ate food.REL   Aisha   (Tuller 1992: 310)
        ɗikɔn]   nɔŋ
        prepared   who
        'who ate the food that Aisha prepared?'

Finally, Tangale also has a clause-final focus position, which is available both for subjects and for non-subjects. Observe that the presence of an adverbial phrase confirms that the object is clause-final rather than in situ in (13b).

(13) a. wa patʊ ayaba   ta luumo   *Tangale subject* wh-*question*
        FUT buy bananas at market   (Tuller 1992: 322)
        dooji   nuŋ
        tomorrow who
        'who will buy bananas at the market tomorrow?'

     b. Mela padʊk landa tu luumon   *Tangale object* wh-*question*
        Mela bought gown at market   (Tuller 1992: 322)
        ti   nuŋ
        for   who
        'who did Mela buy the gown for at the market?'

Kanakuru (West A; Bole-Tangale; SVO)

Newman (1974) describes focus and *wh*-constructions in the SVO Chadic language Kanakuru, which also belongs to the Bole-Tangale subgroup of the West A branch. As in Tangale, Kanakuru focus and *wh*-constructions are syntactically parallel, and as in Tangale, the focus/*wh*-position is after the direct object.

(14) a. at ɗenoi **Balau**   *Kanakuru subject focus*
        ate peanuts Balau   (Newman 1974: 63)
        '**Balau** ate the peanuts'

    b. ànò   aye **kai**   *Kanakuru object focus*
       1s.FUT help 2ms   (Newman 1974: 67)
       'I will help **you**'
    c. na ɗibɔre gami mandai   *Kanakuru subject* wh-*question*
       FUT buy   ram who   (Newman 1974: 63)
       'who will buy the ram?'
    d. kàa   nai mandai   *Kanakuru object* wh-*question*
       2ms.IMPF call who   (Newman 1974: 66)
       'whom are you calling?'

As in Tangale, complex direct objects are 'split' by the focus/wh-phrase. However, this is an obligatory process in Kanakuru:

  (15) aɗe [shiruwoi] **ŋgadlai** [mə   *Kanakuru*
      ate fish   cat   REL   (Newman 1974: 64)
      shée wura ane]
      3fs.PF fry   PRO
      '**the cat** ate up the fish that she fried'

Kanakuru also has a clause-initial focus position. As in Hausa, focus fronting and relativisation condition special inflection (Newman 1974: 45–6).[7] In Kanakuru, only the perfective paradigm has a distinct form in these contexts. Special inflection is accompanied by the suffixation of -*a* to the verb and to any pronominal direct object. Compare the unmarked clause in (16a) with the corresponding focus construction (16b), an example of (string-vacuous) subject focus fronting:[8]

  (16) a. Basha à   tupe yi   *Kanakuru unmarked clause*
       Basha 3ms.PF send 3ms   (Newman 1974: 65)
       'Basha sent him'
      b. **Basha** shée   tupa ya   *Kanakuru subject focus*
       Basha 3ms.FOC.PF send 3ms (Newman 1974: 65)
       '**Basha** sent him':

---

[7] Newman also states that Kanakuru special inflection is conditioned by clausal negation. According to Russell Schuh (p.c.), a special focus-marking inflection is foreign to Bole-Tangale languages and must therefore be an innovation in Kanakuru. Comparative Bole-Tangale data shows that the modern Kanakuru perfective is historically related to the subjunctive (Schuh 1977). Russell Schuh (p.c.) further points out that, as in Hausa, subjunctive clauses in Bole-Tangale languages do not permit wh/focus. Schuh suggests that although modern Kanakuru uses the reflex of the proto Bole-Tangale (probably proto-West Chadic) subjunctive to encode perfectivity in affirmative declarative clauses, the fact that this comes from the subjunctive may be related to its exclusion from negative clauses and clauses with questioned or focused constituents.

[8] These constructions do not contain any copular element. In Kanakuru, non-verbal sentences do not contain a copula, but are formed with an imperfective form of INFL (§ 6.3.2).

c. **shi**   mə́n   tupa   *Kanakuru object focus*
3ms   1pl.FOC.PF send   (Newman 1974: 65)
'we sent **him**'

Mupun (West A; SVO)

Frajzyngier (1993) describes focus and *wh*-constructions in the SVO Chadic language Mupun, the final West A language described here. Unlike the other West A languages surveyed here, Mupun appears to be a *wh*-in situ language across the board: there is no syntactic reordering of subjects or non-subjects in *wh*-questions. Both *wh*-questions and *yes-no* questions are marked by a clause-final (vowel) interrogative particle (Q). However, it is striking that *wh*-expressions are preceded by the copula (COP) *a*. Example (17) illustrates subject and object *wh*-constructions in Mupun.

(17) a. a   mi   ya   jos nə i   *Mupun subject* wh-*question*
COP what catch rat DD Q   (Frajzyngier 1993: 370)
'what caught the rat?'

b. as   nə   ya   a   mi   *Mupun object* wh-*question*
dog DD catch COP what   (Frajzyngier 1993: 371)
'what did the dog catch?'

Contrastive focus can also be marked in the same way, by copula *a* preceding the focused constituent, which also remains in situ. This is illustrated by the examples in (18):

(18) a. ba   a   **surep** fen mo   ɗik   *Mupun subject focus*
NEG COP wives 1s   pl   make   (Frajzyngier 1993: 399)
tul ɗəsə kas   a   **jirap** fen mo
pot this NEG   COP daughters 1s pl
'it was not my **wives** who made this pot, it was my **daughters**'

b. war cet   a   **lua** ba   *Mupun object focus*
3f   cook COP meat   NEG   (Frajzyngier 1993: 401)
a   **pupwap**   kas
COP fish   NEG
'she cooked **meat**, not **fish**'

Frajzyngier also provides examples of the same focus strategy for prepositional phrases, verbs and complement clauses. However, this is not the only means of marking focus in Mupun. Frajzyngier (1993: 407–24) also describes focus in possessive constructions, which involves the obligatory presence 'of both the copula *ā* and the contrastive marker (CM) *mù*. Consider example (19), in which the contrastive marker combines with a first person singular 'personal suffix' to make the form *məne*:

(19) wu hrbet a   reep   **məne**   *Mupun*
3m prefer COP daughter CM.1s   (Frajzyngier 1993: 409)
'he prefers **my** daughter (rather than somebody else's)'

Frajzyngier argues that this construction has been functionally extended to
the construction that marks contrastive focus in complex sentences like
example (20), in which *mini* is the third person masculine singular form of
the contrastive marker:

(20) **Napus** dem **le**   **Darap** dem   *Mupun*
     Napus like cloth Darap like   (Frajzyngier 1993: 412)
     mini   a   **mota**
     CM.3ms COP car
     '**Napus** likes **cloth** while **Darap** likes **cars**'

According to Frajzyngier (1993: 412), 'The function of [these] constructions
… is to indicate that "although the subject of S1 did X, the subject of S2 did
Y".' However, the verb has to be the same in both clauses, so that the
contrastive focus holds between subjects and the complements of the verb,
respectively.

Bade, Ngizim, Duwai (West B; Bade; SVO)

Schuh (1982a) discusses focus and *wh*-constructions in three SVO languages
Bade, Ngizim and Duwai, which belong to the Bade subgroup of the West
B branch of Chadic languages. Schuh (1982a) provides examples from three
different dialects of Bade: Gashua Bade, Southern Bade and Western Bade.
The focus/*wh*-position in these languages is the postverbal position. Schuh
(1982a: 172) states that this strategy is restricted to a subset of the West
Chadic group, in particular the West B languages Bade, Ngizim and Duwai,
and some members of the Bole-Tangale subgroup (West A): Bolanci,
Karekare, Ngamo and Kanakuru.

(21) a. əksə́ bìidəgùr̃ nə́ ndíyè?   *Duwai subject* wh-*question*
        caught giant.rat FM who   (Schuh 1982a: 164)
        'who caught the giant rat?'

     b. áa bə̀nà ábə̀ nə̀n tâi?   *Ngizim subject* wh-*question*
        FUT cook food FM who   (Schuh 1982a: 164)
        'who will cook the food?'

     c. àa bə̀nə̀ kájlùwà n-ái?   *Gashua Bade subject* wh-*question*
        FUT cook tuwo   FM-who   (Schuh 1982a: 165)
        'who will cook the tuwo?'

(22) a. Sáakú bə̀nə́   mù?   *Duwai object* wh-*question*
        Saaku cooked what   (Schuh 1982a: 161)
        'what did Saaku cook?'

     b. Sáfìyà běn   tàm?   *Ngizim object* wh-*question*
        Safiya cooked what   (Schuh 1982a: 161)
        'What did Safiya cook?'

c.   Sáakú   bə̀nə́   támù?   *Gashua Bade object* wh-*question*
        Saku   cooked   what   (Schuh 1982a: 162)
        'what did Saku cook?'

Schuh (1982a: 160) states that 'only subjects are available for syntactic focus. Whenever sentences with constituents other than subjects in focus are offered for translation, speakers of all languages and dialects in this group are consistent in giving sentences with neutral word order, morphology and intonation.'

(23) a. tlə́rmə̀g   zə̀níitìi   nə́ 'ìidə̀m   *Duwai subject focus*
         FUT.tear   my.gown   FM wood   (Schuh 1982a: 166)
         '**wood** will tear my gown'

     b. tlə̀mpìyı-ń   də̀m   *Ngizim subject focus*
         tore-FM   wood   (Schuh 1982a: 166)
         '**wood** tore (it)'

     c. tlə̀mpə̀tə̀ záníináaníi nə́ də̀m   *Gashua Bade subject focus*
         tore   my.gown   FM wood   (Schuh 1982a: 167)
         '**wood** tore my gown'

As demonstrated by these examples, when a subject is either questioned or focused by extraction to the postverbal focus position, it is preceded by a morpheme glossed here as focus marker (FM). Schuh (1982a: 170) suggests that this morpheme has its origins in the demonstrative determiner system, but there is no evidence that this morpheme has evolved a copular function in these languages (Russell Schuh, p.c.).[9] Tuller (1992) points out that examples like those in (22) suggest that non-subject constituents may also occur in the postverbal focus position. Of course, the question that arises in relation to all these languages with postverbal focus is whether direct object focus is in situ or (vacuously) ex situ, the same issue that arises for subject focus fronting in SVO languages.

Miya (West B; Northern Bauchi; SVO/VOS)

Schuh (1998) describes focus and *wh*-constructions in Miya, an SVO/VOS Chadic language belonging to the Northern Bauchi subgroup of the West B branch.[10] This language is rather like the West A language Mupun, in that both subject and non-subject focus/*wh*-constructions lack syntactic reordering (assuming a basic SVO order). Both *yes-no* questions and

---

[9] Tuller (1992: 308) observes that these focus markers resemble copulas (in containing *n*), but argues against a synchronic cleft analysis. While Schuh (1982a) relates this morpheme to the same historical source as the Hausa non-verbal copula (§ 5.3), Russell Schuh (p.c) informs me that there is no evidence that the Bade/Ngizim/Duwai morpheme has ever evolved a copular function (see § 6.3.2).

[10] Miya is described as SVO/VOS because unmarked declarative main clauses license either constituent order, as do consecutive clauses in narrative, complement clauses of verbs and purpose/reason clauses. However, the order VOS is required in relative clauses and adverbial subordinate clauses, and the SVO order is required in focus/*wh*-constructions (Schuh 1998: 281–8).

wh-questions are marked by a clause-final interrogative morpheme *à* or *wà*. When subjects are questioned or focused, they occur clause-initially, and require special inflection:

(24) a. wàa dá   zàra-tlə́n-à   *Miya subject* wh-*question*
        who FOC.PF call-them-Q   (Schuh 1998: 332)
        'who called them?'
     b. **mə̀n** dá   zàra-tlə́n   *Miya subject focus*
        I   FOC.PF call-them   (Schuh 1998: 332)
        'I called them'

When non-subjects are questioned or focused, they remain in postverbal position. Pronominal objects (clitics) are marked as focus by the presence of a clause-final copy pronoun, whereas nominal objects are only identified as focused constituents by the absence of the 'totality' construction *súw...áy* that occurs in neutral unmarked declaratives:[11]

(25) a. à már suw zhàak-áy   *Miya unmarked declarative*
        PF get TOT donkey-TOT   (Schuh 1998: 334)
        'he got a donkey'
     b. à már **zhàakə**   *Miya object focus*
        PF get donkey   (Schuh 1998: 334)
        'he got a **donkey**'

Example (26a) shows an unmarked imperfective clause, and (26b) a similar clause with subject focus. As this example illustrates, the imperfective TAM (INFL) takes on a special form when the subject is in focus.

(26) a. tə̀   gaa zara-fə   *Miya unmarked imperfective*
        PRO.3ms IMPF call-PRO.2ms   (Schuh 1998: 131)
        'he calls/will call you'
     b. **mə̀n** jíy   zàr-uwsə   *Miya imperfective subject focus*
        PRO.1s FOC.IMPF call-PRO.3ms   (Schuh 1998: 333)
        'I will call you'

As this brief survey demonstrates, the Chadic languages illustrate a wide range of syntactic focus/*wh*-positions, including in situ, postverbal, clause-initial and clause-final positions. Of course, an SVO language like Hausa with clause-initial focus might in principle either be described as a language

---

[11] The 'totality extension' is so-called because it is elicited in translations of Hausa grade 4 'totality' constructions such as *zân ƙōnḕ ta* (1s.FUT burn.up 3fs.PRO) 'I'll burn it up' (< grade 1 *ƙōnā̀* 'burn'). However, Schuh (p.c) informs me that in Miya and in the Yobe state languages with the totality extension (see Schuh 2005) the default citation form for verbs occurs with the totality extension. This morphology is unlicensed in negation, focus and *wh*-constructions and in declaratives with nominal objects, but required in declaratives with null/clitic objects and in *yes–no* questions. Schuh points out that this distribution suggests that this morphology might be more insightfully analysed as a case of 'auxiliary focus' (Hyman & Watters 1984). See Schuh (1998: 172–5) for a discussion of this phenomenon in Miya.

that can prepose all focus/*wh*-phrases or (arguably) as a language that preposes non-subjects but leaves subjects 'in situ', given that subjects remain in a preverbal position. A close examination of the morphosyntactic properties of subject focus/*wh*-constructions reveals evidence in favour of the first analysis, which entails that subject focus/*wh*-constructions involve string-vacuous displacement (§ 4.2). Equally, an SVO language with a postverbal focus position might be described as a language that postposes all focus/*wh*-phrases to that position, or as a language that postposes subjects but leaves non-subjects in situ, given that (at least direct) objects remain in their postverbal position. In addition, it is important to distinguish between postverbal (VP-internal) and clause-final (VP-external) focus positions.

In order to establish which of these descriptions is the correct one, it is necessary to examine a range of data that establishes the distribution of adverbials, negation particles, focus/clefting particles and so on, in order to determine whether syntactic reordering occurs in all focus/*wh*-constructions. Although a great deal of valuable descriptive material on the Chadic languages has already been compiled, this enterprise is still at a relatively early stage, and the fact that many of the available published and unpublished sources on the Chadic languages are grammatical sketches compiled from the author's field notes entails that there are often many gaps in the data.[12] It follows that it is not always possible to establish a detailed typology, but the examples presented in this section provide a sense of both the common syntactic properties and the syntactic diversity that characterise this class of constructions in the Chadic languages.

With respect to the distribution of special inflection in Chadic, some authors describe this as a widespread phenomenon. For example, Pawlak (1994: 209) describes relative tense/aspect as a 'common Chadic feature', listing Hausa (West A), the Ron group (West A), the Bole-Tangale group, including Kanakuru (West A) and Tera (Biu-Mandara A). Frajzyngier (1996: 454) lists the West A languages Hausa and Kanakuru, the West B language Pa'a, the Biu Mandara A languages Tera, Hona and Giziga, and the East B languages Dangla and Mukulu.[13] According to Frajzyngier (1996: 458), 'distribution over three out of four branches of Chadic is a strong indication that a similar feature might have existed already at the PC [Proto-Chadic] stage'. However, Schuh (2000) argues that Hausa relative aspects (focus forms of INFL) are a more recent innovation in Hausa or in its immediate ancestor. Schuh suggests that the Hausa focus (relative) TAM

---

[12] In addition, little or no information is available on the prosodic properties of these constructions, features that might reveal, for example, whether the post-verbal focus position is VP-internal or VP-external.

[13] Schuh (2000: 10) suggests that what has been described as 'relative tense' in Pa'a (Skinner 1979: 45) in relative clauses and narrative sequences is in fact a 'clause-level operator', observing that Pa'a uses the unmarked completive in *wh*-questions.

morpheme -*kV* originated as a non-verbal copula, with historical roots in the *k determiner base of Proto-Chadic, but that Hausa special inflection cannot be inherited from Proto-West Chadic:[14]

> ...formally the paired forms in those languages [with a general/relative perfective distinction] could not, by any stretch of imagination, share common ancestral forms with Hausa or with each other. One can therefore assume only a typological drift, perhaps more areal than genetic, since Kanuri [Nilo-Saharan] also makes a similar distinction. (Schuh 2000: 10)

Of the languages surveyed in this section, special inflection can only be claimed as a feature of Kanakuru and Miya.

Finally, a number of the Chadic languages surveyed here have some form of focus marker. Among the West A languages, Bole has a (non-copular) clefting particle *ye*, which precedes questioned or focused subjects. Pero has a (probably non-copular) focus marker *iC*, which precedes clause-initial focus phrases in 'counter-presuppositional' focus constructions, and Mupun has a (copular) focus marker *a* that precedes focus/*wh*-phrases in situ. The three West B languages Bade, Ngizim and Duwai all have a (non-copular) focus marker (*nə́/nən/n*) preceding postverbal focus/*wh*-subjects. This morpheme is historically related to the Hausa copula in the sense that both have evolved from the Proto-Afroasiatic determiner system (§ 5.3), but this morpheme has not evolved a copular function in Bade, Ngizim and Duwai (see also Schuh 2005).

---

[14] Consider the Hausa non-verbal clause in (i), which illustrates that it is possible for the TAM part of the INFL word to occur without the person/number/gender morpheme, in which case the short vowel of the TAM marker lengthens.

     (i) **halinsà**   kè   nan   (Jaggar 2001: 463)
          character.of.3ms   FOC.IMPF there
          'that's just **his character**'

Schuh (2000) outlines his analysis of the evolution of Hausa special inflection as follows: Sentences such as [(i)] must, in fact, represent the original use of *kè*. That is, the original use of Hausa *kè* is as a copula in non-verbal sentences. Its function as a relative TAM marker in verbal sentences is the innovative extension ... Like the *nē/cē~nā/tā* copula, the *kè* copula has its origin in the determiner system, although unlike *nē/cē~nā/tā*, which represent a recent innovation within Hausa, *kè* with copula function must have been inherited as such from the language ancestral to Hausa. Proto-Chadic had a *k determiner base ... which probably originally functioned as a gender neutral marker of definiteness. (Schuh 2000: 5) Schuh (2000) develops an analysis of the extension of relative aspects (special inflection) to the focus/relative perfective TAM form *kà* along similar lines. Schuh's hypothesis is that the Modern Hausa relative/focus-perfective TAM morpheme –*kà* originated as a focus-marking ('clefting') copula, which was preceded by the independent subject pronoun in cases of subject focus (Stage I). As the original verb-final TAM morphemes evolved into pre-verbal TAM markers (Stage IIa) and independent pronouns become person-agreement markers, a new set of independent pronouns evolve (Stage IIb). At some point in this path of change, the complex consisting of the original independent pronoun (person-agreement marker) and the clefting copula, which originally occurs only in cases of subject focus, is reanalysed as a focus form of inflection and is extended to constructions involving the focus fronting of subjects and non-subjects.

In summary, there is considerable typological variation in focus marking in Chadic, and the Hausa pattern, although widespread cross-linguistically, is only a small part of the Chadic picture. As Schuh observes,

> Because of the overwhelming numerical and geographical dominance of Hausa among languages of the Chadic family, there has long been a tendency, spoken or unspoken, in comparative Chadic studies and more broadly in comparative Afroasiatic studies referring to Chadic data to look to Hausa as a sort of prototype for features of grammar. (Schuh 2000: 1)

As the data discussed here demonstrate, the picture is far more complex, not least because many grammatical sketches of Chadic languages contain gaps in the data, and many more Chadic languages have yet to be described.

Theoretical issues

Tuller (1992) develops a (Government and Binding) theoretical account of postverbal focus in Chadic, which rests on the claim that the [+FOCUS] feature is associated with INFL. According to Tuller, this view enables an account of postverbal focus in both SVO and VSO Chadic languages. The first main claim of Tuller's analysis is that postverbal focus results from a VP-adjoined focus position, with the verb raising to adjoin to INFL. This structure is shown in (27) (Tuller 1992: 315):

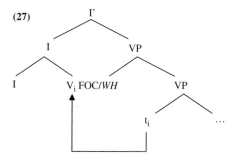

In support of this analysis, recall that Tuller cites evidence from Kenstowicz (1985) relating to two phonological (sandhi) phenomena: final vowel deletion and tone delinking. While these sandhi processes apply between the verb and its direct object in Tangale, they do not apply when the direct object is in focus, suggesting vacuous movement to a VP-external position. Tuller argues that the [+FOCUS] feature is associated with INFL, and that the focus position is VP-adjoined because this places it within the governing domain of INFL. V to INFL raising is motivated by the assumption that INFL must be 'verbal' in order to assign [+FOCUS] (Horvath 1986). The appearance of the relative-marked form of INFL in some Chadic focus constructions also suggests to Tuller a link between INFL and the [+FOCUS] feature.

The second main claim of Tuller's analysis relates to how the relative order of constituents is licensed in postverbal focus constructions. As we have seen, some Chadic languages have a focus position directly after the verb, including Western Bade (SVO) and Podoko (VSO). This gives rise to focus constructions with the constituent order [V FOC/WH DO]. Example (28) illustrates this type of construction in Western Bade.

(28) a. ā   bə̀nà-n   kè   kajlùwaw   *Western Bade subject* wh-*question*
        FUT cook-FM who tuwo   (Schuh 1982a: 166)
        'who will cook the tuwo?'
     b. Sāku ā   bə̀nà kə̀m   *Western Bade object* wh-*question*
        Saku FUT cook what   (Schuh 1982a: 164)
        'what will Saku cook?'

Tuller suggests that the order [V FOC/WH DO] follows from the ability of the verb trace to transmit case (Koopman 1992). In the languages where the focus position follows the verb directly, V raises to INFL, and the (subject) focus/wh-phrase raises from its position within VP to adjoin to VP, falling within the scope of the [+FOCUS] feature in INFL by virtue of its position adjacent to (and governed by) the INFL-V complex. The direct object 'left behind' in VP is case marked by the trace of V, licensing the constituent order [V FOC/WH DO]. The structure for this analysis is shown in (29) (adapted from Tuller 1992: 315).

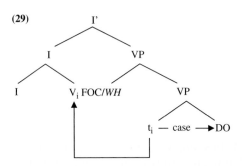

Other Chadic languages have a focus position after the direct object, including Tangale (SVO), Kanakuru (SVO) and Ngizim (SVO). This gives rise to focus constructions with the constituent order [V DO FOC/WH]. The Kanakuru examples in (14) are repeated here in (30):

(30) a. at ɗenoi **Balau**   *Kanakuru subject focus*
        ate peanuts Balau   (Newman 1974: 63)
        '**Balau** ate the peanuts'

b. ànò   aye **kai**   *Kanakuru object focus*
    1s.FUT help 2ms   (Newman 1974: 67)
    'I will help **you**'

c. na   ɗibəre gami mandai   *Kanakuru subject* wh-*question*
    FUT buy   ram who   (Newman 1974: 63)
    'who will buy the ram?'

d. kàa   nai   mandai   *Kanakuru object* wh-*question*
    2ms.IMPF call   who   (Newman 1974: 66)
    'whom are you calling?'

Tuller suggests that the constituent order [v do foc/wh] follows from the inability of the verb trace to transmit case, which entails that the noun must be incorporated into the verb, right-adjoining to the verb in order to be case-licensed. The direct object therefore raises with the verb to INFL. The structure for this analysis is shown in (31) (adapted from Tuller 1992: 318). The third main claim of Tuller's analysis relates to the fact that complex direct object 'splitting' is 'optional' in Tangale and Ngizim but obligatory in Kanakuru. Examples (12) and (15) are repeated here as (32) and (33) respectively.

(31)

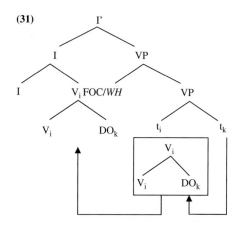

(32) a. shag [wamunjaanan] nɔŋ [nam   *Tangale*
         ate food.REL   who REL   (Tuller 1992: 310)
         Aisha ɗikɔ]
         Aisha prepared
         'who ate the food that Aisha prepared?'

     b. shag [wamunjaanam Aisha   *Tangale*
         ate food.REL   Aisha   (Tuller 1992: 310)
         ɗikɔn]   nɔŋ
         prepared   who
         'who ate the food that Aisha prepared?'

(33) aɗe [shiruwoi] **ŋgadlai** [mə shée   *Kanakuru*
     ate fish   cat   REL 3fs.PF   (Newman 1974: 64)
     wura] ane
     fry   PRO
     '**the cat** ate up the fish that she fried'

Tuller suggests that these facts follow from the alternative focus positions found in these languages. Recall from example (13) that Tangale has a clause-final focus position. Example (34) shows that this option is also available in Ngizim:

(34) ɗəbdə karē ā āsək   nən **Audu**   *Ngizim clause-final focus*
     sold goods in market FM Audu   (Tuller 1992: 322)
     '**Audu** sold the goods in the market'

Tuller suggests that the optionality in these languages is only apparent, and that when the object is not split (32b) the focus/*wh*-phrase is not in the VP-adjoined focus position but in the clause-final focus position (the specifier of CP, in Tuller's analysis). In contrast, the obligatory nature of direct object splitting in Kanakuru follows from the fact that this language does not have a clause-final [Spec CP] focus position. Instead, Kanakuru has a clause-initial alternative focus position (16).

The implications of postverbal focus in Chadic for the focus phrase (FP) analysis were explored by Green (1997), where it was suggested that the FP analysis could in principle be extended to account for postverbal focus by assuming, as in Hausa and other languages with a clause-initial focus position, that focus phrases raise to the specifier of a left-peripheral FP. However, to derive the correct word order facts for postverbal focus languages, the analysis entails that constituents that precede the focus phrase occupy some position higher than FP in the left periphery of the clause: CP and/or TopP. For example, in order to account for the constituent order [v FOC/*WH* DO] in an SVO language like Western Bade, object focus/*wh*-constructions might be derived by raising the object to the specifier of FP, raising V to INFL, and then raising the resulting INFL-V complex to Top, and by assuming that the subject occupies the specifier of the topic phrase (TopP) position. Subject focus constructions, in turn, might be derived by assuming that the subject raises to the specifier of FP, while the INFL-V complex raises to Top and the object remains in situ. The resulting structure is sketched in (35) and (36), for object focus/*wh*- and subject focus/*wh*-constructions, respectively.

Observe that this speculative analysis makes certain empirical predictions, notably that the subject might be expected to display properties of topic in

(35)

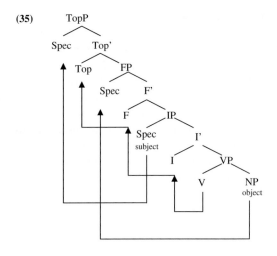

(36)

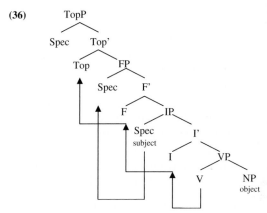

object focus/*wh*-constructions. [15] While the mechanics of a left-peripheral FP structure can be manipulated to account for postverbal focus, this phenomenon requires a considerably more complex derivation than focus fronting. This structure therefore offers a less appealing approach to postverbal focus.

An alternative line of analysis is to postulate a focus position (FP) immediately dominating the verb phrase, and dominated by the inflectional layer (IP) (Belletti & Shlonsky 1995). Assuming that the focused subject or object raises from its VP-internal thematic position to the focus phrase, and

[15] The constituent order [v DO FOC/WH] found in Ngizim,Tangale and Kanakuru can be derived along essentially the same lines, but requires the pied-piping of the object by the verb, while the constituent order [v FOC/WH DO] can be derived for VSO language like Podoko (assuming an underlying SVO order) by raising V to C, raising the focus/*wh*-phrase to the specifier of FP, and leaving either the subject or the object in situ.

that the verb raises to the inflectional layer, this structure would derive the postverbal focus word order, but raises questions about the licensing of subject case when the subject is in focus, a feature standardly associated with the specifier of IP. Whichever line of analysis is pursued, each step in the complex derivation requires some empirical motivation, and the predictions of the analysis can only be addressed by more detailed empirical research into the properties of postverbal focus constructions in Chadic (see French (2004) for a discussion of these theoretical issues as they apply to the Chadic language Bole). An alternative line of investigation might explore further the prosodic properties of these constructions, which may reveal whether the asymmetry between subjects (ex situ) and objects ('in situ') is apparent or real by establishing whether the postverbal focus position is VP-internal or VP-external.

6.2.2 *Arabic*

Descriptive facts

In the syntax of focus/*wh*-constructions, there are a number of striking similarities between Hausa and Modern Standard Arabic, a member of the Semitic branch of the Afroasiatic family.[16] For example, Standard Arabic allows both focus in situ (37a) and focus fronting (37b). However, Ouhalla (1994) argues (after Moutaouakil 1989) that these two strategies encode different types of focus: the in situ strategy encodes new information (or presentational) focus, and the ex situ strategy encodes contrastive (exhaustive) focus. Recall that É. Kiss (1998a) makes the same claim for focus in Hungarian, but that Green and Jaggar (2003) found no evidence for the same form–function correlation in Hausa (§ 4.6.3).

(37) a. ʔallaf-at   Zaynab-u   **riwaayat-an**   *Standard Arabic*
      wrote-3fs   Zaynab-NOM   novel-ACC   (Ouhalla 1999: 337)
      'Zaynab wrote a **novel**'

    b. **riwaayat-an**   ʔallaf-at   Zaynab-u
      novel-ACC   wrote-3fs   Zaynab-NOM
      'Zaynab wrote a **novel**'

Like Hausa, Standard Arabic also allows topic phrases in clause initial position (38).

(38) a. l-shaay-a$_i$, sharib-tu-hu$_i$ *Standard Arabic*
      DD-tea-ACC drank-1s-PRO.3ms   (Ouhalla 1994: 67)
      'the tea, I drank it'

---

[16] Standard Arabic, a case-marking language, permits both VSO and SVO word order, where VSO order is unmarked. However, SVO is the unmarked word order in the spoken dialects discussed here. For discussion of word order in Arabic, see e.g. Fassi-Fehri (1984; 1993); Aoun et al. (1994); Benmamoun (2000); Shlonsky (2000b); Harbert & Bahloul (2002).

b. *shaay-a$_i$, sharib-tu-hu$_i$ *Standard Arabic*
   tea-ACC   drank-1s-PRO.3ms   (Ouhalla 1994: 68)
   'the tea, I drank it'

c. l-kitaab-u$_i$,   qara?-tu-hu$_i$ *Standard Arabic*
   DD-book-NOM read-1s-PRO.3ms   (Ouhalla 1994: 68)
   'the book, I read it'

As the examples in (37) and (38) illustrate, focus fronting and topic constructions differ in Standard Arabic in the same ways that they differ in Hausa. First, focus fronted phrases are not separated from the rest of the clause by an intonational pause, whereas topics are. Secondly, topics are accompanied by a resumptive pronoun lower in the clause and must be definite (hence the ungrammaticality of (38b)), while focus fronted phrases co-occur with a gap lower in the clause. In addition, focus fronted phrases must carry the same case marking as the gap with which they are associated. Observe, for example, that the focus fronted direct object *riwaayat-an* 'novel' bears accusative case in (37b). In contrast, topics are free to bear either nominative or accusative case (compare (38a) and (38c)). Ouhalla (1994) also observes that topic and focus are prosodically distinct: while both in situ and ex situ focus phrases are prosodically prominent, topics are not. As in Hausa, multiple topics are possible, whereas only one focus-fronted phrase is possible, and where focus and topic co-occur within a single clause, topic(s) must precede focus (39).

(39) a. Zayd-un$_i$, **riwaayat-an**   *Standard Arabic*
        Zayd-NOM novel-ACC   (Ouhalla 1994: 71)
        ?a'tay-tu-hu$_i$
        gave-1s-PRO.3ms
        '(as for) Zayd, I gave him **a novel**'

    b. ***riwaayat-an** Zayd-un$_i$?a'tay-tu-hu$_i$
       novel-ACC   Zayd-NOM gave-1s-PRO.3ms
       '(as for) Zayd, I gave him **a novel**'

Example (40) shows that *wh*-phrases pattern together with focus phrases in Standard Arabic, occurring either in left-peripheral position (40a) or in situ (40b). However, constructions like (40b), in which the sole *wh*-phrase appears in situ, do not license a genuine *wh*-interrogative interpretation. Instead, these function as echo questions.

(40) a. maadaa qara?-at Zaynab-u?   *Standard Arabic*
        what   read-3fs Zaynab-NOM   (Ouhalla 1994: 68)
        'what did Zaynab read?'

    b. sharib-a   Zayd-un   maadaa   *Standard Arabic*
       drank-3ms Zayd-NOM what   (Ouhalla 1994: 73)
       'Zayd drank *what*?'

As in Hausa, it is not possible to prepose a *wh*-phrase and a focus phrase simultaneously, irrespective of order, which suggests that they occupy the same syntactic position (41).

(41) a. ***kitaab-an** mataa qaraʔ-ta?   *Standard Arabic*
      book-ACC   when   read-2s   (Ouhalla 1994: 69)
      'when did you read **a book**?'
  b. *mataa **kitaab-an** qaraʔ-ta?
      when   book-ACC   read-2s
      'when did you read **a book**?'

According to Ouhalla & Shlonsky (2002: 19), the spoken dialects of Arabic either permit both in situ and ex situ *wh*-constructions, or prohibit (single) *wh*-phrases in situ and instead require *wh*-fronting. The dialects that allow both in situ and ex situ *wh*-phrases include Egyptian Arabic (Wahba 1984; Jelinek 2002), Iraqi Arabic (Wahba 1991) and Lebanese Arabic (Aoun & Choueiri 1999). The following (subject pro-drop) examples illustrate object *wh*-in situ (42a) and object *wh*-fronting (42b) in Lebanese Arabic.

(42) a. ʃəft   ʔayya mmasil   *Lebanese Arabic*
      saw.2ms which actor   (Aoun & Choueiri 1999: 7)
      b-l-matʕam?
      in-DD-restaurant
      'which actor did you see in the restaurant?'
  b. ʔayya   mmasil ʃəft   b-l-matʕam?
      which   actor   saw-2ms in-DD-restaurant
      'which actor did you see in the restaurant?'

The dialects that require *wh*-fronting include Moroccan Arabic (Ouhalla 1999) and Palestinian Arabic (Shlonsky 2002). Example (43) illustrates the fact that a single *wh*-phrase must be fronted in Moroccan Arabic, while example (44) shows that a *wh*-phrase in situ is marginally acceptable in multiple *wh*-questions.

(43) a. škun šəft-i?   *Moroccan Arabic*
      who see.PF-2s   (Ouhalla & Shlonsky 2002: 19)
      'who have you seen?'
  b. *šəft-i škun
      see.PF-2s who
      'who have you seen?'
(44) ?(qul-li) škun šaf   škun   *Moroccan Arabic*
    (tell-me) who see.PF   who   (Ouhalla & Shlonsky 2002: 19)
    '(tell me) who saw who'

The examples in (45) illustrate *wh*-fronting in Palestinian Arabic.

(45) a. miin l-ʔasad ʔakal   *Palestinian Arabic*
     who DD.lion ate-3fs   (Shlonsky 2002: 138)
     mbaari<u>h</u>?
     yesterday
     'who did the lion eat yesterday?'
   b. miin <u>h</u>all il-muškile?   *Palestinian Arabic*
     who solved DD-problem   (Shlonsky 2002: 142)
     'who solved the problem?'

Focus and *wh*-constructions do not necessarily pattern together in the spoken dialects of Arabic. For example, Moroccan Arabic is a focus in situ dialect that has a cleft construction but not a focus fronting construction (Ouhalla 1999: 338). The cleft focus/*wh*-construction is illustrated in (46). Example (46b) can be compared directly with example (45a). Observe that while the *wh*-fronting example contains a gap in the thematic position of the *wh*-phrase (45a), the cleft construction contains a resumptive pronoun in the associated thematic position (46b). In addition, the cleft construction is characterised by the optional presence of the non-verbal (pronominal) copula and the presence of the relativising complementiser. This construction is discussed in more detail below (§ 6.3.3).

(46) a. **Nadia** hiyya lli   *Moroccan Arabic*
     Nadia PRO.COP.fs COMP   (Ouhalla & Shlonsky 2002: 21)
     qr-at l-ktab
     read-3fs DD-book
     'it's **Nadia** who read the book'
   b. miin$_i$ (hi) ʔilli   *Palestinian Arabic*
     who (PRO.COP.3fs) COMP   (Shlonsky 2002: 147)
     l-ʔasad ʔakal-ha$_i$ mbaari<u>h</u>?
     dd.lion ate-3fs yesterday
     'who did the lion eat (her) yesterday?'
   c. miin ʔilli šafit-hu   *Egyptian Arabic*
     who COMP see.PF-3ms   (Jelinek 2002: 100)
     who was it that she saw (him)?'

Theoretical issues

In his (1994; 1997) analysis of focus in Standard Arabic, Ouhalla argues that fronted focus and *wh*-phrases undergo movement to the same clause-initial position. Ouhalla rejects the possibility that this displacement operation targets the specifier of the complementiser phrase (CP) on the basis that focused-fronted phrases can follow the complementiser ʔanna in embedded clauses (47).

(47) dhanan-tu   ?anna   **kitaab-an**   *Standard Arabic*
     believe-1s   that   book-ACC   (Ouhalla 1994: 70)
     qara?-at   Zaynab-u
     read-3fs   Zaynab-NOM
     'I believe that it was **a book** that Zaynab read'

Ouhalla (1997) therefore argues that the functional projection focus phrase (FP) is the target of focus/*wh*-fronting, and that this displacement operation is motivated by the checking of [+FOCUS] or [+Q] features. In the case of focus fronting, the prosodic prominence associated with focus spells out the [+FOCUS] feature present on the head of the focus phrase. According to Ouhalla, this is due to the 'Identification Requirement' (Ouhalla 1994: 72):

(48) *The Identification Requirement*: Abstract features encoded in
     structural descriptions must be identified (in terms of properties
     of surface strings)

This requirement holds that formal syntactic features have some kind of morphosyntactic realisation, and is also argued to underlie movement of focus phrases to the specifier of FP, a process that identifies the [+FOCUS] feature of the head F under specifier–head agreement. According to Ouhalla's analysis, if the Identification Requirement is satisfied in a given language by the presence of a sentence focus morpheme, this licenses a contrastive focus phrase to remain in situ, because its movement is unnecessary and therefore ruled out by economy. Ouhalla argues that the [+FOCUS] feature is absent from the head F in Standard Arabic new information focus constructions, which entails that the Identification Requirement does not apply, and no movement takes place. In the case of constituent focus fronting in Standard Arabic, no overt focus morpheme is present. However, in the case of sentence focus (where the truth of the whole proposition is in focus), a number of focus particles may occur, such as the focus marker *laqad*. These focus particles lend a contrastive focus interpretation to the sentence, which entails that sentences modified by these elements are not licensed as felicitous answers to *wh*-questions.

(49) laqad   ?arsal-at   Zaynab-u   risaalat-an   *Standard Arabic*
     FM   sent-3fs   Zaynab-NOM letter-ACC   (Ouhalla 1994: 75)
     'Zaynab **did** send a letter'

Ouhalla argues that these sentence focus markers occupy the F position and are the morphological spellout of the [+FOCUS] feature in F. These focus markers also license a contrastive focus phrase to remain in situ, a pattern that follows from Ouhalla's analysis because the presence of the focus

marker in F satisfies the Identification Requirement, so that movement of
the focused constiuent to the specifier of FP is unnecessary and therefore
impossible. Ouhalla suggests that the in situ focus phrase receives its
interpretation by coindexation with F. The interrogative contrastive focus
particle (Q) ?a patterns in a similar way (50).

(50) a. ?a **qara?-ta**   l-kitaab-a   *Standard Arabic*
        Q   read-3ms the-book-ACC   (Ouhalla 1994: 86)
        (?am   ?allaf-ta-hu)?
        or   wrote-2ms-it
        'did he **read** the book (or write it)?'
    b. ?a **kitaab-an** ?allaf-ta   (?am qasiidat-an)?
        Q book-ACC wrote-2ms or   poem-ACC
        'did you write a **book** (or a poem)?'

Ouhalla argues that *?a* has both the features [+FOCUS] and [+Q], and
extends the same analysis to this particle as to the other (non-interrogative)
focus particles. In cases of sentential focus, *?a* occupies the F position and
the rest of the clause remains in situ (50a). In cases of constituent focus, *?a*
is base-generated adjoined to the phrase it modifies, which then raises to the
specifier of FP (50b). This analysis is supported by the ungrammaticality of
example (51), which shows the constituent modified by *?a* remaining in situ.

(51) *?allaf-ta ?a-kitaab-an   (?am qasiidat-an)?   *Standard Arabic*
     write-2ms Q/FM-book-ACC or   poem-ACC   (Ouhalla 1994: 87)
     'did you write a **book** (or a poem)?'

However, if *?a* occurs alone in the left periphery, it licenses in situ
(interrogative) contrastive focus. Compare example (52) with example
(50b).

(52) ?a   ?allaf-ta   **kitaab-an**   *Standard Arabic*
     Q/FM write-2ms book-ACC   (Ouhalla 1994: 87)
     (?am qasiidat-an)?
     or   poem-ACC
     'did you write a **book** (or a poem)?'

As the discussion in this section shows, Hausa and Standard Arabic share a
number of properties in common in relation to the syntax of monoclausal
focus/*wh*-constructions, although they differ with respect to the form–
function correlation that is present in Standard Arabic but absent in Hausa.
Of course, there is far greater dialect variation in Arabic than in Hausa,
which is evident in the fact that different spoken dialects choose different
options among the set of focus/*wh*-strategies. The structure of the cleft
construction discussed by Ouhalla (1999) and Shlonsky (2002) is addressed
in more detail below, since it shares certain properties with the non-verbal
(pronominal) copular clause (§ 6.3.3). In sum, to the extent that Hausa and

Arabic share syntactic properties in the realisation of focus/*wh*-construc-
tions, a largely parallel theoretical analysis is possible, which goes some way
towards capturing these cross-linguistic similarities.

6.2.3 *Hebrew*

Descriptive facts

Modern Hebrew is an SVO language (53a), with VS(O) licensed only in
marked constructions with a clause-initial topic (53b).[17] Observe that the
marked construction in (53b), in which the object is topicalised, places the
postverbal subject in focus, although it is not necessarily prosodically
prominent (Belletti & Shlonsky 1995: 509).

> (53) a. dani   katav et   ha-mixtav   *Modern Hebrew*
>   Dani wrote ACC DD-letter   (adapted from Doron 2000: 42)
>   'Dani has written the letter'
>   b. et   ha-mixtav katav **dani**
>   ACC DD-letter   wrote Dani
>   '**Dani** has written the letter'

The fact that the postverbal subject is in focus is illustrated by the fact that
only VS word order is licensed in response to a subject *wh*-question (54),
whereas VS word order is not licensed in response to an object question
(55). As these examples illustrate, Modern Hebrew is a *wh*-fronting
language.

> (54) Q. mi   ʕacra   ʔet   *Modern Hebrew*
>   who detained ACC   (Belletti & Shlonsky 1995: 509)
>   ha-roceax?
>   dd-murderer
>   'who detained the murderer?'
>   A. ʔet   ha-roceax   ʕacra   **ha-mištara**
>   ACC DD-murderer detained DD-police
>   '**the police** detained the murderer'
>   A'.#ʔet ha-roceax   ha-mištara ʕacra
>   ACC DD-murderer DD-police   detained
>   'the police detained the murderer'
> (55) Q. ma   ʕasta ha-mištara   *Modern Hebrew*
>   what did   DD-police   (Belletti & Shlonsky 1995: 509)
>   ʔetmol?
>   yesterday
>   'what did the police do yesterday?'

---

[17] For discussions of word order in Hebrew, see e.g. Shlonsky & Doron (1992); Borer (1995);
Shlonsky (1997).

A. ʔetmol   ha-mištara   ʕacra   rocxim
   yesterday DD-police detained murderers
   'yesterday the police detained murderers'
A'.#ʔetmol   ʕacra   **ha-mištara** rocxim
   yesterday detained DD-police   murderers
   'yesterday **the police** detained murderers'

Despite this pattern, Belletti & Shlonsky (1995: 509) observe that (54A')
becomes well-formed in response to (54Q) if the postverbal subject *ha-mištara* 'the police' is contrastively focused, suggesting that Hebrew has
access to prosodic strategies for marking focus that may override syntactic
constraints.

Belletti & Shlonsky (1995) argue that focus also underlies the difference
between the unmarked order of verbal complements illustrated in (56a) and
the marked word order in (56b).

(56) a. henaxti ʔet ha-sefer ha.hu   *Modern Hebrew*
      put.1s   ACC DD-book   DEM   (Belletti & Shlonsky 1995: 489)
      ʕal   ha-šulxan
      on   DD-table
      'I put that book on the table'
   b. henaxti **ʕal ha-šulxan** ʔet ha-sefer ha.hu
      put.1s on DD-table   ACC DD-book   DEM
      'I put that book **on the table**'

The fact that the indirect (prepositional) object is in focus in the marked
construction is illustrated by the fact that an indirect object *wh*-question
requires this word order in the response (57).

(57) Q. le-mi   carix le-haxzir   *Modern Hebrew*
      to-whom must to-return   (Belletti & Shlonsky 1995: 512)
      ʔet   ha-maftexot?
      ACC   DD-keys
      'to whom must one return the keys?'
   A. carix   le-haxzir le-**Rina** ʔet ha-maftexot
      (one).must to-return to-Rina ACC DD-keys
      'one must return the keys to **Rina**'
   A'.#carix   le-haxzir ʔet   ha-maftexot le-Rina
      (one).must to-return ACC   DD-keys   to-Rina
      'one must return the keys to Rina'

As Belletti & Shlonsky (1995) observe, if both the postverbal subject in
constructions like (54A) and the indirect object in constructions like (57A)
target the same focus position, it should not be possible for the postverbal
subject and the IO–DO order to occur within a single construction. This is
confirmed by the highly marginal status of examples like (58). In sum, these

data suggest that Modern Hebrew has a single postverbal (new information) focus position.[18]

(58) a. ???etmol,   natan   Dani   *Modern Hebrew*
        yesterday   gave   Dani   (Belletti & Shlonsky 1995: 512)
        le-Rina   matana
        to-Rina   present
        'yesterday, **Dani** gave **Rina** a present'

In addition, Hebrew has a biclausal cleft construction, illustrated in (59). In this construction, the focused NP is linked to a relative clause structure by the pronominal copula. According to Doron & Heycock (1999), this focusing strategy is restricted to subjects.

(59) **Dani**   hu   še   'azar   *Modern Hebrew*
     Dani   PRO.COP.3ms   that   helped   (Doron & Heycock 1999: 77)
     le   Dina
     to   Dina
     'it is **Dani** who helped Dina'

Hebrew also has a pseudocleft construction, which is illustrated by (60). Like the Hausa pseudocleft (§ 5.2), this construction consists of two noun phrases linked by a non-verbal copula, and the pre-copular noun phrase consists of a free relative. This construction is discussed in more detail below (§ 6.3.4).

(60) ma   še-dekart   maca   hu   *Modern Hebrew*
     what that-Descartes found   PRO.COP.ms   (Heller 2002: 253)
     hoxaxa   le-kiyum   ha-el
     proof   to-existence DD-god
     'what Descartes found is/was a proof of God's existence.'

Consider finally the Hebrew 'V(P) fronting construction', sometimes described as a 'predicate cleft' (Landau 2005). In this construction, an infinitive verb occurs in the left periphery of the clause, followed by a fully inflected copy of the verb inside the clause. The complement is either fronted together with the infinitve verb (61a) or stranded in the clause (61b).

(61) a. liknot   et   ha-praxim, hi   kanta   *Modern Hebrew*
        to-buy   ACC   DD-flowers, PRO.3fs   bought (Landau 2005: ex. 8)
        'as for buying the flowers, she bought (them)'
     b. liknot, hi   kanta   et   ha-praxim
        to-buy, PRO.3fs   bought   ACC   DD-flowers
        'as for buying, she bought the flowers'

As the translations indicate, this infinitival V(P) can function as a topic. Landau (2002) observes that this construction is characterised by pause

---

[18] Belletti & Shlonsky (1995) do not provide examples of contrastive focus.

intonation and by high pitch accent on the stressed syllable of the infinitive. However, it is also possible for the construction to contain a contrastive focus interpretation, where the V(P), which is known information, is contrasted with a (prosodically prominent) constituent in the clause. Consider the following examples (prosodic prominence is marked by SMALL CAPITALS).

(62) a. licxok   hi   coxeket rak   *Modern Hebrew*
        to-laugh PRO.3fs laughs   only   (Landau 2005: ex. 16)
        al   **axeRIM**
        on   others
        'as for laughing, she will only laugh at **others**'
     b. licxok   al   acma   hi   LO ticxak
        to-laugh on   herself PRO.3fs NEG will-laugh
        'as for laughing at herself, she **won't** laugh'

Theoretical issues

Belletti & Shlonsky (1995) develop an analysis of the facts illustrated by examples (53)–(58) above in which focused constituents target the specifier of the focus phrase (FP). In Belletti & Shlonsky's analysis, this projection immediately dominates the VP, as shown in (63), adapted from Belletti & Shlonsky (1995: 511).[19]

The VS order that characterises examples like (54A) is derived by raising the subject from its VP-internal position to the specifier of FP, and raising the verb above FP to the inflectional layer. The IO–DO order that

(63)
```
              IP
           /     \
        Spec      I'
               /     \
              I       FP
                   /     \
                Spec      F'
                       /     \
                      F       vP
                          /      \
                       SUBJ       v'
                               /     \
                              v       VP
                                   /     \
                                  V'      IO
                               /     \
                              V       DO
```

[19] Belletti & Shlonsky (1995) assume a split INFL analysis, which is simplified to IP in (64). Belletti & Shlonsky are not specific about the position occupied by the preverbal topic constituents in VS constructions, nor about subject case licensing in VS constructions. For alternative analyses of the VS order, see Borer (1995) and Doron (2000). Borer (1995) argues that nominative case is licensed in the VP, while Doron (2000) argues that it is licensed in the specifier of IP.

characterises examples like (57A) is derived by raising the indirect object
to the specifier of FP, and raising the verb to the inflectional layer.

According to Landau (2005), the V(P)-doubling constructions like (61)
and (62) are derived by displacement, since the dependency between
the left-peripheral V(P) and the clause-internal VP shows characteristics of
movement constraints. For example, (64) shows that the dependency is
sensitive to island constraints: if the clause-internal VP is contained within
a complex noun phrase, the construction is ungrammatical.

(64) a. *likro   et ha-sefer, Gil daxa   et ha-te'ana še-hu
         to-read ACC DD-book   Gil rejected ACC DD-claim that-PRO.3ms
         kvar   kara
         already read
         'as for reading the book, Gil rejected the claim that he had
         already read'

   b *likro, Gil daxa   et ha-te'ana še-hu   kvar   kara
       to-read Gil rejected ACC DD-claim that-PRO.3ms already read
       et   ha-sefer
       ACC   DD-book
       'as for reading, Gil rejected the claim that he had already read
       the book'   *Modern Hebrew* (Landau 2005: ex. 24)

Landau adopts the copy theory of movement (§ 3.4.3), and argues that this
construction involves a movement chain in which both copies are spelled
out. Since the VP-fronting construction is essentially a topic construction,
the target of movement is the specifier of topic phrase (TopP). The structure
proposed by Landau is shown in (65) (adapted from Landau (2005: 57b)).
Landau argues that examples like (61a), in which the infinitival verb is
fronted together with the direct object, involve the raising of vP. In
contrast, examples like (61b), in which only the infinitival verb is raised,
involve the displacement of the verb. The non-identity of the two verbs in
terms of finiteness is accounted for by the assumption that the movement

(65)

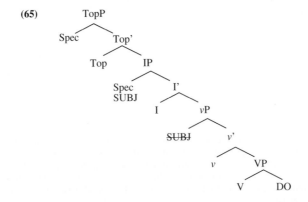

and copying operation precedes the raising of the clause-internal verb to the inflectional layer.

In sum, Hebrew shares some properties with Hausa in terms of the formal features that mark information structure and distinguish declarative and interrogative clauses. Like Hausa, Hebrew has a *wh*-fronting strategy. According to Belletti & Shlonsky's (1995) analysis, Hebrew also has access to a focus-raising operation parallel to the Hausa focus fronting operation in the sense that it targets the specifier of the focus phrase (FP). However, this operation does not result in clause-initial focus in Hebrew, but in a focus position local to the verb, a common typological strategy (§ 3.3.2). Hebrew also has a cleft construction, although this is restricted to subjects. In addition to these syntactic strategies, prosodic prominence also plays an important role in marking contrastive focus in Hebrew.

While both Hebrew and Hausa have a VP fronting strategy that shows characteristics of movement (§ 4.3), there are important differences. First, while Hausa marks the extraction site with a pro-verb, Hebrew marks the extraction site with a fully inflected copy. Secondly, Hausa V(N)P movement results in a focus construction, while its Hebrew counterpart is essentially a topic construction. While Hausa does have a parallel to the Hebrew VP topic construction, this construction does not display properties of movement: recall that Hausa topics are not sensitive to island constraints (§ 4.2.2).

Finally, Hausa and Hebrew both have a similar pseudocleft construction, in which the non-verbal copula links two constituents, one of which has a relative clause structure and expresses the presupposition, and the other of which is the focus of the clause. The properties of the Hebrew pseudocleft, a type of copular construction, are discussed in more detail below (§ 6.3.4).

6.2.4 *Coptic Egyptian*

Descriptive facts

Coptic Egyptian is an SVO language in which the pre-subject inflection word indicates tense, aspect or mood, but does not express person, number or gender features. These features can be marked by subject and object clitic pronouns, which are in complementary distribution with full noun phrases (Reintges 2004). Example (66) illustrates an unmarked declarative sentence in Coptic.[20]

---

[20] Coptic Egyptian, which represents the final stage of Ancient Egyptian, was the indigenous language of late antique and early medieval Christian Egypt, and was spoken from about the third to the eleventh century AD. This branch of the Afroasiatic language family now contains no living languages. The two dominant dialects of Coptic were Sahidic Coptic, spoken in Upper Egypt, and Bohairic Coptic, spoken in Lower Egypt. The data in this section are from Sahidic Coptic, which due to its rich literature represents the main corpus for Coptic Egyptian. The data come mainly from religious texts. See references cited for textual sources, Reintges (2004: 4–6) for a discussion of the Coptic corpus, and Reintges (2004: 597–600) for a list of sources of Coptic texts.

(66) a te-f-sɔne   de   *Coptic unmarked SVO sentence*
        PF DD.fs-3ms-sister PART   (Reintges & Green 2004: ex. 6a)
        ɔl   ən-ne-f-kees
        gather   DO-DD.pl-3ms-bones
        'his sister gathered his bones'

In Coptic, as in Hausa, monoclausal focus and *wh*-constructions are syntactically parallel. Like Hausa, Coptic allows both in situ and ex situ focus/*wh*-constructions. Unlike in Hausa, the in situ strategy is the unmarked (most frequently attested) strategy in Coptic. This is illustrated by the *wh*-constructions in (67), in which *wh*-subject (67a) and *wh*-object (67b) remain in situ, in pre verbal and postverbal positions, respectively.

(67) a. ere   nim   *Coptic subject* wh-*question: in situ*
        RM(FUT) who   (Green & Reintges 2005b: ex. 8b)
        na-na   na-n?
        AUX-have.mercy   for-1pl
        'who will have mercy upon us?'
     b. e-i-na-ti   u   *Coptic object* wh-*question: in situ*
        RM(FUT)-1s-go-give what   (Reintges & Green 2004: ex. 8a)
        na-k?
        to-2ms
        'what shall I give you?'

The examples in (68) illustrate new information focus in situ in a question-answer pair. This strategy is also available for exhaustive/contrastive focus (69).

(68) Q. e-r-βɛk   *Coptic Q–A pair*
        RM(PRES)-2fs-come   *(new information focus in situ)*
        e-tɔn   (Reintges & Green 2004: ex. 13)
        to-where
        'where are you going to?'
     A. e-i-βɛk   **e-p-topos**   **ən apa mɛna** nt-a-ʃlɛl
        RM(PRES)-1s-come to-DD.ms-shrine of Apa Mena CONJ-1s-pray
        'I am on my way **to the shrine of Apa Mêna** to pray'
(69) mpɔr   pa-ʃɛre   *Coptic contrastive focus in situ*
     no   DD.ms.1s-son   (Reintges & Green 2004: ex.15)
     mp-u-toʃ-k   gar **e-ti-oikonomia** alla nt-a p-tʃoeis
     NEG.PF-3pl-appoint-2ms PART to-DEM.fs-service but RM-PF DD.ms-lord
     toʃ-k   **e-u-solsl**   n-ne-snɛu et
     appoint-2ms as-INDEF.s-comfort comp   for-DD.pl-brothers

waaβ		et	ʃoop	həm	pə-tʃaye
be.holy	COMP	live	inside		DD.fs-desert

'no, my son! You have not been appointed (lit. they have not appointed you) for **this career** (as a hermit), but the Lord has appointed you **as a comfort for the holy brothers** who live in the desert'

Like Hausa, Coptic marks its canonical in situ focus/*wh*-construction (as well as relative clauses) with special inflectional forms, traditionally known as SECOND TENSES. Coptic special inflection takes the form of a relative marker (RM) prefixed to the pre-subject inflection word (Reintges 2002; 2003a). The relative marker *ənt-* occurs with the perfect TAM marker *a*, while the default form *e-* occurs in all other contexts. As illustrated by (67)–(69) the relative marker *ere-* and its short form *e-* occur in main clause focus/*wh*-in situ constructions, but are absent from pragmatically neutral declarative clauses like (66). In both Hausa and Coptic, special inflection is realised in present/imperfective and past/perfective inflection systems, but while Hausa has no distinct relative/focus form of INFL in the future paradigm, and places restriction on what modal forms are licensed in focus/*wh*-constructions (§ 2.3.2), the Coptic general/relative distinction has a much wider distribution across TAM categories.

Like Hausa, Coptic allows monoclausal focus/*wh*-ex situ constructions, but these are marked in the sense that they are only sparsely attested in the Coptic corpus. In contrast with the Hausa pattern, special inflection is absent from these constructions, as illustrated by the examples in (70) and (71).

(70) a. nim   a-f-ent-ək   *Coptic subject* wh-*question: ex situ*
        who   PF-3MS-bring-2ms   (Reintges & Green 2004: ex. 19a)
        e-pei-ma?
        to-DEM.ms-place
        'who brought you here?'

     b. u   se-tʃi   wa   ero-i   *Coptic object*
        what 3PL-speak malice against-1s   wh-*question: ex situ*
        həm   p-e-ti-ʃəp   həmot (Reintges & Green
        in   DD.ms-RM(PRES)-1s-take grace   2004: ex. 17a)
        anok   haro-f
        PRO.1s   for-3MS
        'in what can they speak maliciously against me because of that for which I give thanks (lit. 'take grace')?

(71) Q. nim a-f-ent-ək   *Coptic Q-A pair (new*
          who PF-3MS-BRING-2MS   *information focus ex situ)*
          e-pei-ma?   (Reintges & Green
          to-DEM.ms-place   2004: ex. 22)
          'who brought you here?'

      A. **jesus** a-f-ent   e-pei-ma
          Jesus PF-3ms-bring(1s) to-DEM.ms-place
          '**Jesus** brought me here'

Finally, unlike Hausa, Coptic also has a biclausal cleft construction, in
which the copula links the clause-initial (NP) focus/*wh*-phrase with a
relative clause structure (bracketed). Observe that special inflection occurs
within the relative clause structure.

(72) a. nim pe   [ənt-a-f-tɔɔkʸe əmmo-u   *Coptic cleft* (wh)
          who COP.ms RM-PF-3ms-plant of-PRO.3pl   (Reintges 2004: 438)
          əm-pei-ma]?
          in-DD.ms-place
          'who is it that planted them (the trees) here?'

      b. ta-ʃeere   **tu-pistis**   *Coptic cleft (focus)*
          POSS.fs.1s-daughter POSS.fs.2fs-faith.fs   (Reintges et al.
          te   [ənt-a-s-nahm-e]   2005: ex. 19a)
          COP RM-PF-3fs-save-PRO.2FS
          'my daughter, (it is) **your faith** that has saved you.'

Theoretical issues

Reintges (2003a) assumes that the pre-subject TAM markers are generated in
the finiteness phrase (FinP), dominating the IP (Rizzi 1997).[21] As example
(73) illustrates, the fronted *wh*-phrase *eβol tɔn* 'where from' precedes the
perfect TAM marker *a-* and must therefore be located above the FinP.

(73) eβol tɔn   a-tetən-ei   e-pei-ma?   *Coptic*
          PART where PF-2pl-come to-DEM.ms-place   (Reintges et al.
          'from where did you come here?'   2003a: 364)

As illustrated by example (74), the fronted *wh*-phrase follows the
subordinating complementiser *tʃe* 'that' in embedded clauses, which
suggests that the displaced focus/*wh*-phrase is located in some functional
phrase below CP and above FinP/IP.

(74) ti-tʃənu əmmɔ-tən tʃe   hən u   *Coptic*
          1s-ask DO-2pl   COMP in   what   (Reintges & Green
          ən-ʃatʃe   2004: ex. 27a)
          of-word
          a-tetən   ero-i (...)
          PF.2pl-speak   about-1s
          'I ask you with what reason are you saying about me (...)'

---

[21] Coptic has two positions for TAM markers, one preceding the subject and the other following
it. The clause-internal TAM position is limited to root modals (Reintges 2001; 2004: 246–52).

As in Hausa, Coptic topics may precede fronted focus/*wh*-phrases, but unlike in Hausa, Coptic topics may also follow fronted focus/*wh*-phrases. The two available positions for topicalised constituents (underlined) are illustrated by the examples in (75). Note that the Greek loan particle *de* indicates a topic shift.

(75) a. <u>anon</u> de **etße**   **nen-noße**   *Coptic*
        we   PART because.of DD.1pl-sin   (Reintges 2004: 378)
        mar-ən-opt-ən   mawaa-n
        OPT.1pl-lock.up-1PL   SELF-1PL
        '(as for) us, **because of our sins**, let's lock ourselves up!'

    b. ən-aʃ   ən-he   <u>əntok</u>   kə-tʃɔ   *Coptic*
       in-which of-manner PRO.2ms 2ms-say   (Green & Reintges
       əmmo-s [tʃe   tetə(n)-na-ər   2005b: ex. 65b)
       DO-3fs COMP FUT.2pl-aux-make
       rəmhe]?
       free.man
       'how do you say that you will become free?'

Given these facts, Reintges (2003a) argues that the relevant projection that hosts fronted focus/*wh*-phrases in Coptic is the focus phrase (FP), which occurs below CP in embedded clauses, but dominates FinP/IP. In Coptic, as in Hausa, the FP analysis accounts for the fact that neither multiple focus

(76)

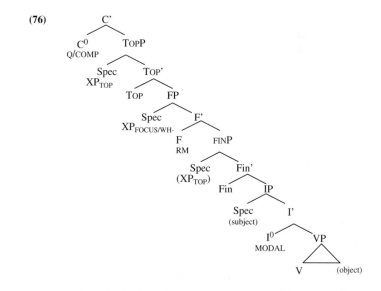

fronting nor a combination of *wh*- and focus fronting is attested. The structure of the Coptic clause is illustrated in (76) (Green & Reintges 2005b: ex. 66).

Recall from Chapter 4 (§ 4.5) that Reintges et al. (2006) develop a typology of special inflection that includes the parameters location (the head that carries special inflectional morphology), recursiveness (whether or not special inflection occurs in every clause through which long-distance extraction passes) and distribution (how wide a class of constructions special inflection occurs in). With respect to the parameter of location, the Coptic pattern roughly corresponds to operator-C agreement in Chamorro as far as the left-peripheral location of special inflection is concerned. With respect to the parameter of recursiveness, Coptic special inflection appears only on the highest designated functional head in cases of long-distance extraction (77). In this respect, Hausa and Coptic show the same pattern.

(77) eye əntɔtən   e-tetən-tšɔ   əmmo-s *Coptic*
      Q   you(pl)   RM(PRES)-2pl-say   DO-2FS (Green & Reintges
      ero-i   tše   ang   nim?   2005b: ex. 37b)
      about-1s COMP   PRO.1s   who
      'who are you saying of me that I (am)?'

Finally, like Hausa, Coptic special inflection shows a relatively wide distribution, occurring in conditional clauses as well as in foregrounded chains of events in narrative discourse. Moreover, it is also found in various types of temporal adjunct clause (Green & Reintges 2005b).

In Hausa, special inflection registers syntactic movement but does not occur with focus/*wh*-in situ (§§ 4.5, 4.6). As the examples in this section illustrate, special inflection in Coptic occurs with focus/*wh*-in situ, but does not occur with focus/*wh*-ex situ. Although the two languages show opposite patterns with respect to the distribution of special inflection, what they share in common is the fact that special inflection occurs in the unmarked strategy but is absent from the marked strategy. The fact that each language has both focus/*wh*-in situ and focus/*wh*-ex situ, and the fact that in each language special inflection occurs in only one of these construction types, entails that special inflection is not simply a morphosyntactic flagging device that distinguishes focus/*wh*-constructions (including relative clauses) from the pragmatically neutral declarative clause.

Recall from Chapter 4 (§ 4.6.5) that Green & Reintges (2005b) develop an analysis of Hausa *wh*-in situ as a case of covert (LF) movement to FP on the basis of the absence of special inflection in focus/*wh*-in situ, the existence of argument–adjunct asymmetries and intervention effects in Hausa *wh*-in situ constructions, and the fact that an echo interpretation of the in situ *wh*-phrase is forced in multiple *wh*-constructions. In this comparative study of special inflection in Hausa and Coptic, Green and Reintges (2005b) argue that, unlike the Hausa case, Coptic *wh*-in situ is most insightfully analysed

as a case of displacement in the syntax rather than at the LF level, in which
the lower rather than the higher copy in the movement chain is pronounced.
This analysis is based on a range of evidence that suggests that *wh*-in situ
phrases in Coptic display characteristic properties of (overtly) moved *wh*-
phrases. The most striking point in favour of this analysis is the presence of
special inflection in Coptic *wh*-in situ: the morphology of extraction is only
expected to surface if the displacement operation takes place before the
derivation is passed to the phonological component. Secondly, the scope
facts are suggestive of a unified account of *wh*-fronting and *wh*-in situ. As
Green & Reintges (2005b) observe, the scope of an overtly moved *wh*-
phrase is contingent on its landing site. When a Coptic *wh*-phrase moves
overtly to the embedded focus phrase to the right of the finite subordinating
complementiser *tše* 'that', it takes embedded scope and the entire
construction is interpreted as an indirect question (78a). If, on the other
hand, the *wh*-phrase undergoes long-distance *wh*-movement across a clause
boundary, it takes matrix scope and the resulting interpretation is that of a
direct question (78b).

(78) a. ti-tʃənu   əmmɔ-tən tʃe   hən u   ən-ʃatʃe a-tetən
       (PRES)1s-ask DO-2PL   COMP in   what of-word PF-2pl-speak
       ero-i (…)
       about-1s
       'I ask you with which reason are you saying about me (…)'
   b. ən-aʃ   ən-he   əntok   *Coptic*
       in-which of-manner PRO.2ms   (Green & Reintges
       kə-tʃɔ   əmmo-s tʃe   tetə(n)-na-ər   2005b: ex. 67)
       (PRES)2ms-say DO-3fs COMP FUT.2pl-AUX-make
       rəmhe?
       free.man
       'how do you say that you will become free?'

Parallel facts can be observed for embedded *wh*-in situ questions. In finite
complement clauses, the in situ *wh*-phrase generally takes embedded
scope, which yields an indirect question interpretation (79). In this
context, special inflection surfaces in the left periphery of the embedded
clause.

(79) e-k-sowən   tʃe ənt-a-k-tʃi   *Coptic*
     RM(PRES)-2ms-know   COMP RM-PF-2ms-get   (Green & Reintges
     sßo   ən-tən   nim   2005b: ex. 68)
     teaching   from-hand who
     'you know by whom you were taught'

However, there are also attested examples where the in situ *wh*-phrase
scopes out of the embedded finite clause and the resulting interpretation is

that of a direct question. When this happens, special inflection surfaces at
the left edge of the matrix clause, as in (80).[22]

(80) a. eye əntɔtən e-tetən-tʃɔ   əmmo-s ero-i   tʃe   ang   nim?
        Q   PRO.2pl RM(PRES)-2pl-say DO-3fs about-1s COMP PRO.1s who
        'who are you saying of me that I (am)?'
     b. e-k-tʃɔ   əmmo-s tʃe   *Coptic*
        RM(PRES)-2ms-say DO-3fs COMP   (Green & Reintges
        u   etßɛɛt-ək   2005b: ex. 69)
        what   about-2ms
        'what are you saying about yourself?'

A different situation obtains in infinitival *wh*-in situ questions where both
wh-arguments and *wh*-adjuncts must take matrix scope, imposing a direct
question interpretation on the entire construction. Special inflection occurs
in the highest clause over which the *wh*-in situ takes scope.

(81) a. ənt-a-tetən-ei   eßol e-t-eremos   *Coptic*
        RM.PF-2pl-come PART to-DD.ms-desert   (Green & Reintges
        e-nau   e-u ?   2005b: ex. 70)
        to-see.INF   at-what
        'what have you come to the desert to to see?'
     b. e-tetən-wɔʃ   e-tra-ka   nim nɛ-tən eßol həm
        RM(PRES)-2pl-want to-CAUS.INF.1s-place who for-2pl PART from
        pe-snau?
        DD.ms-two
        'which of the two do you want me to release to you?'

As with Hausa subjunctive clauses, Coptic infinitivals are defective tense
categories that lack a focus phrase and hence a scope position to which the
in situ *wh*-phrase can be moved. In order to be interpreted, the embedded
wh-in situ phrase must move to the specifier of the focus phrase in the
matrix clause.

   The third argument in favour of a syntactic (pre-LF) movement analysis
is that, unlike Hausa, Coptic *wh*-in situ lacks argument–adjunct
asymmetries: as the examples in this section demonstrate, arguments freely
occur in Coptic *wh*-in situ questions. Finally, unlike Hausa, Coptic *wh*-in
situ lacks the intervention effects that are suggestive of LF movement: it is
insensitive to the blocking effects of quantifier/negation expressions. The
following examples illustrate that Coptic *wh*-in situ can be preceded by a

---

[22] The possibility of taking matrix scope out of an embedded finite clause distinguishes Coptic
wh-in situ from its counterpart in Iraqi and Lebanese Arabic, in which tense and finiteness
block the wide-scope construal of the embedded *wh*-phrase (see Wahba 1991; Ouhalla
1996b; Aoun & Li 2003).

negative TAM (82a), or a universal quantifier (82b), and the scope facts are unaffected.

(82) a. ete-mpe-tʃɔhǝm   hǝn aʃ   ǝm-ma ?   *Coptic*
       RM-NEG.PF.2fs-defile in   what of-place   (Green & Reintges
       'in which place have you (woman)   2005b: ex. 74)
       not been defiled?'

    b. k-nau   tʃe   ǝnt-a-f-sǝnt   ǝm-pɛwe   tɛr-u
       (PRES)2ms-see COMP RM-PF-3ms-establish DD.pl-heavens all-3pl
       ǝn-aʃ   ǝn-he   hǝm   pe.f-logismos
       in-what of-manner through DD.ms.3ms-reasoning
       'you see how He has established all the heavens through His reasoning'

Green and Reintges (2005b) therefore develop an analysis of Coptic *wh*-in situ that is essentially parallel to the analysis of focus/*wh*-fronting developed for both Hausa and Coptic. According to this analysis, the focus/*wh*-phrase raises to the specifier of FP in order to eliminate uninterpretable focus/*wh* features on the left-peripheral head. In Coptic, the TAM inflection incorporates into the relative marker, triggering various complementiser alternations. Reintges (1993: 400–01) views these complementiser alternations as an indication of T^0-to-F^0 movement, which is a corollary of T^0-to-C^0 movement (see Rizzi 1996; Pesestky & Torrego 2000). Finally, the fact that Coptic special inflection does not surface when the top copy of the movement chain is pronounced is reminiscent of the Doubly-filled COMP Filter in English, which allows the pronunciation of either a complementiser or the *wh*-phrase in its specifier, but not both (Chomsky & Lasnik 1977). In a similar way, Coptic allows either the content of the specifier or the head of FP to be phonetically realised, but not both (see Reintges et al. 2006). In this respect, the Coptic pattern is reminiscent of the Modern Standard Arabic pattern described by Ouhalla (1994) (§ 6.2.2).

6.2.5 *Summary*

This section explored focus/*wh*-constructions in a range of related languages, with a view to situating the Hausa pattern within a broader typological context. This section began with a brief descriptive survey of focus/*wh*-constructions in 11 Chadic languages, which revealed that the Chadic group exemplifies a range of ex situ focus/*wh* strategies (clause-initial, clause-final and postverbal), in addition to in situ focus/*wh*-(although it is not always clear from existing descriptions whether the postverbal focus/*wh*-of a direct object in an SVO language is a case of true in situ focus/*wh*-or a case of string-vacuous movement to a designated postverbal focus position). In addition, this survey revealed both the presence and absence of focus markers in these Chadic languages, some of which are copulas and some of which have other origins. Special inflection was also found to occur in a subset of Chadic languages, although this feature may not be as widespread as some researchers suggest. The wide range of focus/*wh*-strategies attested within the Chadic group warns against viewing Hausa as representative of a Chadic pattern (Schuh 2000). Tuller's (1992) analysis of postverbal focus in Chadic was briefly reviewed, according to which postverbal focus emerges from a VP-adjoined focus position, with V raising to INFL. The question of whether the FP analysis can be extended to postverbal focus constructions was briefly considered, and it was shown that this phenomenon presents a challenge to the FP analysis, requiring a considerably more complex derivation than clause-initial focus. Furthermore, despite the existence of a number of excellent reference grammars (notably Schuh's (1998) grammar of Miya), none of the Chadic languages has been as thoroughly described as Hausa, which in many cases makes even a speculative analysis premature.

The syntax of focus/*wh*-constructions in Modern Standard Arabic bears a close resemblance to the Hausa pattern, as do the distinctions between topic and focus constructions. Like Hausa, Standard Arabic has both in situ and ex situ strategies, although Standard Arabic differs from Hausa in that each focus strategy carries a distinct focus interpretation. Ouhalla (1994) develops an analysis of focus/*wh* in Standard Arabic that rests upon the FP structure, but differs from the Hausa analysis developed in the present chapter in that Arabic places a restriction upon overt elements in both head and specifier positions of FP simultaneously, so that a focus/ *wh*-phrase in FP alternates with a focus marker that licenses the focus/*wh*-phrase to remain in situ. A brief survey of focus/*wh*-constructions in some spoken dialects of Arabic reveals that while some dialects pattern like Standard Arabic in permitting both *wh*-in-situ and *wh*-fronting, some dialects only permit the former. Finally, some Arabic dialects have a cleft focus/*wh*-construction, which is discussed in more detail below (§ 6.3.3).

A brief discussion of Hebrew focus/*wh*-constructions reveals that, like Hausa, Hebrew has a *wh*-fronting strategy, but unlike Hausa, there is evidence for a designated (new information) focus position that is local to the verb rather than clause-intial. Hebrew also has a cleft construction that is restricted to subjects. Like Hausa, Hebrew has a VP fronting strategy that shows properties of displacement, but the two languages differ in the discourse function of the resulting construction: while Hebrew VP fronting results in a topic construction, Hausa permits both topic and focus VPs in the left periphery, but only the latter shows properties of a displacement configuration. Finally, Hebrew and Hausa both have a pseudocleft construction. The Hebrew pseudocleft is discussed in more detail below (§ 6.3.3).

Finally, focus/*wh*-constructions in Coptic Egyptian were briefly described. Like Hausa and Arabic, Coptic licenses both in situ and ex situ strategies, but differs from Hausa in that focus/*wh*-in situ is the unmarked strategy. Like Hausa, Coptic has special inflection in focus/ *wh*-constructions, but this correlates with the in situ rather than the ex situ pattern. Rather like Standard Arabic, and unlike Hausa, Coptic allows either the head or the specifier of FP to be filled, but not both, hence the absence of special inflection in focus/*wh*-fronting constructions. Furthermore, unlike Hausa, Coptic also has a biclausal cleft construction. Since the non-verbal copula is central to the syntax of the Coptic cleft, this construction is discussed in more detail below (§ 6.3.5).

6.3 COPULAR/NON-VERBAL CLAUSES

In this section, Hausa non-verbal copular sentences are considered within a broader typological context. The discussion is limited to non-verbal/ copular constructions in Chadic and a small number of other Afroasiatic languages, but it is worth emphasising that the phenomena discussed here are not limited to the Afroasiatic family. The section begins with a typological perspective in the form of a brief overview of a recent cross-linguistic study of copular constructions by Pustet (2003) (§ 6.3.1). The section then compares copular/non-verbal constructions in a range of Chadic languages (§ 6.3.2), in Arabic (§ 6.3.3), in Hebrew (§ 6.3.4) and in Coptic Egyptian (§ 6.3.5). The objective of this section is to explore typological similarties and differences between the Hausa constructions that were discussed in Chapter 5 and non-verbal clauses in a selection of other Afroasiatic languages. No attempt is made to extend the analysis developed in the previous chapter beyond the Hausa constructions, but descriptive and theoretical parallels are discussed as they arise. As the discussion in this section reveals, non-verbal (pronominal) copulas are a common feature of Afroasiatic syntax, although rare within the Chadic family itself. Where copulas exist, they have frequently (but not always) evolved from pronominals, and frequently (but not always) participate in marking focus, demonstrating that the Hausa facts illustrate a relatively common historical and typological pattern.

6.3.1 *Typology of copular sentences*

In a recent empirical study of copulas within the functional-typological framework, Pustet (2003) sampled over 150 languages in order to establish what patterns exist in the properties of copular sentences. With respect to the category and historical origins of copular elements, Pustet points out that while speakers of Indo-European languages will be familiar with verbal copulas, copular elements belonging to other categories are prevalent in the world's languages. Stassen (1997) identifies three distinct

categories of copula: verbal, pronominal and particle copulas. According
to Stassen (1997: 85), the latter type may originate as 'markers of
discourse-oriented categories such as topicalization, backgrounding, or
contrastive focus for subjects or predicates'. Pustet urges caution,
however, in drawing conclusions about the historical origins of particle
copulas:

> 'copulas which are homonymous with markers of pragmatic categories
> do not have to be regarded as historically derived from these markers of
> pragmatic function ... this issue is in need of some systematic cross-
> linguistic research. (Pustet 2003: 61)

As the discussion in this chapter demonstrates, the Hausa copula is
synchronically a focus marker, but recall that the Hausa copula has its
roots in the Proto-Afroasiatic demonstrative/pronominal system (Schuh
1983a). As the discussion in the present section will illustrate, pronominal
copulas are common in the Afroasiatic language family.

The starting point of Pustet's empirical study is a survey of the types of
predicate that can be combined with copulas. Pustet identifies the three
most common language types:[23]

1. AN languages: those that license adjectives and nouns to occur as the
predicates of copular sentences;
2. AV languages: those that license adjectives and verbs to occur as the
predicates of copular sentences;
3. languages of the 'non-copularizing' type: those that lack a copula
altogether.

This finding motivates the implicational hierarchy in (83):

(83) NOMINALS > ADJECTIVALS > VERBALS

According to this hierarchy, if a language licenses any category to occur
with a copula, it will be the category of nouns. If a language licenses a
second category apart from nominals to occur with the copula, it will be the
category of adjectives. Finally, if a language licenses a third category to
occur with copulas, it will be the category of verbs.[24]

In keeping with the functional-typological approach, Pustet explores the
basis for these typological patterns from a semantic perspective. Drawing
on work by typologists Croft (1991), Givón (1979) and Stassen (1997),
Pustet proposes that the explanation lies in the semantic parameters
dynamicity (state vs. process), transience (permanence vs. non-perma-

---

[23] Pustet (2003: 72) also identifies the following 'equally marginal' categories: split-A; split-N;
split-V; and fully copularizing.
[24] Observe that Pustet does not recognise the adpositional phrase as predicate, perhaps
assuming the traditional distinction between predicative complements and adverbial
complements.

Table 6.1 Semantic classification of nouns, adjectives and verbs (Pustet 2003)

	DYNAMICITY	Transience	Transitivity	Dependence
Noun	[− DYNAMIC]	[− TRANSIENT]	[− TRANSITIVE]	[− DEPENDENT]
Adjective	[− DYNAMIC]	[−/+ TRANSIENT]	[−/+ TRANSITIVE]	[+ DEPENDENT]
Verb	[+ DYNAMIC]	[+ TRANSIENT]	[+ TRANSITIVE]	[+ DEPENDENT]

nence), transitivity (requiring two or more arguments) and dependency (autonomous vs. dependent). For example, nominal and adjectival concepts tend to be [− DYNAMIC], describing a state rather than a process, whereas verbal concepts tend to be [+ DYNAMIC]. Nominal concepts tend to be [− TRANSIENT], describing a permanent state, while adjectival concepts are [+/− TRANSIENT] and verbal concepts tend towards [+ TRANSIENT]. Nouns are categorised as [− TRANSITIVE], while adjectives are occasionally [+ TRANSITIVE] and verbs are frequently [+ TRANSITIVE]. Finally, nouns tend to be (semantically) [− DEPENDENT] in the sense that they do not rely on other elements to complete their meaning, while adjectives and verbs are [+ DEPENDENT], requiring participants in the states or processes they describe. Table 6.1 summarises this semantic classification of nouns, adjectives and verbs.

There are obvious parallels between this semantic classification and the distinction between thetic and categorical predication discussed by Basilico (2003) (§ 5.4.3). While nominal and adjectival categories typically involve categorical predication and tend to pattern together with individual level (permanent/stative) meaning, verbs typically involve thetic predication and tend to pattern together with stage-level (temporary/eventive) meaning. This distinction is captured in Pustet's functional-typological classification by means of the features [+/− DYNAMIC] and [+/− TRANSIENT].

Pustet's methodology rests on the existence of 'lexical minimal pairs': pairs of lexemes like *happy* and *rejoice* in English, which are near-synonyms belonging to different categories, where one of the pair is licensed to occur with a copula (*happy*) and one is not (*rejoice*). The patterns observed motivate the following typological principle (Pustet 2003: 131):

(84). *Principle of unidirectionality of semantic distinctions within lexical minimal pairs*: Within a given lexical minimal pair, the feature value of the copularizing member with respect to any one of the four semantic dimensions dynamicity, transience, transitivity and dependency never exceeds the feature value of the non-copularizing member.

In other words, the [+] values of the relevant semantic parameters correlate highly with the absence of the copula, whereas the [−] values correlate highly with the presence of the copula. It follows that in there is a strong tendency either for nouns and adjectives to pattern together in copular constructions or for adjectives and verbs to pattern together, but not for nouns and verbs to pattern together. Indeed, Pustet (2003: 153) states: 'AN and AV languages constitute 90.1 per cent of the sampled languages which have copulas.'[25] Hausa therefore represents one of the most common typological patterns, belonging to the AN language type. As the discussion in the remainder of this section will demonstrate, while most of the Chadic languages belong to the 'non-copularising' type, those that have copulas typically belong, like Hausa, to the AN type, as do Arabic, Hebrew and Coptic Egyptian.

6.3.2 *Chadic*

According to Schuh (1983a), only a minority of Chadic languages have copulas:

> In Chadic languages, copulas of any kind are rather rare. Typically, equational sentences simply juxtapose a subject (noun or pronoun) with a predicate. A few Chadic languages, however, do have morphemes which can be identified as copulas and which have probably developed in a way similar to that outlined by Li and Thompson. (Schuh 1983a: 312)

Indeed, Schuh (2000) states that (unlike Hausa): 'Few other West Chadic language have copulas of any kind and certainly none have an overt copula comparable to, much less cognate with Hausa nē/cē ∼ nā/tā.' Pawlak (1994: 109) provides a (non-exhaustive) list of 12 Chadic languages with copulas.[26] The Chadic languages that lack copulas typically rely either upon simple juxtaposition of subject and predicate in non-verbal clauses or upon imperfective TAM markers. According to Pawlak (1994: 122) the copulas that exist synchronically in Chadic can be traced back to demonstratives, pronouns, prepositions and focus markers. This section presents a brief survey of non-verbal (predicational and specificational) sentences in eight Chadic languages, two from the Biu-Mandara branch (Kilba and Podoko), four West A languages (Bole, Pero, Kanakuru and Mupun) and two West B languages (Ngizim and Miya). This survey illustrates the range of strategies for forming non-verbal clauses in Chadic.

---

[25] Pustet suggests that the distribution of copulas in the world's languages is fully consistent with markedness theory, which is in turn one instantiation of cognitive economy. See Pustet (2003: 186–90) for further discussion.

[26] Pawlak's list of Chadic languages with copulas consists of the East Chadic (B) language Bidiya, the Biu-Mandara (A) languages Lamang and Tera, and the West (A) languages Bokkos, Bolewa, Daffo-Butura, Fyer, Galambu, Gera, Hausa, Mupun and Pero.

Kilba (Biu-Mandara A)

Schuh (1983a) argues that, like Hausa (§ 5.3), Kilba illustrates the pattern of evolution described by Li & Thompson (1977), in which the copula has evolved from pronominal/demonstrative elements. As the examples in (85) demonstrate, non-verbal sentences can be formed without copulas in Kilba. While non-verbal sentences with nominal subjects require the subject to precede the predicate, non-verbal sentences with pronominal (enclitic) subjects require the subject to follow the predicate.

(85) a. ŋgàmə́n ndə̀r zwà   *Kilba*
    Ngamen person.of farming   (Schuh 1983a: 315)
    'Ngamin is a farmer'

    b. ndə̀r zwà-yá
    person.of farming -PRO.1s
    'I am a farmer'

Sentences in which the (independent) pronominal subject precedes the predicate are marginal (86a), but become grammatical when the pronominal enclitic is included (86b).[27]

(86) a. ʔnàyà ndə̀r zwà   *Kilba*
    PRO.1s person.of farming   (Schuh 1983a: 316)
    'I am a farmer'

    b. nàyà ndə̀r zwà-yá
    PRO.1s person.of farming-PRO.1s
    'I am a farmer'

Example (87) illustrates low tone demonstrative determiners, and example (88) illustrates their high tone counterparts, which occur in identificational (specificational) copular sentences:

(87) a. kí nà   *Kilba*
    house DEM   (Schuh 1983a: 315)
    'this house'

    b. kí ndà/ ŋgà
    house DEM
    'that house'

(88) a. nàkə̀-ná   *Kilba*
    PRO.2s-DEM(COP)   (Schuh 1983a: 319)
    'it's you'

    b. nàkə̀-ndá/ŋgà
    PRO.2s-DEM(COP)
    'it was you'

---

[27] Schuh (1983a: 323) suggests that examples like (86b) have their roots in topic structures ('as for me, I'm a farmer'), although there is no evidence that this is a synchronic topic structure.

In example (88), the spatial deixis expressed by the demonstratives is extended to the temporal domain, and these elements also license predication (the functional distinction is reflected in the tonal difference). Now consider the following examples, in which the high tone demonstrative enclitics function as 'true' copulas (Schuh 1983a: 323). In these examples, the prominent deictic feature of the demonstrative enclitics is their tense properties, where proximal forms refer to present time, and distal forms to past time. Example (89c) retains its spatial deixis, however, encoding a distal referent.

(89) a. ùsmân   hə́bà-ná   *Kilba*
        Usman   Kilba-(DEM)COP   (Schuh 1983a: 321)
        'Usman is a Kilba' (Usman is present)
     b. ùsmân   hə́bà-ndá
        Usman   Kilba-(DEM)COP
        'Usman was a Kilba'
     c. ùsmân   hə́bà-ŋgá
        Usman   Kilba-(DEM)COP
        'Usman is a Kilba' (Usman not present)

Finally, compare the examples in (89) with example (90).

(90) ùsmân   hə́bà-cá   *Kilba*
     Usman   Kilba-PRO.3s   (Schuh 1983a: 320)
     'Usman is a Kilba'

Schuh argues that in examples like (90), as well as examples like (86b), the pronominal enclitic functions as a copula. There is evidence, then, that Kilba is in the process of grammaticalising both pronominal enclitics (90) and demonstrative enclitics (89) into copulas, and that in the latter case 'Kilba has exploited the proximal/distal deictic distinction to create a tense distinction for its copulas' (Schuh 1983a: 313). Although it is unusual for Chadic copulas to reflect tense distinctions, the evolution of copulas from demonstratives explains this pattern. Indeed, the extension of spatial expressions to the temporal domain is widely attested cross-linguistically.[28]

Podoko (Biu-Mandara A; VSO)

Podoko does not have a copula. Jarvis (1989) provides a small set of examples of non-verbal clauses In Podoko. According to her description, these constructions are formed by simple juxtaposition of subject and predicate. The predicate can be a noun, a possessive pronoun, an adjective, a locative adverb or a preposition phrase, as illustrated by examples (91a–e), respectively. Observe that the predicate-initial word order that

---

[28] Schuh (1983a: 321, n. 8) suggests that the Margi particle ŋé, which Hoffmann (1963) describes as a demonstrative, might also function as a copula in identificational sentences.

characterises verbal clauses in Podoko is also reflected in non-verbal clauses.

(91) a. ʸmətəbə yá   *Podoko*
    foreigner PRO.1s   (Jarvis 198: 106–7)
    'I am a foreigner'
  b. ngalə   ʸmaná
    PRO.POSS.1s PRO.DEM
    'this is mine'
  c. ʸbarə.ʸbarə haya
    hard   earth
    'the earth is hard'
  d. ʸhakənga kayə   dála
    there   house PRO.POSS.1s
    'my house is (over) there'
  e. də   ʸkwədəgə mamá
    PREP kitchen   mother
    'Mother is in the kitchen'

Bole (West A; SVO)

In Bole, specificational and predicational sentences with nominal or adjectival (stative) predicates are formed by simple juxtaposition of subject and predicate, as illustrated by the examples in (92a) and (92b). Example (92c) illustrates that the non-verbal possessive construction is also formed by simple juxtaposition of subject and predicate, the latter headed by the associative preposition *ga* 'with'.[29]

(92) a. Tijàní Apìnó   *Bole*
    Tijani Hausa.person   (Schuh & Gimba, forthcoming)
    'Tijani is a Hausa person'
  b. gombira tèllèki
    okra   slimy
    'okra is slimy'
  c. Tijàní gà gám   *Bole*
    Tijani PREP ram   (Russell Schuh, p.c.)
    'Tijani has a ram'

Observe, however, that while locative clauses with first and second person subjects are also formed by juxtaposition (93a, b), locative clauses with third person subjects require the element *à* (94):

(93) a. ǹ   ténè̀   *Bole*
    PRO.1s here   (Schuh & Gimba, forthcoming)
    'I am here'

[29] The examples in this section, unless otherwise indicated, are taken from Schuh & Gimba's (forthcoming) unnumbered draft chapters entitled 'The syntax of simplex non-verbal clauses' and 'Equational and identificational sentences'.

  b. ká   ténè
     PRO.2ms here
     'you are here'
(94) a. Bámói à   ténè   *Bole*
        Bamoi PREP/COP here   (Schuh & Gimba, forthcoming)
        'Bamoi is here'
  b. dānde   à   makaranta
     children PREP/TAM/COP school
     'the children are at school'
  c. sun-nì   de   à   bò   tìli-nò
     name-3ms PART PREP/TAM/COP mouth heart-1s
     'his name is on the tip of my tongue'
     (lit. 'his name is at the mouth of my heart')

According to Schuh & Gimba (forthcoming), the element *à* functions both
as a locative preposition and a third person imperfective TAM in Bole.
Although this element is cognate with the locative preposition found in
other Chadic languages (e.g. Hausa *à* 'at') and thus has its source in the
prepositional category, Schuh & Gimba suggest that it is evolving an
auxiliary function and is perhaps more insightfully analysed as a copula in
modern Bole clauses such as those illustrated in (94).[30]

Finally, recall that Bole focus constructions may involve a (non-copular)
clefting particle *yé* (§ 6.2.1). While this particle occurs optionally in verbal
sentences, it is obligatory in non-verbal subject focus sentences. Observe
that the focused subject is postposed in (95), as in verbal clauses.

(95) a. Ásìbítì   yé **sòlûn**   *Bole*
        hospital CP building   (Schuh & Gimba, forthcoming)
        pètìlà **yê**
        white   DD
        '**the white building** is the hospital'

Predicates are typically focused in situ (involving the same consitituent
order as the unmarked declarative). However, while nominal and locative
(prepositional/adverbial) predicates are not focused by means of the clefting
particle, adjectival predicates may (optionally) involve this strategy:

(96) gámnó   (yé) pètìlà   *Bole*
     ram.1s CP   white   (Schuh & Gimba, forthcoming)
     'my ram is **white**'

Pero (West A; SVO)

In Pero, as in Bole, non-verbal clauses with nominal or adjectival predicates
are formed by simple juxtaposition, as illustrated by the following examples:

---

[30] This discussion can be found on the first page of Schuh & Gimba's (forthcoming) draft
chapter entitled 'Locative expressions'.

(97) a. Játtàw   án-cúpèt   *Pero*
     Jattaw s-teacher   (Frajzyngier 1989: 201)
     'Jattaw is a teacher'
   b. cákkà   án-jùkkà   *Pero*
     PRO.3ms s-tall   (Frajzyngier 1989: 202)
     'he is tall'

Example (98) illustrates an inverse equative clause. Observe that the raised predicate is definite.

(98) àn-cúpét-ì   Játtàw   *Pero*
     s-teacher-DD Jattaw   (Frajzyngier 1989: 201)
     'the teacher is Jattaw'

Example (99) illustrates that, as in Hausa, the subject of a non-verbal clause has to be definite, although it is likely that a generic reading will license an indefinite subject.

(99) a. *lándàa díŋ   *Pero*
     shirt   black   (Frajzyngier 1989: 202)
     'a shirt is black'
   b. làndáa-ì díŋ
     shirt-DD black
     'the shirt is black'

Although Frajzyngier provides few examples of non-verbal clauses with locative predicates, the following example shows that a preposition phrase may occur as the predicate of a non-verbal clause. In this example, the element *tí*, which Frajzyngier (1989: 166) describes as a preposition 'whose primary function is locative', marks a benefactive nominal predicate:

(100) cándè-mò tì   Wórì   *Pero*
     yam-DEM PREP Wori   (Frajzyngier 1989: 202)
     'this yam is for Wori'

Despite the fact that non-verbal clauses are typically formed by simple juxtaposition in Pero, a certain class of non-verbal clauses involve a morpheme that Frajzyngier (1989: 204–5) analyses as a copula. Recall the Pero 'counter-presuppositional' or contrastive focus construction, which is a cleft construction in which the focused constituent in the left periphery of the clause is preceded by the focus marker *iC-*, and is followed by the relative marker *ci* (§ 6.2.1). Frajzyngier observes that the same focus marker *iC-* functions as a copula in identificational (specificational) non-verbal sentences that consist of a null subject and a pronominal predicate, as the following examples illustrate.

(101) a. ín-nè   'it's me'   *Pero*
    b. ík-kè   'it's you (ms)' (Frajzyngier 1989: 204)

c. íc-cì   'it's you (fs)'
e. íc-cákkà   'it's him'
f. ít-tè   'it's her'
g. ìm-mínù   'it's us'
h. ìm-má   'it's you (pl)'
i. ìc-cínù   'it's them'

Frajzyngier also provides the following pair of examples, which shows the optional presence of the particle *iC-* (in boldface) in a more complex non-verbal clause. Although Frajzyngier suggests that this particle functions as a copula in (102a), the alternative possibility is that this is the focused counterpart of (102b), given the absence of a copula in most other types of non-verbal clause (97–100) (recall discussion of example (10) above (§ 6.2.1)).

(102) a. nínyà   cín-kà-wé-kò-ì   *Pero*
         people   REL-2m-see-PERF-DD   (Frajzyngier 1989: 205)
         ít-tì-gbándùm
         FM-PREP-Gbandum
         'people you saw are from Gwandum'
      b. nínyà   cín-kà-wé-kò-ì   tì-gbándùm
         people   REL-2m-see-PERF-DD   PREP-Gbandum
         'people you saw are from Gwandum'

Kanakuru (West A; SVO)

In Kanakuru, non-verbal sentences are formed not with a copula but with the imperfective TAM (INFL). Example (103b) illustrates that, as in Hausa, the imperfective TAM occurs with nominalised verb forms (verbal nouns). (These examples have null subjects, licensed by the TAM word.)

(103) a. nà   ta-no   *Kanakuru*
         1s.PF go-ICP   (Newman 1974: 28)
         'I went'
      b. nàa   ta-ma
         1s.IMPF go-NOMIN
         'I am going'

The examples in (104) illustrate non-verbal clauses with nominal (104a), adjectival (104b) and prepositional (104c,d) predicates. The TAM word is optional with overt animate subjects (104a), but is prohibited when the subject is inanimate (104d). However, it is obligatory in possessive constructions like (104c), in which it licenses predication. In its absence, the associative preposition *gən* 'with' is interpreted as a conjunction.

(104) a. Musa (shìi)   namaləm   *Kanakuru*
         Musa 3ms.IMPF teacher   (Newman 1974: 31)
         'Musa is a teacher'

b. shèe   manjoro   *Kanakuru*
   3fs.IMPF old   (Newman 1974: 32)
   'she is old'
c. Ngoje shìi   gən dok   *Kanakuru*
   Ngoje 3ms.IMPF PREP horse   (Newman 1974: 32)
   'Ngoje has a horse' (lit. 'Ngoje is with a horse')
d. takini (*wùn) goro   panda   *Kanakuru*
   shoes 3pl.IMPF under mat   (Newman 1974: 33)
   'the shoes are under the mat'

An independent pronoun only occurs as subject of a non-verbal clause if the subject is in focus. Compare the following examples:

(105) a. shèe   karuwa   *Kanakuru*
        3fs.IMPF harlot   (Newman 1974: 69)
        'she is a harlot'
     b. **shire** shèe   karuwa-i
        PRO.3fs 3fs.IMPF harlot-DD
        '**she** is the harlot'

Finally, a nominal subject can be focused by postposing an independent pronoun that is coreferential with the subject:

(106) **Basha** karuwa-i shire   *Kanakuru*
     Basha   harlot-DD PRO.3fs   (Newman 1974: 70)
     '**Basha** is the harlot'

Newman (1974: 70) states that 'predicate nouns may not be emphasized', although the nominal complements of predicate PPs can be focus fronted. As these examples demonstrate, the Kanakuru imperfective TAM not only licenses verbal noun and prepositional predicates, as in Hausa, but also licenses nominal and adjectival predicates.

Mupun (West A; SVO)

Recall that Mupun marks focus in situ by means of the copula *a*, which precedes the focused constituent (§ 6.2.1). Example (107) illustrates the non-verbal clause with a nominal predicate. Frajzyngier (1993: 252) observes that the subject of a copular clause tends to be definite/specific. As example (108) illustrates, the copula is obligatory in this type of construction.

(107) náàt   nì á   mìskóom nì   *Mupun*
      white.man DD COP chief   DD   (Frajzyngier 1986: 377)
      'the white man is the chief'
(108) a. wur   a   miskoom Mupun   *Mupun*
         PRO.3ms COP chief   Mupun   (Frajzyngier 1989: 377)
         'he is the chief of Mupun'

b. * wur   miskoom Mupun
   PRO.3ms chief   Mupun
   'he is the chief of Mupun'

Example (109) illustrates a non-verbal clause with a nominal predicate that functions adjectivally.[31] Prepositional constructions express locative predicates (110) and possessive predicates (111). Observe that the copula does not occur in any of these constructions, which are formed by simple juxtaposition of subject and predicate.

(109) wùr   ráp   *Mupun*
      PRO.3ms dirty   (Frajzyngier 1986: 378)
      'he is dirty'
(110) a. wur   n-Kano   *Mupun*
         PRO.3ms PREP-Kano   (Frajzyngier 1989: 259)
         'he is in Kano'
      b. caan nə pə təŋ nə kas   *Mupun*
         hoe DD PREP tree DD NEG   (Frajzyngier 1989: 260)
         'the hoe is not by the tree'
(111) a. war   kə́ siwol   *Mupun*
         PRO.3fs PREP money   (Frajzyngier 1989: 264)
         'she has money' (lit. 'she is with money')
      b. war   kə́ muut
         PRO.3fs PREP sickness
         'she is sick' (lit. 'she is with sickness')

Frajzyngier (1986) explains the distribution of the copula on the basis of the role it plays in disambiguating between possessive NPs on the one hand, which are formed by simple juxtaposition of possessed and possessor (112), and nominal clauses on the other hand. According to this functional explanation, because non-verbal clauses with adjectival or prepositional predicates do not give rise to the same ambiguity as those with nominal predicates, the copula is redundant.

(112) mìskóom mòpún   *Mupun*
      chief   Mupun   (Frajzyngier 1986: 377)
      'a chief of Mupun'

Example (113) illustrates contrastive focus on the subject of a copular sentence. According to Frajzyngier (1986: 381), only the first NP (the subject) can be marked for focus.[32]

---

[31] Adjectives do not exist as an independent word class in Mupun. Property concepts are expressed by verb or noun forms (see Frajzyngier 1989: 66–7).
[32] Of course, if equatives like (107) are reversible in Mupun, we might expect that either NP could be focused in this type of construction.

(113)à **náàt** à mìskóom nì   *Mupun*
COP white.man COP chief   DD   (Frajzyngier 1986: 381)
'it is a **white man** who is the chief'

Frajzyngier (1986) argues that in certain West Chadic languages, including Mupun, the copula has evolved from the locative preposition. Example (114a), which is a proverb, shows the same element in its (archaic) prepositional function, and the modern Mupun example in (114b) shows how the morpheme *a* has been replaced by a newer prepositional form *kì*.

(114)a. ndìrít   kìén   kìé   sìwá   *Mupun*
ndirit.bird benefit chicken drinks   (Frajzyngier 1986: 376)
ám   á   kùwór
water   PREP   feeder
'the Ndirit bird benefits when a chicken drinks from a feeder'
b. ás   sìwá   ám   kì   kùwór   *Mupun*
dog drinks water PREP feeder   (Frajzyngier 1986: 376)
'a dog drinks from the feeder'

According to Frajzynger, therefore, Mupun provides evidence for the grammaticalisation of copular elements from prepositions (cf. Schuh & Gimba's analysis of Bole above). Furthermore, the Mupun copula, like the Hausa copula, participates in marking focus.

Ngizim (West B; SVO)

Ngizim patterns rather like Bole in that non-verbal clauses with stative predicates are formed by simple juxtaposition of subject and predicate. Consider example (115), which illustrates a non-verbal clause with a nominal predicate.

(115)waka-tku məshənu   *Ngizim*
tree-DEM   tamarind   (Schuh 2000: 7)
'this tree is a tamarind'

The following example illustrates that possessive non-verbal clauses are also formed by simple juxtaposition of subject (possessor) and predicate (possessed, mediated by the prepositional associative particle).

(116)Kwāna nā   dūka   *Ngizim*
Kwana PREP horse   (Schuh 2000: 8)
'Kwana has a horse' (lit. 'Kwana (is) with a horse')

Example (117) illustrates a non-verbal clause with an adjectival predicate, which is also formed by simple juxtaposition.

(117) ama-w   jagəla   *Ngizim*
      woman-DD   clean   (Russell Schuh p.c.)
      'the woman is clean'

The Ngizim imperfective TAM (INFL) morpheme *ā* occurs not only in imperfective verbal clauses (118a), but also in locative non-verbal clauses (118b) (cf. Schuh & Gimba's discussion of Bole, above).

(118) a. Āmadu   ā   dlamau   *Ngizim*
        Ahmadu   IMPF   do   (Schuh 2000: 7)
        'Ahmadu will do (it)'
     b. garū-gā   ā   miya   mavgī-gā
        goats.1S   IMPF   mouth.of   doorway.1S
        'my goats are at my doorway'

Miya (West B; Northern Bauchi; SVO/VOS)

Miya does not have a copula. In Miya, non-verbal clauses with nominal and adjectival predicates are formed by simple juxtaposition, as illustrated by the following examples:

(119) a. Ndùwya   miy-dzəhə   *Miya*
        Nduya   Miya-man   (Schuh 1998: 316)
        'Nduya is a Miya man'
     b. və́rkə   ka   gàɓəna   *Miya*
        boy   DD   small   (Schuh 1998: 319)
        'the boy is small'

Locative and possessive non-verbal clauses are also formed by simple juxtaposition of subject and prepositional predicate (120). However, possessive clauses also permit the imperfective TAM (121).[33]

(120) a. mə̀n   aakyar-wásə   *Miya*
        PRO.1S   behind-PRO.3ms   (Schuh 1998: 322)
        'I am behind him'
     b. Ndùwya   áa   dùwakə   Miya
        Nduya   PREP   horse   (adapted from Schuh
                                  1998: 321)
        'Nduya has a horse' (lit. 'Nduya is with a horse')
(121) Ndùwya   g-áa   mìr   *Miya*
       Nduwya   IMPF-PREP   money   (Schuh 1998: 320)
       'Nduya has money'

Finally, Schuh (1998) also provides examples of focused non-verbal clauses. While focus on the predicate is not morphosyntactically marked, focus on the

---

[33] As in many languages, the 'prepositional' forms are typically derived from body-part nouns (Schuh 1998: 213).

Table 6.2 Survey of non-verbal clauses in Chadic

	Ø/IMPF.TAM/COP	Category of predicate
Kilba Biu-Mandara A	COP (pronominal/demonstrative)	N (no other data)
Podoko Biu-Mandara A	Ø	N/A/P/Adv$_{LOC}$
Bole West A	Ø IMPF.TAM/COP (< PREP)	N/A/P/Adv$_{LOC}$ N$_{LOC}$/Adv$_{LOC}$ (3rd person subject)
Pero West A	Ø ʔcop iC- (focus/cleft marker)	N/A/P$_{LOC}$ pronominal
Kanakuru West A	IMPF.TAM	N/A/P$_{LOC}$/POSS
Mupun West A	COP (< prep) á (focus marker) Ø	N A/P$_{LOC}$/POSS
Ngizim West B	Ø IMPF.TAM	N/A P$_{LOC}$/POSS
Miya West B	Ø IMPF.TAM	N/A/P$_{LOC}$/POSS P$_{POSS}$

subject (which remains in clause-initial position) requires the TAM *jíy*, which also occurs with focus/*wh* subjects of imperfective verbal clauses (§ 6.2.1).

(122) **Ròoya**   jíy   malvɔ́ dɔ̀   maa   *Miya*
      Roya   FOC.IMPF chief IMPF NEG   (Schuh 1998: 320)
      Ndùwya-w
      Nduya-NEG
      '**Roya** is chief, not Nduya'

As this brief survey illustrates, Chadic languages employ a range of strategies in the formation of non-verbal clauses. While the most widely attested strategy is simple juxtaposition of subject and predicate, the presence of the imperfective TAM is also relatively frequent in these constructions, and some languages used a mixed system, sometimes distinguishing between nominal and adjectival predicates on the one hand and prepositional predicates on the other. Nouns represent the most common predicate category for non-verbal clauses in Chadic, and typically pattern together with adjectives, suggesting that Chadic illustrates two of the most common patterns observed by Pustet (2003): the 'non-copularizing' pattern and the AN pattern. In the small subset of languages that have copulas, these elements are thought to have evolved from pronominal/demonstrative elements, or from locative prepositions. In addition, the copula typically participates in marking focus in verbal clauses. Table 6.2 summarises the findings of this brief survey.[34]

---

[34] The symbol Ø indicates that non-verbal clauses are formed by simple juxtaposition of subject and predicate.

6.3.3 *Arabic*

Descriptive facts

Recall Li & Thompson's (1977) hypothesis that anaphoric/demonstrative
pronouns evolve into copulas as topic–comment structures are reanalysed
as subject–predicate structures (§ 5.3). The Semitic languages with
pronominal copulas provide striking evidence in support of Li &
Thompson's hypothesis, representing a stage in the grammaticalisation
process at which the pronominal element functions both as a straightforward pronoun and as a copula. Palestinian Arabic illustrates this
phenomenon. In example (123a), the third person singular pronoun *hiyye*
functions as pronominal subject of the non-verbal clause. In example
(123b), the same element co-occurs with a nominal subject, and functions as
a copula. As example (123c) shows, the pronominal copula is required for
grammaticality.

(123) a. hiyye   le   mʕalme   *Palestinian Arabic*
        pro.3fs DD   teacher.f   (Li & Thompson 1977: 431)
        'she is the teacher'
    b. il   bint   hiyye   le   mʕalme
        DD   girl   PRO.COP.fs   DD   teacher.f
        'the girl is the teacher'
    c. *il   bint   le   mʕalme
        DD   girl   DD   teacher.f
        'the girl is the teacher'

As the examples in (124) illustrate, the third person pronominal copula can
co-occur with first and second person subjects, showing its grammaticalisation as a copula.

(124) a. ana   huwwe   il   ista:z   alli   Fari:d   ʕallak
        PRO.1s   PRO.COP.ms   DD   teacher.m   COMP   Farid   talked
        ʕanno
        about.3ms
        'I am the teacher that Farid talked about'
    b. inta   huwwe   il   *Palestinian Arabic*
        PRO.2ms   PRO.COP.ms   DD   (Li & Thompson 1977: 432)
        ista:z   alli   Fari:d   ʕallak   ʕanno
        teacher.m   COMP   Farid   talked   about.3ms
        'you are the teacher that Farid talked about'

Egyptian Arabic has a copular verb that functions in the past tense (125a)
the future tense (125b) and in the habitual present (125c), but not in the
'continuous present' tense (125d), which illustrates a predicational non-
verbal clause with an adjectival predicate.

(125)a. il-mudarris kaan   latiif   *Egyptian Arabic*
        DD-teacher   was-(he) nice   (Eid 1983: 197–8)
        'the teacher was nice'
     b. il-mudarris   ha-y-kuun latiif
        DD-teacher   FUT-he-be nice
        'the teacher will be nice'
     c. il-mudarris ʕadatan bi-y-kuun latiif lamma ʔa-kallim-u
        DD-teacher   usually PRES-he-be nice   when   I-talk-him
        'the teacher is usually nice when I talk to him'
     d. il-mudarris   latiif
        DD-teacher   nice
        'the teacher is nice'

Example (126) shows that when the predicate is a definite NP, the pronominal copula is required:

(126) il-mudarris huwwa   il-latiif   *Egyptian Arabic*
       DD-teacher PRO.COP.ms DD-nice   (Eid 1983: 204)
       'the teacher is nice / the nice one'

According to Eid, the pronominal copula is required in nominal clauses to prevent ambiguity in interpretation (cf. Frajzyngier 1986). In the absence of the pronominal copula, only a phrasal interpretation is possible, in which the adjective functions attributively rather than predicatively:

(127) il-mudarris il-latiif   Eid (1983: 203)
       DD-teacher   DD-nice
       'the nice teacher'

According to Eid, the distribution of the pronominal copula is due to the fact that, in Arabic, attributive adjectives must agree in definiteness (as well as gender and number) with the NP that they modify. The absence of the definite article on the adjective in (125d) rules out the possibility of a phrasal interpretation, so that the presence of the pronominal here is not necessary to force a sentential interpretation. Eid suggests that the reason why pronominals are licensed to function as copulas in present-tense nominal sentences relates to their rich morphological agreement: pronominals, like verbs, agree in person, number and gender with the subject. In a number of dialects, such as Egyptian, Iraqi, Palestinian and Makkan Arabic, the same pronoun that performs the copular pronoun also functions as a question marker.

(128)a. ʕali katab   il-gawaab   *Egyptian Arabic*
        Ali   wrote.3ms DD-letter   (Eid 1992: 108)
        'Ali wrote the letter'
     b. (huwwa)   ʕali katab   il-gawaab?
        PRO.COP.3ms Ali   wrote.3ms DD-letter'
        'did Ali write the letter?'

Edwards & Ouhalla (1996) argue that there is a designated focus position in
Arabic pronominal copular clauses. Because these clauses are equatives
(specificational sentences, in Declerck's terminology), they are reversible, and
the NP in clause-initial position is licensed to receive a contrastive or corrective
focus interpretation. For example, (129a) would be licensed in response to an
utterance asserting that someone other than Said is the teacher, and (129b) in
response to an utterance identifying some other individual as Said.

(129) a. **Said**   huwwa   l-mudrris   *Moroccan Arabic*
      Said   PRO.COP.ms   DD-teacher   (Jamal Ouhalla, p.c.)
      '**Said** is the teacher'

    b. **l-mudrris**   huwwa   Said   *Moroccan Arabic*
      DD-teacher   PRO.COP.ms   Said   (Jamal Ouhalla, p.c.)
      '**the teacher** is Said'

In a non-verbal clause with an adjectival predicate, which entails that the
sentence is predicational rather than specificational, the pronominal copula
is optional and there is no contrastive focus (130a). In order to place the
subject in contrastive focus, a cleft construction is required (130b).

(130) a. Saida   (hiyya)   zwina   *Egyptian Arabic*
      Saida   PRO.COP.fs   pretty   (Edwards & Ouhalla 1996)
      'Saida is pretty'

    b. **Saida**   (hiyya)   lli   zwina
      Saida   PRO.COP.fs   COMP   pretty
      '**Saida** is pretty'

Example (131) illustrates *wh*-in situ (131a) and *wh*-ex situ (131b) in
Egyptian Arabic (non-verbal clauses).

(131) a. il-baab   maftuu<u>h</u>   leeh?   *Egyptian Arabic*
      DD-door   open   why   (Ouhalla & Shlonsky 2002: 19)
      'why is the door is open?'

    b. (huwwa)   leeh   ?il-baab   maftuu<u>h</u>
      (PRO.3ms)   why   DD-door   open
      'why is the door open?'

Recall that Standard Arabic allows focus fronting (§ 6.2.2). As the
following examples illustrate, the same mechanism of focus marking applies
to non-verbal clauses. Observe that the examples in (132) have a (locative)
preposition phrase predicate. Example (132b) illustrates (string-vacuous)
focus fronting of the subject, while example (132c) illustrates focus fronting
of the predicate.

(132) a. Zayd-un   fii   l-bayt-i   *Standard Arabic*
      Zayd-NOM   in   DD-house-GEN   (Ouhalla 1994: 74)
      'Zayd is in the house'   *unmarked*

b. **Zayd-un**   fii   l-bayt-i   (laa   Khaalid-un)   *subject focus*
   Zayd- NOM   in   DD-house- GEN   not   Khaalid- NOM

'**Zayd** is in the house (not Khalid)'

c. **fii l-bayt-i**   Zayd-un   (laa fii al-maqhaa) *predicate focus*
   in   DD-house- GEN   Zayd- NOM   not   in   DD-cafe
   'Zayd is **in the house** (not in the cafe)'

Finally, recall that in Moroccan and Palestinian Arabic the pronominal copula occurs not only in equatives but also in clefts (§ 6.2.2). Example (46) is repeated here as (133)

(133) a. **Nadia**   hiyya   lli   *Moroccan Arabic*
       Nadia   PRO.COP.fs   COMP   (Ouhalla & Shlonsky 2002: 21)
       qr-at   l-ktab
       read-3fs DD-book
       'it's **Nadia** who read the book'

b. miin$_i$ (hi)   ?illi   *Palestinian Arabic*
   who   (PRO.COP.3fs)   comp   (Shlonsky 2002: 147)
   l-?asad ?akal-ha$_i$ mbaari<u>h</u>?
   DD.lion ate-3fs   yesterday
   'who did the lion eat (her) yesterday?'

c. miin   ?illi   šafit-hu   *Egyptian Arabic*
   who   COMP   see.PF-3ms   (Jelinek 2002: 100)
   who was it that she saw (him)?'

Theoretical issues

Ouhalla (1999) points out that the Moroccan Arabic cleft construction (133a) has an identical structure to the equative non-verbal copular clause illustrated in examples like (129): DP PRO.COP DP. The difference between the two construction types is that the predicate DP consists of a free relative clause in the cleft construction. However, the cleft does not pattern like the equative clause, because it is not reversible. On the basis that the independent pronouns that function as copulas have a marked focus interpretation (as in many pro-drop languages with rich agreement morphology), Ouhalla (1999: 354) argues that the pronominal copula in the cleft construction originates in INFL, alternating with clitic pronouns and agreement morphology, and differing from these in that it has a [+ FOCUS] feature in addition to its person, number and gender features. This position receives support from the fact that either the pronominal copula or the cleft ed constituent can receive focal stress (indicated by SMALL CAPITALS), with no apparent difference in interpretation:

(134) a. NADIA   hiyya   lli   *Moroccan Arabic*
         Nadia   PRO.COP.fs COMP   (Ouhalla 1999: 354)
         ʔllf-at   l-ktab
         wrote-3fs   DD-book
         'it's **Nadia** who wrote the book'
      b. Nadia   HIYYA   lli   ʔllf-at   l-ktab
         Nadia   PRO.COP.fs REL   wrote-3fs   DD-book
         'it's **Nadia** who wrote the book'

According to Ouhalla's analysis, the complement of INFL is a small clause
structure (SC) containing the subject and predicate DPs. The subject DP
raises to the specifier of IP, and subsequently to the specifier of FP. The
cleft construction receives its focus interpretation as a result of the [+ FOCUS]
feature associated with the pronominal copula in INFL, which raises to the
head position of the left periphery of the clause (FP) and links the clefted
constituent in its specifier position with the open position in the relative
clause. This analysis, which captures the parallels between focus/*wh*-
fronting and the cleft construction, is illustrated in (135). Ouhalla (1999:
355–6) argues that the analysis he develops for clefts in Moroccan Arabic
can also be extended to focus in situ and focus fronting in the relevant
dialects.

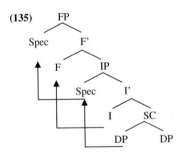

Shlonsky (2002) develops a similar analysis of the Palestinian Arabic cleft
wh-construction illustrated in (133b). Like Ouhalla, Shlonsky argues that
the *wh*-phrase is the underlying subject of a non-verbal copular construction of which the free relative is the predicate. However, Shlonsky adopts
the standard CP analysis of *wh*-constructions, and assumes that the *wh*-
phrase raises to the specifier of CP.
    The cleft construction discussed by Ouhalla (1999) and Shlonsky (2002) is
structurally more similar to the Hausa pseudocleft (§ 5.2) than to the focus/
wh-fronting construction, in the sense that it is a non-verbal copular
construction in which one of the consitutents is a free relative that expresses
the presupposition, while the other constituent is a focused nominal. Of
course, the Hausa pseudocleft and the Arabic *wh*-cleft are functionally
distinct, despite their syntactic similarities, since only the latter has an

interrogative function. Furthermore, the Hausa pseudocleft is reversible, suggesting that it is closer to the simple equative in terms of its derivational properties than the Arabic cleft construction.

As the discussion in this section illustrates, the similarities between Arabic and Hausa are rather striking. Not only does Arabic have a copula that is related to a pronoun, as Schuh (1983a; 2000) argues for Hausa, but the copula also participates in marking focus in certain construction types, although it is not a feature of monoclausal focus fronting constructions. Furthermore, a wider range of focus constructions exist across the dialects of Arabic than Hausa, and the pronominal origins of the Arabic copula are still very much evident synchronically: the same element has a dual function, a property that is characteristic of the layering or polysemy that indicates gramaticalisation in process. Finally, like Hausa, Arabic falls within Pustet's (2003) AN category in terms of the categorial status of the predicate in copular constructions. As the discussion of Ouhalla's (1999) analysis of clefts in Moroccan Arabic illustrates, the similarities between Hausa and Arabic focus constructions (with or without the copula) can be accounted for by assuming a rather similar syntactic analysis built around the functional projection focus phrase (FP). The most striking difference between the FP analysis developed for in this book and the analysis developed by Ouhalla (1999) for Morocan Arabic relates to the category of the non-verbal copula. While the Hausa non-verbal copula is analysed as a grammaticalised focus marker, the Arabic non-verbal copula is analysed as a type of INFL category that participates in both non-verbal copular clauses and cleft sentences (cf. Doron 1986; Tuller 1986a). This accounts for its absence in monoclausal focus fronting constructions in the relevant dialects of Arabic.

6.3.4 *Hebrew*

Descriptive facts

As Li & Thompson (1977) observe, the facts for the two Semitic languages Hebrew and Arabic are very similar. Hebrew copular sentences are formed in the past or future tense with the verb *h-y-y*, but this verb has no present tense form. Present tense copular sentences are formed with a pronominal copula, identical to third person pronouns, which has masculine and feminine forms, both singular and plural. Like Arabic and Hausa, Hebrew represents Pustet's (2003) AN pattern. This type of construction licenses AP, NP and PP predicates, and the pronominal copula, which usually agrees in number and gender with the subject, is optional unless the postcopular NP is a referring expression. Examples (136a–c) illustrate predicational copular sentences with adjectival, nominal and prepositional predicates, respectively, and example (136d) illustrates an equative (specificational) copular sentence with a definite NP predicate.[35]

(136) a. Dani (hu)   nexmad   *Hebrew*
          Dani PRO.COP.ms   nice   (Rothstein 1995: 28)
          'Dani is nice'

     b. Dani (hu)   rofe
         Dani PRO.COP.ms   doctor
         'Dani is a doctor'

     c. Dani (hu)   al   ha-gag
         Dani PRO.COP.ms   on   DD-roof
         'Dani is on the roof'

     d. Dani *(hu)   mar   yosef
         Dani PRO.COP.ms   Mr   Yosef
         'Dani is Mr Yosef'

The Hebrew pronominal copula has received considerable attention in the literature, and there exist a number of quite different accounts of the structure in which it participates (see e.g. Berman & Grosu 1976; Doron 1983; 1986; Rapoport 1987; Rothstein 1995; Shlonsky 2000a; Greenberg 2002; Heller 2002). Some of these analyses are summarised below.

Theoretical issues

Doron (1986) argues that the Hebrew pronominal copula is not an independent NP, but the phonological realisation of INFL features (cf. Ouhalla 1999). Doron (1983) argues that the explanation for the obligatory presence of the pronominal copula in 'identity' (specificational/equative) sentences like (136d) lies in the fact that referring NPs are arguments and must have theta-roles assigned to them, whereas predicational NPs are themselves theta-role assigners. Essentially, then, Doron proposes an analysis wherein the pronominal copula may, but need not, be a theta-role assigner.

Rothstein (1995) adopts Doron's view that the pronominal copula is the spellout of agreement features in INFL, but argues that it is thematically vacuous, pointing out that the pronominal copula is not in fact obligatory in identity sentences containing either negation (137a,b), or a pronominal subject (137c):

(137) a. Dani (hu)   lo   mar yosef   *Hebrew*
          Dani PRO.COP.ms   not   Mr Yosef   (Rothstein 1995: 34–5)
          'Dani is not Mr Yosef'

     b. Dani (*hu)   eyno   mar   yosef
         Dani PRO.COP.ms   not.ms   Mr   Yosef
         'Dani is not Mr Yosef'

---

[35] Some of Rothstein's (1995) examples are attributed to Doron (1983).

c. ani   (hu)   mar   yosef
    I   PRO.COP.ms   Mr   Yosef
    'I am Mr Yosef'

Rothstein argues that the pronominal copula is obligatory in identity sentences because no syntactic predication relation holds between the two NPs. This relation is introduced by the pronominal copula, which nevertheless does not assign thematic roles. This analysis therefore captures the fact that the pronominal copula licenses predication without assigning a thematic role. According to Rothstein's analysis, clauses with the pronominal copula contain a full inflectional (IP) clause structure that mediates between subject and complement, while clauses without the pronominal copula lack this structure and are simply small clauses (see also Rapoport 1987).

Greenberg (1998; 2002) takes a different tack, and argues that the optionality of the pronominal copula in predicational non-verbal clauses is only apparent, since its presence attributes a generic interpretation to the subject. This is illustrated by the following examples, where the pronominal copula is obligatorily present in clauses with a generic interpretation (138a,c), and obligatorily absent in clauses with a non-generic interpretation (138b,d).

(138) a. orvim   *(hem)   *Modern Hebrew*
          ravens   PRO.COP.3pl   (Greenberg 2002: 269)
          (yecurim)   šxorim
          creatures   black
          'ravens are black (creatures)'
      b. Rina   (*hi)   yafa   ha-yom
          Rina   PRO.COP.3fs pretty DD-day
          'Rina is pretty today'
      c. ha-šamayim   hem   kxulim
          DD-sky   PRO.COP.3pl blue
          'the sky is generally blue/blue by its nature'
      d. ha-šamayim   kxulim
          DD-sky   blue
          'the sky is blue now/today'

Greenberg (1998; 2002) adopts Rothstein's claims concerning the structural differences between Hebrew non-verbal clauses with and without the pronominal copula, and links the property of genericity to the distinct positions of the subject in each type of clause: while the generic subject occupies the specifier of IP, the non-generic subject occupies the small clause subject position. From this perspective, the pronominal copula is a generic operator in predicational non-verbal clauses.

Greenberg (2002) acknowledges that the obligatory presence of the pronominal copula in equative (specificational) non-verbal clauses cannot be explained by the genericity account, since equative clauses can also express non-generic meaning, as illustrated by example (139).

(139) ha-yom ha-'axot ha-toranit   *Modern Hebrew*
      DD-day DD-nurse DD-duty   (Greenberg 2002: 293)
      *(hi)   Rina
      PRO.COP.3fs   Rina
      'today the duty nurse is Rina'

However, Greenberg (2002) argues that it is possible to maintain the generalisation concerning the correlation between syntactic struture and genericity by assuming that while generic subjects of predicational clauses raise to the specifier of IP from the small clause, the subjects of equative clauses are base-generated in the specifier of IP. This draws on Rothstein's (1995) analysis, according to which the postcopular NP in equative clauses is an argument rather than a predicate, and therefore occurs as the complement of the inflectional head rather than as part of a small clause structure. The three distinct structures assumed by Rothstein (1995) and Greenberg (2002) are summarised in (140).

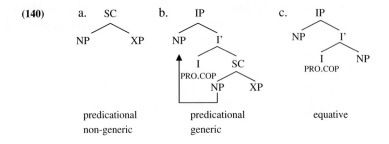

Shlonsky (2000a) develops an analysis that focuses on the distribution of the pronominal copula in Hebrew equative clauses. Shlonsky points out that the pronominal copula is usually described as obligatory in equative clauses with a lexical (i.e. non-pronominal) NP subject (136d) but optional in equative clauses with a pronominal subject (137c). However, Shlonsky argues that this 'optionality' is also apparent: the pronominal copula is only licensed in the latter case when the pronominal subject is in focus, which is marked by prosodic prominence (141).

(141) **hi**   hi   gveret Levi   *Modern Hebrew*
      PRO.3fs PRO.COP.fs Mrs   Levi   (adapted from Shlonsky 2000a: 338)
      '**she** is Mrs Levi'

Example (142) shows that when the pronominal subject *hi* is old information (linking back to the discourse-old *Rina*), the pronominal copula is not licensed.

(142)'ata   lo   yod'ea mi   Rina? Hi   *Modern Hebrew*
     PRO.2ms NEG know   who Rina   PRO.3fs   (Shlonsky 2000a: 338)
     (*hi)   gveret Levi
     PRO.COP.fs   Mrs   Lev
     'you don't know who Rina is? She is Mrs Levi'

Shlonsky explains this pattern by positing that the Hebrew clause has two subject positions, one (higher) topic-subject position, which licenses nominative case, and one lower subject position which does not license nominative case. This claim is independently motivated by the behaviour of subjects in verbal clauses. Consider the following examples.

(143)a. 'eyn Rina mədaberet rusit   *Modern Hebrew*
        NEG Rina speak.fs Russian   (Shlonsky 2000a: 326)
        'Rina does not speak Russian'
     b. Rina 'eyn-a   mədaberet rusit
        Rina NEG.3fs speak.fs   Russian
        'Rina does not speak Russian'

These examples illustrate that the Hebrew subject can occupy two different positions relative to the negation morpheme. Observe that when the negation morpheme follows the subject, it agrees with the subject (143b). The fact that the subject in (143b) precedes the negation morpheme indicates that the subject is VP-external. Example (144) shows that the subject below negation in (143a), together with the verb, precedes VP(-adjoined) adverbs. According to Shlonksy, this suggests that the verb has raised out of the VP and that this subject must therefore also be in some VP-external subject position.

(144)'eyn Rina mədaberet heitev rusit   *Modern Hebrew*
     NEG Rina speak.fs well   Russian (Shlonsky 2000a: 326)
     'Rina doesn't speak Russian well'

Despite the fact that Hebrew licenses null subjects, Shlonsky demonstrates that the subject position below the (non-agreeing) negation morpheme (143a) does not license null subjects. This is illustrated by the ungrammaticality of the weather sentence in example (145).

(145)*'eyn yored gešem bə-Telaviv   *Modern Hebrew*
     NEG   falls rain   in-Tel.Aviv   (Shlonsky 2000a: 328)
     'rain doesn't fall in Tel-Aviv' (lit. 'it isn't raining in Tel-Aviv')

In contrast, the subject position above the (agreeing) negation morpheme licenses null referential subjects, as illustrated by example (146a), but not null non-referential subjects, as illustrated by (146b).

(146) a. 'eyn-(ən)i   mədaberet rusit   *Modern Hebrew*
        NEG.1s   speak.fs   Russian   (Shlonsky 2000a: 329)
        'I don't speak Russian'
    b. *'eyn-o   yored   gešem   bə-Telaviv   *Modern Hebrew*
        NEG-3MS   falls   rain   in-Tel.Aviv   (Shlonsky 2000a: 330)
        'rain doesn't fall in Tel-Aviv' (lit. 'it isn't raining in Tel-Aviv')

Shlonsky analyses the subject position above (agreeing) negation as the position that licenses nominative case, hence the fact that lexical subjects must raise to that position when the negation morpheme bears the agreement features. Compare example (143b) with the ungrammatical example in (147).

(147) *'eyn-a   Rina   mədaberet   rusit   *Modern Hebrew*
      NEG.3fs   Rina   speak.fs   Russian   (Shlonsky 2000a: 330)
      'Rina does not speak Russian'

Shlonsky claims that the subject position above (agreeing) negation only licenses referential subjects because this position is an argument topic position (distinct from a left-dislocated topic position). The conclusion that emerges from Shlonsky's discussion is therefore that Hebrew has two subject positions: one higher nominative topic-subject position that dominates and therefore precedes (agreeing) negation, and one lower non-nominative subject position that is dominated by and therefore follows (non-agreeing) negation.

    Now consider the following non-verbal clauses. Example (148a) illustrates a predicative non-verbal clause, and example (148b) an equative non-verbal clause. Recall that the pronominal copula is required in the latter case.

(148) a. Rina   zameret   rok   *Modern Hebrew*
        Rina   singer   rock   (Shlonsky 2000a: 334)
        'Rina is a rock singer'
    b. Rina   hi   gveret   Levi
        Rina   PRO.COP.fs   Mrs   Levi
        'Rina is Mrs Levi'

Example (149) demonstrates that the subject of the predicative non-verbal clause can occupy the subject position below (non-agreeing) negation, while the subject of the equative clause cannot.

(149) a. 'eyn Rina   zameret   rok   *Modern Hebrew*
        NEG Rina   singer   rock   (Shlonsky 2000a: 335)
        'Rina is not a rock singer'
    b. *'eyn   Rina   (hi)   gveret   Levi
        NEG   Rina   PRO.COP.fs   Mrs   Levi
        'Rina is not Mrs Levi'

Instead, the subject of the equative clause must occupy the topic-subject position that precedes (agreeing) negation:

(150) Rina 'eyn-a   gveret Levi   *Modern Hebrew*
      Rina NEG-3fs singer Levi   (Shlonsky 2000a: 334)
      'Rina is not Mrs Levi'

Shlonsky argues that NP_1 in equative clauses like (148b) occupies the higher of the two Hebrew subject positions (the topic-subject position), occupying the specifier of a functional projection whose head is realised by the pronominal copula. He further argues that the referential NP_2 occupies the lower of the two Hebrew subject positions, in the specifier of a functional projection whose head is null in Hebrew. In contrast, Shlonsky (2000a: 337) argues that the subject of a predicative non-verbal clause occupies the lower subject position, and is not 'forced up' to the higher subject position because the non-referential predicative XP does not compete for the lower subject position.

Recall Shlonsky's observation that the pronominal copula is only licensed in non-verbal clauses with pronominal subjects if the pronominal subject is in focus. Example (141) is repeated here as (151).

(151) **hi**   hi   gveret   *Modern Hebrew*
      PRO.3fs PRO.COP.fs Mrs   (adapted from Shlonsky 2000a: 338)
      Levi
      Levi
      '**she** is Mrs Levi'

Shlonsky argues that the underlying structure for this example is an 'inverse' construction in which the NP *gveret Levi* originates in the higher subject position, in the specifier of the projection headed by the pronominal copula, while the pronominal subject *hi* originates in the lower subject position. According to Shlonsky's analysis, the pronominal subject then raises to SpecFP, while the pronominal copula, bearing the [+ FOCUS] feature, raises to F. This derivation is illustrated in (152), where the higher (topic) subject position is the specifier of Agr(eement)P_1, and the lower subject position is the specifier of AgrP$_2$.

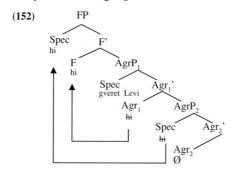

According to Shlonsky, this analysis explains why the pronominal copula agrees in person with the NP *gveret Levi* (third person), rather than with the pronominal subject: the NP *gveret Levi* and the pronominal copula originate in a specifier–head configuration. This point that is made clearer by an example like (153), in which the pronominal subject is in the first person:

(153) **ani**   hi   gveret Levi   *Modern Hebrew*
      PRO.1S PRO.COP.fs Mrs   Levi   (Shlonsky 2000a: 338)
      'I am Mrs Levi'

This analysis also explains why the higher subject position [SpecAgrP$_1$] cannot host (nominal or pronominal) focused constituents: it is a topic position. In other words, this analysis correctly predicts the ungrammaticality of the following example:

(154) *hi   hi   gveret **Levi**   *Modern Hebrew*
      PRO.3fs PRO.COP.fs Mrs   Levi   (Shlonsky 2000a: 338)
      (lo   gveret   Cohen)
      NEG   Mrs   Cohen
      'she is Mrs Levi (not Mrs Cohen)

It follows that examples like (151) and (153), which contain a focused pronominal subject, involve a different underlying structure from examples like (148b), which contain a non-focused lexical subject. As Shlonsky (2000a: 339) observes, however, this raises the questions of why an example like (148b) is not licensed with a (non-focused) pronominal subject in the higher topic-subject position. Shlonsky (2000a) argues that this position is restricted to 'strong nominals': lexical NPs and strong pronouns. Non-focused pronouns are not strong pronouns, and while focused pronouns are strong, they are excluded from the topic-subject position because of the incompatibility between topic and focus. Shlonsky's analysis receives further support from the ungrammaticality of the following example, in which an indefinite NP occupies the topic-subject position:

(155) *yeled hu   Dani   *Modern Hebrew*
      child   PRO.COP.ms Dani   (Shlonsky 2000a: 340)
      'Dani is a child'

Since topics relate to discourse-given information, they are not licensed to be indefinite, unless generic. This means that a predicate nominal (indefinite) cannot occupy the topic-subject position, as predicted by the analysis. It can, however, raise to the focus position: according to Shlonsky (2000a: 340), example (155) is licensed with 'heavy, contrastive stress on the indefinite'. Finally, consider example (156), in which a non-focused pronominal subject (NP$_1$) occurs in simple juxtaposition with NP$_2$.

(156) ani   gveret Levi   *Modern Hebrew*
      I   Mrs   Levi   (Shlonsky 2000a: 338)
      'I am Mrs Levi'

Given the evidence that a (weak) pronominal subject cannot occupy the topic-subject position (Sub₁), but that the NP2 in an equative clause occupies the lower subject position (Sub₂), Shlonsky (2000a: 342) posits an additional subject position above Sub₂ that is specialised for pronominal subjects.

Finally, recall that Hebrew also has a pseudocleft construction (§ 6.2.3). Example (60) is repeated here as (157).

(157) ma   še-dekart   maca   *Modern Hebrew*
      what   that-Descartes   found   (Heller 2002: 253)
      hu   hoxaxa   le-kiyum   ha-el
      PRO.COP.ms proof   to-existence DD-god
      'what Descartes found is/was a proof of God's existence.'

Recall that pseudoclefts are often but not always specificational (§ 5.2.2). As has often been observed (Akmajian 1970; Higgins 1973 [1979]), English examples like (158) are ambiguous between the predicational and the specificational reading.

(158) what John is is important (Heller 2002: 247)

The specificational reading of this sentence can be paraphrased as *John is important*, while the predicational reading means that John's role or position (e.g. his job as bank manager) is important. Heller points out that Hebrew relies upon distinct forms of the pronominal copula in order to distinguish predicational and specificational pseudoclefts, with the result that this ambiguity does not arise. As the following examples illustrate, the third person pronominal copula *hu* identifies a predicational pseudocleft, while the neutral form of the impersonal pronominal copula *ze* identifies a specificational pseudocleft.

(159) a. ma   še-dan   haya   *Modern Hebrew*
         what   that-Dan   was   *predicational pseudocleft*
         hu   mo'il   la-xevra
         PRO.COP.3ms   helpful   to-society
         'what Dan was is helpful to society.'
      b. ma   še-dan   haya ze   *Modern Hebrew*
         what that-Dan was   PRO-COP.4n   *specificational pseudocleft*
         mo'il   la-xevra   (Heller 2002: 248)
         helpful to-society
         'what Dan was was helpful to society'

While specificational pseudoclefts display connectivity effects such as reflexive pronoun binding between the pre-copular and the post-copular constituents (160a), predicational pseudoclefts do not (160b) (see Heycock & Kroch (1999) for a discussion of connectivity in English pseudoclefts).

(160) a. ma   še-dan   haya ze   *Modern Hebrew*
         what   that-Dan   was   PRO.COP.4n   *specificational pseudocleft*
         mesukan   le-acmo
         dangerous   to-himself
         'what Dan was was dangerous to himself'

      b. *ma še-dan   haya   *Modern Hebrew*
         what that-Dan   was   *predicational pseudocleft*
         hu   mesukan   le-acmo   (Heller 2002: 248)
         PRO.COP.3ms   dangerous to-himself
         'what Dan was was dangerous to himself'

In addition, Heller identifies a third type of pseudocleft that is characterised
by the agreeing form of the impersonal pronominal copula (161). Compare
the following examples.

(161) a. ma   še-kaninu ba-šuk   *Modern Hebrew*
         what   that-bought.1pl   in.DD-market   (Heller 2002: 245)
         ze   *(et)   ha-xulca   ha-kxula
         PRO.COP.4n   ACC   DD-shirt(f)   DD-blue(f)
         'what we bought in the market was the blue shirt'

      b. ma   še-kaninu
         what   that-bought.1pl
         ba-šuk   zot   (*et) ha-xulca   ha-kxula
         in.DD-market   PRO.COP.4f   ACC   DD-shirt(f)   DD-blue(f)
         'what we bought in the market was the blue shirt'

While (161a) illustrates the specificational pseudocleft, which is characterised by the neutral form of the impersonal pronominal copula, in the
pseudocleft construction illustrated in (161b) the impersonal pronominal
copula agrees in gender with the postcopular NP. In addition, these
examples also illustrate a difference in connectivity effects. While the
specificational pseudocleft requires accusative case marking on the
postcopular NP, linking this constituent to the gap in the complement
position of the relative clause, the pseudocleft with the agreeing form of
the impersonal pronominal copula does not license accusative case
marking on the post-copular NP. Heller further observes that while
pseudoclefts with the neutral impersonal pronominal copula license a
range of post-copular categories (CP, VP, AP, NP), the agreeing copular
pseudocleft is resticted to taking what Heller (2002: 258) describes as 'real
world' individual-denoting postcopular NPs, ruling out, for example,
property-denoting NPs. Heller argues that this semantic constraint
accounts for the fact that constructions like (161a) display a range of
connectivity effects that the agreeing counterpart illustrated in (161b)
lacks. While Heller's account focuses on the semantic properties of the
Hebrew pseudocleft rather than a syntactic analysis, it demonstrates that

the semantic properties of the construction are reflected in its grammatical behaviour, which in turn has implications for a syntactic analysis of the construction (see Heycock & Kroch (1999) for a recent syntactic treatment of pseudoclefts).

In sum, as the discussion in this section illustrates, the constructions in which the Hebrew pronominal copula participates have been subject to a range of different syntactic analyses, which share the assumption that the pronominal copula is a realisation of inflectional features. According to Shlonsky (2000a), Hebrew patterns rather like Arabic, in that the pre-copular NP position in an equative clause is associated with focus, although Shlonsky's discussion suggests that this is restricted to pronominal rather than nominal subjects. Although the facts concerning the focus (and topic) position in copular clauses are slightly different in Arabic and Hebrew on the one hand and in Hausa on the other, this discussion nevertheless reveals cross-linguistic support for an analysis in which the copula heads a functional projection that is associated with focus. Furthermore, Shlonsky's analysis of Hebrew also relies upon a topic position for the subject of a certain type of non-verbal clause, an analysis that is similar in spirit to the analysis proposed for Hausa in the previous chapter (§ 5.4) (cf. also Basilico 2003). Finally, Heller's account of Hebrew pseudoclefts raises many questions concerning the syntax and semantics of the corresponding construction in Hausa (§ 5.2). An in-depth analysis of Hausa pseudoclefts awaits future research.

6.3.5 Coptic Egyptian

Descriptive facts

Coptic Egyptian has two types of non-verbal clauses: those formed by simple juxtaposition of subject pronoun and predicate, and those formed with a pronominal copula. Reintges (2004) refers to these by the traditional terms 'bipartite' and 'tripartite' non-verbal clauses, respectively. The bipartite clause type is illustrated in (162).

(162) a. ang-u-pneuma   *Coptic*
    PRO.1s-INDEF.ms-ghost   (Reintges 2004: 175)
    'I am a ghost'

  b. u-rɔme-pe   *Coptic*
    INDEF.ms-man-PRO.3ms   (Reintges 2004: 173)
    'he is a man'

  c. ntetn-hen-at-ʃipe   *Coptic*
    PRO.2pl-INDEF.pl-NEG-shame   (Reintges 2004: 179)
    'you are shameless'

d. ntetn-n-ʃere   m-p-petwaaβ   *Coptic*
   PRO.2pl-DD.pl-children   of-DD.ms-holy   (Reintges 2004: 178)
   Apa   Mɔsɛs
   Apa   Moses
   'you are the children of the holy Apa Moses'

Examples (162a) and (162b) illustrate predicational non-verbal clauses, in
which the nominal predicate ascribes a property to the subject. Example
(162c) illustrates a predicational clause with an adjectival noun predicate.[36]
Example (162d) illustrates an equative non-verbal clause.

In this type of non-verbal clause, only personal pronouns are licensed in
subject position. As the examples in (162) illustrate, first and second
person pronouns are proclitic forms, while third person pronouns are
enclitics. Example (163) shows that first and second person independent
pronouns substitute for clitic forms when the pronominal subject is
in focus. Third person pronouns do not have a distinct independent form.

(163)a. **anok**   u-ʃɔs   *Coptic*
        pro.1s INDEF.ms-shepherd   (Reintges 2004: 172)
        'I am a shepherd'
     b. **ntok**   u-rm-tɔn   *Coptic*
        PRO.2ms INDEF.ms-man-where   (Reintges 2004: 173)
        '**you** are a man from whence?'

The Coptic non-verbal clause has a default present tense interpretation. For
a past tense reading, the auxiliary *ne* is added, as illustrated by example
(164). Observe that this example has a locative (preposition phrase)
predicate.

(164)   ne   hən-ebol-ne   *Coptic*
        PRET INDEF.pl-from-PRO.3pl   (Reintges 2004: 180)
        t-metropolis   et-tajeu̯   nte kɛme
        DD.fs-capital   DD.fs-glorious   of Egypt
        'they were from the glorious capital of Egypt'

The following examples illustrate non-verbal clauses with a topic-comment
structure. In example (165a), the topic noun phrase *n-nute n-n-hethnos* 'the
gods of the pagans' is co-referential with the third person plural resumptive
pronoun *ne* in the subject position of the non-verbal clause. In example
(165b), the topic *anok* 'me' is co-referential with the first person singular
resumptive subject pronoun *ang-* 'I'.

---

[36] Adjectives do not exist as a separate word class in Coptic, but the language borrowed many
forms from Greek, which does have an adjective word class (Reintges 2004: 90–91).

(165) a. n-nute   n-n-hethnos   *Coptic*
DD.PL-gods   of-DD.pl-pagans   (Reintges 2004: 176–7)
hn-daimɔnion   ne
INDEF.pl-demons   PRO.3pl
'as for the gods of the pagans, they are demons'

b. anok   de   ang-u-kah   awɔ ang-u-plasma   nte
PRO.1s PART PRO.1s-INDEF-earth and PRO.1s-INDEF-creature of
ne-f-kʲitʃ
DD.pl-3ms-hands
'as for me, I am earth, and a I am creature of his (God's) hands'

Reintges (2004: 178) suggests that the topic position in this type of non-verbal clause has been reanalysed as a subject position, given the restriction on lexical noun phrases as subjects. According to this perspective, the pronominal element evolves from a resumptive pronoun into a pronominal copula, a position that blurs the boundary somewhat between the 'bipartite' non-verbal clause and its 'tripartite' counterpart, although the two constructions show different linear properties in the third person. Observe that this analysis is consistent with Li & Thompson's (1977) hypothesis concerning the evolution of copulas (§ 5.3).

The tripartite non-verbal clause is illustrated in (166). As these examples illustrate, the canonical constituent order in this type of sentence is [SUBJECT PRO.COP PREDICATE]. As in Arabic and Hebrew, the pronominal copula is the third person form, and takes either masculine/feminine singular forms or the plural form, agreeing with the subject. Like the other Afroasiatic languages discussed in this section, Coptic illustrates the AN typological pattern.

(166) a. pai   pe   pa-hai   *Coptic*
DEM.ms   PRO.COP.ms DD.ms.1s-husband   (Reintges 2004: 182)
'this is my husband'

b. tai   te   ta-shime
DEM.fs   PRO.COP.fs DD.fs.1s-wife
'this is my wife'

c. nai   ne   na-ʃēre
DEM.3pl PRO.COP.pl DD.pl.1s-children
'these are my children'

Example (167) illustrates that, as in Arabic and Hebrew, the third person pronominal copula is licensed with first and second person subjects.

(167) a. anok   pe   pe-tʃoei̯s   *Coptic*
PRO.1s   PRO.COP.ms DD.ms-christ   (Reintges 2004: 184)
'I am the christ'

b. ntok   an   pe   pɔ-rro
PRO.2ms NEG PRO.COP.ms DD.ms-king
'you are not the king'

Reintges (2004: 183) suggests that the Coptic pronominal copula licenses a clausal structure by distinguishing the non-verbal clause from its phrasal equivalent (e.g. 'this husband of mine' in example (166a)) (cf. Eid 1983).

Unlike the bipartite non-verbal clause, the tripartite non-verbal clause licenses both lexical NP subjects as well as pronominal subjects. However, Reintges (2004: 184) observes that this subject must be definite, a familiar restriction on non-verbal clauses. The examples in (168) illustrate equative clauses, which are clearly reversible.

(168) a. pef-ran   pe   Paulos   *Coptic*
          poss.3ms-name pro.cop.ms Paul   (Reintges 2004: 186)
          'his name was Paul'

     b. Nahrow   pe   pa-ran   *Coptic*
         Nahrow   pro.cop.ms DD.ms.1s-name (Reintges 2004: 191)
         'Nahrow is my name'

Example (169) illustrates predicative tripartite non-verbal clauses with indefinite adjectival noun predicates. It appears that inversion of subject and predicate is common in this type of construction.

(169) a. alɛthɔs, u-nok^j m-magos   *Coptic*
          really   INDEF.ms-great of-magician (Reintges 2004: 187)
          pe   pei-rɔme
          pro.cop.ms   DEM.ms-man
          'really, this man is a great magician'

     b. u-nok^j pe   *Coptic*
         INDEF.ms-great   pro.cop.ms (Reintges 2004: 186)
         pek-klɛros
         poss.2ms-heritage
         'your heritage is great'

As the examples in this section demonstrate, Coptic Egyptian has a similar syntactic strategy to the Semitic languages for forming non-verbal clauses. In addition, the reader will have observed that the morphology of the Coptic pronominal/demonstrative system shows some striking similarities to the Hausa system, in possessing sound features that have been reconstructed for Proto-Afroasiatic. In particular, plural forms are characterised by /n/ and feminine singular forms by /t/. These sound features are evident in the Hausa pronominal/demonstrative system, and Schuh (1983a) argues that the same features underlie the Hausa non-verbal copula nē/cē/nē (§ 5.3). These similarities are most evident in the examples in (166), in which demonstrative pronouns, pronominal copulas and bound possessive pronouns share the same sound features. A close comparison of Hausa and Coptic copular constructions awaits future research.

Theoretical issues

Recall that Coptic Egyptian has a biclausal cleft construction, in which the pronominal copula participates (§ 6.2.4). Example (72) is repeated here as (170).

(170) a. nim   pe   *Coptic*
     who PRO.COP.ms   (Reintges 2004: 438)
     ənt-a-f-tɔɔkʸe   mmo-u   əm-pei-ma?
     RM-PF-3ms-plant   of-PRO.3pl   in-DD.ms-place
     'who is it that planted them (the trees) here?'

    b. ta-ʃeere   **tu-pistis**   *Coptic*
     DD.fs.1s-daughter DD.fs.2fs-faith   (Reintges, et al 2005: ex. 19a)
     te   ənt-a-s-nahm
     PRO.COP.fs   RM-PF-3fs-save(-PRO.2fs)
     'my daughter, it is **your faith** that has saved (you)'

Example (170a) illustrates a *wh*-cleft, in which the clefted constituent *nim* 'who' is separated from the remainder of the construction by the pronominal copula, which is followed by a relative clause containing a gap or a resumptive pronoun corresponding to the clefted constituent. Example (170b) illustrates a similar construction in which the clefted constituent *tu-pistis* 'your faith' is in focus. The clefted constituent is restricted to the NP category: it must either be a lexical noun phrase, a pronoun or a *wh*-pronoun. Furthermore, while this construction typically expresses contrastive focus, it can also express new information focus (Reintges 2003b).

Reintges, et al. (2005) argue that the presence of the pronominal copula in the Coptic cleft suggests an analysis in which this construction is analysed as a straightforward equative copular structure [DP PRO.COP DP], like the tripartite copular sentences illustrated above in (166)–(169), the only difference being that the postcopular DP is a free relative. However, Reintges, et al. provide evidence that the relative clause structure in the cleft construction does not pattern like the free relative in equative clauses. For example, (171) illustrates that it is possible for the element *pe* to occur twice in the tripartite equative, once as a pronominal copula and once as as a determiner in the free relative. Because the nominal head is null, the determiner cliticises to the complementiser. This doubling of the pronominal element is not found in cleft constructions.

(171)   u-athεt   de   *Coptic*
      INDEF.s-stupid PART   (Reintges *et al.* 2005: ex. 16a)
      pe   p-et   moste   n-ne-tʃpio
      pro.COP.3ms   DD.ms-COMP   hate   DO-DD.pl-criticism
      'the one who hates criticism is stupid'

On the basis of this and other evidence, Reintges, *et al.* conclude that the relative clause structure cannot be analysed as a free relative, and does not therefore have the status of a DP. Instead, it is analysed as a CP consituent that originates in the complement position of a small clause structure that is headed by the pronominal copula. This small clause structure is dominated by a focus phrase (FP) layer. The clefted constituent originates in the small clause subject position, and raises to the specifier of FP. This analysis is illustrated in (172) (adapted from Reintges, et al. (2005: ex. 30).

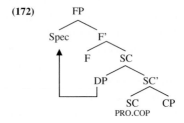

In sum, as in many languages, the Coptic copula not only licenses predication in non-verbal clauses, but participates in marking focus in verbal clauses.

6.3.6 *Summary*

The comparisons drawn in this section show that although Hausa is relatively unusual in the Chadic family in having a copula, a relatively consistent typological pattern can nevertheless be observed, particularly with respect to the fact that nominal and adjectival predicates pattern together (§ 6.3.2). There are some clear parallels between Hausa and Arabic, in that both languages have a copula that is related to a pronoun, which also participates in marking focus in certain construction types (§ 6.3.3). However, the copula is not a feature of monoclausal focus fronting constructions in Arabic. A discussion of Ouhalla's (1999) analysis of clefts in Moroccan Arabic shows that although the Arabic copula is analysed as a type of INFL category that participates in both non-verbal copular clauses and cleft sentences, the similarities between Hausa and Arabic focus constructions (with or without the copula) can be accounted for by assuming a rather similar syntactic analysis built around the focus phrase (FP). Like Arabic, Hebrew has a pronominal copula that has also been analysed as the realisation of inflectional features (§ 6.3.4). This element also participates in the Hebrew cleft construction. According to Shlonsky (2000a), Hebrew patterns rather like Arabic, in that the pre-copular NP position in an equative clause is associated with focus. Shlonsky develops an analysis built around an FP structure in order to account for this fact, which also relies upon a topic position for the subject of a certain type of non-verbal clause. This analysis is similar in spirit to the analysis proposed for Hausa in the previous chapter (§ 5.4) Finally, like Arabic and Hebrew,

Coptic Egyptian also has a pronominal copula, which participates in tripartite non-verbal clauses as well as in the biclausal cleft (§ 6.3.5). Reintges *et al.* analyse the Coptic pronominal copula not as an INFL category, but as the head of a small clause structure that, in the case of clefts, is dominated by an FP layer.

6.4. CONCLUSIONS

This chapter explored focus/*wh*-constructions and copular/non-verbal clauses in a range of Chadic and other Afroasiatic languages, with a view to situating the Hausa pattern within a broader typological context. A brief descriptive survey of focus/*wh*-constructions in 11 Chadic languages reveals that the Chadic group exemplifies a range of ex situ and focus/*wh*-strategies (clause-initial, clause-final and postverbal), in addition to in situ focus/*wh*. This survey also reveals that some but not all Chadic languages have focus markers, some of which are copulas and some of which have other origins. Special inflection also occurs in a subset of Chadic languages, although this feature may not be as widespread as some researchers suggest.

Turning to the more distant Afroasiatic relatives, the syntax of focus/*wh*-constructions in Modern Standard Arabic bears a close resemblance to the Hausa pattern, as do the distinctions between topic and focus constructions. A brief survey of focus/*wh*-constructions in some spoken dialects of Arabic reveals that while some dialects pattern like Standard Arabic in permitting both *wh*-in situ and *wh*-fronting, some dialects only permit the former. In addition, some Arabic dialects have a cleft focus/*wh*-construction. The similarities between Hausa and Hebrew focus constructions are less striking. Like Hausa, Hebrew has a *wh*-fronting strategy, but unlike Hausa, there is evidence for a designated (new information) focus position that is local to the verb rather than clause-initial. Hebrew also has a cleft construction that is restricted to subjects, and a VP fronting strategy that results in a topic construction. Like Hausa and Arabic, Coptic Egyptian licenses both in situ and ex situ focus/*wh*-strategies, but differs from Hausa in that focus/*wh*-in situ is the unmarked strategy. In Coptic, special inflection correlates with the in situ rather than the ex situ pattern. Furthermore, unlike Hausa, Coptic also has a biclausal cleft construction.

While non-verbal copulas are rare in the Chadic family, similarities can be observed between Hausa and its more distant Afroasiatic relatives Arabic, Hebrew and Coptic Egyptian. First, with respect to the historical origins of the copula, these languages appear to have undergone similar grammaticalisation processes whereby copulas have evolved from analogous expressions. Secondly, similarities are evident in the morphosyntactic and information structuring properties of the constructions in which copulas participate. From a historical perspective, cleft constructions and monoclausal focus fronting constructions of the Hausa type, in which a copula has evolved into a focus marker, can be seen as related points on a continuum. This accounts both for synchronic similarities and for synchronic differences between the two construction types. In addition, the pseudocleft construction also falls within this broader class of focus constructions, displaying properties associated with both the biclausal cleft construction and the simple non-verbal clause. Although there are clear similarities between the Hausa pseudocleft and its counterparts in the Afroasiatic languages discussed here, a detailed account of the Hausa pseudocleft awaits future research.

Finally, this chapter provides an overview of the range of recent theoretical analyses of focus/*wh*- and non-verbal copular constructions in the languages discussed here, including clefts. This reveals how the relatively simple FP analysis explored in this book for focus and copular constructions in Hausa has also been usefully exploited in accounting for a broader class of focus/*wh*-constructions in related languages.

7

SUMMARY AND CONCLUSIONS

The present study set out to achieve two main objectives: to provide a detailed description of the morphosyntax, semantics and pragmatics of focus and non-verbal copular constructions in Hausa, and to develop a syntactic analysis of these constructions from a current generative perspective. The first three chapters detailed the background of the study: Chapter 1 presented an overview of the book, Chapter 2 provided a descriptive overview of the morphosyntactic features of the Hausa language, introducing readers to the data that is the focus of the present study, and Chapter 3 explored ways of defining focus, a linguistic phenomenon that involves the complex interaction of phonology, morphosyntax, semantics and pragmatics. This chapter also discussed the development of generative theories of the syntax of focus, setting the scene for the theoretical analysis developed in subsequent chapters.

Chapter 4 concentrated upon the syntax, semantics and discourse properties of focus fronting constructions in Hausa, in which a single constituent can be focus fronted, optionally followed by the non-verbal focus marking copula, a process that typically requires gapping rather than resumption in the base position of the displaced constituent. In addition, focus fronting requires special inflection (the 'relative' or 'focus' form of INFL) in the clause whose left periphery hosts the extracted focus phrase. In each of these respects, focus fronting is morphosyntactically distinct from the superficially similar topic construction. A syntactic analysis of focus fronting was developed, according to which the focused constituent is displaced to the specifier position of the left-peripheral functional projection, the focus phrase (FP), a process that is motivated in the recent versions of the Chomskyan framework by the requirement to match and eliminate non-semantic features. This analysis accurately characterises the properties of the focus construction, in particular the restriction to a single focus fronted phrase and the presence of the non-verbal copula, which is reanalysed as a focus marker that instantiates the head of the focus phrase.

The syntactic parallels between focus fronting and *wh*-fronting entail that the FP analysis can be straightforwardly extended to *wh*-fronting. In addition, an analysis of 'special inflection' (relative aspects) developed by Green & Reintges (2005b) was discussed, according to which special inflection surfaces as the morphological realisation of agreement features between functional heads. Finally, Chapter 4 compared and contrasted the properties of in situ focus/*wh* in Hausa with the properties of ex situ focus/*wh*, with particular emphasis on the question of whether the two types of construction are distinct in terms of semantics or discourse function. While all speakers accept *wh*-in situ with echo interpretation, genuine interrogative *wh*-in situ appears to have relatively marginal status. While *wh*-subjects in situ are uniformly rejected, there is evidence of an argument–adjunct asymmetry, with non-argument *wh*-phrases in situ more widely accepted than arguments. In contrast, focus in situ appears to be more widespread in Hausa, and a number of recent studies suggest that, like its ex situ counterpart, the in situ construction licenses both new information and exhaustive/contrastive focus interpretations. In addition, presentational focus is restricted to the in situ construction.

It was concluded that the interpretation of focus is underspecified by the syntax in Hausa. Instead, it is the discourse context that determines which focus interpretation is selected from the range of options provided by the syntax. Multiple focus/*wh*-constructions (with one in situ and one ex situ phrase) were found to be acceptable only with two contrastively focused constituents, or where the *wh*-in situ phrase receives an echo interpretation. With respect to the syntactic analysis of focus/*wh*-fronting proposed earlier in the chapter, the fact that in situ *wh*-phrases are restricted to an echo interpretation in multiple *wh*-constructions suggests that the genuine wh-interrogation interpretation is linked to extraction, either in the overt syntax or covertly. In contrast, echo questions and presentational focus constructions are thought to lack movement altogether, hence their distinct morphosyntactic and functional properties.

Chapter 5 focused upon the syntax, semantics and information packaging properties of non-verbal copular sentences in Hausa, the other major context in which the non-verbal focus marking copula occurs. The main empirical question addressed in this chapter was whether the reanalysis of the non-verbal copula as a grammaticalised focus marker is upheld by its function in the non-verbal clause. According to the perspective explored in this chapter, the Hausa non-verbal copula evolved from pronominal elements (Li & Thompson 1977; Schuh 1983a), and is in the process of evolving via its function in focus/*wh*-fronting constructions into a fully grammaticalised focus marker. It was argued that while the non-verbal copula shows a 'less grammaticalised' status in the non-verbal clause, in the sense that its function is partly to license predication or equation, there is also evidence in this construction type of its evolving function as a focus marker, hence the fact that there is a designated focus position in both canonical and non-canonical non-verbal copular clauses: both predicational and equative copular sentences in Hausa permit a range of constituent order permutations that are unified by the fact that focus falls on the constituent left-adjacent to the copula. It was further argued that the FP analysis of focus/*wh*-fronting developed in Chapter 4 can be usefully extended to the non-verbal copular clause, enabling a simple account of these constructions that accurately captures both their morphosyntactic properties and their information packaging properties.

Chapter 6 set the discussion of the Hausa facts in a broader typological context by taking a within-family cross-linguistic perspective on focus/*wh*-constructions and non-verbal clauses. This discussion focused on a subset of Chadic languages and on Arabic, Hebrew and Coptic Egyptian. A brief descriptive survey of focus/*wh*-constructions in 11 Chadic languages revealed that the Chadic group exemplifies a range of ex situ and focus/*wh*-strategies (clause-initial, clause-final and post-verbal), in addition to in situ focus/*wh*. This survey also showed that some but not all Chadic languages have focus markers, some of which are copulas and some of which have other origins. Special inflection also occurs in a subset of Chadic languages, although this feature may not be as widespread as some researchers suggest.

With respect to the more distant Afroasiatic relatives, the syntax of focus/*wh*-constructions in Modern Standard Arabic bears a close resemblance to the Hausa pattern, as do the distinctions between topic and focus constructions. In contrast, the similarities between Hausa and Hebrew focus constructions are less striking. Like Hausa and Arabic, Coptic Egyptian licenses both in situ and ex situ focus/*wh*-strategies, but differs from Hausa in that focus/*wh*-in situ is the unmarked strategy, which correlates with special inflection. Furthermore, unlike Hausa, Coptic also has a biclausal cleft construction.

While non-verbal copulas are rare in the Chadic family, similarities can be observed between Hausa and its more distant Afroasiatic relatives Arabic, Hebrew and Coptic Egyptian, particularly in that these languages appear to have undergone similar grammaticalisation processes whereby copulas have evolved from comparable types of expressions. In addition, similarities are evident in the morphosyntactic and information structuring properties of the constructions in which copulas participate. From a historical perspective, it was argued that cleft constructions and monoclausal focus-fronting constructions of the Hausa type, in which a copula has evolved into a focus marker, can be seen as related points on a continuum. This accounts both for synchronic similarities as well as synchronic differences between the two construction types. The pseudocleft construction also falls within this broader class of focus constructions, displaying properties associated both with the biclausal cleft construction and with the simple non-verbal clause. Although there are clear similarities between the Hausa pseudocleft and its counterparts in the Afroasiatic languages discussed here, a detailed account of the Hausa pseudocleft awaits future research.

Finally, Chapter 6 provided an overview of the range of recent theoretical analyses of focus/*wh*- and non-verbal copular constructions in the languages discussed here, including clefts. This discussion showed that the relatively simple FP analysis explored in the present study of Hausa has also been usefully exploited in accounting for a broader class of focus/*wh*-constructions in related languages.

In sum, while the morphosyntactic properties of Hausa focus/*wh*-fronting constructions are well understood, research into the properties of Hausa focus/*wh*-in situ constructions is at a relatively early stage. In addition, further research into the prosodic properties of Hausa focus constructions is required, which is expected to cast light on some of the questions raised but left unanswered in Chapter 4 (Green, in preparation).

The word-internal phonology of Hausa tone is well understood (e.g. Hyman and Schuh 1974; Leben 1978; Schuh 1978; Newman 1995). Intonation in Hausa was the focus of much research during the 1980s (e.g. Newman & Newman 1981; Miller & Tench 1980; 1982; Lindau 1986; Inkelas, et al. 1987). These studies focused particularly on the intonational patterns that distinguish clause types such as declaratives, *yes-no* questions and *wh*-questions, and revealed that Hausa 'clause-type' intonation is consistent with cross-linguistic patterns. For example, statements are characterised by 'downdrift' (a progressive lowering of pitch over the utterance as a whole) and *yes-no* questions by the suspension of downdrift and the raised pitch of the final high tone.

Typological approaches divide languages into 'tone', 'pitch accent' and 'stress accent' languages. A consequence of this typology is that prosodic prominence has received relatively little attention in the literature on Hausa (Hunter 1980; Möhlig 1983; Wolff 1993; Hartmann & Zimmermann fourthcoming, a). Indeed, Jaggar (2001:16) describes 'the existence of stress and its possible overlap with tone in Hausa [as] a controversial and under-researched phenomenon'. However, some authors (e.g. McCawley 1978; Hyman 1978; Hirst 1987; Odden 1995) argue that tone and accent (in the sense of 'prominence') are not mutually exclusive. For example, Selkirk & Shen (1990) describe focal prominence in Chinese, the textbook example of a tone language. Although Inkelas et al. (1987) and Inkelas & Leben (1990) briefly report 'emphatic raising' in Hausa focus fronting constructions – a process whereby the first high tone of a word or phrase is raised in order to express 'emphasis' – the prosodic properties of such constructions have received little attention. In addition, a systematic investigation of the prosodic properties of the recently described focus/*wh*-in situ constructions would settle a number of empirical and theoretical questions. For example, while Green & Jaggar (2003) suggest that the restriction on subject focus/*wh*-in situ might be explained by the prosodic structure of the Hausa sentence, such analyses remain speculative without further instrumental investigation.

From an empirical perspective, therefore, a careful investigation of this aspect of Hausa prosody is the 'missing link' that will enable a full description of the complex relationships between sound, meaning, grammar and discourse in this major world language. From a theoretical perspective, this investigation is also expected to cast light upon the nature of the syntax–phonology interface (Inkelas 1988; Selkirk 1984; Ladd 1996; Zec & Inkelas 1990; Zubizarreta 1998), contributing to the debate on the existence and nature of typological universals.

REFERENCES

REFERENCES

Abdoulaye, Mahamane L., 1992. *Aspects of Hausa morphosyntax in role and reference grammar*, doctoral dissertation, State University of New York at Buffalo.

Abdoulaye, Mahamane L., 1997. 'Presupposition and realis status in Hausa', *Sprachtypologie und Universalien Forschung* 50(4), 308–28.

Abdoulaye, Mahamane L., 2004. 'Four uses of relative marking in Hausa', paper presented at Syntax of the World's Languages (SWL 1), Leipzig, 5–8 August 2004.

Abney, Steven, 1987. *The English noun phrase in its sentential aspects*, doctoral dissertation, MIT.

Abraham, R. C., 1941. *A modern grammar of spoken Hausa*, London: Crown Agents for the Colonies (published on behalf of the Government of Nigeria).

Abraham, R. C., 1946. *Dictionary of the Hausa language*, London: University of London Press.

Abraham, R. C., 1959. *The language of the Hausa people*, London: University of London Press.

Abraham, R. C., 1962. *Dictionary of the Hausa language*, 2nd edn, London: University of London Press.

Adger, David, & Gillian Ramchand, 2003. 'Predication and equation', *Linguistic Inquiry* 34, 325–59.

Agbayani, Brian, 2000. '*Wh*-subjects in English and the vacuous movement hypothesis', *Linguistic Inquiry* 31, 703–13.

Akmajian, Adrian, 1970. 'On deriving cleft sentences from pseudo-cleft sentences', *Linguistic Inquiry* 1, 140–68.

Akmajian, Adrian, 1979. *Aspects of the grammar of focus in English*, New York: Garland.

Aoun, Joseph, 2000. 'Resumption and last resort', *DELTA (Revista de Documentaçäo de Estudos em Lingüística Teórica e Aplicada)* 16, 13–43.

Aoun, Joseph, Elabbas Benmamoun & Dominic Sportiche, 1994. 'Agreement, conjunction and word order in some varieties of Arabic', *Linguistic Inquiry* 25, 195–220.

Aoun, Joseph, & Lina Choueiri, 1999. 'Modes of interrogation', in Elabbas Benmamoun (ed.), *Perspectives on Arabic linguistics*, Amsterdam: John Benjamins, 7–25.

Aoun, Joseph, Norbert Hornstein & Lina Choueiri, 2001. 'Resumption, movement and derivational economy', *Linguistic Inquiry* 32, 371–403.

Aoun, Joseph, & Yen-hui Audrey Li, 1993. 'Wh-elements in situ: syntax or LF?', *Linguistic Inquiry* 24, 199–238.

Aoun, Joseph, & Yen-hui Audrey Li, 2003. *Essays on the representational and derivational nature of grammar* [*Linguistic Inquiry* monograph 40], Cambridge, Mass.: MIT Press.

Artstein, Ron, 2002. 'A focus semantics for echo questions', in Ágnes Bende-Farkas and Arndt Riester (eds.), *Workshop on information structure in context*, University of Stuttgart: IMS, 98–117.

Bagari, Dauda M. 1976. *Subordinate adverbial clauses in Hausa*, PhD dissertation, UCLA.

Bahloul, Maher, 1993. 'The copula in Modern Standard Arabic', in Mushira Eid & Clive Holes (eds.), *Perspectives on Arabic linguistics V*, Amsterdam: John Benjamins, 209–29.

Bargery, G. P., 1934. *A Hausa–English dictionary and English–Hausa vocabulary*, London: Oxford University Press.

Barreteau, Daniel, & Paul Newman, 1978. 'Les langues Tchadiques', in Daniel Bareteau (ed.), *Inventaire des études linguistiques sur les pays d'Afrique noire d'expression française et sur Madagascar*, Paris: Conseil International de la Langue Française, 291–330.

Basilico, David, 2003. 'The topic of small clauses', *Linguistic Inquiry* 34, 1–35.

Bearth, Thomas, 1999. 'The contribution of African linguistics towards a general theory of focus: update and critical review', *Journal of African Languages and Linguistics* 20, 126–56.

Bearth, Thomas, forthcoming 'Countervalue', in Jost Gippert & Rainer Vossen (eds.), *Sentence types and sentence structures*, special issue of *Sprachtypologie und Universalienforschung*.

Beck, Sigridk, & Shin-Sook Kim, 1997. 'On *wh-* and operator scope in Korean', *Journal of East Asian Linguistics* 6, 339–84.

Belletti, Adriana & Ur Shlonsky, 1995. 'The order of verbal complements: a comparative study', *Natural Language and Linguistic Theory* 13, 489–526.

Benmamoun, Elabbas, 2000. 'Agreement asymmetries and the PF interface', in Jacqueline Lecarme, Jean Lowenstamm & Ur Shlonsky (eds.), *Research in Afroasiatic grammar* [Current Issues in Linguistic Theory 202], Amsterdam: John Benjamins, 23–40.

Berman, Ruth & Alex Grosu, 1976. 'Aspects of the copula in Modern Hebrew', in Peter Cole (ed.), *Studies in Modern Hebrew syntax and semantics*, Amsterdam: North-Holland, 265–85.

Bobaljik, Jonathan D., 2002. 'A-chains at the PF-interface: copies and "covert" movement', *Natural Language and Linguistic Theory* 20, 197–267.

Bolinger, Dwight, 1954. 'English prosodic stress and Spanish sentence order', *Hispania* 37, 152–6.

Bolinger, Dwight, 1972a. 'Accent is predictable (if you're a mind reader)', *Language* 48, 634–44.

Bolinger, Dwight, 1972b. 'A look at equatives and cleft sentences', in Evelyn S. Firchow, Kaaren Grimstad, Nils Hasselmo & Wayne A. O'Neil (eds.), *Studies for Einar Haugen*, The Hague: Mouton, 96–114.

Bolinger, Dwight, 1985. *Intonation and its parts: melody in spoken English*, Stanford, Calif.: Stanford University Press.

Borer, Hagit, 1984. *Parametric syntax*, Dordrecht: Foris.

Borer, Hagit, 1995. 'The ups and downs of Hebrew verb movement', *Natural Language and Linguistic Theory* 13, 527–606.

Bošković, Željko, 2002. 'On multiple *wh-*fronting', *Linguistic Inquiry* 33, 351–83.

Bowers, John, 1993. 'The syntax of predication', *Linguistic Inquiry* 24, 591–656.

Bresnan, Joan, 2001. *Lexical-functional syntax*, Oxford: Blackwell.

Brody, Michael, 1990.'Some remarks on the focus field in Hungarian', *UCL Working Papers in Linguistics* 2, 201–25.

Brody, Michael, 1995a. *Lexico-logical form: a radically minimalist theory*, Cambridge, Mass.: MIT Press.

Brody, Michael, 1995b. 'Focus in Hungarian and bare checking theory', in I. Kolhof & Suzanne Winkler (eds.), *Arbeitspapiere des Sonderforschungsbereichs* 340, Proceedings of the Goettingen Focus Workshop, University of Tübingen, 197–210.

Brody, Michael, 1996. 'Focus in perfect syntax', paper presented at the International Workshop on Focus, Universities of Paris III and Paris X.

Browning, Maggie, 1987. *Null operator constructions*, doctoral dissertation, MIT.

Büring, Daniel, 1997. *The meaning of topic and focus: the 59th Street Bridge accent*, London: Routledge.

Burzio, Luigi, 1986. *Italian syntax*, Dordrecht: Reidel.

Caron, Bernard, 2000. *Topicalisation et focalisation dans les langues africaines*, Paris: Peeters.

Chafe, Wallace, 1976a. 'Language and consciousness', *Language* 50, 111–33.

Chafe, Wallace, 1976b. 'Givenness, contrastiveness, definiteness, subjects, topics and points of view', in Charles N. Li (ed.), *Subject and topic*, New York: Academic Press, 25–56.

Chang, Lisa, 1995. *Wh-in-situ phenomena in French*, Ph.D. dissertation, University of British Columbia.

Cheng, Lisa Lai-Shen, 1991. *On the typology of* wh-*questions*, doctoral dissertation, MIT. [Published 1997, New York: Garland.]

Cheng, Lisa Lai-Shen, & Johan Rooryck, 2000. 'Licensing *wh*-in-situ', *Syntax* 3, 1–19.

Chiu, Bonnie Hui-Chun, 1993. *The inflectional structure of Mandarin Chinese*, doctoral dissertation, UCLA.

Chomsky, Noam, 1957. *Syntactic structures*, The Hague: Mouton.

Chomsky, Noam, 1959. 'Review of B.F. Skinner's *Verbal behaviour* 1957', *Language* 35, 26–58.

Chomsky, Noam, 1965. *Aspects of the theory of syntax*, Cambridge, Mass.: MIT Press.

Chomsky, Noam, 1970a. 'Remarks on nominalization', in R. A. Jacobs & P. S. Rosenbaum (eds.), *Readings in English transformational grammar*, Waltham, Mass.: Ginn-Blaisdell.

Chomsky, Noam, 1970b. 'Deep structure, surface structure and semantic interpretation', in Roman Jakobson & Shiego Kawamoto (eds.), *Studies in general and Oriental linguistics presented to Shiro Hattori on the occasion of his sixtieth birthday*, Tokyo: TEC Co., 52–91. [Reprinted in Noam Chomsky, *Studies on semantics in generative grammar*, The Hague: Mouton, 1972, 62–119.]

Chomsky, Noam, 1973. 'Conditions on transformations', in Stephen Anderson & Paul Kiparsky (eds.), *A festschrift for Morris Halle*, New York: Holt, Rine hart and Winston.

Chomsky, Noam, 1977. 'On wh-movement', in Peter W. Culicover, Thomas Wasow & Adrian Akmajian (eds.), *Formal syntax*, New York: Academic Press, 71–132.

Chomsky, Noam, 1980. 'On binding', *Linguistic Inquiry* 11, 1–46.

Chomsky, Noam, 1981. *Lectures on government and binding*, Dordrecht: Foris.

Chomsky, Noam, 1982. *Some concepts and consequences of the theory of government and binding*, Cambridge, Mass.: MIT Press.

Chomsky, Noam, 1986. *Knowledge of language: its nature, origin and use*, New York: Praeger.

Chomsky, Noam, 1991. 'Some notes on economy of derivation and representation', in Robert Freidin (ed.), *Principles and parameters in comparative grammar*, Cambridge, Mass.: MIT Press, 417-454. [Reprinted in Chomsky (1995: 129–66).]

Chomsky, Noam, 1993. 'A minimalist program for linguistic theory', in Kenneth Hale & Samuel Keyser (eds.), *The view from Building 20*, Cambridge, Mass.: MIT Press, 1–52.

Chomsky, Noam, 1995. *The minimalist program*, Cambridge, Mass.: MIT Press.

Chomsky, Noam, 2000. 'Minimalist inquiries', in Roger Martin, David Michaels & Juan Uriagereka (eds.), *Step by step: essays on minimalist syntax in honor of Howard Lasnik*, Cambridge, Mass.: MIT Press, 89–156.

Chomsky, Noam, 2001a. 'Derivation by phase', in Michael Kenstowicz (ed.), *Ken Hale: a life in language* [Current Studies in Linguistics 36], Cambridge, Mass.: MIT Press, 1–52.

Chomsky, Noam, 2001b. 'Beyond explanatory adequacy', *MIT Occasional Papers in Linguistics* 20, Department of Linguistics, MIT.

Chomsky, Noam & Morris Halle, 1968. *The sound pattern of English*, New York: Harper & Row.

Chomsky, Noam, & Howard Lasnik, 1977. 'Filters and control', *Linguistic Inquiry* 8, 425–504.

Chung, Sandra, 1998. *The design of agreement: evidence from Chamorro*, Chicago: University of Chicago Press.

Cinque, Guglielmo, 1990. *Types of A'-dependencies*, Cambridge, Mass.: MIT Press.

Cinque, Guglielmo, 1993. 'A null theory of phrase and compound stress', *Linguistic Inquiry* 24(2), 239–97.

Cinque, Guglielmo, 1999. *Adverbs and functional heads: a cross-linguistic perspective* [Oxford Studies in Comparative Syntax], Oxford: Oxford University Press.

Clark, Herbert & Susan E. Haviland, 1977. 'Comprehension and the given–new contrast', in Roy O. Freedle (ed.), *Discourse production and comprehension*, Hillsdale, NJ: Lawrence Erlbaum, 1–40.

Clements, George N., 1984. 'Binding domains in Kikuyu', *Studies in the Linguistic Sciences* 14, 37–57.

Clements, George N., James McCloskey, Joan Maling & Annie Zaenen, 1983. 'String-vacuous rule application', *Linguistic Inquiry* 14, 1–17.

Comorovski, Ileana, 1996. *Interrogative phrases and the syntax–semantics interface* [Studies in Linguistics and Philosophy], Dordrecht: Kluwer.

Comrie, Bernard, 1988. 'Topics, grammaticalized topics, and subjects', in Shelley Axmaker, Annie Jaisser & Helen Singmaster (eds.), *Proceedings of the Fourteenth Annual Meeting of the Berkeley Linguistics Society*, University of California, Berkeley, 265–79.

Cornillon, Jeanne, & Wynn Chao, 1995. 'Association with focus and the *ne ... que* construction in French', *SOAS Working Papers in Linguistics and Phonetics* 5, 271–83.

Cottell, M. Siobhan, 1996. 'Verb-movement, the copula and verb-second phenomena in Irish', paper presented at LAGB Spring Meeting, University of Sussex.

Cottell, M. Siobhan, 1997. 'Irish copular constructions and the clefting of predicates', in T. Cambier (ed.), *Proceedings of ConSole* 5, The Hague: Holland Academic Graphics, 1–14.

Cowan, J. Ronayne, & Russell G. Schuh, 1976. *Spoken Hausa*, New York: Spoken Language Services.

Croft, William, 1991. *Syntactic categories and grammatical relations*, Chicago: University of Chicago Press.

Croft, William, 2003. *Typology and universals*, 2nd edn, Cambridge: Cambridge University Press.

Cruttenden, Alan, 1997. *Intonation,* 2nd edn, Cambridge: Cambridge University Press.

Culicover, Peter W. & Michael S. Rochemont, 1983. 'Stress and focus in English', *Language* 59, 123–65.

Curnow, Timothy Jowan, 2000. 'Towards a cross-linguistic typology of copula constructions', in John Henderson (ed.), *Proceedings of the 1999 Conference of the Australian Linguistic Society* [on-line publication at http://www.arts.uwa.edu.au/LingWWW/als99/proceedings].

Dayal, Veneeta (Srivastav), 1991. 'Subjacency effects at LF: the case of Hindi *wh*', *Linguistic Inquiry* 22, 762–70.

Dayal, Veneeta (Srivastav), 2002. 'Single-pair versus multiple-pair answers: w*h*-in-situ and Scope', *Linguistic Inquiry* 33, 512–20.

Déchaine, Rose-Marie, 1993. *Predicates across categories: towards a category-neutral syntax*, PhD dissertation, University of Massachusetts.

Declerck, Renaat, 1988. *Studies on copular sentences, clefts and pseudoclefts*, Dordrecht: Foris.

den Dikken, Marcel, 1993. *Predicate inversion and minimality*, MS, Free University Amsterdam.

Devitt, Daniel, 1994. *Copula constructions in cross-linguistic and diachronic perspective*, PhD dissertation, University of Buffalo.

Diesing, Molly, 1992. *Indefinites*, Cambridge, Mass.: MIT Press.

Diesing, Molly, & Eloise Jelinek, 1995. 'Distributing arguments', *Natural Language Semantics* 3, 123–76.

Dik, Simon C., 1980. 'Cleft and pseudocleft in functional grammar', in Wim Zonneveld & Fred Weerman (eds.), *Linguistics in the Netherlands 1977-1979*, Dordrecht: Foris, 26–43.

Dik, Simon C., 1981a. *Functional grammar*, Dordrecht: Foris.

Dik, Simon C., 1981b. 'On the typology of focus phemomena', in Teun Hoekstra, Harry van der Hulst & Michael Moortgat (eds.), *Perspectives on functional grammar*, Dordrecht: Foris, 41–74.

Doetjes, Jenny, Georges Rebuschi & Annie Rialand, 2003. 'Cleft sentences', in Henriette de Swart and Francis Corblin (eds.), *Handbook of French semantics*, Stanford, Calif.: CSLI.

Doron, Edit, 1983. *Verbless predicates in Hebrew*, doctoral dissertation, University of Texas at Austin.

Doron, Edit, 1986. 'The pronominal "copula" as agreement clitic', in Hagit Borer (ed.), *The syntax of pronominal clitics* [Syntax and Semantics 19], Orlando, Fla.: Academic Press, 313–32.

Doron, Edit, 2000. 'Word order in Hebrew', in Jacqueline Lecarme, Jean Lowenstamm & Ur Shlonsky (eds.), *Research in Afroasiatic Grammar* [Current Issues in Linguistic Theory 202], Amsterdam: John Benjamins, 41–56.

Doron, Edit, 2003. 'Agency and voice: the semantics of the Semitic template', *Natural Language Semantics* 11, 1–67.

Doron, Edit, & Caroline Heycock, 1999. 'Filling and licensing multiple specifiers', in David Adger, Susan Pintzuk, Bernadetter Plunkett & George Tsoulas (eds.), *Specifiers: minimalist approaches*, Oxford: Oxford University Press, 69–89.

Drubig, Hans Bernard, 2003. 'Toward a typology of focus and focus constructions', *Linguistics* 41, 1–50.

Edwards, Malcolm, & Jamal Ouhalla, 1996. 'Questions, pronouns and operators in spoken Arabic', paper presented at LAGB Spring Meeting, University of Sussex.

Eid, Mushira, 1983. 'The copula function of pronouns', *Lingua* 59, 197–207.

Eid, Mushira, 1991. 'The copula pronoun in Arabic and Hebrew', in Bernard Comrie & Mushira Eid (eds.), *Perspectives on Arabic linguistics* III, Amsterdam: John Benjamins, 31–61.

Eid, Mushira, 1992. 'Pronouns, questions and agreement', in Mushira Eid & John McCarthy (eds.), *Perspectives on Arabic linguistics* IV, Amsterdam: John Benjamins, 107–41.

Emonds, Joseph, 1969. *Root and structure-preserving transformations*, doctoral dissertation, MIT.

Erades, P.A., 1949. 'On identifying and classifying sentences', *English Studies* 30, 299–308.

Erteschik-Shir, Nomi, 1986. '*Wh*-questions and focus', *Linguistics and Philosophy* 9, 117–49.

Erteschik-Shir, Nomi, 1997. *The dynamics of focus structure* [Cambridge Studies in Linguistics 84], Cambridge: Cambridge University Press.

Erteschik-Shir, Nomi, 1999. 'Focus structure and scope', in Georges Rebuschi & Laurice A. Tuller (eds.), *The grammar of focus*, Amsterdam: John Benjamins, 119–50.

Fanselow, Gisbert, & Anoop Mahajan, 2000. 'Towards a minimalist theory of *wh*-expletives, *wh*-copying, and successive cyclicity', in Uli Lutz, Gereon Müller & Armin van Stechow (eds.), *Wh-scope marking* [Linguistik Aktuell 37], Amsterdam: John Benjamins, 195–230.

Fassi-Fehri, Abdelkader, 1984. 'Agreement in Arabic, binding and coherence', in Michael Barlow & Charles Ferguson (eds.), *Agreement in natural language*, Stanford, Calif.: CSLI, 107–58.

Fassi-Fehri, Abdelkader, 1993. *Issues in the structure of Arabic clauses and words*, Dordrecht: Kluwer.

Felser, Claudia, 2004. '*Wh*-copying, phases and successive cyclicity', *Lingua* 114, 543–74.

Firbas, Jan, 1992. *Functional sentence perspective in written and spoken communication*, Cambridge: Cambridge University Press.

Fodor, Jerry, 1983. *The modularity of mind*, Cambridge, Mass.: MIT Press.

Fodor, Jerry A., 2000. 'Precis of *The modularity of mind*', in Robert Cummins & Denise Dellarosa Cummins (eds.), *Minds, brains and computers: the foundations of cognitive science*, Oxford: Blackwell, 493-9

Frajzyngier, Zygmunt, 1986. 'From preposition to copula', *BLS* 12, 371–86.

Frajzyngier, Zygmunt, 1989. *A grammar of Pero,* Berlin: Dietrich Reimer.

Frajzyngier, Zygmunt, 1993. *A grammar of Mupun,* Berlin: Dietrich Reimer.

Frajzyngier, Zygmunt, 1996. *Grammaticalization of the complex sentence: a case Study in Chadic*, Amsterdam: John Benjamins.

Frank, Robert, 1992. *Syntactic locality and tree adjoining grammar: grammatical acquisition and processing perspectives*, doctoral dissertation, University of Pennsylvania.

French, Andrew, 2004. 'All is not as right as it seems: *wh*-questions in Bole', paper submitted in partial fulfilment of the requirements for the MA in Linguistics, UCLA.

Fukui, Naoki, & Margaret Speas, 1986. 'Specifiers and projection', *MIT Working Papers in Linguistics* 8, 128–72.

Furniss, Graham L., 1991. *Second level Hausa: grammar in action*, SOAS, University of London.

Furniss, Graham L., 1996. *Poetry, prose and popular culture in Hausa* [International African Library 16], London: Edinburgh University Press for the International African Institute, London.

Gazdar, Gerald, Ewan Klein, Geoffrey Pullum & Ivan Sag, 1985. *Generalized phrase structure grammar*, Cambridge, Mass.: Harvard University Press.

Georgopoulos, Carol, 1985. 'Variables in Palauan syntax', *Natural Language and Linguistic Theory* 3, 59–94.

Georgopoulos, Carol, 1991. 'On A- and A'-agreement', *Lingua* 85, 135–69.

Givón, Talmy, 1979. *On understanding grammar*, New York: Academic Press.

Green, Melanie, 1992. *Operators and agreement in Hausa*, MA dissertation, SOAS, University of London.

Green, Melanie, 1993. 'Focus and copular constructions in Hausa', *SOAS Working Papers in Linguistics and Phonetics* 3, 205–18.

Green, Melanie, 1996. 'Focus in copular sentences: the interface between semantics, syntax and prosody', *SOAS Working Papers in Linguistics and Phonetics* 6, 154–78.

Green, Melanie, 1997. *Focus and copular constructions in Hausa*, doctoral dissertation, SOAS, University of London.

Green, Melanie, in preparation. *Prosody and focus in Hausa*, MS., University of Sussex.

Green, Melanie, & Philip J. Jaggar, 2003. 'Ex-situ and in-situ focus in Hausa: syntax, semantics and discourse', in Jacqueline Lecarme (ed.), *Research in Afroasiatic grammar II* [Current Issues in Linguistic Theory 241], Amsterdam: John Benjamins, 187–213.

Green, Melanie, & Chris H. Reintges, 2003. 'Copy theory of movement, special inflection and the syntax-PF interface', paper presented at the 26th GLOW colloquium, Lund, April 2003.

Green, Melanie, & Chris H. Reintges, 2004. 'Syntactic anchoring in Hausa and Coptic *wh*-constructions', in Andrew Simpson (ed.), *Proceedings of the Twenty-Seventh Annual Meeting of the Berkeley Linguistics Society*, University of California, Berkeley, 61–72.

Green, Melanie, & Chris H. Reintges, 2005a. 'Syntactic conditions on special inflection: evidence from Hausa and Coptic Egyptian interrogative and focus constructions', *University of Sussex Working Papers in Linguistics and English Language* (LxWP14/05). [Electronic working papers series available at www.sussex.ac.uk/linguistics/1-4-1.html]

Green, Melanie, & Chris H. Reintges, 2005b. 'Syntactic conditions on special inflection: evidence from Hausa and Coptic Egyptian interrogative and focus constructions' [revised], MS, University of Sussex.

Greenberg, Joseph H., 1950. 'Studies in African linguistic classification: IV, Hamito-Semitic', *Southwestern Journal of Anthropology* 6 47–63.

Greenberg, Joseph H., 1960. 'An Afro-Asiatic pattern of gender and number agreement', *Journal of the American Oriental Society* 80, 317–21.

Greenberg, Yael, 1998. 'An overt syntactic marker for genericity in Hebrew', in Susan Rothstein (ed.), *Events and Grammar*, Dordrecht: Kluwer, 125–43.

Greenberg, Yael, 2002. 'The manifestation of genericity in the tense aspect system of Hebrew', in Jamal Ouhalla & Ur Shlonsky (eds.), *Themes in Arabic and Hebrew syntax* [Studies in Natural Language and Linguistic Theory 53], Dordrecht Kluwer, 267–98.

Grimshaw, Jane, 1991. 'Extended projection', MS, Brandeis University.

Groat, Erich, & O'Neil, John, 1996. 'Spell-out at the LF interface: achieving a unified syntactic computational system in the minimalist framework', in Werner Abraham, Samuel D. Epstein, Höskuldur Thráinsson & Jan-Wouter Zwart (eds.), *Minimal ideas: syntactic studies in the minimalist framework*, Amsterdam: John Benjamins, 113–39.

Guéron, Jacqueline, 1980. 'On the syntax and semantics of PP extraposition', *Linguistic Inquiry* 11, 637–78.

Gundel, Jeanette K., 1977. 'Where do cleft sentences come from?', *Language* 53, 543–59.

Gundel, Jeanette K., 1999. 'On different kinds of focus', in Peter Bosch & Rob van der Sandt (eds.), *Focus: linguistic, cognitive and computational perspectives*, Cambridge: Cambridge University Press, 293–305.

Gussenhoven, Carlos, 1984. *On the grammar and semantics of sentence accents,* Dordrecht: Foris.

Haegeman, L., 1994. *Introduction to government and binding theory*, 2nd edn, Oxford: Blackwell.

Haïk, Isabelle, 1990. 'Anaphoric, pronominal and referential INFL', *Natural Language and Linguistic Theory* 8, 347–74.

Haiman, John, 1978. 'Conditionals are topics', *Language* 54, 564–89.

Hale, Kenneth, & Samuel J. Keyser, 1993. 'On argument structure and the lexical expression of syntactic relations', in Kenneth Hale & Samuel J. Keyser (eds.), *The view from Building 20: essays in honour of Sylvain Bromberger,* Cambridge, Mass.: MIT Press, 53-109.

Halle, Morris, & Alex Marantz, 1993. 'Distributed morphology', in Kenneth Hale & Samuel J. Keyser (eds.), *The view from Building 20: essays in honour of Sylvain Bromberger*, Cambridge, Mass.: MIT Press, 111–76.

Halliday, Michael, 1967. 'Notes on transitivity and theme in English, Part II', *Journal of Linguistics* 3, 199–244.

Harbert, Wayne, & Maher Bahloul, 2002. 'Postverbal subjects in Arabic and the theory of agreement', in Jamal Ouhalla & Ur Shlonsky (eds.), *Themes in Arabic and Hebrew syntax* [Studies in Natural Language and Linguistic Theory 53], Dordrecht, Kluwer, 45–70.

Harries-Delisle, Helga, 1978. 'Contrastive emphasis and cleft sentences', in Joseph Greenberg (ed.), *Universals of human language, Vol. 4: Syntax*, Stanford, Calif.: Stanford University Press, 419–86.

Harris, Alice C., & Lyle Campbell, 1995. *Historical syntax in cross-linguistic perspective*, Cambridge: Cambridge University Press.

Hartmann, Katharina, 2006. 'Focus constructions in Hausa', in Valéria Molnár & Suzanne Winkler (eds.), *The architecture of focus* [Studies in Generative Grammar], Berlin: Mouton de Gruyter.

Hartmann, Katharina, & Malte Zimmermann, forthcoming, a. 'In place – out of place: focus in Hausa', in Kerstin Schwabe and Suzanne Winkler (eds.), *Proceedings of the Workshop on Information Structure and the Architecture of Grammar*, Amsterdam: John Benjamins.

Hartmann, Katharina, & Malte Zimmermann, forthcoming, b. 'Exhaustivity marking in Hausa: a reanalysis of the particle nee/cee', in Enoch Aboh, Katharina Hartmann & Malte Zimmermann (eds.), *Focus strategies: evidence from African languages*, Berlin: Mouton de Gruyter.

Heggie, Lorie A., 1988. *The syntax of copular structures*, doctoral dissertation, University of Southern California.

Heggie, Lorie A., 1992. 'On reference in copular contexts', in Paul Hirschbühler and Konrad Koerner (eds.), *Romance languages and modern linguistic theory*, Amsterdam: John Benjamins, 105–22.

Heggie, Lorie A., 1993. 'The range of null operators: evidence from clefting', *Natural Language and Linguistic Theory* 11, 45–84.

Heine, Bernd, & Tania Kuteva, 2002. *World lexicon of grammaticalization*, Cambridge: Cambridge University Press.

Heine, Bernd, & Mechthild Reh, 1984. *Grammaticalization and reanalysis in African languages*, Hamburg: Buske.

Heller, Daphna, 2002. 'On the relation of connectivity and specificational pseudoclefts', *Natural Language Semantics* 10, 243–84.

Heycock, Caroline, 1992. 'Layers of predication and the syntax of the copula', *Belgian Journal of Linguistics* 7, 95–123.

Heycock, Caroline, 1994. 'The internal structure of small clauses: new evidence from inversion', *Proceedings of NELS* 25, 223–38.

Heycock, Caroline & Anthony Kroch, 1996. 'Identity, predication and connectivity in pseudo-clefts', paper presented at the 19th GLOW Colloquium, Athens.

Heycock, Caroline & Anthony Kroch, 1999. 'Pseudocleft connectedness: implications for the LF interface level', *Linguistic Inquiry* 30, 365–98.

Higginbotham, James, & Robert May, 1981. 'Questions, quantifiers and crossing', *Linguistic Review* 1, 41–79.

Higgins, Francis Roger, 1973. *The pseudo-cleft construction in English*, doctoral dissertation, MIT.

Higgins, Francis Roger, 1979. *The pseudo-cleft construction in English*, New York: Garland.

Hirst, Daniel, 1987. *La représentation linguistique des systèmes prosodiques: une approche cognitive*, thèse de Doctorat d'Etat, Université de Provence.

Hoffmann, Carl F., 1963. *A grammar of the Margi language*, London: Oxford University Press.

Horvath, Julia, 1986. *Focus in the theory of grammar and the syntax of Hungarian*, Dordrecht: Foris.

Horvath, Julia, 1995. 'Structural focus, structural case and the notion of feature assignment', in Katalin É. Kiss (ed.), *Discourse configurational languages*, Oxford: Oxford University Press, 28–64.

Horvath, Julia, 1996. 'The status of wh expletives and the partial movement construction in Hungarian', MS, Tel Aviv University.

Huang, James C.-T., 1982. *Logical relations in Chinese and the theory of grammar*, doctoral dissertation, MIT.

Huang, James C.-T., 1984. 'Move WH in a language without WH movement', *Linguistic Review* 1, 369–416.

Huddleston, Rodney, 1971. *The sentence in written English*, Cambridge: Cambridge University Press.

Huddleston, Rodney, & Geoffrey K. Pullum, 2002. *The Cambridge grammar of the English language*, Cambridge: Cambridge University Press.

Hunter, Linda, 1980. 'Stress in Hausa: an experimental study', *Studies in African Linguistics* 11, 353–74.

Hyman, Larry, 1978. 'Tone and/or accent', in Donna J. Napoli (ed.), *Elements of tone, stress and intonation*, Washington, DC: Georgetown University Press, 1–20.

Hyman, Larry, 1999. 'The interaction between focus and tone in Bantu', in Georges Rebuschi & Laurice Tuller (eds.), *The grammar of focus* [Linguistik Aktuell 24], Amsterdam: John Benjamins, 151–78.

Hyman, Larry, & Russell Schuh, 1974. 'Universals of tone rules: evidence from West Africa', *Linguistic Inquiry* 5, 81–115.

Hyman, Larry and John Watters, 1984. 'Auxiliary focus', *Studies in African Linguistics* 15, 233–73.

Inkelas, Sharon, 1988. 'Prosodic effects on Hausa "fa"', *Proceedings of the Seventh West Coast Conference on Formal Linguistics*, Stanford Linguistics Association.

Inkelas, Sharon, & William R. Leben, 1990. 'Where phonology and phonetics intersect: the case of Hausa intonation', in John Kingston & Mary E. Beckman (eds.), *Between the grammar and the physics of speech*, New York: Cambridge University Press, 17–34.

Inkelas, Sharon, William R. Leben & Mark Cobler, 1987. 'The phonology of intonation in Hausa', in Joyce McDonough & Bernadette Plunkett (eds.), *Proceedings of the Annual Meeting of the North Eastern Linguistic Society* (NELS) 17, 327–41.

Jackendoff, Ray, 1972. *Semantic interpretation in generative grammar*, Cambridge, Mass.: MIT Press.

Jackendoff, Ray, 1983. *Semantics and cognition*, Cambridge, Mass.: MIT Press.

Jackendoff, Ray, 2002. *Foundations of language*, Oxford: Oxford University Press.

Jaggar, Philip J., 1978. '"And what about ...": topicalization in Hausa', *Studies in African Linguistics* 9, 69–81.

Jaggar, Philip J., 1985. *Factors governing the morphological coding of referents in Hausa narrative discourse*, doctoral dissertation, UCLA.

Jaggar, Philip J., 1988. 'Affected-subject (grade 7) verbs in Hausa: what are they and where do they come from?', in Masayoshi Shibatani (ed.), *Passive and voice* [Typological Studies in Language 16], Amsterdam: John Benjamins, 387–416.

Jaggar, Philip J., 1992. *An advanced Hausa reader*, SOAS, University of London.

Jaggar, Philip J., 1997. 'Reflexives in Hausa', in Dymitr Ibriszimow, Rudolf Leger & Uwe Seibert (eds.), *Von Aegypten zum Tschadsee. Eine Linguistische Reise durch Afrika (Festschrift für Herrmann Jungraithmayr zum 65 Geburtstag)*, Cologne: Rüdiger Köppe, 100–127.

Jaggar, Philip J., 1998. 'Restrictive vs. nonrestrictive relative clauses in Hausa: where morphosyntax and semantics meet', *Studies in African Linguistics* 27, 199–238.

Jaggar, Philip J., 2001. *Hausa* [London Oriental and African Language Library 7], Amsterdam: John Benjamins.

Jaggar, Philip J., 2006a. 'More on in situ *wh-* and focus constructions in Hausa', in Dymitr Ibriszimow, Henry Tourneux & Ekkehard H. Wolff (eds.), *Chadic Linguistics*, vol. 3, Cologne: Rüdiger Köppe.

Jaggar, Philip J., 2006b. 'The Hausa perfective tense-aspect used in *wh-*/focus constructions and historical narratives: a unified account', in Larry M. Hyman & Paul Newman (eds.), *West African Linguistics: descriptive, comparative and historical studies in honor of Russell G. Schuh* [Studies in African Linguistics, special issue].

Jarvis, Elizabeth, 1981. 'Some considerations in establishing the basic word order of Podoko', *Studies in African Linguistics* 12, 155–67.

Jarvis, Elizabeth, 1989. 'Esquisse grammaticale du Podoko', in Daniel Barreteau & Robert Hedinger (eds.), *Descriptions de langues camerounaises*, Paris: Orstom, 39–127.

Jelinek, Eloise, 2002. 'Agreement, clitics and focus in Egyptian Arabic', in Jamal Ouhalla & Ur Shlonsky (eds.), *Themes in Arabic and Hebrew syntax* [Studies in Natural Language and Linguistic Theory 53], Dordrecht: Kluwer, 71–106.

Junaidu, Ismail, 1987. *Topicalization in Hausa*, doctoral dissertation, Indiana University.

Junaidu, Ismail, 1990. 'The relation between topicalisation and left dislocation in Hausa', *African Languages and Cultures* 3, 57–70.

Jungraithmayr, Herrmann, & Kiyoshi Shimizu, 1981. *Chadic lexical roots, Vol. 2: Tentative reconstruction, grading and distribution*, Berlin: Dietrich Reimer.

Kahn, C.H., 1973. *The verb 'be' in Ancient Greek*, Dordrecht: Reidel.

Kaplan, Ronald, & Joan Bresnan, 1982. 'Lexical-functional grammar: a formal system for grammatical representation', in Joan Bresnan (ed.), *The mental representation of grammatical relations*, Cambridge, Mass.: MIT Press, 173–281.

Kayne, Richard, 1984. *Connectedness and binary branching*, Dordrecht: Foris.

Kayne, Richard, 1994. *The antisymmetry of syntax*, Cambridge, Mass.: MIT Press.

Kenesei, István, 1993. *A minimalist program for the syntax of focus*, MS, University of Szeged.

Kenstowicz, Michael, 1985. 'The phonology and syntax of wh-expressions in Tangale', *Studies in the Linguistic Sciences* 15, 79–91.

Kidda, Mairo, 1985. *A Tangale phonology: a descriptive analysis*, doctoral dissertation, University of Illinois, Urbana-Champaign.

Kidwai, Ayesha, 1996. 'Focus positions in universal grammar and Hindi–Urdu scrambling', paper presented at UCL Linguistics Department Seminar.

Kidwai, Ayesha, 1999. 'Word order and focus positions in universal grammar', in Georges Rebuschi & Laurice Tuller (eds.), *The grammar of focus* [Linguistik Aktuell 24], Amsterdam: John Benjamins, 213–44.

Kihm, Alain, 1999. 'Focus in Wolof: a study of what morphology may do to syntax', in Georges Rebuschi & Laurice Tuller (eds.), *The grammar of focus* [Linguistik Aktuell 24], Amsterdam: John Benjamins, 245–74.

Kiss, Katalin É., 1995a. 'Introduction', in Katalin É. Kiss (ed.), *Discourse configurational languages*, Oxford: Oxford University Press, 3–27.

Kiss, Katalin É., 1995b. 'NP movement, operator movement and scrambling in Hungarian', in Katalin É. Kiss (ed.), *Discourse configurational languages*, Oxford: Oxford University Press, 207–43.

Kiss, Katalin É., 1996. 'The focus operator and information focus', *Working papers in the theory of grammar* 3(2), Budapest University.

Kiss, Katalin É., 1998a. 'Identificational focus versus information focus', *Language* 74, 245–73.

Kiss, Katalin É., 1998b. 'On generic and existential bare plurals and the classification of predicates', in Susan Rothstein (ed.), *Events and grammar*, Dordrecht: Kluwer, 145–172.

Klingenheben, A., 1927/28. 'Die Silbenauslautgesetze des Hausa', *Zeitschrift für Eingeborenen-Sprachen* 18, 272–97.

Koopman, Hilda, 1992. 'On the absence of case chains in Bambara', *Natural Language and Linguistic Theory* 10, 555–94.

Kornfilt, Jaqueline, 1997. *Turkish*, London: Routledge.

Kuno, Susumo, 1971. 'The position of locatives in existential sentences', *Linguistic Inquiry* 2, 333–78.

Kuno, Susumo, 1972. 'Functional sentence perspective: a case study from Japanese and English', *Linguistic Inquiry* 3, 269–320.

Kuno, Susumo, & Etsuko Kaburaki, 1977. 'Empathy and syntax', *Linguistic Inquiry* 8, 627–72.

Kuno, Susumo, & Jane G. Robinson, 1972. 'Multiple wh-questions', *Linguistic Inquiry* 3, 463–87.

Kuno, Susumo, & Preya Wongkhomthong, 1981. 'Characterizational and identificational sentences in Thai', *Studies in Language* 5, 65–109.

Ladd, D. Robert, 1980. 'Intonation, main clause phenomena and point of view', in Linda R. Waugh & Cornelis H. Van Schooneveld (eds.), *The melody of language*, Baltimore: University Park Press, 49–63.

Ladd, D. Robert, 1996. *Intonational phonology* [Cambridge Studies in Linguistics 79], Cambridge: Cambridge University Press.

Lambrecht, Knud, 1994. *Information structure and sentence form: topic, focus and the mental representations of discourse referents* [Cambridge Studies in Linguistics 71], Cambridge: Cambridge University Press.

Lambrecht, Knud, 2001. 'A framework for the analysis of cleft constructions', *Linguistics* 39, 463–516.

Landau, Idan, 2005. 'Chain resolution in Hebrew V(P) fronting', MS, Ben Gurion University.

Langacker, Ronald, 2000. 'A dynamic usage-based model', in Michael Barlow and Suzanne Kemmer (eds.), *Usage-based models of language*, Stanford, Calif.: CSLI, 1–63.

Larson, Richard, 1988a. 'On the double object construction', *Linguistic Inquiry* 19, 335–91.

Larson, Richard, 1988b. 'Light predicate raising', *Lexicon Project Working Papers* 27, Center for Cognitive Science, MIT.

Larson, Richard, 1990. 'Double objects revisited: reply to Jackendoff', *Linguistic Inquiry* 21, 589–632.

Lasnik, Howard, 1992. 'Case and expletives: notes toward a parametric account', *Linguistic Inquiry* 23, 381–407.

Lasnik, Howard, 1995. 'Case and expletives revisited: on greed and other human failings', *Linguistic Inquiry* 26, 615–33.

Layton, Bentley, 2000. *A Coptic grammar with chrestomathy and glossary* [*Porta Linguarum Orientalium* N.S. 20], Wiesbaden: Harrassowitz.

Leben, William R., 1978. 'The representation of tone', in Victoria Fromkin (ed.), *Tone: a linguistic survey*, New York: Academic Press, 177–219.

Lecarme, Jacqueline, 1999. 'Focus in Somali', in Georges Rebuschi & Laurice Tuller (eds.), *The grammar of focus* [Linguistik Aktuell 24], Amsterdam: John Benjamins, 275–310.

Lehmann, Christian, 2002. 'Thoughts on grammaticalization', *Arbeitspapiere des Seminars für Sprachwissenschaft der Universität Erfurt*, 9.

Levin, Beth, and Malka Rappaport Hovav, 1995. *Unacccusativity: at the syntax–lexical semantics interface,* Cambridge, Mass.: MIT Press

Lewis, David, 1975. 'Adverbs of quantification', in Edward L. Keenan (ed.), *Formal semantics of natural languages,* Cambridge: Cambridge University Press, 3–15.

Li, Charles, & Sandra A. Thompson, 1976. 'Subject and topic: a new typology of language', in Charles N. Li (ed.), *Subject and topic,* New York: Academic Press, 457–90.

Li, Charles, & Sandra A. Thompson, 1977. 'Mechanisms for the development of copula morphemes', in Charles N. Li (ed.), *Mechanisms of syntactic change,* Austin: University of Texas Press, 419–44.

Li, Charles, & Sandra A. Thompson, 1981. *Mandarin Chinese: a functional reference grammar,* Berkeley: University of California Press.

Lindau, Mona, 1986. 'Testing a model of intonation in a tone language', *Journal of the Acoustical Society of America* 80, 757–64.

Loprieno, Antonio, 1995. *Ancient Egyptian: a linguistic introduction,* Cambridge: Cambridge University Press.

Lukas, Johannes, 1936. 'The linguistic situation in the Lake Chad area in Central Africa', *Africa* 5, 1–42.

Marantz, Alex, 1997. 'No escape from syntax: don't try morphological analysis in the privacy of your own lexicon', in A. Dimitriadis, L. Siegel, C. Surek-Clark & A. Williams (eds.), *Proceedings of the 21st Annual Penn Linguistics Colloquium* [University of Pennsylvania Working Papers in Linguistics 4.2], Philadelphia: University of Pennsylvania, 201–25.

Matthews, Stephen, & Virginia Yip, 1994. *Cantonese: a comprehensive grammar,* London: Routledge.

May, Robert, 1985. *Logical form,* Cambridge, Mass.: MIT Press.

McCawley, James, 1978. 'What is a tone language?', in Victoria Fromkin (ed.), *Tone: a linguistic survey,* New York: Academic Press, 113–31.

McCloskey, James, 1979. *Transformational syntax and model theoretic semantics: a case study in Modern Irish,* Dordrecht: Reidel.

McCloskey, James, 1990. 'Resumptive pronouns, A'-binding, and levels of representation in Irish', in Randall Hendrick (ed.), *The syntax of modern Celtic languages* [Syntax and Semantics 23], New York: Academic Press, 199–248.

McCloskey, James, 2001. 'The morphosyntax of WH-extraction in Irish', *Journal of Linguistics* 37, 67–100.

McConvell, Patrick, 1973. *Cleft sentences in Hausa? A syntactic study of focus,* doctoral dissertation, SOAS, University of London.

McDaniel, Dana, 1989. 'Partial and Multiple WH-movement', *Natural Language and Linguistic Theory* 7, 565–604.

Miller, Jennifer, & Paul Tench, 1980. 'Aspects of Hausa intonation 1: utterances in isolation', *Journal of the International Phonetic Association* 10, 45–63.

Miller, Jennifer, & Paul Tench, 1982. 'Aspects of Hausa intonation 2: continuous text', *Journal of the International Phonetic Association* 12, 78–93.

Mittwoch, Anita, 1979, 'Final parentheticals with English questions – their illocutionary function and grammar', *Journal of Pragmatics* 7, 401–12.

Möhlig, Wilhelm J.G., 1983. 'Basic principles of Hausa prosodological structure at the distinctive level', in Ekkehard Wolff & Hilke Meyer-Bahlburg (eds.), *Studies in Chadic and Afroasiatic linguistics,* Hamburg: Helmut Buske, 373–96.

Moro, Andrea, 1990. 'There-raising: principles across levels', paper presented at the XVI GLOW Conference, St John's College, Cambridge.

Moro, Andrea, 1997. *The raising of predicates,* Cambridge: Cambridge University Press.

Moro, Andrea, 2000. *Dynamic antisymmetry* [Linguistic Inquiry Monograph 38], Cambridge, Mass.: MIT Press.

Moutaouakil, Ahmed, 1989. *Pragmatic functions in a functional grammar of Arabic*, Dordrecht: Foris.

Muriungi, Peter, 2003. *Focus constructions in Kitharaka*, PhD dissertation, University of the Witwatersrand, Johannesburg.

Newman, Paul, 1974. *The Kanakuru language* [West African Language Monographs 9], Leeds: Institute of Modern English Language Studies, University of Leeds, in association with the West African Linguistic Society.

Newman, Paul, 1977. 'Chadic classification and reconstruction', *Afroasiatic Linguistics* 5, 1–42.

Newman, Paul, 1980. *The classification of Chadic within Afroasiatic*, Leiden: Universitaire Pers.

Newman, Paul, 1995. 'Hausa tonology: complexities in an "easy" tone language', in John A. Goldsmith (ed.), *The handbook of phonological theory*, Oxford: Blackwell, 762–81.

Newman, Paul, 1996. *African linguistics bibliographies: Hausa and the Chadic language family*, Cologne: Rüdiger Köppe.

Newman, Paul, 2000. *The Hausa language: an encyclopedic reference grammar*, New Haven, Conn.: Yale University Press.

Newman, Paul, and Roxana Ma Newman, 1977. *Sabon kamus na Hausa zuwa Turanci*, Ibadan: University Press.

Newman, Paul, and Roxana Ma Newman, 1981. 'The question morpheme *Q* in Hausa', *Afrika und Übersee* 64, 35–46.

Newman, Paul, & Russell G. Schuh, 1974. 'The Hausa aspect system', *Afroasiatic Linguistics* 1, 1–39.

Nissenbaum, Jonathan, 2000. *Investigations of covert phrase movement*, PhD dissertation, MIT.

Nunes, Jairo, 1995. *The Copy Theory of movement and linearization of chains in the minimalist program*, doctoral dissertation, University of Connecticut.

Nunes, Jairo, 2004. *Linearization of chains and sideward movement* [Linguistic Inquiry Monographs 43], Cambridge, Mass.: MIT Press.

Odden, David, 1995. 'Tone: African languages', in John A. Goldsmith, (ed.), *The handbook of phonological theory*, Oxford: Blackwell, 444–75.

Omoruyi, Thomas, 1989. 'Focus and question formation in Edo', *Studies in African Linguistics* 23, 279–300.

Ortiz de Urbina, Jon, 1986. *Parameters in the grammar of Basque*, doctoral dissertation, University of Illinois at Urbana-Champaign.

Ortiz de Urbina, Jon, 1995. 'Residual verb second and verb first in Basque', in Katalin É. Kiss (ed.), *Discourse configurational languages*, Oxford: Oxford University Press, 99–121.

Ouhalla, Jamal, 1990. 'Focusing in Berber and Circassian and the V2 phenomenon', paper presented at UCL Linguistics Department seminar.

Ouhalla, Jamal, 1993. 'Negation, focus and tense: the Arabic *maa* and *laa*', *Rivista di Linguistica* 5, 275–300.

Ouhalla, Jamal, 1994. 'Focus in Standard Arabic', *Linguistics in Potsdam* 1, 65–92.

Ouhalla, Jamal, 1996a. 'Focus in Standard Arabic (revised)', MS, QMW, University of London.

Ouhalla, Jamal, 1996b. 'Remarks on the binding properties of *wh*-pronouns', *Linguistic Inquiry* 27, 676–707.

Ouhalla, Jamal, 1997. 'Remarks on focus in Standard Arabic', in Mushira Eid & Robert R. Ratcliffe (eds.), *Perspectives on Arabic linguistics*, Amsterdam: John Benjamins, 9–45.

Ouhalla, Jamal, 1999. 'Focus and Arabic clefts', in Georges Rebuschi & Laurice Tuller (eds.), *The grammar of focus* [Linguistik Aktuell 24], Amsterdam: John Benjamins, 335–60.

Ouhalla, Jamal, & Ur Shlonsky, 2002. 'Introduction', in Jamal Ouhalla & Ur Shlonsky (eds.), *Themes in Arabic and Hebrew syntax* [Studies in Natural Language and Linguistic Theory 53], Dordrecht: Kluwer, 1–43.

Parsons, F. W., 1960. 'The verbal system in Hausa', *Afrika und Übersee* 44, 1–36.

Parsons, F. W., 1961. 'The operation of gender in Hausa: the personal pronoun and genitive copula', *African Language Studies* 2, 100–124.

Parsons, F. W., 1981. *Writings on Hausa grammar: the collected papers of F.W. Parsons*, ed. G.L. Furniss, SOAS, University of London.

Pawlak, Nina, 1994. *Syntactic markers in Chadic*, University of Warsaw.

Pesetsky, David, 1987. '*Wh*-in-situ: movement and unselective binding' in Eric J. Reuland & Alice G.B. ter Meulen (eds.), *The representation of (in)definiteness* [Current Studies in Linguistics 14], Cambridge, Mass.: MIT Press, 98–129.

Pesetsky, David, 1997. 'Optimality Theory and syntax: movement and pronunciation', in Diana Archangeli & D. Terence Langendoen (eds.), *Optimality Theory: an overview*, Oxford: Blackwell, 134–70.

Pesetsky, David, 1998. 'Some Optimality principles of sentence pronunciation', in Pilar Barbosa, Danny Fox, Paul Hagstrom, Martha McGinnis & David Pesetsky (eds.), *Is the best good enough?*, Cambridge Mass.: MIT Press, 337–83.

Pesetsky, David, 2000. *Phrasal movement and its kin* [Linguistic Inquiry Monographs 37], Cambridge, Mass.: MIT Press.

Pesetzky, David, & Esther Torrego, 2000. 'T-to-C movement: causes and consequences', in Michael Kenstowicz (ed.), *Ken Hale: a life in linguistics* [Current Studies in Linguistics 36], Cambridge, Mass.: MIT Press, 355–426.

Pinker, Steven, 1994. *The language instinct*, London: Penguin.

Pollard, Carl, & Ivan Sag, 1994. *Head-driven phrase structure grammar*, Stanford, Calif.: CSLI and Chicago: University of Chicago Press.

Pollock, Jean-Yves, 1989. 'Verb movement, UG and the structure of IP', *Linguistic Inquiry* 20, 365–424.

Prince, Ellen, 1981. 'Towards a taxonomy of given–new information', in Peter Cole (ed.), *Radical pragmatics*, New York: Academic Press, 223–55.

Pustet, Regina, 2003. *Copulas: universals in the categorization of the lexicon* [Oxford Studies in Typology and Linguistic Theory], Oxford: Oxford University Press.

Quirk, Randolph, Sidney Greenbaum, Geoffrey Leech & Jan Svartvik, 1985. *A comprehensive grammar of the English language*, London: Longman.

Radford, Andrew, 1988. *Transformational Grammar: a first course*, Cambridge: Cambridge University Press.

Randell, Richard, Abdullahi Bature & Russell G. Schuh, 1998. *Hausar Baka: elementary and intermediate lessons in Hausa language and culture*, Windsor, Calif.: World of Languages [www.humnet.ucla.edu/humnet/aflang/hausarbaka]

Rapoport, Tova R., 1987. *Copular, nominal and small clauses: a study of Israeli Hebrew*, PhD dissertation, MIT.

Rebuschi, Georges, & Laurice Tuller, 1999. 'The grammar of focus: an introduction', in Georges Rebuschi & Laurice Tuller (eds.), *The grammar of focus* [Linguistik Aktuell 24], Amsterdam: John Benjamins, 22.

Reinhart, Tanya, 1998. '*Wh*-in-situ in the framework of the minimalist program', *Natural Language Semantics* 6, 26–56.

Reinhart, Tanya, 1995. 'Interface strategies', *OTS Working Papers*, University of Utrecht.

Reintges, Chris H., 2001. 'Aspects of the morphosyntax of subjects and objects in Coptic Egyptian', in Hans Broekhuis & Ton van der Wouden (eds.), *Linguistics in the Netherlands 2001*, Amsterdam: John Benjamins, 177–88.

Reintges, Chris H., 2002. 'A configurational approach to Coptic second tenses', *Lingua Aegyptia* 10, 343–88.

Reintges, Chris H., 2003a. 'Syntactic conditions on special inflection in Coptic interrogatives', in Jacqueline Lecarme (ed.), *Research in Afroasiatic grammar II* [Current Issues in Linguistic Theory 241], Amsterdam: John Benjamins, 363–408.

Reintges, Chris H., 2003b. 'The syntax and semantics of the Coptic cleft construction', *University of Sussex Working Papers in Linguistics and English Language* (LxWP4/03). [Electronic working papers series available at www.sussex.ac.uk/linguistics/1-4-1.html]

Reintges, Chris H., 2004. *Coptic Egyptian: Sahidic dialect* [Afrikanistische Studienbücher], Cologne: Köppe.

Reintges, Chris H., 2005. 'Variable pronunciation sites and types of *wh*-in-situ', MS, University of Leiden.

Reintges, Chris H., and Melanie Green, 2004. 'Coptic second tenses and Hausa relative aspects: a comparative view', *Lingua Aegyptia* 12, 157–77.

Reintges, Chris H., Phil LeSourd & Sandra Chung, 2006. 'Movement, *wh*-agreement, and apparent *wh*-in-situ', in Lisa Lai-Shen Chen & Norbert Korver (eds.), Wh-*movement on the move*, Cambridge, Mass.: MIT Press.

Reintges, Chris H., Anikó Lipták and Lisa Lai-Shen Cheng, 2005. 'The nominal cleft construction in Coptic Egyptian', in Katalin É. Kiss (ed.), *Universal Grammar in the reconstruction of ancient languages* [Studies in Generative Grammar 83], Berlin: Mouton de Gruyter, 105–35.

Rizzi, Luigi, 1990. *Relativized minimality* [Linguistic Inquiry Monograph 16], Cambridge, Mass.: MIT Press.

Rizzi, Luigi, 1996. 'Residual verb second and the *wh*-criterion', in Adriana Belletti & Luigi Rizzi (eds.), *Parameters and functional heads*, Oxford: Oxford University Press: 63–90.

Rizzi, Luigi, 1997. 'The fine structure of the left periphery', in Liliane Haegeman (ed.), *Elements of grammar*, Dordrecht: Kluwer: 281–337.

Rochemont, Michael S., 1986. *Focus in generative grammar*, Amsterdam: John Benjamins.

Rochemont, Michael S., & Culicover, Peter W., 1990. *English focus constructions and the theory of grammar*, Cambridge: Cambridge University Press.

Rooth, Mats, 1992. 'A theory of focus interpretation', *Natural Language Semantics* 1, 75–116.

Rooth, Mats, 1996. 'Focus', in Shalom Lappin (ed.), *The handbook of contemporary semantic theory*, Oxford: Blackwell: 271–97.

Ross, John Robert, 1967. *Constraints on variables in syntax*, doctoral dissertation, MIT.

Rothstein, Susan, 1995. 'Small clauses and copular constructions', in Anna Cardinaletti & Maria Teresa Guasti (eds.), *Small clauses* [Syntax and Semantics 28], New York: Academic Press, 27–48.

Rudin, Catherine, 1988. 'On multiple questions and multiple *wh* fronting', *Natural Language and Linguistic Theory* 6, 445–501.

Rufa'i, Abba, 1977. *Grammatical agreement in Hausa*, doctoral dissertation, Georgetown University.

Rufa'i, Abba, 1983. 'Defining and non-defining relative clauses in Hausa', in H. Ekkehard Wolff & Hilke Meyer-Bahlburg (eds.), *Studies in Chadic and Afroasiatic linguistics*, Hamburg: Helmut Buske, 419–27.

Saeed, John, 1984. *The syntax of topic and focus in Somali*, Hamburg: Helmut Buske.

Saeed, John, 1999. *Somali*, Amsterdam: John Benjamins.

Sag, Ivan, & Thomas Wasow, 1999. *Syntactic theory: a formal introduction*, Stanford, Calif.: CSLI.

Saito, Mamoru, 1985. *Some asymmetries in Japanese and their theoretical implications*, doctoral dissertation, MIT.

Samek-Lodivici, Vieri, 1998. 'Opposite constraints: left and right focus-alignment in Kanakuru', *Lingua* 104, 111–30.

Schachter, Paul, 1966. 'A generative account of Hausa *ne/ce*', *Journal of African Languages* 5, 34–53.

Schachter, Paul, 1973. 'Focus and relativization', *Language* 49, 19–46.

Schlenker, Philippe, 2004. 'Conditionals as definite descriptions (a referential analysis)', *Research on Language and Computation* 2, 417–62.

Schmerling, Susan F., 1976. *Aspects of English sentence stress*, Austin: University of Texas Press.

Schön, James Frederick, 1843. *Vocabulary of the Haussa language (Part I. English and Haussa, Part II. Haussa and English) and phrases and specimens of translations; to which are prefixed the grammatical elements of the Haussa language*, London: Church Missionary Society.

Schuh, Russell G., 1971. 'Reconstruction of the syntax of subject emphasis in certain Chadic languages', *Studies in African Linguistics* Supplement 2, 67–77.

Schuh, Russell G., 1972. *Aspects of Ngizim syntax*, doctoral dissertation, UCLA.

Schuh, Russell G., 1977. 'West Chadic verb classes', in Paul Newman & Roxana Ma Newman (eds.), *Papers in Chadic linguistics*, Leiden: Afrika-Studiecentrum, 143–66.

Schuh, Russell G., 1978. 'Tone rules', in Victoria Fromkin (ed.), *Tone: a linguistic survey*, New York: Academic Press, 221–56.

Schuh, Russell G., 1982a. 'Questioned and focussed subjects and objects in Bade/Ngizim', in Herrmann Jungraithmayr (ed.), *The Chad languages of the Hamitosemitic-Nigritic border area*, Berlin: Dietrich Reimer, 160–74.

Schuh, Russell G., 1982b. 'The Hausa language and its nearest relatives', *Harsunan Nijeriya* 12, 1–24.

Schuh, Russell G., 1983a. 'Kilba equational sentences', *Studies in African Linguistics* 14, 311–26.

Schuh, Russell G., 1983b. 'The evolution of determiners in Chadic', in H. Ekkehard Wolff & Hilke Meyer-Bahlburg (eds.), *Studies in Chadic and Afroasiatic linguistics*, Hamburg: Helmut Buske, 157–210.

Schuh, Russell G., 1985. 'Hausa tense/aspect/mood (TAM) system', MS, UCLA.

Schuh, Russell G., 1998. *A Grammar of Miya* [University of California Publications in Linguistics 130], Berkeley: University of California Press.

Schuh, Russell G., 2000. 'On the origin of the Hausa relative aspects and the "stabilizer"', MS, UCLA.

Schuh, Russell G., 2003. 'Chadic overview', in M. Lionel Bender, Gabor Takacs & David L. Appleyard (eds.), *Selected comparative-historical Afrasian linguistic studies in memory of Igor M. Diakonoff*, Munich: Lincom Europa, 55–60.

Schuh, Russell G., 2005. 'Yobe State, Nigeria as a linguistic area', paper presented at the Berkeley Linguistics Society 31st Annual Meeting, 18-20 February 2005, MS, UCLA.

Schuh, Russell G., & Alhaji Maina Gimba, forthcoming. 'Bole grammar, dictionary and texts'. MS, UCLA.

Schwarz, Florian, 2004. 'Focus without intonation? Syntactic focus marking in Kikuyu and Kitharaka', paper presented at Intonation Matters conference, UMASS, May 2004.

Selkirk, Elisabeth, 1984. *Phonology and syntax*, Cambridge, Mass.: MIT Press.

Selkirk, Elisabeth, & Tong Shen, 1990. 'Prosodic domains in Shanghai Chinese', in Sharon Inkelas & Draga Zec (eds.), *The phonology–syntax connection*, Chicago: University of Chicago Press, 313–37.

Shlonsky, Ur, 1997. *Clause structure and word order in Hebrew*, Oxford: Oxford University Press.

Shlonsky, Ur, 2000a. 'Subject positions and copular constructions', in Hans Bennis, Martin Everaert & Eric Reuland (eds.), *Interface strategies*, Amsterdam: Royal Netherlands Academy of Arts and Sciences, 325–47.

Shlonsky, Ur, 2000b. 'Remarks on the complementiser layer of Standard Arabic', in Jacqueline Lecarme, Jean Lowenstamm & Ur Shlonsky (eds.), *Research in Afroasiatic grammar* [Current Issues in Linguistic Theory 202], Amsterdam: John Benjamins, 325–44.

Shlonsky, Ur, 2002. 'Constituent questions in Palestinian Arabic', in Jamal Ouhalla & Ur Shlonsky (eds.), *Themes in Arabic and Hebrew syntax* [Studies in Natural Language and Linguistic Theory 53], Dordrecht: Kluwer, 137–60.

Shlonsky, Ur, & Adriana Belletti, 1995. 'The order of verbal complements: a comparative study', *Natural Language and Linguistic Theory* 13, 489–526.

Shlonsky, Ur, & Edit Doron, 1992. 'Verb-second in Hebrew', *WCCFL (Proceedings of the West Coast Conference in Formal Linguistics)* 10, 431–46.

Simpson, Andrew, 1995. *Wh-movement, licensing and the locality of feature checking*, doctoral dissertation, SOAS, University of London.

Simpson, Andrew, 1999. 'Wh-movement, licensing and the locality of feature checking', in David Adger, Susan Pintzuk, Bernadette Plunkett & George Tsoulas (eds.), *Specifiers: minimalist approaches*, Oxford: Oxford University Press, 231–47.

Skinner, Margaret G., 1979. *Aspects of Pa'anci Grammar*, doctoral dissertation, University of Wisconsin.

Skinner, Neil, 1965. *Kamus na Turanci da Hausa*, Zaria: Northern Nigeria Publishing Company.

Skinner, Neil, 1979. *A grammar of Hausa*, Zaria: Northern Nigeria Publishing Company.

Sperber, Dan, & Deirdre Wilson, 1995. *Relevance: communication and cognition*, 2nd edn, Oxford: Blackwell.

Stassen, Leon, 1997. *Intransitive predication*, Oxford: Oxford University Press.

Stenson, Nancy, 1981. *Studies in Irish syntax*, Tübingen: Gunter Narr.

Stockwell, Robert P., 1960. 'The place of intonation in a Generative Grammar', *Language* 36, 360–67.

Stowell, Tim, 1978. 'What was there before there was there', in Donka Farkas (ed.), *Proceedings of the 13th regional meeting of the Chicago Linguistics Society*, 458–71.

Stowell, Tim, 1991. 'Small clause restructuring', in Robert Freidin (ed.), *Principles and parameters in comparative grammar*, Cambridge, Mass.: MIT Press, 182–218.

Stucky, Susan, 1979. 'Focus of contrast aspects in Makua: syntactic and semantic evidence', in Christine Chiarello (ed.), *Proceedings of the fifth annual meeting of the Berkeley Linguistics Society*, Berkeley: University of California at Berkeley, 362–72.

Surányi, Balázs, 2002. *Multiple operator movements in Hungarian* [LOT Dissertation Series 72], Utrecht: LOT.

Svenonius, Peter, 1994. *Dependent nexus: subordinate predication structures in English and the Scandinavian languages*, doctoral dissertation, UCSC.

Svolacchia, Marco, Lunella Mereu & Annarita Puglielli, 1995. 'Aspects of discourse configurationality in Somali', in Katalin É. Kiss (ed.), *Discourse configurational languages*, Oxford: Oxford University Press, 65–98.

Szabolcsi, Anna, 1981a. 'The semantics of topic-focus articulation', in Jan Groenendijk, Theo Janssen & Martin Stokhof (eds.), *Formal methods in the study of language* 2, Amsterdam: Matematisch Centrum, 513–41.

Szabolcsi, Anna, 1981b. 'Compositionality in focus', *Folia Linguistica* 15, 141–63.

Szabolcsi, Anna, 1983. 'Focussing properties, or the trap of first order', *Theoretical Linguistics* 10, 125–45.

Szendröi, Kriszta, 2001. *Focus and the syntax–phonology interface*, doctoral dissertation, University College London.

Szendröi, Kriszta, 2003. 'A stress-based approach to the syntax of Hungarian focus', *Linguistic Review* 20, 37–78.

Tancredi, Christopher, 1992. *Deletion, deaccenting and presupposition*, doctoral dissertation, MIT.

Tsai, W.-T. Dylan, 1999, 'On lexical courtesy', *Journal of East Asian Linguistics* 8, 39–73.

Tsimpli, Ianthi Maria, 1995. 'Focusing in Modern Greek', in Katalin É. Kiss (ed.), *Discourse configurational languages*, Oxford: Oxford University Press, 176–206.

Tuller, Laurice A., 1982. 'Null subjects and objects in Hausa', *Journal of Linguistic Research* 2, 77–99.

Tuller, Laurice A., 1986a. *Bijective relations in universal grammar and the syntax of Hausa*, doctoral dissertation, UCLA.

Tuller, Laurice A., 1986b. 'Tense features and operators in Hausa', MS, University of Quebec at Montreal.

Tuller, Laurice A., 1988. 'Resumptive strategies in Hausa', in Graham L. Furniss & Philip J. Jaggar (eds.), *Studies in Hausa language and linguistics,* London: Kegan Paul International, 132–48.

Tuller, Laurice A., 1989. 'Variation in focus constructions', in Zygmunt Frajzyngier (ed.), *Current progress in Chadic linguistics,* Amsterdam: John Benjamins, 9–33.

Tuller, Laurice A., 1992. 'Postverbal focus constructions in Chadic', *Natural Language and Linguistic Theory* 10, 303–34.

Tuller, Laurice A., 1996. 'Rich and strong inflection: object agreement in Hausa', in Jacqueline Lecarme, Jean Lowenstamm & Ur Shlonsky (eds.), *Studies in Afroasiatic grammar II*, The Hague: Holland Academic Graphics, 431–50.

Vallduví, Enric, 1992. *The informational component,* New York: Garland.

Vallduví, Enric, 1995. 'Structural properties of information packaging in Catalan', in Katalin É. Kiss (ed.), *Discourse configurational languages,* Oxford: Oxford University Press, 122–52.

Wahba, Wafa, 1984. *Wh-constructions in Egyptian Arabic,* PhD dissertation, University of Illinois at Urbana-Champaign.

Wahba, Wafa, 1991. 'LF movement in Iraqi Arabic', in C.-T. James Huang & Robert May (eds.), *Logical structure and linguistic theory,* Dordrecht: Kluwer, 253–76.

Watanabe, Aikira, 1996. *Case absorption and wh-agreement,* Dordrecht: Kluwer.

Watters, John, 1979. 'Focus in Aghem: a study of its formal correlates and typology', in Larry Hyman (ed.), *Aghem grammatical structure* [Southern California Occasional Papers in Linguistics 7], Los Angeles: University of Southern California, 137–97.

Wolff, H. Ekkehard, 1993. *Referenzgrammatik des Hausa* [Hamburger Beiträge zur Afrikanistik 2], Münster: LIT.

Yalwa, Lawan Danladi, 1995. *Issues in Hausa complementation,* doctoral dissertation, UCLA.

Yusuf, Mukhtar Abdulkadir, 1991. *Aspects of the morphosyntax of functional categories in Hausa,* doctoral dissertation, University of Essex.

Zaenen, Annie, 1983. 'On syntactic binding', *Linguistic Inquiry* 14, 469–504.

Zamparelli, Roberto, 2000. *Layers in the determiner phrase,* New York: Garland.

Zec, Draga, and Sharon Inkelas, 1990. 'Prosodically constrained syntax', in Sharon Inkelas & Draga Zec (eds.), *The phonology–syntax connection,* Chicago: University of Chicago Press, 365–78.

Zubizarreta, Maria Luisa, 1994. 'Word order, prosody and focus', MS, University of Southern California.

Zubizarreta, Maria Luisa, 1998. *Prosody, focus and word order* [LI Monograph 23], Cambridge, Mass.: MIT Press.

Zwicky, Arnold, 1977. *On clitics,* Indiana University Linguistics Club.

INDEX

Abdoulaye, Mahamane L. 7, 97n
Abraham, R. C. 6
adequacy
 descriptive 28–9
 explanatory 28–9, 32–3
 observational 27
Adger, David 177–81
adjectives 18, 226–7, 227*t*
adverbial clauses 96n
Afroasiatic languages 4
Aghem 44, 46
Agree 34, 35, 36, 56
alternative semantics 39
Amharic 42
Aoun, Joseph 206
Arabic
 copular/non-verbal clauses 240–5, 260
 descriptive facts 204–7, 240–3
 focus/*wh*-constructions 47*t*, 185, 204–10, 224
 theoretical issues 207–10, 243–5
 Egyptian Arabic 206, 207, 240–1, 242, 243
 Iraqi Arabic 206
 Lebanese Arabic 206
 Moroccan Arabic 206, 207, 242, 243–4, 245
 Palestinian Arabic 206–7, 240, 243, 244
 Standard Arabic 185, 204–6, 207–10, 242–3
Artstein, Ron 116
aspect 9–10
Austronesian languages *see* Chamorro; Malayo-Polynesian languages; Palauan; Tagalog

Bade 74n, 194–5, 198, 200
Bantu languages *see* Aghem; Kihung'an; Kikuyu; Makua
Bargery G. P. 6
Basilico, David 172–5, 227
Basque 44, 46, 47*t*
Belletti, Adriana 210–12, 213, 215
Bengali 42, 47*t*
Berber languages 4, 5
Binding Theory 28
Bole 5, 187–8, 198, 231–2, 239*t*
broad and narrow focus 39–40
Brody, Michael 48–50, 55, 71

Catalan 46, 47*t*
Chadic languages 46, 184–5
 as Afroasiatic languages 4
 classifications 5
 copular/non-verbal clauses 228–39, 239*t*
 descriptive facts 186–99
 distribution 5
 focus markers 198–9
 focus/*wh*-constructions 185, 186–204, 223–4
 morphology 4
 phonology 4
 special inflection 197–8
 syntactic features 4–5
 theoretical issues 199–204
 Angas sub-group 5
 Bade 74n, 194–5, 198, 200
 Biu-Mandara sub-group 5, 186–7, 197, 229–31
 Bole 5, 187–8, 198, 231–2, 239*t*
 Bole-Tangale sub-group 5, 190–3, 194, 197
 Duwai 194–5, 198
 East Chadic 5, 197
 Gude 5, 186
 Gwandara 5
 Kanakuru 44–5, 47*t*, 74n, 191–3, 194, 197, 198, 200–1, 202, 234–5, 239*t*
 Kilba 229–30, 239*t*
 Lamang 5
 Margi 5
 Masa 5
 Miya 5, 195–6, 198, 238–9, 239*t*
 Mupun 5, 193–4, 195, 198, 235–7, 239*t*
 Ngizim 74n, 194–5, 198, 200, 201, 202, 237–8, 239*t*
 Pero 5, 188–90, 198, 232–4, 239*t*
 Podoko 5, 44–5, 47*t*, 74n, 186–7, 200, 230–1, 239*t*
 Ron sub-group 5, 197
 Tangale 74n, 190–1, 200, 201, 202
 West A 187–94, 197, 198, 231–7
 West B 194–6, 197, 198, 237–9
 West Chadic 5, 186
 see also Hausa language
Chafe, Wallace 153
Chamorro 43, 47*t*, 90–1, 92
Chang, Lisa 102
Chinese 47*t*, 115, 136

Hebrew 185, 210–15, 224
Kihung'an 41–2, 47*t*
summary 223–5
see also focus constructions in Hausa
focus constructions in Hausa 23–4, 47*t*, 58–118
conclusions 116–18, 263–4
focus fronting: descriptive facts 58, 59–70, 116
focus fronting: FP analysis 58, 70–83, 116
focus/*wh*-in situ 59, 100–16, 117
special inflection 59, 60, 90–100, 117
wh-fronting 58–9, 83–90, 116–17
Focus Criterion 49–50
'focus form' 9n
focus fronting: descriptive facts 58, 59–70, 116
focus fronting 60–4
focus vs topic 64–7
vs clefting 67–70
focus fronting: FP analysis 58, 70–83, 116
empirical evidence 73–7
extension 114–16
proposal 71–3
theoretical issues 77–83
focus in situ: descriptive facts 104–6
focus markers 16, 198–9
focus movement 43–5, 47*t*, 48, 51, 52
focus particles 42–3, 47*t*
focus projection 40
focus/*wh*-in situ 59, 100–16, 117
extending the FP analysis 114–16
focus in situ: descriptive facts 104–6
form–function correlation 106–12
multiple focus/*wh*-constructions 112–14
wh-in situ: descriptive facts 101–4, 141
formal tradition 38
FP (focus phrase) analysis
focus fronting 58, 70–83, 116
focus/*wh*-in situ 114–16
FP (focus phrase) analysis of non-verbal copular clauses 139–83
displacement 155–9
empirical evidence 145–59
focus position 146–7
IP analysis 159–65
predicate raising analysis 165–77
PredP analysis 177–82
proposal 140–5
summary 182–3
theoretical issues 159–82
topic and subject prominence 147–54, 148*t*

Frajzyngier, Zygmunt 5, 188–90, 193–4, 197, 233–4, 235–7
French 47*t*
functional tradition 38

generative framework 25–36
Minimalist Program 30, 32–6, 50, 56, 78n
philosophical assumptions 25–9
transformational model 29–30
X-bar syntax 30–2, 33n, 48
generative grammar 26–9
generative theories of focus 47–57
model of focus in present study 55–7
prosody-based theories 50–5
syntax-based theories 47–50
German 80n
Gimba, Alhaji Maina 5, 187–8, 231–2
Government and Binding Theory 30, 47, 48, 56
grammar 28
grammaticalisation 135–6, 135*t*, 139, 146–7, 148
Greek 43, 44, 46, 47*t*
Green, Melanie 52, 56n, 64, 79, 82, 86, 97–9, 99n, 102, 103–4, 105, 106, 109, 110–11, 112, 113–14, 115–16, 132n, 202, 204, 216, 217–19, 220–3
Greenberg, Joseph H. 5
Greenberg, Yael 247–8
Gude 5, 186
Gwandara 5

Haida 46
Halle, Morris 51
Harries-Delisle, Helga 41–3, 42n, 45
Hartmann, Katharina 64, 106n, 109n, 110n, 111n, 112
Hausa dictionaries and grammars 6
Hausa language 4–24
adjectives 18
adverbial clauses 96n
aspect 9–10
copular verbs 15n, 121
deictic system 18
dialects 3, 6, 92n, 137, 161, 175
distribution 5–6
Eastern Hausa 137
echo questions 101, 102n
focus constructions 23–4, 47*t*, 58–118
intonation 8
modal/adverbial particles 20, 24, 64